Oil Wealth and Development in Uganda an

Oil Wealth and Development in Uganda and Beyond

Prospects, Opportunities and Challenges

Edited by
Arnim Langer, Ukoha Ukiwo, and Pamela Mbabazi

LEUVEN UNIVERSITY PRESS

Published with the support of the
KU Leuven Fund for Fair Open Access

Published in 2020 by Leuven University Press / Presses Universitaires de Louvain / Universitaire Pers Leuven. Minderbroedersstraat 4, B-3000 Leuven (Belgium).

ISBN 978 94 6270 200 4 (Paperback)
ISBN 978 94 6166 309 2 (ePDF)
ISBN 978 94 6166 310 8 (ePUB)

https://doi.org/10.11116/9789461663092

D/2020/1869/7
NUR: 741

Layout: Crius
Cover design: Frederik Danko
Cover illustration: Single petrol pump in Uganda, Africa (Dennis Diatel/Shutterstock.com)

GPRC
Guaranteed
Peer Reviewed
Content
www.gprc.be

Contents

Part II — Macroeconomic and Fiscal Framework, Policies and Challenges

Part III — Other Major Governance Polices and Challenges

Part IV — International Comparison

Part V — A Way Forward

List of Figures

List of Tables

Foreword

Uganda stands at an important crossroad in its history. In 2006, large quantities of oil and gas were discovered in the Albertine Western Region of Uganda. Now more than a decade later, Uganda is on the verge of becoming a significant oil producer and exporter in Africa. The people of Uganda are awaiting the moment that oil starts flowing with great anticipation. This is expected to happen around 2021/22. And while Ugandans hope and pray that their country's oil wealth will soon translate into improved social and economic outcomes for them, there exists a widespread sense of unease and concern among the population about whether Uganda is ready for the inflow of large amounts of oil revenues.

Given the history of oil exploration and exploitation in Africa, these concerns are not unfounded. Unfortunately, there are cases, both in Africa and elsewhere, that demonstrate that natural resource wealth, if mismanaged, will not be the route to development Eldorado but will produce the opposite result of poverty in the midst of plenty. However, the negative political, social and economic impacts of oil wealth—a situation also known as the 'resource curse'—is not inevitable, as some countries with credible governance of the oil-producing class have shown (e.g. Norway). In this respect, everything depends on how a country's oil resources and revenues are being managed. Moreover, countries with more effective, efficient and transparent institutions are clearly better able to take full advantage of their oil wealth.

The development of a sound and well-functioning oil governance regime is therefore arguably the major public policy challenge Uganda is currently facing. While the Government of Uganda, together with other important local stakeholders including the Parliament of Uganda, local businesses, civil society, the Ugandan Chamber of Mines and Petroleum, and Oil and Gas Service Providers, have been preparing for the moment that oil is expected to start flowing in the early 2020s, a major question remains how well prepared Uganda is to manage the oil production and revenues effectively, efficiently and transparently. This crucial question lies at the heart of this important book. More specifically, the current book aims to answer the following question: to what extent is Uganda ready to effectively harness its oil revenues for national and human development, thereby avoiding the oil governance curse?

In order to answer this crucial question, the current book brings together original scholarship by a stellar group of African researchers (mainly from

Uganda) concerning Uganda's oil governance regime. It includes detailed chapters on the institutional, legal-regulatory, fiscal, environmental, social, macroeconomic, political and financial dimensions of the country's oil regime. It also includes comparative insights from three other African cases, namely: Ghana, Kenya and Nigeria. These case studies provide interesting insights and policy lessons which are extremely useful for Uganda.

Overall, this book constitutes a fascinating read and offers insightful reflections concerning Uganda's oil governance regime, its main challenges and shortcomings as well as possible ways to improve it. It is my sincere hope that the Government of Uganda and all other local stakeholders will draw on the findings and policy lessons of this book to further strengthen Uganda's oil governance regime, thereby ensuring that the country's oil wealth will be managed wisely and for the benefit of all Ugandans.

Hon. Richard H. Kaijuka F.C.I.B.

Chairperson of the Board of Trustees of the Uganda Chamber of Mines and Petroleum and former Minister of Energy and Mineral Development in Uganda.

Preface

This book is the result of close research collaboration between the Centre for Research on Peace and Development (CRPD), KU Leuven (Belgium) and Mbarara University of Science and Technology, Mbarara (Uganda), as part of the VLIR-UOS-funded research project entitled 'Is Uganda Ready to Avoid the Governance Curse? A Comprehensive Analysis of the Country's Oil Governance Regime'. The successful completion of this book project would not have been possible without the invaluable support we have received since the start of the project in 2015 from a number of corporate and individual partners.

First, we owe a large debt of gratitude to the VLIR-UOS (a Flemish development funder which aims to support inter-university collaborations and partnerships), which made the above-mentioned research project possible by awarding us generous research funding (Grant number: ZEIN2015PR412). We would also like to thank Mr. Herman Diels and Ms. Kathleen Wuytack, who both acted as VLIR-UOS Programme Manager for Uganda at different stages of the project, for providing technical and administrative support and guidance to the project.

Second, we would like to thank all chapter contributors for their continued commitment to this book project. It has been a long time since we met in Kampala in December 2016 to present draft papers and discuss the outlines of this book. The sustained interest in the project, which demonstrates recognition of the significance of the study, is evidenced by the efforts of the contributors to update their chapters with recent developments.

Third, we would also like to express our profound gratitude to all scholars and practitioners who have provided invaluable inputs and feedback to our research project as well as the individual chapters along the way. In addition, we also thank the anonymous reviewers of our book proposal for their helpful and insightful comments and suggestions.

Fourth, we wholeheartedly thank the publication team at Leuven University Press for their excellent guidance and support during the preparation of this book.

Fifth, we wish to thank Ms. Ingrid De Wachter, the project's financial administrator at KU Leuven, for her invaluable logistical and administrative

support, and Ms. Ninotsjka Callens and Ms. Clara Rabelo Caiafa Pereira for
their editorial assistance at the final stages of preparing this book.

Finally, it is important to note that while the VLIR-UOS funded the
research project, the views and opinions expressed in this book are those
of the individual authors. The perspectives expressed in the book do not
necessarily reflect those of the VLIR-UOS.

Arnim Langer, Ukoha Ukiwo, and Pamela Mbabazi

1

Oil Wealth and Development in Uganda and Beyond: Prospects, Opportunities and Challenges

Arnim Langer, Ukoha Ukiwo and Pamela Mbabazi

1.1   Setting the Stage

With an increasing number of African countries having discovered commercially viable quantities of oil and gas in recent years, including, for example, Kenya, Chad, Ghana and Uganda, there is both excitement and trepidation about the prospects for increased incomes and investments, economic growth and development on the continent. This is due to comparative historical evidence of the link between natural resource exploitation, economic growth and development on the one hand and natural resource exploitation, economic decline and socio-political crises on the other hand (see, for example, Ross, 2003; 2012; Sachs and Warner, 2001; Torres, Afonso and Soares, 2012). Indeed, a substantial body of empirical studies has shown that many countries 'blessed' with natural resources have paradoxically faced economic decline and severe socio-political crises (see, for example, Mehlum, Moene and Torvik, 2006; Ross, 2012; Sachs and Warner, 1995).

The observation that countries rich in oil, gas or other minerals often end up facing serious economic, social and political challenges rather than economic progress and political stability has led some scholars to claim that these countries experienced a so-called 'resource curse' (see, for example, Ross, 2012; Sachs and Warner, 2001). More specifically, the Natural Resource Governance Institute (NRGI) refers to the resource curse as 'the failure of many resource-rich countries to benefit fully from their natural resource wealth, and for governments in these countries to respond effectively to public welfare needs' (NRGI, 2015, p.1). It is noteworthy that many developing countries seem to be plagued by the resource curse. As noted by Arthur (2014, p.39) in this respect, '... there is increasing evidence that extractive natural resources have not helped developing countries, especially those in

Africa, to achieve prosperity and their desired socioeconomic ends' (see also Obi, 2010a). In Africa, Nigeria and D.R. Congo are often seen as prominent examples of countries where the resource curse has manifested itself. To illustrate this point, Sala-i-Martin and Subramanian (2012) posit that despite earning more than US$ 350 billion in cumulative oil revenues between 1965 and 2000, Nigeria's GDP per capita did not improve over this period. Instead the country has been plagued by endemic corruption, institutional failure and violent conflicts (see Ukiwo, 2008, 2011; Obi, 2010b).

A range of economic, social and political problems and challenges have been associated with the extraction and exploitation of natural resources. In terms of political challenges, Michael Ross—one of the leading scholars on the politics of resource-rich countries and the causes and consequences of the resource curse—asserts:

> ... there is strong evidence that one type of resource wealth—petroleum— has at least three important [political] effects: It tends to make authoritarian regimes more durable; it leads to heightened corruption; and it helps trigger violent conflict in low- and middle-income countries, particularly when it is located in the territory of marginalized ethnic groups (Ross, 2015, p.240).

The possible ruinous impact of natural resource wealth on a country's political institutions and the state of democracy is often linked to the issue of taxation. In particular, as noted by the Natural Resource Governance Institute (NRGI):

> ... governments are more responsive to their citizens and are more likely to transition to democracy when government spending is reliant on citizen taxation. When countries collect large revenues from natural resources, they are less dependent on levying taxes on citizens, and thus citizens feel less invested in the national budget. Politicians and government officials are also less directly tied to citizen requests or demands (NRGI, 2015, p.2).

With respect to the apparent empirical association between natural resource wealth and violent conflict risk, myriad plausible mechanisms have been proposed to explain this relationship (see, for example, Tadjoeddin, 2012; Humphreys, 2005; Ross, 2004). More specifically, Humphreys (2005, p.510) argues that there are 'at least six rival families of mechanisms that could explain the relationship between natural resources and war onset'. These are: 1) the greedy rebels mechanism, 2) the greedy outsiders mechanism, 3) the grievance mechanism, 4) the feasibility mechanism, 5) the weak states mechanism, and 6) the sparse networks mechanism. Importantly, empirical support seems to be stronger 'for the weak state structures and grievance [mechanisms] than for the booty futures or state capture [mechanisms]' (Humphreys, 2005, p.534).

While in the last two decades a large amount of research has focused on the relationship between natural resource wealth and its associated *political* consequences—or the so-called *'political* resource curse' (Ross, 2015, p.239, emphasis added)—the original resource curse hypothesis was mainly concerned with possible negative *economic* consequences associated with an abundance of natural resources (Tadjoeddin, 2012). Indeed, the British economic geographer Richard Auty, who introduced the resource-curse concept in 1993, was predominantly concerned with the adverse effects of an abundance of natural resources on a country's economic growth (see Auty, 1993). In this respect, Auty (1993) observed that 'a growing body of evidence suggests that a favourable natural resource endowment may be less beneficial to countries at low and mid-income levels of development than the conventional wisdom might suppose' (cited in Toedjaddin, 2012, p.111).

There are essentially three channels through which natural resource abundance can lead to lower economic grow (Sala-i-Martin and Subramanian, 2012). First, 'natural resources generate rents which lead to rapacious rent-seeking (the voracity effect), whose adverse manifestation is felt through political economy effects ... and [through] increased corruption ... which adversely affects long-run growth' (Sala-i-Martin and Subramanian, 2012, p.574). Second, resource-rich countries are vulnerable to volatility in international commodity prices and ipso facto resource revenue volatility, with potentially adverse implications for economic growth. With regard to the volatility in resource revenues, the Natural Resource Governance Institute (NRGI) further observes:

> ... it is very difficult to effectively spend fluctuating and unpredictable revenues. Governments often get trapped in boom-bust cycles where they spend on legacy projects, such as airports and monuments, when revenues are rising and then must make painful cuts when revenues decline. Resource-rich governments have a tendency to over-spend on government salaries, inefficient fuel subsidies and large monuments and to underspend on health, education and other social services (NRGI, 2015, p.2).

Third, countries with an abundance of natural resources also appear to be more susceptible to the adverse effects of the 'Dutch disease' (see, for example, Larsen, 2006; Tadjoeddin, 2012; Sala-i-Martin and Subramanian, 2012). Tadjoeddin (2012, p.112) explains that the Dutch disease refers to the 'economic disruption in the form of de-industrialization or de-agriculturalization (in accordance with what is the tradable sector in the economy) originating from the large inflow of foreign currencies from natural resource exports'. Similarly, Di John (2011, p.169) notes that the Dutch disease is a situation in which the export of natural resources leads to an appreciation of the exchange rate, which in turn 'leads to a decline in the competitiveness, and hence production and employment, of the traded goods sector' (Di John, 2011, p.169).

Given the potentially disastrous political, social and/or economic problems and challenges facing resource-rich countries, it is understandable that the discovery of large quantities of mineral resources, especially in developing countries, has provoked a mixed reception from policy makers, civil society organisations and the general population. There are four important points to be made in this regard, however. First, it is worth emphasising that the resource curse is absolutely *not* inevitable. Indeed, there are a range of resource-rich countries, including, for example, Botswana, Canada and Norway, that have been able to prevent the resource curse from taking hold by introducing sound policies and developing an effective and transparent resource governance regime (see, for example, Holden, 2013; Lewin, 2011). Moreover, resource-rich countries with effective institutions and sound resource governance regimes, with Norway arguably being the benchmark in this regard, can enormously benefit from their resource wealth.

Second, in recent years scholars and policy makers have increasingly started using the term 'governance curse' instead of 'resource curse'. This is a welcome change in terminology because 'governance curse' more accurately identifies governance failures—and not resources *per se*—to be the cause of the negative social, political and economic consequences often associated with the extraction of natural resources, such as oil, gas and other minerals (see, for example, NORAD, 2013; Pegg, 2006; Shaxson, 2007). Moreover, Germano Mwabu, one of the contributors to this book (see Chapter 16), argues that oil and gas resources are essentially 'welfare neutral', and that any welfare or efficiency consequences that may result from these resources fundamentally depend on how these resources are being extracted, managed, shared, and how their proceeds are being spent—or, in other words, it depends on the nature of the resource governance regime in place.

While the causes of ineffective management of natural resources are to some extent country-specific, it appears that natural resource-rich countries characterised by undemocratic and exclusionary regimes and/or a weak institutional and administrative capacity are more likely to manage their natural resource wealth badly and ineffectively (see Obi, 2011; Roll, 2011;

Ross, 2015). Furthermore, an increasing amount of research has shown that the relationship between the presence of natural resources and development outcomes is to a large extent dependent on and mediated through the *quality* of a country's institutions (for example, Brunnschweiler, 2006; Cabrales and Hauk, 2011; Mehlum *et al.*, 2006). In addition, poor institutional quality and weak administrative capacity are usually associated with insufficient knowledge and experience among government institutions and decision makers to design appropriate policies and implement these policies effectively and efficiently (for example, Roll, 2011).

Third, it is also important to note that countries that have recently discovered commercially viable quantities of oil, gas or other mineral resources, and hence are facing the herculean task of developing a country-specific resource governance regime, do not have to reinvent the wheel completely in this regard. Indeed, in the last two decades an enormous amount of research and scholarship has been devoted to understanding the potential impact and governance challenges associated with the extraction and export of natural resources. In addition, a huge amount of knowledge is currently available globally to help emerging oil- or gas-producing countries in their efforts to develop an effective and suitable resource governance regime. There is widespread recognition in this respect that resource-rich countries can learn from each other in terms of how best to manage their mineral resources and revenues. Unsurprisingly, given Norway's successful track-record in transforming its oil wealth into economic development and prosperity, several emerging and prospective oil-exporting countries in Africa, including Uganda, have looked towards Norway for guidance and technical assistance in the development of their oil governance regimes (Polus and Tycholiz, 2017). The recognition that resource-rich countries are facing similar challenges and hence can learn from each other's governance approaches also partly explains why the comparative analysis of policy choices and pathways of resource-rich countries has continued to attract a lot of scholarship in recent times (see, for example, Akanni, 2007; Lewis, 2007; Pinto, 1987; Roll, 2011).

Fourth, it is also worth emphasising that the quality of a country's resource governance should not be seen in binary terms, i.e. good versus bad governance. Instead there is a lot of variation over time within countries (meaning that governance regimes are not fixed and can thus be strengthened or can become less effective over time) and between countries. To illustrate the latter point, Table 1.1 shows the variation in the quality of resource governance for a number of African countries. The resource governance index (RGI) shown in this table is composed by the Natural Resource Governance Institute

(NRGI) and measures how well countries govern their extractive resources.[1] From the table it is immediately clear that there is substantial variation in how well different African countries manage their resources. In particular, while Ghana (being ranked 13th out of 89 countries) and Botswana (ranked 18th) are doing extremely well in both an African and a global context, Nigeria (ranked 55th), Angola (Ranked 70th) and D.R. Congo (ranked 75th) on the other hand are clearly not managing their resources very effectively, and these countries need to explore opportunities to improve and strengthen their resource governance regimes.

Table 1.1: Resource Governance Index Scores for Selected African countries

Country	Index Score	Global Rank
Ghana (Oil and Gas)	67	13
Botswana (Mining)	61	18
South Africa (Mining)	57	23
Côte d'Ivoire (Oil and Gas)	55	28
Nigeria (Oil and Gas)	42	55
Angola (Oil and Gas)	35	70
D.R. Congo (Oil and Gas)	33	75

Source: Data drawn from the 2017 Resource Governance Index, Natural Resource Governance Institute (NRGI). Available at: https://resourcegovernanceindex.org/.

1.2   The Objective of this Book

Given the potential impact of natural resource wealth on countries' development trajectories and socio-political situation, the development of a sound oil governance regime is undoubtedly one of the key public policy challenges for Uganda as well as other African countries with large oil and/ or gas endowments (see Kimenyi and Lewis, 2016). Following the discovery of large oil reserves in 2006, the Government of Uganda started preparing for the future oil windfall by developing a governance regime for the exploration, development and management of its oil resources. Yet, as we get closer to the moment that oil and gas will actually start flowing (now expected in late 2021

---

1   For a detailed description of the underlying methodology of Resource Governance Index (RGI), please visit https://resourcegovernanceindex.org/about/global-report.

or early 2022), it is unclear how well prepared the country is to manage its oil wealth effectively, efficiently and transparently. Uganda's record in terms of governance effectiveness, administrative capacity, institutional quality, and transparency and accountability is not particularly good, as evidenced by the country's low rankings on the World Bank's governance indicators.[2] Given the challenges that Uganda is facing in terms of promoting and advancing good governance, this raises serious questions and concerns about how the country will manage its newly found oil and gas wealth. The objective of the current book is to analyse how Uganda is preparing to deal with its expected oil wealth in order to ensure that it will contribute to national development. The collection of chapters in this book together aim to answer the following overarching question: *to what extent is Uganda ready to effectively harness its oil revenues for national and human development, thereby avoiding the oil governance curse?*

In order to answer this question, the book aims to analyse how Uganda is planning to deal with the challenge of effectively, efficiently and transparently harnessing and managing its oil sector and resources, and to identify possible shortcomings and weaknesses that need to be addressed in order to realise the full potential of its oil and gas wealth. The book therefore provides a comprehensive analysis of the emerging Ugandan oil governance regime, which involves analysing institutional, legal, fiscal, environmental, social, macroeconomic, political and financial dimensions. In order to analyse these different dimensions of Uganda's oil governance regime we take a decidedly multidisciplinary approach, and hence we combine political, legal, public policy, economic, gender and sociological perspectives and analyses. The book also includes comparative analysis and insights from other African countries, including Nigeria, Kenya and Ghana. While Nigeria has been exporting oil for more than four decades, Kenya and Ghana have only very recently become oil exporters. In the next section we will briefly review the different chapters that make up this book.

1.3   Overview of the Book

The book contains 17 chapters, including an introductory chapter and a conclusion. The chapters are grouped into the following five parts: I) Institutional and Regulatory Framework, Policies and Challenges; II) Macroeconomic and

---

2   See the World Bank's Worldwide Governance Indicators (WGI), retrieved from: https://info.worldbank.org/governance/wgi/#home.

Fiscal Framework, Policies and Challenges; III) Other Major Governance Policies and Challenges; IV) International Comparison; and V) A Way Forward.

Part I, containing four chapters, is aimed at critically analysing Uganda's legal-institutional and political framework for managing its oil resources and revenues. In Chapter 2, Pamela Mbabazi and Martin Muhangi analyse the role and functioning of the main formal institutions that have been established to manage, oversee and regulate Uganda's oil exploration, development and revenue management. The authors argue that while Uganda has attempted to embrace the principles of good resource management, serious challenges remain. They further assert that the main challenge for Uganda lies not in the application of technical approaches to managing oil revenues, but rather in the political context in which these policies and approaches have to be implemented and/or managed.

Complementing Chapter 2, J. Oloka-Onyango analyses Uganda's legal-regulatory oil regime in Chapter 3. In line with Mbabazi and Muhangi (Chapter 2), Oloka-Onyango also concludes that Uganda has not yet complied with the best practices for managing natural resources and revenues. He asserts that there is too much space and leeway for abuse and misappropriation of oil funds in Uganda.

Chapter 4 by Kathleen Brophy and Peter Wandera further expands on the important theme of possible misappropriation and abuse of oil resources and revenues. In particular, the authors systematically examine the risks of corruption in Uganda's burgeoning oil sector by mapping the opportunities for revenue mismanagement onto the standard oil revenue chain. They conclude that it is crucial to monitor 'the interplay of corruption, oil and democracy in Uganda' vigorously, thereby ensuring 'that oil strengthens, rather than erodes Uganda's democracy through a strong governance framework that limits all opportunities for corruption in the oil revenue chain'.

In Chapter 5, Badru Bukenya and Jaqueline Nakaiza investigate and analyse the dynamics of deal making between the Government of Uganda and international oil companies (IOC), as well as the strategies employed by the Government to remain in charge of the oil sector. The authors discuss the dominant role that is being played in these negotiations by the President of Uganda, Yoweri Museveni. Despite the secretive way in which Museveni proceeds in arranging oil deals with IOCs, the authors nonetheless conclude that 'the deals reached so far appear to be in the national interest as they give few concessions to IOCs'. Yet, they rightly caution that this situation is clearly not sustainable and may lead to a lot of instability and tensions, when the current president is no longer holding the reins of power.

Part II also consists of four chapters which together aim to provide a comprehensive analysis and assessment of Uganda's macroeconomic and fiscal framework and policies. In Chapter 6, Corti Paul Lakuma analyses Uganda's macroeconomic management regime and also the fiscal rules the Government of Uganda has put in place to achieve a balance between spending and saving of the expected oil revenues. The author makes a strong case for a 'prudent management of these oil resources' among other things by smoothing the production—and hence oil revenues—over time, and by committing 'to making realistic and relatively conservative projections of future oil prices in order to mitigate unaffordable expenditure commitments in the event of oil revenues falling short of the forecasted levels'.

Chapter 7 by Joseph Mawejje explores the opportunities that the oil revenues offer with regard to social development. The author argues that 'oil revenues can support social development if a people-centred approach is taken that prioritises investments in agricultural sector transformation, human capital development, social protection, and harnesses the demographic dividend by focusing on interventions that can lead to sustainable improvements in mortality and fertility outcomes'. However, he stresses that Uganda's governance structures need to be strengthened across the board in order to ensure that the opportunities for social development are not missed.

In Chapter 8, Wilson Bahati Kazi examines Uganda's fiscal regime in detail. On the basis of his analysis, he argues that Uganda's fiscal regime is competitive and ensures certainty and stability. Moreover, he concludes positively that the 'government has done enough preparatory work in terms of putting in place the necessary legal and institutional framework, including staff training and enhancing the capacities to deal with intricacies of assessing, collecting and managing oil revenues'.

Jackson Mwakali and Jackson Byaruhanga, who in Chapter 9 analyse the human resource challenges and opportunities facing Uganda's emerging oil sector, come to a more sober conclusion concerning the preparatory work conducted by the Government of Uganda. In particular, despite a serious lack of skilled Ugandan people who could work in the oil and gas sectors, so far the Government has insufficiently remedied this situation. The authors offer a range of policy interventions that could help to address these important human resources challenges.

Part III again contains four chapters, each analysing an important governance aspect related to the exploration and exploitation of oil and gas resources. In Chapter 10, Moses Isabirye reflects on the main environmental issues linked to the oil development and assesses the adequacy of the existing environmental regulatory systems in regulating potential problems associated with the upstream oil and gas activities in Uganda. The author warns that environmental challenges and issues are currently not a priority, despite the fact that environmental sustainability and considerations remain key determinants for the sustainable development of the oil and gas sector. He subsequently discusses a number of ways in which these environmental challenges can be addressed before oil exploitation and production will really take off.

In Chapter 11, Roberts K. Muriisa and Specioza Twinamasiko systematically examine the processes of land grabbing as a result of oil exploration and exploitation in Uganda. Based on their analysis, it is clear that land grabbing is a widespread problem in the oil production areas in the Western part of the country, and it has affected the livelihoods of a large number of people, especially women. The authors conclude that it is crucial to deal with this problem in an effective, constructive and transparent manner.

In Chapter 12, Musiime Chris Byaruhanga analyses the expectations of Ugandans concerning their country's oil and gas resources, and how far the government and the oil companies have managed these expectations appropriately. It is noteworthy that most Ugandans appear to know relatively little about how the oil resources and revenues may potentially impact their country. But unsurprisingly most Ugandans hope that they will somehow benefit from the oil revenues, although there is a lot of doubt whether the oil wealth will be spent transparently and fairly. In line with this observation, the author argues that 'the government's biggest task should be to build trust and confidence with the population that oil money will be used for the greater public good and will not be stolen through corruption'.

The final chapter (Chapter 13) in Part III belongs to Tom Ogwang, who analyses the emergent social tensions and conflicts linked to the advent of oil exploration and exploitation in Uganda. Given the fact that most tensions and conflicts are related to land, and that more land will be needed for the expanding oil infrastructures, the author argues that 'it would be prudent to develop and provide a clear description of the potential extent/magnitude of displacement of persons/settlements, including a clear compensation and livelihoods restoration plans (LRPs)'.

Part IV contains three additional African case studies. In Chapter 14, Ukoha Ukiwo analyses the Nigerian case; the Ghanaian case is analysed by Peter Quartey and Emmanuel Abbey in Chapter 15, and Germano Mwabu focuses on the Kenyan case in Chapter 16. These additional case studies provide important comparative insights into how these countries have managed their natural resources and revenues. As noted above, while Ghana and Kenya have only fairly recently started exporting oil and gas resources,

Nigeria, on the other hand, has been Africa's largest oil producer for many decades. Moreover, comparing Uganda's oil governance regime with the regimes in Kenya, Nigeria and Ghana is extremely useful in terms of gaining insights concerning best practices, policies and institutions to manage oil and gas resources effectively, efficiently and transparently..

Part V contains the concluding chapter, in which we will draw a number of conclusions concerning the effectiveness and soundness of Uganda's oil governance regime. A major conclusion is that oil wealth has enormous potential to accelerate development in Uganda as well as other African countries blessed with oil resources, but only if Uganda and other emerging as well as 'old' oil-exporting countries get both their politics and institutions right. In the final chapter, we also formulate a set of actionable policy recommendations which could contribute to improving the (future) governance of Uganda's oil windfall as well as that of other African countries, thereby not only preventing the governance curse from taking hold, but also ensuring that the oil windfall benefits as many people as possible.

References

Akanni, O.P. (2007), 'Oil Wealth and Economic Growth in Oil Exporting African Countries'. *AERC Research Paper*, No. 170. Retrieved from: https://aercafrica.org/wp-content/uploads/2018/07/RP_170.pdf.

Arthur, P. (2014), 'Governance of Natural Resource Management in Africa: Contemporary Perspectives', in K.T. Hanson, C. D'Alessandro and F. Owusu (eds.), *Managing Africa's Natural Resources* (pp.39–65). London: Palgrave Macmillan.

Auty, R.M. (1993), *Sustaining Development in the Mineral Economies: The Resource Curse Thesis*. London: Routledge.

Brunnschweiler, C.N. (2006), 'Cursing the Blessings? Natural Resource Abundance'. *CER-ETH Working Paper*, 06(51). Retrieved from: http://dx.doi.org/10.2139/ssrn.928330.

Cabrales, A., and E. Hauk (2011), 'The Quality of Political Institutions and the Curse of Natural Resources', *The Economic Journal*, 121(551), 58–88. Retrieved from: https://doi.org/10.1111/j.1468-0297.2010.02390.x.

Di John, J. (2011), 'Is There Really a Resource Curse? A Critical Survey of Theory and Evidence', *Global Governance: A Review of Multilateralism and International Organizations*, 17(2), 167–184. Retrieved from: https://www.jstor.org/stable/23033728?seq=1#metadata_info_tab_contents

Holden, S. (2013), 'Avoiding the Resource Curse the Case Norway', *Energy Policy*, 63, 870–876. Retrieved from: https://doi.org/10.1016/j.enpol.2013.09.010.

Humphreys, M. (2005), 'Natural Resources, Conflict, and Conflict Resolution: Uncovering the Mechanisms', *The Journal of Conflict Resolution*, 49(4), 508–537. Retrieved from: http://www.jstor.org/stable/30045129.

Kimenyi, M., and Z. Lewis (2016), 'Managing Natural Resources for Development in East Africa: Examining Key Issues with the Region's Oil and Natural Gas Exploration'. Retrieved from the Brookings Institution website: https://www.brookings.edu/research/managing-natural-resources-for-development-in-east-africa-examining-key-issues-with-the-regions-oil-and-natural-gas-discoveries/.

Larsen, E.R. (2006), 'Escaping the Resource Curse and the Dutch Disease?', *American Journal of Economics and Sociology*, 65(3), 605–640. Retrieved from: https://doi.org/10.1111/j.1536-7150.2006.00476.x

Lewin, M. (2011), 'Botswana's Success: Good Governance, Good Policies, and Good Luck', in M. Angwafo and P. Chuhan-Pole (eds.), *Yes Africa Can: Success Stories from a Dynamic Continent*. Washington, DC World Bank. Retrieved from: http://siteresources.worldbank.org/AFRICAEXT/Resources/258643-1271798012256/Botswana-success.pdf.

Lewis, P. (2007), *Growing Apart: Oil, Politics and Economic Change in Indonesia and Nigeria*. Ann Arbor, Michigan: The University of Michigan Press. Retrieved from: http://www.jstor.org/stable/10.3998/mpub.206785.

Mehlum, H., K. Moene and R. Torvik (2006), 'Institutions and the Resource Curse', *The Economic Journal*, 116(508), 1–20. Retrieved from: https://doi.org/10.1111/j.1468-0297.2006.01045.x.

Norad Evaluation Department (2013), *Facing the Resource Curse: Norway's Oil for Development Program*. Oslo: Norwegian Agency for Development Cooperation.

NRGI (2015), 'The Resource Curse: The Political and Economic Challenges of Natural Resource Wealth', *NRGI Reader*, March 2015. New York: Natural Resource Governance Institute (NRGI). Retrieved from: https://resourcegovernance.org/sites/default/files/nrgi_Resource-Curse.pdf.

Obi, C. (2010a), 'Oil as the "Curse" of Conflict in Africa: Peering through the Smokes and Mirrors', *Review of African Political Economy*, 37(126), 483–495. Retrieved from: 10.1080/03056244.2010.530947.

—— (2010b), 'Oil Extraction, Dispossession, Resistance and Conflict in Nigeria's Oil Rich Niger Delta', *Canadian Journal of Development Studies*, 30(1), 219–236. Retrieved from: 10.1080/02255189.2010.9669289.

—— (2011), 'Democratising the Petro-State in West Africa: Understanding the Challenges', in S. Sperling and M. Roll (eds.), *Fuelling the World-Failing the Region? Oil Governance and Development in Africa's Gulf of Guinea* (pp.102–120). Abuja: Fredrich-Ebert Stiftung.

Ovadia, J.S. (2016), *Petro-Developmental States in Africa: Making Oil Work in Angola, Nigeria and Gulf of Guinea*. London: Hurst and Company.

Pegg, S. (2006), 'Can Policy Intervention Beat the Resource Curse? Evidence from the Chad-Cameroon Pipeline Project', *African Affairs*, 105(418), 1–25. Retrieved from: http://www.jstor.org/stable/3518786.

Pinto, B. (1987), 'Nigeria Before and After the Oil Boom: A Policy Comparison with Indonesia', *The World Bank Economic Review*, 1(3), 419–445. Retrieved from: http://documents.worldbank.org/curated/en/198091468775789095/Nigeria-during-and-after-the-oil-boom-a-policy-comparison-with-Indonesia.

Polus, A., and W.J. Tycholiz (2017), 'The Norwegian Model of Oil Extraction and Revenues Management in Uganda', *African Studies Review*, 60(3), 181–201. Retrieved from: https://doi.org/10.1017/asr.2017.88.

Roll, M. (2011), 'Conclusion: Solutions to the Resource Curse Reconsidered', in S. Sperling and M. Roll (eds.), *Fuelling the World-Failing the Region? Oil Governance and Development in Africa's Gulf of Guinea* (pp.208–224). Abuja: Fredrich-Ebert Stiftung.

Ross, M.L. (2003), 'Nigeria's Oil Sector and the Poor'. *Position Paper for DFID-Nigeria*, 1–27. Retrieved from: https://www.sscnet.ucla.edu/polisci/faculty/ross/papers/other/NigeriaOil.pdf.0

————— (2004), 'How Do Natural Resources Influence Civil War? Evidence from Thirteen Cases', *International Organization*, 58(1), 35–67. Retrieved from: http://www.jstor.org/stable/3877888.

————— (2012), *The Oil Curse: How Petroleum Wealth Shapes the Development of Nations*. Princeton, New Jersey: Princeton University Press.

————— (2015), 'What Have We Learned about the Resource Curse?', *Annual Review of Political Science*, 18(1), 239–259. Retrieved from: https://doi.org/10.1146/annurev-polisci-052213-040359.

Sachs, D.J., and A.M. Warner (1995), 'Natural Resource Abundance and Economic Growth'. *NBER Working Paper*, no. 5398. Retrieved from: https://www.nber.org/papers/w5398.

————— and ————— (2001), 'The Curse of Natural Resources', *European Economic Review*, 45(4), 827–838. Retrieved from: https://www.earth.columbia.edu/sitefiles/file/about/director/pubs/EuroEconReview2001.pdf.

Shaxson, N. (2007), 'Oil, Corruption and the Resource Curse', *International Affairs*, 83(6), 1123–1140. Retrieved from: http://www.jstor.org/stable/4541914.

Tadjoeddin, Z. (2012), 'Conflict, Natural Resources and Development', in G.K. Brown and A. Langer (eds.), *Elgar Handbook of Civil War and Fragile States* (pp.110–124). Cheltenham: Edward Elgar Publishing.

Torres, N., O. Afonso and I. Soares (2012), 'Oil Abundance and Economic Growth: A Panel Data Analysis', *The Energy Journal*, 32(2), 119–148. Retrieved from: https://www.iaee.org/en/publications/ejarticle.aspx?id=2479&id=2479.

Ukiwo, U. (2008), 'Nationalization versus Indigenization of the Rentier Space: Oil and Conflict in Nigeria', in K. Omeje (ed.), *Extractive Economies and Conflicts in the Global South: Multiregional Perspectives on Rentier Politics* (pp.75–91), Aldershot: Ashgate.

————— (2011), 'The Nigerian State, Oil and the Resolution of the Niger Delta Crisis', in C. Obi and S.A. Rustad (eds.), *Oil Insurgency in the Niger Delta: Managing the Complex Politics of Petro-violence* (pp.17–27). London: Zed Press.

PART I

INSTITUTIONAL AND REGULATORY FRAMEWORK, POLICIES AND CHALLENGES

2

Uganda's Oil Governance Institutions: Fit for Purpose?

Pamela Mbabazi and Martin Muhangi

2.1 Introduction

The discovery of commercially viable quantities of oil in the Albertine Graben in Western Uganda was announced by the Government of Uganda in 2006 (Veit, Excell and Zomer, 2011). By the end of 2017/2018 Uganda had 21 oil and gas discoveries with an estimated accumulation of 6.5 billion barrels of oil equivalent, of which 1.3 billion barrels is recoverable (Ministry of Energy and Mineral Development [MEMD], 2018). Uganda's gas reserves are estimated at 672 billion cubic feet of gas, with 499 billion barrels of non-associated gas and 173 of associated gas. There is still considerable potential for discovering more petroleum, given that less than 40 per cent of the total area in Albertine Graben with the potential for petroleum production has been explored (MEMD, 2017). For instance, two more petroleum production licences were cleared by the Cabinet, and on 14 September 2017 the Government signed a production-sharing agreement with an Australian company, Armour Energy Limited.[1]

This is in addition to some eight licences that were previously granted over oil fields in Exploration Area 1 (EAI), Exploration Area 2 (EA2) and Kingfisher Area, and shared out between Tullow Uganda Operations Pty Limited, Total E&P Uganda B.V. and China National Offshore Oil Corporation (CNOOC) Uganda Limited (MEMD, 2017). There are also efforts to search for oil and gas in other prospective areas of the country, including Amuru in Northern Uganda and the Karamoja area (MEMD, 2017).

---

[1]   The production-sharing agreement that Uganda signed with Australia's Armour Energy Limited covers approx. 133 square miles of the Albertine Graben region. The area was previously licensed to existing operators (Total, CNOOC and Tullow) but the firms gave control of the block back to the Government in 2012 after explorations failed to find viable deposits. (Source: Biryabarema, E., 14 Sept. 2017. Uganda signs Oil Exploration deal with Australia's Armoury Energy. Retrieved from: www.reuters.com).

Cumulative foreign direct investment in petroleum exploration in Uganda since 1998 was estimated to be over US$ 3 billion at the end of 2016 (MEMD, 2017). From 2017 to 2019 there has been little activity as the development phase is yet to commence pending the final investment decision by the international oil companies. Investment in the petroleum sector is expected to increase significantly as the country enters the development, and subsequently the production, transportation and refining phases of the petroleum value chain.

To add value to oil and gas resources there are plans to develop the Uganda Refinery with a capacity of 60,000 barrels per day and the associated down-stream infrastructure. In addition, feasibility studies on the development of a crude oil export pipeline from the Albertine Graben in Uganda to the East African coast were undertaken, with a view of selecting the least-cost route for transporting Uganda's crude oil to the coast (MEMD, 2017). The Hoima (Uganda)–Tanga (Tanzania) route was selected for being more secure, and cheaper in terms of cost.[2] Consequently, a 1,445 km long, 24-inch diameter, heated East Africa crude oil pipeline (EACOP) will be developed to transport crude oil from Uganda to Tanga Port in Tanzania. The development of this pipeline is spearheaded by the licensed upstream oil companies in Uganda, with participating interests by the governments of Uganda and Tanzania (MEMD, 2017) through the Uganda National Oil Company and the Tanzania Petroleum Development Corporation respectively.

These developments are indicative of the expectations that oil production will increase government revenue, improve economic growth and promote development in Uganda (Veit *et al.*, 2011). However, since the experiences of some oil-producing countries suggest that the oil discovery does not always lead to economic prosperity, there have been conscious efforts among recent discoverers of oil and gas to chart paths that would lead to oil becoming a source of blessing rather than a curse. This is the notion that countries that are richly endowed with natural resources such as oil and gas tend to be enmeshed in widespread poverty, with the benefits of the resources not enjoyed by the populace, and instead are beset by negative economic growth, entrenched corruption and political oppression (Deacon and Rode, 2012; Mehlum, Moene and Torvik, 2006; Mähler, 2010).

In Uganda, expectation of national benefits from oil production has sparked interests in the governance of oil wealth to avoid the experiences of other countries where discovery and exploitation of oil have attracted woes rather than wealth (Kiiza, Bategeka and Ssewanyana, 2011). This is against the background of growing recognition that the 'oil curse' is not an inevitable

2   http://petroleum.go.ug/uploads/resources/Status_of_Policy_2017_dl.pdf.

occurrence and that its negative effects can be avoided (see Anthonsen, Löfgren and Nilsson, 2009; Mehlum, Sachs and Warner, 1995; Thuber and Istad, 2010; Thuber, Hults and Heller, 2011). Indeed, the Ugandan president has promised its citizens that the Ugandan case will be different, and noted in this respect:

> ... There is a lot of nonsense that the Oil will be a curse. No way! The Oil of Uganda cannot be a curse. Oil becomes a curse when you have got useless leaders, and I can assure you that we don't approach that description even by a thousandth of a mile... The Oil is a blessing for Uganda and money from it will be used for development .... (as cited in Kiiza *et al.*, 2011, p.25).

In his Address to the Nation on 31 December 2009, President Yoweri Museveni promised to ensure that oil becomes a blessing to Uganda and detailed how the oil resource will be well managed for national development: He is quoted to have noted that:

> ... The development of Oil resources will go hand in hand with the continued efforts to develop other sectors of the economy that is, the diversification of the economy will continue to be among the top priorities of Government in spite of the Oil wealth. The Government recognizes the critical importance of managing Oil resources well; to avoid the mistakes many other countries have faced. ... Hence, Government will ensure that these resources are managed in a manner that facilitates sustainable development and avoids distortions such as a sharply appreciated exchange rate, which would destroy other sectors of the economy, by making them uncompetitive in terms of export. In other words, Oil and Gas resources will be managed in a manner that is consistent with the macro framework of the country. Since Oil is a finite resource, Oil revenues will be used to develop durable and competitive competences that will increase productivity in key sectors of the economy (as cited in Veit *et al.*, 2011, p.5).

From the foregoing it is evident that the Ugandan political leadership has been influenced by the growing recognition that the 'oil curse' is attributable not to the discovery of abundant natural resources but to the nature of institutional arrangements that guide the exploitation and management of natural resource deposits and revenues (Okuku, 2015).

Ahead of the next chapter which provides detailed analysis of Uganda's oil governance institutions, this chapter reviews evolving theoretical perspectives on the implications of the governance of natural resources for economic development. It explores the challenges of implementation of institutions developed for good resource management. In particular, the authors address how the political economy context affects the full realisation of the objectives of the governance institutions in order to find sustainable options for maximally harnessing oil for national development.

The chapter proceeds as follows: the next section looks at the existing debates in oil governance. This is followed in section 3 with a discussion of the apex oil governance framework in Uganda and its myriad challenges. The concluding section raises a number of reform measures needed to strengthen the governance framework in order to maximise the benefits of oil wealth to Uganda.

2.2   Beyond the Resource Curse Perspective

There is no doubt that historically natural resources have had a decisive and positive role in supporting countries to attain economic growth (Karabegović, 2009; Mikesell, 1997). Countries that have had sustainable growth because of natural resources include Australia, Canada, the United States, New Zealand, Norway, Denmark and Finland (Karabegović, 2009). There are also examples to indicate that the presence of natural resources is not by itself a conclusive basis for attaining economic growth and eradicating poverty (Ross, 2012; 2015).

Several empirical studies seeking to explain the absence of economic growth and development in some resource-rich countries have shown the high probability of the resource curse phenomenon in such resource-rich countries from the onset (see Ross, 2012; 2015; Sachs and Warner, 1995, 2001). The resource curse refers to the context where expected dividends of development do not follow the export of natural resources but ironically stimulate trends that stall development.

One of the noticeable signs of the resource curse is the 'Dutch disease'. This occurs when economic resources are moved from the productive sector, such as agriculture and manufacturing, known for stimulating economic growth, to a newly booming sector of an economy, especially in the natural resource field (Sachs and Warner, 1995). This often results in neglecting the productive sectors of the economy due to increasing dependence on revenues from the extractive sector.

A major consequence of the disease is the appreciation of a country's currency relative to other currencies, which is often due to the windfall in government revenues from the booming extractive sector of the economy

(Ross, 2012; 2015). The problem is usually manageable as long as prices of the natural resources remain stable and revenue flows are uninterrupted. However, the volatility of global market prices of natural resources, especially oil and gas, creates conditions for the manifestation of the curse phenomenon (Sachs and Warner, 1995; 2001). This is because of the balance of payments issues that arise from dependence on commodities experiencing glut and price slump.

Consequently, Frankel (2010) conducted an econometric analysis and concluded that possession of abundant natural resources does not necessarily lead to the resource curse syndrome, but rather factors such as commodity price volatility, the Dutch disease, political and civil unrest and poor institutional quality set the stage for a resource curse. Karl (2005) emphasises that the resource curse problem is more political than economic. Barma, Kaiser and Vinuela (2012) have also shown that the poor governance indicators in most resource-rich developing countries are an attestation that the resource curse phenomenon has an institutional dimension.

Anthonsen, Löfgren and Nilsson (2009) submit that the quality of institutions is the independent variable that explains the consequence of resources in the economy. This is a marked departure from the previous perspectives that regarded the quality of institutions as the intermediate or intervening variable. Institutions have been defined as the constraints devised by humans that structure political, economic and social interaction such as constitutions, laws and property rights (North, 1991).

Much historical evidence suggests that the quality of institutions or governance is more instrumental in cultivating economic growth than the availability of resources *per se* (Schubert, 2006). Considerable research has been undertaken to determine how countries richly endowed with natural resources such as oil and gas are building and using the quality of institutions to attain good governance and optimum benefits from the resources (Anthonsen *et al.*, 2009; Collier and Hoeffler, 2005; Isham, Wookcock, Pritchett and Busby, 2005; Mehlum *et al.*, 2006; Sachs and Warner, 1995; Mbabazi, 2013). This is focused on determining how political and economic actions taken by governments typified by the quality of decisions made, policies and regulatory models selected, and institutional frameworks adopted, affect the management of the resources (Ibadildin, 2011; Weinthal and Jones, 2006).

Several scholars have rightly argued that the quality of institutions determines whether natural resources would be a blessing or curse to a given country (Kaznacheev, 2017; Mehlum *et al.*, 2006; Hunter, 2014; Ibadildin, 2011). The most appropriate illustration of the impact of the quality of institutions is the two neighbouring Southern African states of Botswana[3] and Angola. At independence in 1966, Botswana had 12 kilometres of paved roads and two secondary schools; but with the discovery of diamonds, the country was catapulted into a middle-income country with growth hovering at about 16 per cent in the 1970s and 1980s, and revenue to GDP ratio climbing as high as 60 per cent by the year 2010 (Hammond, 2011). The 2016 Human Development Index (HDI) graded the country at a score of 0.698 (ranked as 106 out of 188 participating countries) and it is categorised as a medium human development[4] country (UNDP, 2017).

On the other hand, Angola is more often presented as the graphic example of a developing country richly endowed with natural resources but experiencing armed conflict and poor performance in economic and social development (Hodges, 2004). Though the oil and gas sector contributes 45 per cent of its GDP, the country has experienced rising poverty levels and political instability (Hammond, 2011). It is designated as a low human development country with a score of 0.532 and ranked at 150 out of the 188 countries surveyed (UNDP, 2017).

This abysmal position is replicated in other resource-rich sub-Saharan African States such as the Democratic Republic of Congo (DRC), Chad and the Republic of Sudan whose HDI-rankings are within the bottom 20 places (UNDP, 2017). Table 2.1 shows how a country's enabling environment, precipitated by the quality of governance institutions and practices, impacts on the resource management. This draws on pre-existing research to measure the broader governance context. A total of 89 resource countries were ranked. It is clear that the index scores for Angola and Equatorial Guinea suggest weak or failing natural resource governance.

It is important to note, therefore, that there is a correlation between strong and efficient institutions with better oil and gas management systems. This has been shown in case studies documenting the experience of Norway and Botswana (Mehlum *et al.*, 2006). The question to be settled, however, is how the Ugandan model will work to achieve the successes evidenced in the Norwegian and Botswanan models.

---

3   Botswana does not have oil, but is a flagbearer for responsible management of natural resources in the form of diamonds.

4   The UNDP categorises four classes of HDI group: (1) countries with an index over 0.800 are categorised as Very High Human Development group; (2) countries with an index between 0.700 and 0.800 are categorised as High Human Development, (3) countries with an index between 0.550 and 0.700 are categorised as Medium Human Development and (4) countries with an index below 0.550 are categorised as Low Human Development group.

Table 2.1: Resource Governance Index Scores for Selected Countries

Index Rank	Country	Index Score	Value Realization Score	Revenue Management Score	Enabling Environment Score
1	Norway (Oil and Gas)	86	77	84	97
2	Chile (Mining)	81	74	81	90
13	Ghana (Oil and Gas)	67	65	65	70
18	Botswana (Mining)	61	40	62	81
36	Tanzania (Oil and Gas)	53	65	40	53
51	Uganda (Oil and gas)	44	42	42	47
70	Angola (Oil and Gas)	35	50	31	25
85	Equatorial Guinea (Oil and Gas)	22	29	18	17

Source: Data drawn from the 2017 Resource Governance Index, Natural Resource Governance Institute (NRGI). Available at: https://resourcegovernanceindex.org/.

Van Alstine *et al.* (2014) performed a qualitative study to investigate the dynamics of resource governance in Uganda. The research findings highlight four significant governance gaps, namely: lack of coherence among civil society organisations (CSOs); limited civil society access to communities and the deliberate centralisation of oil governance; industry-driven interaction at the local level; and weak local government capacity. Other available evidence posits that the political setting, citizen vigilance and societal institutions determine and shape how natural resources are exploited, and the way the proceeds are harnessed for the benefit of the society (Lederman and Maloney, 2012; Okuku, 2015).

2.3   Uganda's Governance Framework for Oil and Gas

This section examines the different institutions and practices that have been put in place in Uganda to manage and regulate the oil and gas sector. The Constitution of the Republic of Uganda vests the ownership and control of petroleum in the Government on behalf of the people (Article 244 of the Constitution of Uganda). Accordingly, the Government of Uganda holds in trust for the people of Uganda all the natural resources, such as minerals and petroleum.

The oil and gas sector is also being developed and governed in accordance with the national development plan that is underscoring programmes such as fiscal expansion for front-loading physical infrastructure investment, industrialisation through resource beneficiation, fast-tracking skills development and strengthening governance or enabling business environment.

Within the constitutional context, the primary framework that guides the management of oil resources in Uganda is the national oil and gas policy (NOGP) (MEMD, 2008; 2014). With the overarching theme of using the resource to eradicate poverty and create lasting value to Ugandans, NOGP recognises that to attain the ultimate goal it should have as a primary objective the 'development of institutions, including legislation and manpower necessary for effective management and regulation of the sub-sector'.

Prior to the coming in force of the NOGP, Uganda's oil and gas activities were regulated under the Petroleum Exploration and Production Act, 1985, CAP 150 of the Laws of Uganda, which was implemented by the Petroleum Exploration and Production Department under the Ministry of Energy and Mineral Development (MEMD). This was a single department handling all the oil and gas activities in the country. This 1985 law covered exploration operations but did not have adequate provisions to cover development and production operations. The NOGP recommended the establishment of 1) the Petroleum Authority of Uganda to handle the regulatory functions; 2) the National Oil Company to handle the commercial interest of the state; and, 3) the Directorate of Petroleum to advise on policy issues and resource management.

These were eventually established under the Petroleum (Exploration, Development and Production) Act, 2013. Figure 2.1 shows the interaction of the recently established institutions together with other government ministries, departments and agencies.

Uganda's oil and gas sector shares similar characteristics with East Timor's governance framework which is internationally recognised as a robust system. Both Timor Leste and Uganda's model of oil and gas revenue management were developed with assistance from the Norwegian Government. The Timor Leste model shows the interconnectedness of various institutions including civil society organisations for the prudent management of oil and gas revenues. The Timor-Leste oil and gas revenue management model has been hailed for providing a strong foundation for fiscal stability, investing oil and gas revenues in foreign portfolios and reducing the possibility of the 'Dutch disease' (Mackechnie, 2013).

One of the key features of a robust governance model is the role of the Parliament. The degree of parliamentary involvement varies among different

Figure 2.1:   **Oversight and Governance Institutions for Petroleum Sector in Uganda**

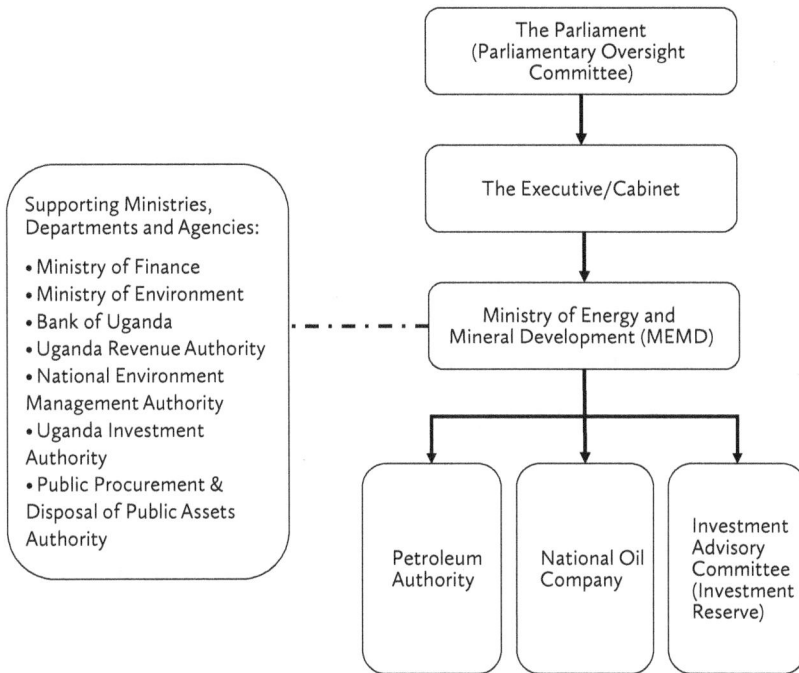

countries, and this usually starts at the point of initial licensing and contract-ing with the companies extracting the resource. Given the importance of this level in developing a framework in which the resource will be exploited, some countries raise the profile of Parliament in having powers to approve and/or veto resource contracts (WBI, 2012). In Azerbaijan and Georgia, the Parliament has constitutional powers to ratify or veto international agreements, including extractive industry contracts. In Egypt, a production-sharing contract can take effect only if approved by the legislature. In Liberia, investment contracts are ratified by Parliament (WBI, 2012).

The Constitution of the Republic of Uganda mirrors the above practices, as it places considerable responsibility on the Parliament to provide the oversight role in the management and exploitation of resources and other operations of the State of Uganda.[5] The Parliament of Uganda is accordingly

5   Section 79 of the Constitution provides that '[s]ubject to the provisions of this Constitution, Parliament shall have power to make laws on any matter for the peace, order, development and

the apex institution mandated to make laws for the regulation management and exploitation of the minerals and natural resources such as oil and gas in the country and the sharing of royalties arising from petroleum exploitation and other related activities.

However, the legal regime in Uganda is not as strong as that of Liberia or Egypt, where the international agreements or investment contracts are given effect only after parliamentary approval/ratification. In Uganda, the Minister responsible for petroleum (Minister of Energy) negotiates and enters into petroleum agreements (section 9 of the Upstream Act and section 8 of the Midstream Act) and does not require parliamentary approval. Although there is a national resources committee of Parliament, there is no oversight role of Parliament during the negotiation and contracting process. As a result, Parliament has no control of the negotiated contract terms and appears to be merely a bystander or spectator in the process. The Minister is part of the executive, and as such this process is prone to political interference and direction.

The Parliament of Uganda has enacted laws to regulate oil operations in Uganda. However, most of the laws passed by Parliament concentrate powers in the hands of the executive (the Minister of Energy and Minerals Development), and this has implications for ensuring accountability and transparency in the oil sector. This is largely attributable to the governance system that has Cabinet Ministers who are Members of Parliament selected from the majority party (WBI, 2012). In such a situation, where the ruling party has an overwhelming majority, Parliament will have no firm basis to develop independent capacities (Barkin, 2009; WBI, 2012). It is a common practice in the Ugandan Parliament for the ruling party, the National Resistance Movement (NRM), which currently controls 293 out of 400 Members of Parliament, to make critical decisions ahead of parliamentary deliberations in its caucus. In effect Parliament ends up endorsing decisions agreed upon from the party caucus. The Parliament also seems to have ceded some of its oversight responsibilities by allowing the executive to have absolute powers in the governance of the oil sector.

There is evident political interference in the management of Uganda's oil and gas sector. The President has arguably been adamant about maintaining firm control over the oil industry. He has been quoted to have said, 'In the case of petroleum and gas, I direct that no agreement should ever be signed without my express written approval of that arrangement' (Watkins, 2010). This poses a major challenge to the oil sector and undermines the authority of the oil governance institutions (Patey, 2015). Moreover, the powers

good governance of Uganda'.

vested in the Minister of Energy and Mineral Development in Uganda are arguably rather excessive and provide a conducive milieu for possible misuse and abuse (Golombok and Jones, 2015; International Alert, 2009; Veit *et al.*, 2011). This explains why the Minister of Energy could refuse to have the production-sharing agreements debated on the floor of Parliament on the pretext of protecting proprietary rights (WBI, 2012).

There has been some undisclosed information on the Government's management of the oil and gas industry in Uganda that are undermining the credibility and quality of governance institutions and practices. In Uganda, there is limited access to information on oil and gas activities. A case in point is that the production-sharing agreements (PSAs) remain inaccessible to the public. This may be due to different statutes/laws giving contradictory positions on the right of citizens to access information (Veit *et al.*, 2011). For instance, section 151 of the Petroleum Act on accessing information on petroleum activities by the public is not robust enough. Whereas the provision avers that the Minister may provide information about the petroleum agreement to the public, it does not indicate how much of the information regarding the contents of the agreement can be provided; are they details as to the parties or all the clauses in the agreement in question? This lack of transparency has created negative perceptions and worries as to whether the PSAs were well negotiated for the benefit of the people of Uganda.[6]

There is also concern that the Ministry of Energy and Mineral Development, and more specifically the Directorate of Petroleum, is simply too lean to fully execute its role in the petroleum sector. The effort to reorganise and strengthen the Ministry has been constrained by limited funding. The constrained funding has also affected both the strategic and operational business activities of fully developing the oil and gas sector in the country (MEMD, 2016; Parliament of Uganda, 2016). Government has been slow in developing and skilling human resources for the sector. Not all the staff are well grounded in technical petroleum and ancillary matters such as negotiation, licensing and contract management (Kashambuzi, 2010).

Although Uganda's oil industry is operating outside communities, degradation of the ecological biodiversity of the Lake Albert region is increasingly becoming a reality due to poor environmental governance (Patey, 2015). Oil companies are basically self-regulating. Uganda's National Environment Management Authority is underfunded, understaffed and lacks political

---

6   The Black Monday protestors used these restrictions as one of the justifications for protesting against corruption in government (see www.monitor.co.ug: 3 December 2012:   'Anti-corruption Activities Call for Black Money Protests').

authority. Environmental impact assessments have been conducted, but there are few guidelines on waste management.

2.4   Conclusions: Towards Strengthening Uganda's Oil Governance Institutions

Karl (1997) suggests that oil states have little interest in developing sound institutions because stronger institutions demand higher accountability. It has also been argued that weak institutions are chiefly responsible for the lack of growth and development in many of the oil-rich countries in the global south (Acemoglu *et al.*, 1999). The case of Uganda shows that attempts have been made to develop sound institutions to manage the oil sector. Uganda is undoubtedly at a crossroads and how it manages its oil resources will have a profound impact on its future. For Uganda to take full advantage of its oil resources and become one of Africa's oil success stories, it must strengthen its oil governance institutions and become more transparent and accountable in the way it manages its emerging oil industry. This chapter has explored the institutional framework under which Uganda's emerging oil sector is being managed. It is clear that the Government has made efforts to establish a number of institutions which are required to effectively manage the industry, but a number of gaps exist still. A lot more needs to be done to strengthen the institutions.

As argued in this chapter, there is also need for more checks and balances to ensure that the industry is well regulated. The autonomy of most of the institutions is still lacking especially in light of the excessive powers vested in the Minister of Energy. Following the consideration of the performance of the different institutions, it is only pertinent that recommendations are made for improving oil governance in Uganda. We therefore propose the following policy recommendations:

– There is need to set good practice in management and governance of the sector through giving effect to the institutions as defined in the legal and regulatory framework. The President's oversight role should be operationalised through Cabinet, and not through direct instructions on agreements and other operational matters. It is important that governance institutions' roles are clearly spelt out, and conflicting and grey areas cleared out.

– There is need to review the powers of the Minister to prevent abuses. The powers need to be tempered with clear lines of accountability and transparency.

- There is need for enhancement of the powers of Parliament so that it can effectively provide oversight to the executive and other regulatory institutions in the sector.
- The executive needs to show greater transparency and accountability in its dealings with the oil companies. The Government should provide full disclosure of activities in the sector.
- The contradictions in accessing information on oil governance need to be cleared to ensure transparency and accountability in the management of the oil resources. It is a principle of giving with one hand and taking away with the other. For example, the executive claims to have laid the signed PSAs before Parliament but the actual fact is that Members of Parliament can only look at them, without being allowed to take any notes, copy, or even take a screen shot of any of the contents therein. The Government would do well to amend the Petroleum Act (2002) and enact laws creating the environment for transparency, accountability and good resource management.
- The Bank of Uganda should take an active role in influencing the policies and practices in revenue management and align with agents of restraint. A good starting point would be to encourage Government to fast track the process of joining the Extractive Industries Transparency Initiative (EITI).
- There is need for active focus on ensuring that there are policies to stop the callous degradation of the environment especially in light of the rich biodiversity in the Albertine Graben. The oil is projected to flow for barely 25–30 years; it would be foolhardy to allow such a short stint of a non-renewable resource to run down the environment.

References

Acemoglu, D., S. Johnson and J.A. Robinson (1999), 'On the Political Economy of Institutions and Development', *American Economic Review,* 91(4), 938–963.

Anthonsen M., Å. Löfgren and K. Nilsson (2009), 'Natural Resource Dependency and Quality of Government'. *Working Papers in Economics,* No. 415. Retrieved from the University of Gothenburg website: http://hdl.handle.net/2077/21512.

Barma, N. H., K. Kaiser, T.M. Le and L. Vinuela (2012), *Rents to Riches? The Political Economy of Natural Resource-led Development.* Washington, DC: The World Bank. Retrieved from: http://documents.worldbank.org/curated/en/545221468150583397/Rents-to-riches-The-political-economy-of-natural-resource-led-development.

Deacon, R., and A. Rode (2012), *Rent Seeking and the Resource Curse* (Manuscript). Retrieved from the University of California website: http://www.econ.ucsb.

Golombok, R., and M.L. Jones (2015), *Oil Governance in Uganda and Kenya: A Review of Efforts to Establish Baseline Indicators on the Impact of the Oil Sector in Uganda and Kenya*. Nairobi: UNEP.

Hammond, J.L. (2011), 'The Resource Curse and Oil Revenues in Angola and Venezuela', *Science & Society*, 75(3), 348–378.

Hodges, T. (2004), 'The Role of Resource Management in Building Sustainable Peace', *Conciliations Resources Accord*, 15, 48–53. Retrieved from: https://www.c-r.org/accord/angola/role-resource-management-building-sustainable-peace.

Hunter, T. (2014), 'The Role of Regulatory Frameworks and State Regulation in Optimising the Extraction of Petroleum Resources: A Study of Australia and Norway', *The Extractive Industries and Society*, 1(1), 48–53. Retrieved from: https://www.sciencedirect.com/science/article/pii/S2214790X14000148

Ibadildin, N. (2011), *Role of the Old and New Institutional Framework in Combating the Resource Curse in Kazakhstan* (Academic Dissertation). Retrieved from the University of Tampere website: http://urn.fi/urn:isbn:978-951-44-8391-2.

International Alert (2009), *Investing in Peace, Issue No. 2:   Harnessing Oil for Peace and Development in Uganda*. Kampala: International Alert.

Isham, J., M. Wookcock, L. Pritchett and G. Busby (2005), 'The Varieties of Resource Experience: Natural Resource Export Structures and the Political Economy of Economic Growth', *The World Bank Economic Review*, 19(2), 141–174.

Karabegović, A. (2009), *Institutions, Economic Growth, and the 'Curse' of Natural Resources*. Retrieved from the Fraser Institute Studies in Mining Policy website: https://www.fraserinstitute.org/sites/default/files/CurseofNaturalResources2009.pdf.

Karl, T.L. (1997), *The Paradox of Plenty: Oil Booms and Petro-States*. Berkeley, California: University of California Press.

—— (2005), 'Understanding the Resource Curse', in S. Tsalik and A. Schiffrin (eds.), *Curse, in Covering Oil: A Reporter's Guide to Energy and Development* (pp.22–29). New York: Open Society Institute.

Kashambuzi, R. (2010), *The Story of Petroleum Exploration in Uganda*. Kampala: Impro Publications Ltd.

Kaznacheev, P. (2017), 'Curse or Blessing? How Institutions Determine Success in Resource-Rich Economies', *Policy Analysis*, 808, 1–48. Retrieved from: https://www.cato.org/publications/policy-analysis/curse-or-blessing-how-institutions-determine-success-resource-rich.

Kiiza, J., L. Bategeka and S. Ssewanyana (2011), 'Righting Resource Curse Wrongs in Uganda: The Case of Oil Discovery and the Management of Popular Expectations', *The Journal of Humanities and Social Sciences*, 10(3), 183–203.

Lederman, D., and W. Maloney (2012), *Does What You Export Matter? In Search of Empirical Guidance for Industrial Policy*. Washington, DC: World Bank.

Mähler, A. (2010), 'Nigeria: A Prime Example of the Resource Curse? Revisiting the Oil-Violence Link in the Niger Delta'. *GIGA Working Paper No. 120*. Retrieved from: http://dx.doi.org/10.2139/ssrn.1541940.

Mbabazi, P. (2013), *Oil in Uganda: A Blessing in Disguise or an All Too Familiar Curse?* Uppsala: North Africa Institute.

McKechnie, A. (2013), *Managing Natural Resource Revenues: The Timor-Leste Petroleum Fund*. London: Overseas Development Institute.

Mehlum, H., K. Moene and R. Torvik (2006), 'Institutions and the Resource Curse', *The Economic Journal*, 116(508), 1–20. Retrieved from; https://doi.org/10.1111/j.1468-0297.2006.01045.x.

Mikesell, R. (1997), 'Explaining the Resource Curse, with Special Reference to Mineral-Exporting Countries', *Resources Policy Elsevier*, 23(4), 191–199. Retrieved from: http://www.sciencedirect.com/science/article/pii/S0301420797000366.

Ministry of Energy and Mineral Development (MEMD) (2017), *Ministerial Policy Statements*. Retrieved from: www.energyandminerals.go.ug.

—— (2018), *Sector Performance Report*. Kampala: Government of Uganda.

North, D.C. (1991), 'Institutions', *The Journal of Economic Perspectives*, 5(1), 97–112. Retrieved from: https://www.aeaweb.org/articles?id=10.1257/jep.5.1.97

Okuku, J.A. (2015), 'Politics, the State and Limits of Oil-led Development in Uganda'. Paper presented at Makerere Institute of Social Research (MISR) Seminar, Kampala. Retrieved from: https://misr.mak.ac.ug/sites/default/files/events/UGANDA%20OIL-LED%20DEVELOPMENT.pdf.

Parliament of Uganda (2016), *The Report of the Parliamentary Committee on Natural Resources for the 2016/17*. Kampala: Government of Uganda.

Patey, L. (2015), 'Oil in Uganda: Hard Bargaining and Complex Politics in East Africa', *OIES Working Paper* 660. Retrieved from the Oxford Institute for Energy Studies website: https://doi.org/10.26889/9781784670405.

Ross, M.L. (2012), *The Oil Curse: How Petroleum Wealth Shapes the Development of Nations*. Princeton, New Jersey: Princeton University Press.

—— (2015), 'What Have We Learned about the Resource Curse?', *The Annual Review of Political Science*, 18(1), 239–259.

Sachs, J.D., and A.M. Warner (2001), 'The Curse of Natural Resources', *European Economic Review*, 45(4), 827–838.

—— and —— (1995), 'Natural Resource Abundance and Economic Growth'. *NBER Working Paper Series*, 5398.

Schubert, S.R. (2006), 'Revisiting the Oil Curse: Are Oil Rich Nations Really Doomed to Autocracy and Inequality?', [2006] *Oil and Gas Business* 1. Retrieved from: http://mpra.ub.uni-muenchen.de/10109/.

Thuber, M.C., and B.T. Istad (2011), 'Norway's Evolving Champion: Statoil and the Politics of State Enterprise', in D. Victor, D. Hults and M. Thurber (eds.), *Oil and Governance: State-Owned Enterprises and the World Energy Supply* (pp.599–654). Cambridge: Cambridge University Press.

——, D.R. Hults and P.R.P. Heller (2011), 'Exporting the "Norwegian Model": The Effect of Administrative Design on Oil Sector Performance', *Energy Policy*, 39(9), 5366–5378. Retrieved from: https://doi.org/10.1016/j.enpol.2011.05.027.

Van Alstine, J., J. Manyindo, L. Smith, J. Dixon and I. Amaniga Ruhanga (2014), 'Resource Governance Dynamics: The Challenge of "New Oil" in Uganda', *Resources Policy*, 40, 48–58. Retrieved from: https://doi.org/10.1016/j.resourpol.2014.01.002.

Veit, P., C. Excell and A. Zomer (2011), 'Avoiding the Resource Curse: Spotlight on Oil in Uganda'. *WRI Working Paper*. Retrieved from the World Resources Institute website: http://www.wri.org/project/equity-poverty-environment.

Watkins, E. (2010), Uganda's President Wants Final Approval of All Oil, Gas Deals', *The Oil and Gas Journal*, 108(32), 25–27. Retrieved from: https://www.ogj.com/general-interest/government/article/17282811/ugandas-president-wants-final-approval-of-all-oil-gas-deals.

Weinthal, E., and P.J. Luong (2006), 'Combating the Resource Curse: An Alternative Solution to Managing Mineral Wealth', *Perspectives on Politics*, 4(1), 35–53. Retreived from: https://doi.org/10.1017/S1537592706060051.

World Bank Institute (2012), 'Parliamentary Oversight of the Extractives Industries Sector'. Retrieved from: https://www.agora-parl.org/sites/default/files/parliamentary_oversight_and_the_extractive_industries.pdf.

3
Courting the Oil Curse or Playing by the Rules? An Analysis of the Legal and Regulatory Framework Governing Oil in Uganda

J. Oloka-Onyango

3.1   Introduction

Although indications of the availability of oil can be traced to the 1920s, exploration for the resource in Uganda was not taken very seriously until the early 1980s. The colonial government did not believe that oil was available in sufficient quantities to justify its exploitation (Okuku, 2015, p.4). Post-colonial governments took a similar view until a survey 'indicated a possibility of the existence of hydrocarbons in the Albertine area in the north-western part of the country' (Okuku, 2015, p.4). From the 1990s onwards, more serious efforts were devoted to exploration in the area. However, no petroleum exploration or production took off in Uganda until 2000 (Bainomugisha *et al.*, 2006, p.23).

It is therefore not surprising that Uganda lacked a comprehensive legal framework to regulate her oil sector. The law applicable to the management of all activities in Uganda's oil and gas sector was the Petroleum (Exploration and Production) Act, No. 20 of 1985.[1] The law covered exploration, discovery and production; the obligations of licensees, and the registration, transfer and cancellation of licences; restrictions and surface rights, and financial matters. However, given that no oil had yet been discovered in exploitable quantities, that legislation was barely used. The primary source of regulation of the Ugandan oil sector is the 1995 Constitution of Uganda, which *inter alia* requires the Government to ensure that resources are used for the benefit of all Ugandans.[2] Article 244(2) of the Constitution further mandates the

---

1   Since repealed by the Petroleum (Exploration, Development and Production) Act 2013.
2   See ObjectiveXIII of the National Objectives and Directive Principles of State Policy, and Article 244(1) of the 1995 Constitution of Uganda.

Parliament of Uganda to make laws regulating the exploitation of petroleum and minerals, and the sharing of royalties arising from petroleum exploitation and other related activities. As a result, Uganda currently has a number of laws, policies and regulations in place to govern the oil and gas sector. Some of these include the National Oil and Gas Policy (NOGP), 2008, the Oil and Gas Revenue Management Policy (OGRMP), 2012, the Petroleum (Exploration, Development and Production) Act, 2013 (the 'Upstream Act'); the Petroleum (Refining, Conversion, Transmission and Midstream Storage) Act, 2013 (the 'Midstream Act'); and the Public Finance Management Act (PFMA) of 2015.

This chapter critically analyses the laws and regulations adopted to manage the oil sector, highlighting their strengths and weaknesses. The discussion in the remainder of this chapter will be structured around the following issues: ownership of oil resources in Uganda (Section 2), access to information about oil resources and revenues in Uganda (Section 3), Uganda's exploration and production regime (Section 4), and Uganda's oil revenue management regime (Section 5).The chapter concludes by addressing the extent to which Uganda's legal and policy regime governing the oil sector sufficiently protects the country from the proverbial oil curse.

3.2   Ownership of Oil Resources

The issue of 'ownership' is linked to and has an impact on how oil resources are controlled, by whom and on whose behalf. Understanding ownership therefore provides important insights into who controls the resources and who is likely to benefit from them. Article 244(1) of the 1995 Constitution of Uganda, as amended in 2005, places the entire property in and control of all minerals and petroleum in, on or under any land or water in the hands of the Government on behalf of the Republic of Uganda. It also prohibits the unlicensed exploration or development of petroleum. The guiding philosophy behind this provision is the public trust doctrine which obliges the Government to account to its people as principals/owners, ensuring they participate in the management of their affairs either by themselves or through elected representatives (International Alert, 2011, p.15).

Article 244(2) of the 1995 Constitution further mandates Parliament to make laws to regulate the exploitation of minerals and petroleum, the sharing of royalties arising from petroleum exploitation, conditions for the payment of indemnities arising out of the exploitation of petroleum and minerals, and the restoration of derelict lands. Consequently, various pieces of legislation have been enacted by Parliament to give effect to the relevant constitutional provisions. Section 4 of the Petroleum (Exploration, Development and Pro-duction) Act and Chapter 4 of the Oil Gas Revenue Management Policy, 2012 respectively affirm the position of the Constitution that Government shall hold petroleum rights on behalf of and for the benefit of the people of Uganda. At the time of writing this chapter, the Petroleum (Exploration, Development and Production) Act, 2013 is the major legal regime governing the oil industry in Uganda.

Consequently, the people of Uganda are the largest and most important stakeholders in the country's oil resource exploitation. The question conse-quently shifts to how the people can ensure that their government, as the controller of the resource, abides by the rules in managing this finite resource for their benefit. Access to information becomes crucial at this stage, which is an issue we turn to in the next section.

3.3   Access to Information and the Law in Uganda

In Uganda, all oil resources belong to the Government, which must control and exploit them for the benefit of the people in a fiduciary arrangement. It is this fiduciary arrangement which naturally imposes the need for transparency and accountability on the part of the Government, and also necessitates access to information so that the people—as the principal beneficiaries of the resources—can ably gauge the same Government's performance and hold it accountable. Simply put, therefore, access to information enhances the ownership structure as by law established. This section examines the above concepts within the context of Uganda's prevailing legal regime.

Under Article 41 of the 1995 Constitution, every citizen of Uganda has the right of access to information in the possession of the State or any organ or agent of the State, except where the release of such information is likely to prejudice security or interfere with the right to privacy of another person. It is on this basis that the Access to Information (A2I) Act, 2005 was enacted. The Act was also designed to promote an efficient, effective, transparent and accountable government and to empower the public effectively to scrutinise and participate in government decisions that affect them.[3]

Guiding Principle 3 of the NOGP is about transparency and accountability which entails openness and access to information. This information enables stakeholders to assess how their interests are being affected. The NOGP seeks to promote high standards of transparency and accountability in licensing,

---

3   Section 3 of the A2I Act, 2005.

procurement, exploration, development and production operations, as well as in the management of revenues from oil and gas. Both the Upstream and Midstream Acts allow for public access to information relating to petroleum activities such as the announcement of new areas for petroleum exploration, the publication of application notices and bidding processes,[4] and access to some information/reports from the Petroleum Fund and the Petroleum Revenue Investment Reserve (PRIR).[5]

Section 61 of the PFMA requires the Minister of Finance to present to Parliament the estimated inflows and outflows of the Petroleum Fund of each financial year. One major criticism of this provision is that there is no requirement for the Minister to ensure that such payments are disaggregated in accordance with the Extractive Industries Transparency Initiative (EITI) standards stipulating the payment type, origin and source. This makes it impossible to follow company payments with government receipts, since the national budget recognises only one single figure from the oil and gas industry (Avocats Sans Frontières, 2015, p.7).

Under section 151 of the Upstream Act, the Minister may make available to the public details of all agreements and licences or approved field development plans upon payment of a prescribed fee. However, use of the word 'may' rather than 'shall' implies that the availability of such information is provided at the discretion of the Minister, who may choose to disclose only selected information while withholding other such. Section 153 goes on to prohibit the disclosure of information furnished or in a report submitted by a licensee, to any person who is not a minister or an officer in the public service except with the consent of the licensee. Government employees are even subjected to an oath of secrecy and strict penal sanctions are imposed for its breach. While the Government should honour its commitment to join the EITI and make it an open policy to publish all the contracts on the ministry's website, there is also a need for the transnational oil companies to publicly demonstrate their willingness to disclose the information they have (Avocats Sans Frontières, 2015, p.7). This will increase public trust in government and bring about enhanced transparency and accountability in Uganda's petroleum industry.

Even with such information being accessed, there remains a challenge in ensuring that Ugandans—the majority of whom are illiterate or know only basic English—are able to be included in its dissemination and debate (International Alert, 2011, p.21). Furthermore, the processes of accessing

---

4   Sections 52 and 54 of the Upstream Act.
5   Sections 57–75 of the PFMA.

information are tedious and can be expensive. Finally, the culture of government secrecy over state affairs remains deeply entrenched, to the extent that even the courts of law have been shy to enforce provisions that would compel the Government to divulge information on the agreements made in the oil sector.

Such reluctance was apparent in the *Charles Mwanguhya Mpagi & Angelo Izama v. The Attorney General* case[6] in which two journalists sought copies of agreements made between the Government of Uganda and various companies involved in prospecting for and the exploitation of oil.[7] Although the Permanent Secretary to the Ministry of Energy did not directly reject the request, he responded to it by stating that more time was needed to consult other government bodies before he could properly react. The Solicitor General also stepped in to argue that the agreements could not be accessed due to a confidentiality clause prohibiting their disclosure. Using section 18 of the A2I Act, the petitioners took the PS's non-committal response and the SG's opinion as a refusal to release the information, and filed a complaint in the Chief Magistrates' Court at Nakawa under section 37 of the Act.[8] The court dismissed the Government's argument that the information could not be released for fear of breaching a confidentiality clause contained in the agreements because to do so would mean that the State would be able to restrict all information arising out of agreements by simply inserting language which covered this angle. This was a positive response to the Government's attempt to place a blanket cover over the release of the agreements.

However, the court went on to assess both the public interest and the harm contemplated by the disclosure and declared that it was not satisfied that the public interest in the disclosure was greater than the harm contemplated. After examination, the court held that the two journalists did not show how they would use the information for the benefit of the public. According to the court, 'Government business is not in its entirety, supposed to be in the public domain'. The court determined that demonstrating such a benefit was necessary to prove a public interest in disclosure.[9]

6 Miscellaneous Case No. 751 of 2009.
7 The analysis in the following paragraphs is taken from Africa Freedom of Information Centre, *Analysis of the Court Ruling in Charles MwanguhyaMpagi and Angelo Izama vs. Attorney General (Miscellaneous Cause No. 751 of 2009) against the Framework of the Uganda Access to Information Act, 2005 and International Access to Information Standards,* retrieved from: http://www.right2info.org/cases/r2i-charles-mwanguhya-mpagi-and-izama-angelo-v.-attorney-general.
8 *Ibid.,* at 3.
9 *Ibid.,* at 6.

The *Mwanguhya & Izama* case can be criticised on two main grounds. First of all, it is for the public authority to prove that any disclosure of information in its possession would be more harmful to the public interest that its non-disclosure. It is not for the persons requesting that information to prove it. Secondly, there is no provision in the law that requires the person requesting the information to justify how they are going to use it.[10] Nevertheless, the decision was arrived at within the context of a heated exchange between Parliament and the executive, with threats issued by the President that eventually deterred the legislature from further pursuing the matter. When eventually accessed, Global Witness found many loopholes in the agreements (Global Witness, 2015a; 2015b).[11] While Government claims that the agreements have been provided to Parliament, MPs continue to complain of a lack of information and transparency about the sector (Odyek, 2016, p.7).

Signs of an early disconnect between laws and practice are thus beginning to show, even with the same laws containing various inconsistencies. Consequently, it is plausible to say that unless Uganda fully adheres to the requirements of full disclosure of information, it is bound to make the same mistakes as many other earlier oil-producing countries have, and to fall into the same traps they fell into or are in. Without access to information, the public will be blindsided as to the Government's actual activities, thereby providing a cloak for the same embezzlement and misappropriation of oil revenues that befell (and continue to befall) countries like Nigeria, Gabon, Angola and Equatorial Guinea (Gary and Karl, 2003, pp.25–42). It is however hoped that the signing into law of the Dodd-Frank Wall Street Reform and Consumer Protection Act (the Wall Street Reform Act) in the US will have a positive impact on access to information by compelling oil companies registered with the US Securities and Exchange Commission annually to disclose information on payments made to foreign governments (Veit *et al.*, 2011, p.2). This is so especially since 29 of the 32 largest global oil companies are registered with the Commission. However, only Total SA and CNOOC, in Uganda's case, would 'appear' to be bound by this law. Further questions are raised by the recent changes to the Dodd-Frank Law engineered by the Republican-dominated Congress with the support of President Donald Trump's administration (Lane, 2017). Many of the provisions in the law relating to tighter accountability and transparency have been dismantled.

---

10   *Ibid.*, at 6.
11   Also see Global Witness, 'A Good Deal Better? Uganda's Secret Oil Contracts Explained', September 2014, Retrieved from: https://www.globalwitness.org/en/reports/good-deal-better/.

Putting aside the negative developments in the United States, it is imperative that the Ugandan Government adopt a binding practice of full disclosure and unhampered access to information in order to enhance accountability and public confidence and avert the threat of a resource curse. Inevitably, this also means ending the reign of confidentiality clauses in oil-related contracts or agreements and following through with the planned application to join the EITI, amongst other initial steps.

3.4 Uganda's Exploration and Production Regime

This section examines the following three concepts which broadly fall within the ambit of Uganda's exploration and production regime: 1) licensing and the regulation of oil exploitation activities in general, 2) national oil companies, and 3) the issue of local content.

3.4.1 Licences and Concessions

The 2008 National Oil and Gas Policy (NOGP) was designed to ensure that the country's oil and gas resources contribute to the early achievement of poverty eradication and create lasting value to society. The NOGP sets out its first objective as ensuring efficiency in licensing areas with the potential for oil and gas production in the country. The policy provides for the initiation of gradual licensing as against licensing all areas at once; open and transparent bidding; execution of due diligence on companies applying for licences and avoiding the undesirable situation of a monopoly by licensing and maintaining several oil companies.

The Petroleum (Exploration, Development and Production) Act, 2013 (the 'Upstream Act') and the Petroleum (Refining, Conversion, Transmission and Midstream) Act, 2013 (the 'Midstream Act') also govern licensing. The Upstream Act regulates the licensing and participation of commercial entities in petroleum activities and provides for an open, transparent and competitive process of licensing. Section 5 of the Act prohibits petroleum activities in Uganda without an authorisation licence, permit or approval. Anybody who contravenes the provision commits an offence and is liable on conviction to a fine not exceeding 100,000 currency points or imprisonment for a maximum of ten years, or both.[12] For a body corporate, the fine is a maximum of 1,000,000

---

12   A currency point is equivalent to UGX.20,000. As at the time of writing, US$1 is equivalent to UGX.3,700.

currency points.[13] Section 6 gives power to the Government to enter into agreements relating to petroleum activities with any person with respect to granting or renewing a licence. Section 8 of the Act empowers the Minister to grant and revoke licences, issue petroleum regulations and to negotiate and endorse petroleum agreements, among other functions.

The Minister is also tasked to develop a model production-sharing agreement or any other model agreement which must be approved by Cabinet and laid before Parliament. Once approved by Cabinet, this model is supposed to guide future agreements. In November 2015, a model production-sharing agreement that had been approved by Cabinet was laid before Parliament and referred to its Committee on Natural Resources (Ekwau, 2016, p.8).

At present, the Uganda National Oil Company makes Uganda's model production-sharing agreement publicly available on its website.[14] Importantly, the Act does not provide any penalties for failure to disclose model production-sharing agreements to Parliament and it has been correctly argued that Parliament's role as regards such model agreements is merely advisory (Ekwau, 2016, p.8). This has created the situation where the Government has consistently refused to make the main agreements on exploration, development and production of oil publicly available, thereby violating the constitutional right of access to information and thus rendering this provision ineffective (Avocats Sans Frontières, 2015, p.10). Moreover, an attempt to seek disclosure of the contents of these agreements was rejected by a magistrates' court ostensibly because the applicants failed to show that the public benefit in their disclosure outweighed the harm to the third parties, i.e. the Government and the oil companies.[15]

The situation of non-disclosure raises the risks of poorly negotiated production-sharing agreements. Full disclosure forces the Government to negotiate tougher and better terms because any slips will stir controversial public debate to its detriment. Secrecy creates an incentive for either corruptly or incompetently bargained terms that are unfavourable to the nation's interest as a whole.

Section 52 of the Upstream Act requires the Minister, with Cabinet approval, to announce areas open for bidding for a petroleum exploration licence. The announcement must be published in the official *Gazette* and in newspapers of national and international circulation. Direct applications may be accepted

---

13   Section 5(2)(a) and (b).

14   See https://www.unoc.co.ug/wp-content/uploads/2018/06/MPSA.pdf, last accessed on 14 August 2019.

15   See ***Charles Mwanguhya Mpagi and Izama Angelo v. Attorney General***, Misc. Cause No.751 of 2009. For a critique of the case see Oloka-Onyango (2015), pp.27–28.

in exceptional circumstances and in consultation with the authority, and must also be published in the *Gazette* and at least one national newspaper of wide circulation.[16] In response to the announcements made, a person intending to carry out petroleum exploration activities must apply in writing to the Minister. The Minister must then require an applicant to make arrangements for the execution of a bond or other form of security and to take out insurance policies necessary to protect against liabilities that may arise as a result of activities carried out under the petroleum exploration licence.[17] Section 58 stipulates that the licence may be granted by the Minister in consultation with the petroleum authority and with the approval of Parliament on conditions made by the Minister. Unless otherwise determined, the duration of such licence should not exceed two years after the date of grant, although the licence can be renewed for another two years upon application.[18] When granted, this licence remains in force and confers on the licensee the right to explore for petroleum and carry on petroleum exploration activities.[19] As of the present time, there is no plan for companies applying for the reconnaissance permits and petroleum exploration licence to prevent social and environmental destruction, yet drilling is an extremely dangerous activity with significant risks (Minio-Paluello, 2012, p.4).

Section 69 of the Upstream Act gives exclusive rights to the holder of a petroleum exploration licence who has made the discovery of petroleum in his or her exploration area to apply for the grant of a production licence. Any other person may apply notwithstanding that he or she does not hold the petroleum exploration licence in respect of the exploration area.[20] Application for a licence may be made to the Minister in the manner prescribed by the regulations and must, under section 71, be accompanied by a report on the petroleum reservoir and a field development plan. Such plan should contain information related to proposals for the development and production of the reservoir; estimated production profiles; cost estimates; safety measures to be adopted in the course of the production of petroleum; the applicants' proposals for employment and training of Ugandan citizens and the applicants' proposals with respect to the procurement of goods and services from Uganda.

The petroleum production licence must be granted on the basis of technical competence, capacity, experience and financial strength; the applicants'

16   Section 53.
17   Section 56(8)(a)(b).
18   Section 61.
19   Section 60.
20   Section 69(4).

understanding of the petroleum reservoir as well as other conditions as determined by the Minister.[21] Under section 75, the Minister may grant a production licence after consultation with the authority and approval by Cabinet in such manner as the Minister may determine. A petroleum production licence may continue in force for a period not exceeding 20 years and can be renewed for another period on conditions determined by the Minister.[22] Once granted, such a licence confers on the licensee exclusive rights to carry on petroleum activities and to sell or otherwise dispose of the licensee's share of petroleum recovered in accordance with the field development plan. Under section 87, a licence cannot be transferred without the written consent of the Minister in consultation with the Authority, and may be cancelled or suspended under section 90 where a licensee is in default because of violations of Ugandan law. In such a case, the Minister may, in consultation with the authority and with the approval of Cabinet by notice in writing served on the licensee, proceed to do so.

The Act generally gives the Minister too much discretionary power to approve licences and their content. Given such power, if there is no tightly-defined model licence there is a likelihood that one licence could substantially differ from another in terms of content. This risks creating an incentive for companies forcefully to negotiate and influence the Minister to ensure favourable conditions for themselves and possibly to water down liability and social and environmental protection measures (Global Witness, 2012, p.8). The extensive ministerial powers also pose a threat of a concentration of political (and economic) power, common to oil-endowed nations where mismanagement reigns supreme, with the potential to reinforce corruption as there are few or no checking safeguards to counteract it (Gary and Karl, 2003, p.24).

The Midstream Act, which provides for midstream operations including the planning, preparation, installation and execution of operations related to refining, conversion, transmission and storage of petroleum products, has similar provisions related to licensing contained in the Upstream Act.[23] Anyone who operates without a licence is liable on conviction to a fine not exceeding 100,000 currency points or imprisonment of up to ten years, and for a company a fine of up to 200,000 currency points.[24] All conditions and

---

21   Section 73.
22   Sections 77 and 80.
23   Section 2 of the Petroleum (Refining, Conversion, Transmission and Midstream Storage) Act, 2013.
24   Section 9(1) and (2) of the Midstream Act.

procedures related to the application, grant duration and cancellation of licences are similar to those in the Upstream Act.

3.4.2   National Oil Companies

The national oil company is provided for under the NOGP and is born out of the State's need to create an entity to handle its commercial interests in the oil sector. Under regulatory best practice 7.2.5 of the NOGP, the intended roles of the oil company are outlined and include: managing the business aspects of state participation, developing in-depth expertise in the oil and gas industry, participating in contracts and investigating and proposing new upstream, midstream and downstream ventures locally, and later internationally. The policy correctly observes that financing the national oil company will be difficult in the initial period and, therefore, the oil company will not be able to attract shareholders. The proposal is for the national oil company to be supported as an embryonic unit at the beginning, thus starting with minimal resources and growing steadily by learning from experienced actors.[25]

Section 42 of the Upstream Act provides that the national oil company is to be incorporated and wholly owned by the State to manage the commercial aspects of Uganda's petroleum activities. The Act also provides for some functions of the national oil company and under section 44 introduces a board of directors for the company who shall be appointed by the President with the approval of Cabinet. The Board of Directors is expected to submit audited accounts of revenues and expenditure to the annual general meeting with respect to the State's participating interests, together with an annual report containing an overview of the participating interests managed by the company.

The Midstream Act acknowledges that the national oil company shall be deemed to be established for its purposes. However, section 7(3) makes it clear that it is up to the Minister with the approval of Parliament to decide that the national oil company shall participate in midstream operations. Whereas provision for the national oil company in the various policies and laws is commendable, the provisions are not as comprehensive as should be expected and need to be improved in detail. This background will later allow us to turn to the most recent development in the area of oil legislation, *viz.*, the Public Finance Management Act of 2015.

---

25   Principle 8.1.3 on financing the national oil and gas policy.

3.4.3   The Question of Local Content

The failure to exploit resources sustainably and to ensure that citizens take part in decision making and employment greatly contributes to conflicts emanating from natural resource endowments (Mushemeza and Okiira, 2016). Furthermore, the lack of involvement of citizens in the exploitation and use of the natural resource sector greatly hinders the trickle-down effect of a resource like oil, resulting in negative effects to the economy (Gwayaka, 2014, p.2). Placing an emphasis on local content ensures that non-tax benefits stay in-country or in the backyard of resource regions, and local ownerships and capital are guaranteed in the long term (Avocats Sans Frontières, 2015, p.11).

Objective 7 of the NOGP aims at ensuring optimum national participation in oil and gas activities through strategies such as promoting state participation in production-sharing agreements; promoting use of the country's materials, goods and services in the oil and gas sector, and promoting the employment of Ugandans in the sector, among others. In the same spirit, Objective 8 of the NOGP seeks to support the development and maintenance of national expertise through strategies such as the provision of goods and services to the sector by national enterprises and entrepreneurs and broadening the national education curricula to prepare the necessary workforce for engagement with the sector.

These objectives are reflected in both the upstream and midstream laws such that, while applying for a licence, the application must contain a state-ment on how the applicant intends to employ and train Ugandan citizens.[26] However, there is no strategy listed in the Acts to ensure that licensees follow up this training. Section 125 of the Upstream Act provides that licensees and their contractors shall give preference to goods produced or available in Uganda and to services rendered by Ugandan citizens and companies. Although well-intentioned, this section has been criticised for its ambiguity. The law does not define what a 'Ugandan' company is, thereby leaving a gap for exploitation. Strict interpretation of the word 'company' versus 'business entity' limits the application of the section only to companies. This leaves out other well-recognised commercial entities such as partnerships and cooperative societies, among others (Gwayaka, 2014, p.12).

The Midstream Act attempts to correct the ambiguity by providing that the licensee and its contractors shall give priority to citizens and registered entities owned by Ugandans in the provision of goods and services. Unlike the Upstream Act, the Midstream Act therefore considers other business entities

---

26   Sections 56(3)(f) of the Upstream Act and 10(6)(s) of the Midstream Act.

in addition to companies. However, both Acts lack provisions to ensure that Ugandans employed by the oil companies receive the same treatment, pay and opportunities at the workplace as their foreign counterparts (Avocats Sans Frontières, 2015, p.12). The legislation is also silent on other forms of inclusion and equity including gender, ethnic and social status.

An estimated 996 Ugandan-owned companies prospected in 2018 to provide oil-related services by registering with the Petroleum Authority's national supplier database for the oil and gas sector, a register of service providers in the oil and gas sector (Musisi, 2018). It is also estimated that the sector will create 150,000 jobs at peak oil production, and 30,000 at the start of production, which is expected to occur in 2022 based on revised forecasts (URN, 2018). Most Ugandan entities are expected to participate extensively in the sectors reserved to promote local content: logistics, clearing and forwarding, supply chain management, catering, light air transportation, security and camp management. If legislation is strengthened and practice is made to accord with the rules contained in that legislation therefore, the benefits accruing from the resulting effective promotion of local content will be valuable for meaningful growth and development.

3.5   Uganda's Oil Revenue Management Regime

Revenue management is the most important link in the chain of oil exploita-tion. Even the best production process cannot cure the debilitating effects of a poor use of oil proceeds. It determines whether the oil-exploitation process laboured through for years at a huge cost yields real benefit so as to become a great asset to the nation, or results in a resource curse. Flawed revenue management has the power to cripple nascent economies, extraordinarily grow poverty and income inequality, breed more entrenched autocracies and catalyse conflict, amongst other possibilities. This section therefore critically analyses Uganda's existing oil revenue management legal regime and its potential impact on the whole oil story. In this respect, the Public Financial Management Act (PFMA) of 2015 plays a particularly important role. The PFMA repealed the Public Finance and Accountability Act, 2003 and can be credited for its effort to provide strong checks against government expenditure and conformity of sector budgets to gender and equity budget guidelines. The PFMA mainly addresses four critical issues, namely the Petroleum Fund, the Petroleum Revenue Investment Reserve (PRIR), the Investment Advisory Committee and the issue of royalty-revenue sharing. These are separately discussed below.

3.5.1   The Petroleum Fund

The PFMA establishes a Petroleum Fund into which all the revenues which accrue to Government from the resource shall be paid.[27] All petroleum revenue due to the Government is to be collected by the Uganda Revenue Authority (URA) by the seventh day of the next month.[28] The Act makes provision for petroleum as a form of payment other than cash using a value calculated in an international and freely convertible currency.[29] This will enable the country to have its own petroleum reserve under the fund. Section 57(5) stipulates that such petroleum received as payment shall be received and recorded by the national oil company, which must then submit a copy of the record to the Minister, URA, the Secretary to the Treasury, the Accountant General, as well as to the Auditor General. This practice will ensure the maintenance of clear records, thereby encouraging transparency in the management of the Petroleum Fund. Section 58 of the Act permits withdrawals from the fund only under authority granted by an Appropriation Act and a warrant of the Auditor General. Although section 59(3) guarantees that money from the fund shall be used to finance the infrastructure and development projects of Government and not recurrent expenditure, no extra measures are given under the Act to distinguish between the two, and the resultant ambiguity could therefore result in the misuse of Petroleum Funds by the Government.

This ambiguity has already manifested itself in practice. In August 2016, the President authorised payment of 6 billion shillings out of oil revenues to 42 public officials for their contribution towards recovering capital gains tax from Heritage Oil and Gas Limited and Tullow Oil Uganda in the course of an arbitration case in London (Musoke, 2017; COSASE, 2017). While this transaction—referred to as the 'presidential handshake'—was justified by many of its beneficiaries and the President on the ground that it was an appreciation of a job well done amidst 'pressures and temptations', the fact that it was not sanctioned by law and was in fact prohibited by section 59 of the PFMA shows that there is little regard for laws and rules.

More recently, the Government withdrew 200 billion shillings from the Petroleum Fund to fund a budget deficit for the 2018/2019 financial year that ended in June 2019 (Musisi and Kyeyune, 2019). The Accountant General also claimed that this and other withdrawals will be 'offset'

27   *Ibid.,* section 56(1) and (2).
28   *Ibid.,* section 57(1).
29   *Ibid.,* section 57(4).

when oil production commences, at which time the fund will be 'better managed'. In November 2017, the Government had also withdrawn 125.6 billion shillings to finance the 2017/2018 budget. The fund, which initially stood at over 470 billion shillings in June 2018 primarily because of capital gains tax inflows, was reduced to 288 billion shillings by May 2019, without any clear indication of what precise expenditures the money was used to finance (URN, 2019). In defence of these withdrawals, the Accountant General is quoted as having said, 'It does not make sense at all to keep money in the Fund lying idle yet we have a deficit' (Musisi and Kyeyune, 2019). In response to these withdrawals, Parliament has called on the Government to establish a petroleum investment framework (URN, 2019). Without clear indications of the nature of expenditures financed and a demonstration of prudential self-control on the part of Government rather than seemingly impulsive withdrawals, the Petroleum Fund is at a high risk of mismanagement.

For purposes of accountability, section 60 of the Act requires the Accountant General to maintain proper books of accounts and proper records. The Accountant General must submit semi-annual and annual reports to the Minister, Secretary to the Treasury and the Auditor General. Section 61 of the Act requires the Minister to present to Parliament the estimated petroleum revenue for the financial year, as well as both semi-annual and annual reports indicating the various transactions in and out of the Petroleum Fund. These reports are to be published in newspapers and on the website. This provision not only enhances transparency over the monies collected, but also ensures public involvement in the same. However, the Act gives the Minister (of Energy and Mineral Development) the responsibility for the overall management of the Petroleum Fund, which is anomalous to the effort of reducing the concentration of power in a single individual without making provision for the necessary checks and balances. The aim should be to create multi-tiered mechanisms of accountability rather than to concentrate power in the hands of a single individual.

3.5.2   The Petroleum Revenue Investment Reserve (PRIR)

The PRIR is another significant feature created by the PFMA. The PRIR operates in such a way that by warrant of the Auditor General Parliament is given the power to appropriate money to be paid from the Petroleum Fund to the PRIR, which money shall be invested in accordance with the petroleum revenue investment policy issued by the Minister in consultation with the

Secretary to the Treasury and on the advice of the Investment Advisory Committee.[30]

Section 63(2)(a)-(c) imposes an obligation on the investment policy to include a requirement that investments should not jeopardise the macroeconomic stability of Uganda and that the money in the reserve must be invested in an internationally convertible currency, a debt instrument denominated in internationally convertible currency that bears interest, or any qualifying instrument prescribed by the Minister. Although the Act requires the Minister to lay such instrument before Parliament, the fact that there is no mechanism put in place to assist the Minister in determining the qualifying instrument means that the Act may be said to give the Minister fairly wide discretionary powers which can possibly result in miscalculated and unchecked decisions that could ultimately prove costly to the investment reserve.

Under section 64(1)–(3), the operational management of the PRIR is placed in the hands of the Bank of Uganda (BoU) to be managed within the framework of a written agreement between the Minister and the Governor. This agreement is to be based on the principles of transparency, accountability, intergenerational fairness and equity and shall provide for liability for paying to the Government damages that may arise out of negligence on the part of the BoU or an external manager/service provider operating under an agreement with the Bank.[31] There is also a provision for the PRIR to be managed separately from the other reserves of the BoU. The Act adequately covers the issue of undue risk under section 64(6)(a)-(b) by requiring the BoU to establish satisfactory risk management arrangements for instruments to be used in the management of the reserve. The BoU must also appoint an external investment manager in accordance with the Public Procurement and Disposal of Public Assets Act, 2003 who must adhere to the petroleum investment policy and have the necessary qualifications stipulated in the Act.[32]

The Minister may also issue policy guidelines to the BoU concerning government expectations regarding the performance of the PRIR which must first be tabled before Parliament, thus helping to check the Minister's powers.[33] Section 69 imposes a duty upon the BoU to maintain proper books of accounts and records for the reserve. The Bank must prepare and submit semi-annual and annual financial statements of the reserve to the Minister with a copy to the Auditor General, the Secretary to the Treasury and the

---

30   *Ibid.*, sections 62 and 63.
31   *Ibid.*, section 64(4)(a)-(b).
32   *Ibid.*, section 64(7), (8) and (9).
33   *Ibid.*, section 65.

Accountant General. This provision denies Parliament and the public access to these financial statements.

The Bank must also submit to the Minister monthly performance reports which shall be made publicly available.[34] Under section 71, the BoU must prepare an annual plan for each financial year for the reserve which must be submitted to the Minister for approval. The Minister must then submit the annual plan to Parliament for approval. This too is required by the Act to be published, thus fulfilling the constitutional right of access to information. An annual report is also required by the Bank to be submitted to the Minister and the Auditor General and must be tabled before Parliament by 1 April of the following financial year.[35]

Unfortunately, the independence of the Bank of Uganda has recently been questioned. First of all, the Bank's Governor has on several occasions given in to executive pressure to ill-advisedly facilitate questionable transactions. In 2011, the Governor facilitated the use of US$ 740 million for the purchase of fighter jets from Russia without prior Parliamentary approval, on the understanding that oil revenues would be used to replenish the money spent (Mugerwa, 2011). The Bank has also been criticised for indirectly facilitating electoral financing for the presidency during election seasons (Kalinaki, 2014) and for facilitating unlawful payments to a city businessman in 2011 (Sserunjogi, 2011). Furthermore, the Bank's activities regarding the supervision of financial institutions have been the subject of a parliamentary inquiry which was concluded in February 2019 and revealed inefficiency, recklessness and a disregard of rules by Bank officials in the execution of the Bank's main mandate (COSASE, 2019).

To ensure accountability and transparency in the petroleum sector, section 73 requires the Petroleum Fund and the PRIR to be audited in accordance with the National Audit Act, 2008. In order to ensure total safety of the assets in the Petroleum Fund, section 74 prohibits the financial assets of the Petroleum Fund from being earmarked, pledged, loaned out or otherwise encumbered by any person or entity. Government shall not borrow money from the Petroleum Fund or hold a financial instrument that may place a contingent liability on the fund. Consequently, any contract that encumbers a financial asset of the Petroleum Fund is null and void. It is clear that the purchase of fighter jets referred to above, which was done on the understanding that the monies used would be refunded using oil revenues, violated section 74. Also, the claim that monies withdrawn from the Petroleum Fund

34   *Ibid.*, section 70(1) and (2).
35   *Ibid.*, section 72.

will be offset when oil production commences is irrationally circular because it is a claim that money 'borrowed' from the fund will be repaid using the fund's future resources. In essence, nothing will be repaid to the fund.

3.5.3   Investment Advisory Committee

In the spirit of transparency and accountability, section 66 of the Act creates the Investment Advisory Committee to advise the Minister on the investments made under the reserve. The committee is to consist of seven members with representatives from the Ministry of Finance and the ministry in charge of petroleum activities, one from the National Planning Authority, and four who are not public officers, all to be appointed by the Minister, who will consider gender representation in the appointment. All members must have substantial experience, training and expertise in financial investment. Again, the terms of appointment of the committee members are left to the Minister for determination, although the Act requires all the names of those appointed to be published.[36]

Section 68 sets out the functions of the committee as being to include advising the Minister on the performance of the PRIR as well as other related issues. In giving its advice, the committee must take into account the economic conditions, opportunities and constraints in the investment markets and the constraints under which the BoU operates.[37] The committee is also tasked within 30 days of the end of each period of three months with submitting a report on its performance to the Minister.[38] This will enable the Minister to keep track of the committee's performance and provide accountability. However, there is no stipulation requiring these reports to be presented to Parliament or shared with the public.

3.5.4   Sharing Revenues from Royalties

According to the current law, the Central Government is to retain 94 per cent of the revenue from petroleum production, while 6 per cent will be shared among local governments located within the petroleum production areas. 50 per cent of the revenue from the royalties due to the local governments will be shared among the local governments involved, based on the level of production of each local government. The balance of 50 per cent due to the

36   *Ibid.*, section 67(1)-(8).
37   *Ibid.*, section 68(3).
38   *Ibid.*, section 68(4).

local governments shall be shared among all the local governments based on population size, geographical area and terrain. Government shall grant 1 per cent of the royalty due to the central government to a gazetted cultural or traditional institution.[39]

Several observations can be made about the manner in which the issue of revenue-sharing is formulated in the law. First of all, there is no individual reporting line for these payments to enable local communities and subjects to hold their local governments accountable for such monies. Using local government budget lines makes it complicated for ordinary stakeholders within the districts to know if the local governments are getting a fair share (Avocats Sans Frontières, 2015, p.8). Secondly, the percentages allocated to the local government and cultural institutions are peanuts compared to what the central government retains, yet it is the local governments that interact directly with the people and bring services directly to them. This also runs counter to the expressed principles of devolution and decentralisation embedded in the 1995 Constitution, aside from providing more avenues for corruption at the centre. Finally, because these provisions are not enshrined in the Constitution but are merely ordinary legislation, they can easily be changed to the detriment of the local actors. There is thus a need to achieve consensus on the sharing formulae, especially with the communities based within the production areas and a sufficiently entrenched codification of the same in order to avoid disruptive and illegitimate tampering. It is in the best interests of the nation that this be done to avoid even the remotest possibility of any forms of conflict that usually arise from revenue/royalty-sharing arrangements as is the case with Nigeria (Oyefusi, 2007).

3.6   Conclusion: Edging Beyond the Oil Curse?

This chapter has explored a fairly rich collection of laws, policies and regulations. Looking on the bright side of things, the legal regime in Uganda appears to be determined to avoid the debt trap associated with oil-producing states in Africa in which the future is mortgaged on the basis of oil, a finite resource. It is often the case that rents accruing from oil booms create a tendency of governments to inflate expenditure, especially in sectors that do not have a sustainable and positive impact on development. When the unreliability of oil revenues causes discrepancies between projected and realised revenues, governments often resort to heavy borrowing on the basis of oil, thereby

39   *Ibid.*, section 75.

endangering their economies and future generations (Gary and Karl, 2003, p.27). Oil-backed loans, for example, are endangering Angola's future. As of March 2016, its oil-backed debts were estimated to total US$ 25 billion (George, 2016). The result, as is often the case, is that more and more of Angola's crude oil flows to its creditors to offset the debts, leaving less of it available as 'profit' for the state (George, 2016).

Section 74 of the PFMA of 2015 prohibits the placement of any encumbrance whatsoever on the Petroleum Fund's assets by way of lending, pledging, committing, earmarking or otherwise. This means that the assets of the Petroleum Fund cannot be used as collateral for a debt, and neither can the Government borrow from the fund. The Petroleum Fund is thus the designated reservoir for all petroleum revenues due to the Government and is distinct from the Consolidated Fund, from which all moneys for public expenditure are derived. Even when payment due to the state is made in the form of oil, the National Oil Company holds such oil as an asset belonging to the Petroleum Fund, and upon its sale all proceeds must be paid into that fund. Any withdrawal from the Petroleum Fund must also be made under the authority of an Appropriation Act and a warrant of the Auditor General for only two purposes, support of the annual budget or for investment purposes by the Petroleum Revenue Investment Reserve. Money withdrawn from the Petroleum Fund to support the annual budget must also be channelled to the Consolidated Fund first, before extraction for its approved expenditure. The separation of oil monies from other monies of the State is thus a positive element of prudential management whose effect will also enhance the State's ability better to execute fiscal controls for macroeconomic stability. This is a promising enactment that should be able to largely curtail the risk of the debt trap that the likes of Gabon have succumbed to (Gary and Karl, 2003).

Additionally, Uganda's national oil company as envisaged is also less likely to have the same negative impacts as have most of its counterparts in other oil-producing States in Africa. In particular, it is less susceptible to the shortcomings that afflict the likes of Sonangol (Angola's national oil company) whose participation in the oil sector exceeds the bounds of simply pursuing the Government's strict commercial interests and enters the arena of mainstream industry management by, for example, collecting revenue and regulating the sector. Such a concentration of power creates glaring conflicts of interest and avenues for mismanagement, as can be seen from Sonangol which is used as a vehicle for under-reporting oil revenues in Angola (Gary and Karl, 2003). Separation of the Government's role as regulator and its revenue collection department from the national oil company's mission as a pursuer of the State's commercial interests is thus ideal and imperative.

Uganda has taken the first step towards achieving the separation. Regulation is placed in the hands of Government and bodies such as the Petroleum Authority; revenue collection is placed within the ambit of the Uganda Revenue Authority; custody of collected oil revenue is entrusted to the Petroleum Fund, while investment of the same revenue is in the hands of the petroleum revenue investment reserve. Pursuance of the Government's commercial interests in the oil sector is a preserve of the national oil company. This proliferation of duties is key to the deconcentration of power and a further deterrence to mismanagement. The hiccup however, as already mentioned, lies in the fact that the PFMA places control and overall management of the Petroleum Fund in the hands of the Minister, which is problematic. The national oil company is also subject to influence from the Minister who, under section 46 of the Upstream Act, may issue instructions to it in the execution of its tasks. Given Uganda's track record in deviating from sound policies and laws on paper to adopt the contrary paths in practice, any benefits from the positivity in these parts of the legal regime will greatly depend on the Government's own adherence to the rules. As already mentioned, the upstream law requires improvements that include a tightening up of the bidding process, greater oversight of the licensing and allocation process, and a greater role for Parliament. There is also the need to buttress the independent oversight role of institutions such as the Auditor General and for the introduction of a much more robust regulatory framework that limits the scope of companies to negotiate on key terms such as revenue rates and environment and social safeguards, among others (Global Witness, 2015a; 2015b). Furthermore, the licence allocation process is still quite opaque. The long title to the Petroleum (Exploration, Development and Production) Act, 2013 stipulates commitment to an open, transparent and competitive licensing process. However, the Minister of Energy and Mineral Development is accorded unfettered powers to circumvent the bidding process in certain instances. Indeed, on the whole, the powers conferred on the Minister are excessive.

The Government of Uganda has, after several years of pressure from civil society and international development institutions, agreed to join the global Extractive Industries Transparency Initiative (EITI). The EITI framework promotes open and accountable management of oil, gas and mining industries through public participation in holding governments accountable as trustees of their natural resources. Several African countries including Nigeria, Sierra Leone, Ghana, and Liberia have enacted the EITI into their domestic laws. Both neighbouring Tanzania and Kenya have adopted progressive and transparent policy and legislative frameworks in line with the EITI. Countries like Ghana have witnessed positive outcomes with the EITI in place.[40] Sierra Leone has taken extractive transparency one step further, with the establishment of an online electronic mining cadastre administration system (MCAS) which has improved the recording and reporting of mining revenues. All information related to mineral processing and any financial transactions in the sector are thus available to the general public in real time.

Despite making a commitment to joining the EITI as far back as the NOGP in 2008, none of the legislation on oil production took this commitment further. This commitment was renewed under the 2012 Oil and Gas Revenue Management Policy (OGRMP), but found no mention in the Petroleum (Exploration, Development and Production) Act of 2013. This raised critical questions as to the actual commitment of the Government to the transparency guidelines enshrined in the ETTI. In January 2019, however, Cabinet resolved that Uganda would join the EITI and the Government is expected to make a formal application to do so in October 2019 (Draku, 2019; Kamugisha, 2019). On 12 August 2019, civil society organisations led by the Africa Institute for Energy Governance penned an open letter to the Minister of Finance, stating that the Government of Uganda was not ready to join and utilise the EITI (Kamugisha, 2019). In the letter, the CSOs argue that, based on the Government's conduct regarding the 6 billion shilling 'presidential handshake', the recent withdrawal of 200 billion shillings from the Petroleum Fund to finance a budget deficit, the raiding of the treasury to buy fighter jets in 2011 and other similar events, the Government is unprepared to comply with the EITI unless it undertakes urgent reform. The CSOs recommend that the Government should make the EITI guidelines binding through enacting legislation, undertake a national audit of conditions necessary for the successful implementation of the EITI, and amend the PFMA to create individual liability.

There is a further problem relating to transparency, in that the three oil companies operating in Uganda, namely Total, CNOOC and Tullow, are currently not required by domestic law to disclose information regarding the payments they make to the Government (Veit *et al.*, 2011, p.10). Reliance is thus, for now, placed on foreign law to bind them. As mentioned earlier, the Wall Street Reform (Dodd-Frank) Act may have been binding on Total and CNOOC to disclose information on payments made to the Government of Uganda by way of an annual report to the Securities and Exchange Commission of the US Government. However, the recent amendments to the law

40   Since signing on to the EITI in 2003, Ghana`s corporate income tax has risen from 25 to 35 per cent; it has fixed the mineral royalty rate at 5 per cent and developed guidelines for the allocation and use of mineral royalties (Oil in Uganda Newsletter, June 2016, p.8).

could change this. On the other hand, Tullow has, in the past, voluntarily disclosed payment information in line with mandatory European Union (EU) standards. Companies which, however, receive licences in future may not be covered by the EU or US laws on disclosure (Global Witness, 2015a; 2015b). This makes it even more imperative that domestic law step in to create such a requirement.

In the end, the strongest determinant of whether Uganda will learn from the experiences of other oil-producing countries and avoid the oil curse depends on the choices that the governing regime will make and continues to make. At the moment, few of those choices can be considered reassuring. Indeed, the choices thus far made are worrying, to say the least. But, perhaps even more importantly, public pressure and joint activism from the media, civil society organisations, international financial institutions and even the countries of origin or domicile of the multinational oil companies entering into agreements with the Ugandan Government can and should influence government choices and, ultimately, the path Uganda will take in relation to its nascent oil sector.

In sum, the Government of Uganda has largely not yet fully complied with the best practices in the oil sector. This creates space for the abuse and misappropriation of oil funds, ultimately culminating in the oil curse. A genuine allegiance to the principles of openness and full access to information that enables the various stakeholders to participate fully in the oil sector is still lacking. While the legal regime can be commended for creating certain prudent parameters of operation necessary to stave off the onset of the resource curse, several improvements are necessary. These include a tightening up of the bidding process, greater levels of oversight of the licensing and allocation process, and a much stronger role for Parliament.

References

Avocats Sans Frontières (2015), *Business, Human Rights and Uganda's Oil and Gas industry: A Briefing of Existing Gaps in the Legal and Policy Framework*. Kampala: ASF.

Bainomugisha, A., H. Kivengyere and B. Tusasirwe (2006), 'Escaping the Oil Curse and Making Poverty History: A Review of the Oil and Gas Policy and Legal Framework for Uganda'. *ACODE Policy Research Series*, No.20. Retrieved from: https://www.africaportal.org/publications/escaping-the-oil-curse-and-making-poverty-history-a-review-of-the-oil-and-gas-policy-and-legal-framework-for-uganda/.

Draku, F. (2019, 1 February), 'Uganda Cleared to Join Extractive Initiative', *Daily Monitor*. Retrieved from: https://www.monitor.co.ug/News/National/Uganda-cleared-join-extractive-initiative/688334-4960686-t0khtq/index.html.

Ekwau, I.F. (2016), *Alternative Policy Statement for Energy and Mineral Development Financial Year 2016/17*. Kampala: Office of the Leader of Opposition, Parliament of the Republic of Uganda.

Gary, I., and T.L. Karl (2003), *Bottom of the Barrel: Africa's Oil Boom and the Poor*. Baltimore, Maryland: Catholic Relief Services.

George, L. (2016, 14 March), 'Growing Chinese Debt Leaves Angola with Little Spare Oil', *Reuters*. Retrieved from: http://www.reuters.com/article/angola-oil-finance-idUSL5N16H3EV.

Global Witness (2012), 'Uganda`s Oil Laws'. Retrieved from: https://www.globalwitness.org/en/archive/ugandas-oil-laws-global-witness-analysis/.

——— (2015a), 'How Compliant is Uganda with the Key Requirements of the Extractive Industries Transparency Index (EITI)?'. Retrieved from: https://www.globalwitness.org/en/campaigns/uganda/how-compliant-uganda-extractive-industries-transparency-initiative-eiti/.

——— (2015b), 'Blessing or Curse?'. Retrieved from: https://www.globalwitness.org/en/campaigns/uganda/blessing-or-curse/.

Gwayaka, P.M. (2014), 'Local Content in Oil and Gas Sector: An Assessment of Uganda's Legal and Policy Regimes'. *ACODE Policy Briefing Paper Series*, No.28. Retrieved from: https://www.business-humanrights.org/sites/default/files/documents/Acode%20-%20Local%20Content.pdf.

International Alert (2011), 'Oil and Gas Laws in Uganda: A Legislators' Guide', *Oil Discussion Paper No.1*. Retrieved from: https://www.international-alert.org/sites/default/files/publications/18-Oil-web.pdf.

Kalinaki, D. (2014, 14 November), 'Mutebile Lifts Lid on Patronage and Electoral Financing in Uganda', *The East African*. Retrieved from: https://www.theeastafrican.co.ke/news/Mutebile-lifts-lid-on-patronage-electoral-financing-in-Uganda/2558-2523800-view-printVersion-lutsw/index.html.

Kamugisha, D. (2019), 'CSO Open Letter to the Minister of Finance: Ugandan Government not Ready to Comply with EITI'. Kampala: Africa Institute for Energy Governance.

Lane, S. (2017, 9 June), 'Trump Praises House Vote to Dismantle Dodd-Frank', *The Hill*. Retrieved from: http://thehill.com/policy/finance/337107-trump-praises-house-vote-to-dismantle-dodd-frank.

Minio-Paluello, M. (2012), 'The Ugandan Upstream Oil Law: A Search in Vain for Accountability and Democracy Oversight'. *Platform Briefing Paper*. Retrieved from: https://www.platform-london.org/carbonweb/documents/uganda/2012_Uganda_analyis_of_upstream_bill_Platform_briefing.pdf.

Mugerwa, Y. (2011, 27 March), 'Uganda Government Takes Shs. 1.7 Trillion for Jet Fighters', *Daily Monitor*. Retrieved from: https://www.monitor.co.ug/News/National/688334-1133504-aohn4hz/index.html.

Mushemeza, E.D., and J. Okiira (2016), 'Local Content Frameworks in the African Oil and Gas Sector: Lessons from Angola and Chad'. *ACODE Policy Research Series*, No.72. Retrieved from: https://www.acode-u.org/.

Musisi, F. (2018, 31 August), 'Firms Scramble to Cash in on Oil Cash', *Daily Monitor*. Retrieved from: https://www.monitor.co.ug/News/National/Firms-scramble-cash-in-oil-cash/688334-4736932-lmcjanz/index.html.

——— and M. Kyeyune (2019, 3 April), 'Government Raids Oil Fund to Finance Budget', *Daily Monitor*. Retrieved from: https://www.monitor.co.ug/News/National/Government-oil-fund-finance-budget-Semakula-Mutebile/688334-5053972-cq27o1/index.html.

Musoke, R. (2017, 16 January), 'Scandal over Museveni's Shs 6bn "handshake"', *The Independent*. Retrieved from: https://www.independent.co.ug/scandal-musevenis-shs-6bn-handshake/.

Odyek, J. (2016, 28 July), 'MPs Want Information on Oil and Gas Sector', *New Vision*. Retrieved from: https://www.newvision.co.ug/new_vision/news/1430974/mps-information-oil-gas-sector.

Oil in Uganda (2016), 'EITI is a Viable Option for Uganda'. *Oil in Uganda Newsletter*, Issue 11. Retrieved from: http://www.oilinuganda.org/wp-content/plugins/downloads-manager/upload/Issue%2011%20June%202016%20EITI%20is%20a%20viable%20option%20for%20Uganda.pdf.

Okuku, J.A. (2015), 'Politics, the State and Limits of Oil-led Development in Uganda'. Paper presented at Makerere Institute of Social Research (MISR) Seminar, Kampala. Retrieved from: https://misr.mak.ac.ug/sites/default/files/events/UGANDA%20OIL-LED%20DEVELOPMENT.pdf.

Oloka-Onyango, J. (2015), 'Free at Last? Assessing the Impact of the High Court Decision in the Case of Sulaiman Kakaire & Another v. The Parliamentary Commission', *Makerere Law Journal* 22. Retrieved from: https://makererelawjournal.org/gallery/mlj%202015.pdf.

Oyefusi, A. (2007), 'Oil-dependence and Civil Conflict in Nigeria'. *CSAE Working Paper Series 2007–09*. Retrieved from: https://core.ac.uk/download/pdf/6250435.pdf.

Parliamentary Committee on Commissions, Statutory Authorities and State Enterprises (2017), *Report on the Investigations into the Circumstances under which the Reward of UGX 6 Bn was Given to the Public Officers who Participated in the Heritage Oil and Gas Arbitration Case*. Retrieved from: https://www.parliament.go.ug/cmis/browser/Sites/parliament/documentLibrary/Committee%20Reports/Standing%20Committees/Committee%20on%20Commissions%2C%20Statutory%20Authorities%20and%20State%20Enterprises.

———— (2019), *Report on the Special Audit Report of the Auditor General on Defunct Banks*. Retrieved from: https://www.parliament.go.ug/cmis/browser/Sites/parliament/documentLibrary/Committee%20Reports/Standing%20Committees/Committee%20on%20Commissions%2C%20Statutory%20Authorities%20and%20State%20Enterprises.

Sserunjogi, E.M. (2011, 10 September), 'Basajjabalaba: The Merchant of Trouble', *The Independent*. Retrieved from: https://www.independent.co.ug/basajjabalaba-merchant-trouble/.

URN (2018, 20 December), 'Uganda's First Oil Production Now Pushed to 2022', *The Observer*. Retrieved from: https://observer.ug/news/headlines/59510-uganda-s-first-oil-production-now-pushed-to-2022.

———— (2019, 24 May), 'Uganda's Petroleum Fund not Growing', *The Independent*. Retrieved from: https://www.independent.co.ug/ugandas-petroleum-fund-not-growing/.

Veit, P., C. Excell and A. Zomer (2011), 'Avoiding the Resource Curse: Spotlight on Oil in Uganda'. *WRI Working Paper*. Retrieved from: https://www.wri.org/publication/avoiding-resource-curse.

4
Keeping Corruption in Check in Uganda's Oil Sector? Uganda's Challenge to Let Everybody Eat, and Not Just the Lucky Few

Kathleen Brophy and Peter Wandera

4.1   Introduction

The discovery of oil and subsequent transition into an oil-producing State is a complex task for any country. The social, political and economic impacts of oil are multifaceted and far-reaching and the transition into an oil-producing State is a unique process for every country. Though there is no exact formula for success in harnessing oil extraction for shared prosperity and widespread development, certain best and worst practices have certainly emerged. When managed well, oil revenues can transform a country's economy and significantly contribute to development and poverty alleviation. But, in many countries around the world oil has served to enrich only the select elite, entrenching and exacerbating pre-existing systems of clientelism and corruption.

According the popular 'resource curse' theory, discovery of natural resources in developing countries can often lead to more harm than benefit and can cause widespread instability in a country (Kathman and Shannon, 2011). Experts have cited this as the catalyst for breakdown in many countries including the Democratic Republic of the Congo, Sierra Leone and Nigeria (Shepherd, 2013). This paradoxical phenomenon refers to the inverse effect that increased resource rents can have on the standard of living in a given country. According to Bategeka and Mawejje:

> The natural resource curse refers to a situation in which, exploitation of newly discovered natural resources does not lead to a reduction in poverty and improvements in human development, but instead, exacerbates poverty

and negatively affects the people's living standards (Bategeka and Mawejje, 2013, p.1).

In fact, the 'curse' itself has little to do with the resource. Instead, the resource curse refers to the challenges associated with successful governance and management of resource benefits and revenues (Kiiza, Bategeka and Sswanyana, 2011). The negative effects associated with resource discovery are due to a complex set of interrelated factors. As stated in a 2012 African Development Bank study:

> These counter-intuitive trends however are more complex ... The abundance of a resource is after all, not the cause of poor growth. Rather, the abundance of a resource creates incentives for poor wealth management which in turn result in less rather than more growth (Castel and Ximena Meijia, 2012, p.2).

While the resource curse refers to many different negative impacts of resource extraction, this chapter focuses on one particular element, i.e. corruption and mismanagement of resource revenues. For the purposes of this chapter corruption will be defined in line with Transparency International's definition as 'the abuse of entrusted power for private gain' (see Transparency International, 2018). This includes any unauthorised and deliberate manipulation of circumstances leading to private benefit derived from public revenue.

Based on this definition of corruption, this chapter will examine the risks of corruption in Uganda's burgeoning oil sector by mapping the opportunities for revenue mismanagement onto the standard oil revenue chain. Then the various vectors for corruption will be explained and analysed in the context of Uganda. Finally, the chapter will explore the various frameworks and initiatives in place aiming to prevent corruption in the development of Uganda's oil sector. The chapter will then close with reflections on the interplay between oil, democratic governance and corruption with prescriptions for Uganda.

4.2   Natural Resources in Uganda: Some Basic Facts

When Uganda announced the discovery of commercially viable reserves of oil in 2006 reactions were mixed. Many were naturally excited that oil would lead to investment and transformative development. On the other hand, some were sceptical that the oil would in fact lead to widespread prosperity due to the country's history of endemic corruption. It is certainly true that the discovery of oil will endow Uganda with significant returns—once commercial production begins the reserves are expected greatly to impact on government revenue annually for at least 25 years. What is less certain is who will benefit from these revenue windfalls and, furthermore, who will suffer the consequences of mismanagement. In a 2012 brief by Global Witness, the watchdog organisation summarised these concerns as follows:

> The industry is born into a deteriorating governance environment, characterized by the consolidation of Uganda's neo-patrimonial regime; increasing perceptions of corruption and high-level state looting; and some early warning signs that the government's own commitments to good governance standards laid out in its oil and gas policy are not being implemented (Global Witness, 2012, p.1).

According to projections by the organisation, the outlook for good governance of oil revenues is concerning 'in a country with Uganda's recent history of deteriorating governance standards, high-level corruption and nepotism', and 'the succession of scandals surrounding the misappropriation of public and donor funds over the last ten years' (Global Witness, 2010, p.16).

According to 2012 World Bank worldwide governance indicators, Uganda loses US$ 286 million annually from corruption.[1] Instances of bribery, embezzlement and graft persist from the most local levels of government up to the highest executive offices. For instance, in 2012 the Office of the Prime Minister was alleged to have stolen US$ 12.7 million in donor funds intended to go to recovery programmes in war-torn Northern Uganda (Reuters, 2012). Unfortunately, this type of scandal has been continuously repeated in the country's recent history, leading some to believe that a general level of impunity has set in among government officials.

Despite the country's history of corruption, Government has not put in place adequate safeguards to prevent malfeasance in Uganda's burgeoning oil sector. Discounting international best practice guidance promoting enhanced transparency and accountability in the extractive industries, the Government has continued to operate in secrecy, keeping critical information about oil-sector developments hidden from the general public. This opacity presents a serious risk that oil and mining revenues may be wasted or corruptly diverted instead of spent on much needed public services.

---

1   See World Governance Indicators. Available at: http://info.worldbank.org/governance/wgi/index.aspx#home.

Oil has not yet left the ground in Uganda but there is already sufficient evidence of mismanagement associated with pre-production revenues. Instead of seeing the benefits of oil revenues in the form of local school renovations and improvements in the country's lacking electrical grid, Ugandans learn about oil revenue expenditures in the headlines of local newspapers detailing the latest scandals uncovered.

In 2011, the Government struck a deal with a Russian arms exporter for a US$ 740 million advance for the purchase of six fighter jets. Addressing Members of Parliament, the Governor of the Bank of Uganda said he consented to the advance on the assurance that it would be repaid by future oil revenues (Mugerwa, 2015). This one-off discretionary expenditure represents a quarter of the entire 2011/2012 national budget and over four times the combined education and health budgets for that year.

That same year, Members of Parliament alleged that three senior members of Cabinet, including the Prime Minister, had received 'oil bribes' from certain oil exploration firms. However, the parliamentary ad hoc committee in charge of the resulting investigation found no evidence to support the allegations due to the inability to access the necessary information (Republic of Uganda, 2013). The committee's report of findings did note huge sums of oil revenues unaccounted for, including discrepancies at times amounting to nearly US$ 500,000 missing in several account transfers between the different government entities tasked with collecting oil revenue (Republic of Uganda, 2013, p.13).

More recently, in January 2017 it was discovered that US$ 1.6 million had been paid as a reward to 42 government officials loosely involved in the recovery of Shs 1.5 trillion in capital gains tax owed from Heritage Oil and Gas. The scandal, named the 'presidential handshake' controversy, revealed a disturbing lack of regard for the protocols outlined in the petroleum section of the Public Finance Management Act, 2015 (PFMA) governing withdrawals from the Petroleum Fund.

These instances, described in more detail below, paired with a continuous lack of access to information for citizens, mean that the oil sector is developing in Uganda with little transparency or accountability. Citizens simply lack the information necessary to hold Government accountable. According to the needs analysis performed in the creation of *The National Communication Strategy for Oil and Gas*, a widely evidenced information gap exists between the Government and people related to oil and gas sector development (Republic of Uganda, 2013, p.13). According to the analysis, over 50 per cent of the people sampled had little knowledge of the policy and regulations around the sector, and many people also believed that information surrounding the oil activities was shared only among elites (Republic of Uganda, 2013, p.14).

According to political scientist Michael Ross, without coherent and insistent demands from an informed public, the Government-citizen relationship could break down in the process of resource extraction and the Government could become increasingly despondent (Ross, 2001). Unless this is averted through greater access to information for citizens regarding oil sector developments, the industry will continue to operate in secrecy, devoid of public scrutiny.

4.3 Conceptualising Corruption as 'Leakages' in the Petroleum Revenue Chain

There are many risks in ensuring transparency and accountability in the emerging extractive industries in Uganda, as in any country. These risks can be divided between the horizontal (company to government) and vertical (intra-government) opportunities for corruption in the petroleum revenue chain. 'Horizontal' risks can be summarised as *illicit reductions* in the revenue base paid to government while 'vertical' risks can be thought of as *illicit diversions* of the oil revenue once paid to government. In other words, these risks can be phrased as two separate but interrelated questions—did the Government get what it was rightfully owed and did those revenues paid to Government successfully reach citizens? This conceptualisation is based on the standard petroleum revenue chain, modelled in this case according to the petroleum revenue management scheme established in Uganda's Public Finance Management Act, 2015, as depicted in Figure 4.1.

According to the Constitution, petroleum is a national resource, to be managed by Government in trust of the citizens. Therefore, the Government is the agent, managing natural resource extraction on behalf of the citizens as ultimate owner and principal. In this framework, revenue derived from oil extraction must be returned to citizens Similarly, when Government allocates extraction rights to companies, companies also take on the role of the agent, extracting on behalf of Government as the principal. In both cases, there is an opportunity for the principal-agent problem to arise, wherein 'the agent pursues his own interests rather than those of the principal who hired [or in this case elected] the agent' (Bategeka and Mawejje, 2013, p.19). In either case, such an issue leads to agents behaving out of individual self-interest, so that either less oil revenue goes into government coffers or is taken out of government coffers. Either way, the result leads to less oil revenues distributed to citizens for public benefit.

Conceptually, 'corruption' in the petroleum revenue chain can also be thought of as 'revenue leakages' or instances where money may go 'missing'.

Figure 4.1:   **Uganda's petroleum revenue management scheme**

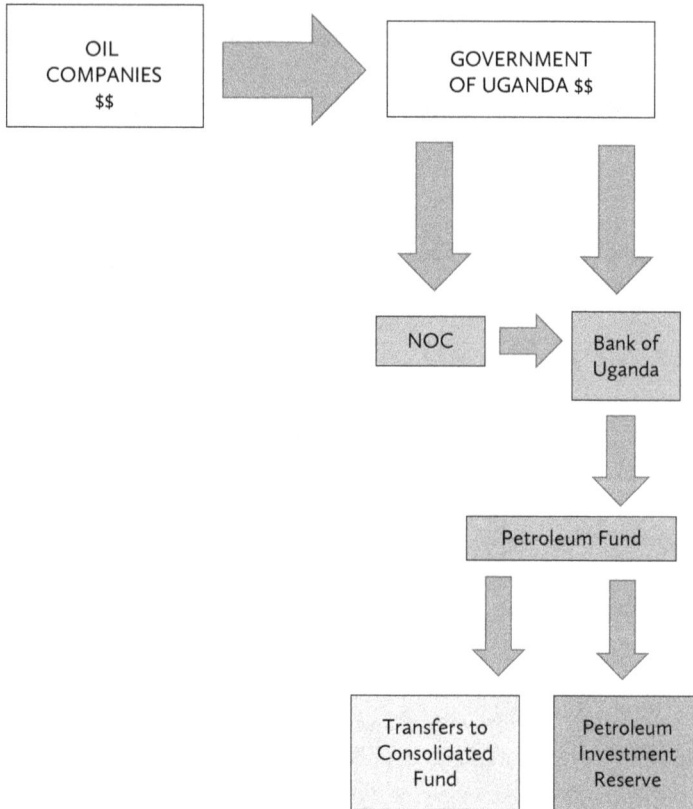

Weak areas in the revenue chain can cause revenue leakage in so far as they may be exploited to divert money from the public financial realm into the private in an unauthorised manner. This must also include money that never formally entered the public domain in the first place, but rightfully should have, as explained further below in the horizontal leakages section. Thus, standards for good governance dictate that oil revenue management schemes should be insulated and protected from this sort of discretionary diversion through statutory requirements for transparency, accountability and oversight throughout the entire revenue chain.

4.4 Horizontal Leakages and Risk Areas for Uganda

As depicted in Figure 4.2, the horizontal relationship between companies and Government represents the cadre of transactions and agreements that take place between the two entities prior to and during extraction. There are many instances during these transactions where corruption could occur, limiting the maximum amount of money that could then be introduced into the revenue chain and later transformed into public benefit. First, companies must bid for the right to extract. As with any public contract, the public procurement process may be corrupted in many ways, especially when the contract is of high value.

Figure 4.2: **Horizontal relationship between the Government and oil companies**

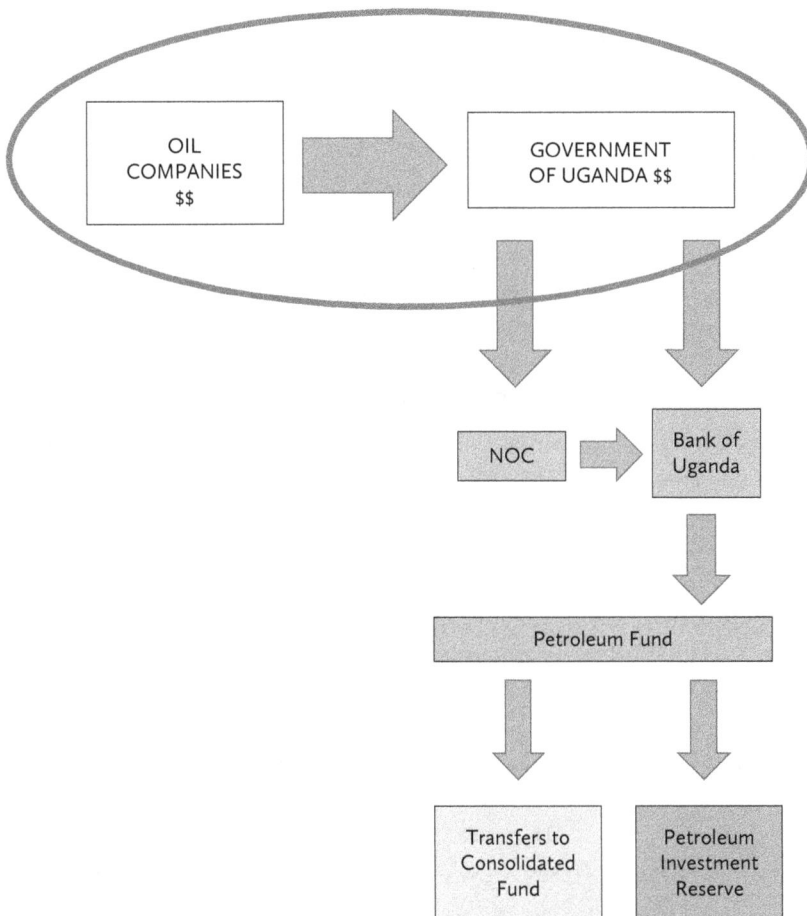

4.4.1   Contract Negotiations and Corruption in the Bidding Process

Often, procurement and negotiation processes for oil sector contracts happen behind closed doors in an ad hoc fashion. This is especially true in the oil industry for frontier areas that have not yet been fully explored where the reserve potential is not widely known. In such cases, companies are often handled on a first-come-first-serve basis, with little formal regulation or oversight of the bidding and negotiation process. During such processes, a small number of government officials are given the discretion to negotiate the contract directly with the company. In such a setting, officials may be tempted to accept suboptimal terms of contract with the promise of individual benefit on the side. In this way, government officials may be compromised and negotiate a poor deal for the country, due to an offer for some sort of compensation by the company for doing so. Therefore, the individual government official gains while the country loses out on future revenues due to corrupted negotiations.

Procurement processes may also be manipulated by relevant decision makers, with conflicts of interest illicitly influencing the choice of bidder. Often, these conflicts of interest are undisclosed by politically exposed persons and relate to a company's ultimate beneficial owners. Politically exposed persons with high-powered connections often manipulate contract processes and win licences based on patronage associations or clientele relationships rather than the merit and quality of the bid. According to a 2012 report by Global Witness:

> Too often private 'shell' companies with opaque ownership structures are awarded lucrative concessions with little information available as to who the beneficial owners of the company are, how much (if anything) the company has paid for the license, and what the country has gained in return (Global Witness, 2012, p.3).

These opaque licensing procedures are used to award contracts to government officials or their private sector proxies outside a fair, open and competitive bidding process (Global Witness, 2012). For instance, in Nigeria in 2005 a company named Conoil Producing Ltd partnering with local company New Tigerhead PSTI Limited, won an offshore oil licence. Based on investigations, it was later found that the Chair of the Nigerian Senate Committee on Petroleum Resources Upstream responsible for bid allocation, was the majority shareholder of New Tigerhead PSTI Limited (Global Witness, 2012, pp.22–23). Of course, such a stark conflict of interest taints the integrity of the bidding process, and also brings into question the actual merits of the selected bidder.

In worst case scenarios, the chosen bidder lacks the qualifications to carry out the contract and ends up transferring the contract to another company for a profit, at the cost of the State. In such cases involving corruption in rights allocation, the State sells the licence to the politically exposed person for less than market value due to the conflict of interest held by an influential official, and the country loses out on revenues that could have been gained in a non-corrupted, market-based transaction.

Conflicts of interest can taint the rights allocation process at many steps in the bidding process. Thus, international best practice recommends that countries allocate rights using fair, open and competitive bidding processes that are standardised and closely regulated. That way, undue influence cannot easily manipulate the process. Considering contract negotiation and procurement manipulation to be a form of corruption, the Ugandan case has already proven problematic. The first set of exploration and production licences to Tullow, Total and CNOOC were granted in direct, non-competitive closed negotiations. While some could argue that this was necessary based on the state of oil-sector development at the time, it led to many issues.

First, in 2010, the production-sharing agreement (PSA) between the Government of Uganda and Heritage Oil was leaked to the public. This leak allowed civil society to undertake joint work and engage in dialogue with the Government on the weaknesses and risk areas illustrated in the agreement and ways to improve the terms of contract. The agreement included many problematic components. Upon review, the Norwegian Agency for Development, NORAD, ultimately declared, '[The PSAs] cannot be regarded as being in accordance with the interests of the host country' (Civil Society Coalition on Oil and Gas in Uganda, 2010, p.16). The Petroleum Exploration and Production Development (PEPD) Commissioner also admitted that the heritage PSAs were not in Uganda's best interest. The agreement was later revised when Heritage Oil was acquired by Tullow Oil, which entered into a joint venture partnership with oil majors Total and CNOOC.

Due to the continuous secrecy of oil sector contracts and suspicions of malfeasance, in 2011 the Parliament of Uganda passed a motion establishing a moratorium on the issue of new oil sector agreements (Parliament of Uganda, 2011). This motion mandated the executive to pass updated oil laws and publicly share all signed oil sector agreements before new licences could be issued. It also authorised the investigation into allegations of oil sector bribery involving the then Prime Minister, Rt. Hon Amama Mbabazi, the current

Foreign Affairs Minister, Hon. Kutesa Kahamba Sam, and the former Internal
Affairs Minister, Hon. Obaloker Hillary Onek (Parliament of Uganda, 2011).

All three officials were accused of various high-level revenue manipulation
and embezzlement offences in collusion with oil companies. Kutesa was
alleged to have received payments from Tullow Oil PLC, amounting to over
€30,000,000 through transfers to his company, East Africa Development
Limited (Republic of Uganda, 2013). Similarly, Onek was accused of receiving
transfers from a Tullow account to his foreign account in Dubai. Onek,
along with Mbabazi, was also accused of personally benefiting from the sale
of production rights from Eni SpA to Heritage Oil (Republic of Uganda,
2013). Mbabazi was also accused of receiving money from a shell company
called TKL Holdings set up for his benefit in London by Eni SpA (Republic
of Uganda, 2013). The parliamentary investigation committee eventually
exonerated all the three of the oil bribery allegations but cited a general
inability to perform its investigation due to lack of access to information from
banks and lack of cooperation by government institutions as key weaknesses
hindering the outcomes of the investigation (Republic of Uganda, 2013).

Subsequently, for over two years, the Government of Uganda then spent
public monies battling Tullow Oil in court over a discretionary tax incentive
offered by Energy Minister Irene Muloni in closed-door negotiations with
the oil company (Larsen, 2014). During negotiations, Muloni's team offered a
capital gains tax exemption which, according to Article 152 of the Constitution,
is outside their mandate (Larsen, 2014). Then, when the Uganda Revenue
Authority later charged the company its full capital gains tax liability, the
company took the Government to court. Even though the two parties eventually settled, the Government spent thousands of dollars fighting the case in
Ugandan courts and eventually international tribunals. Although corruption
on the part of Muloni was never alleged, the discretionary incentive offered
in the closed-door negotiations eventually cost the Ugandan Government
hundreds of thousands of dollars in public revenues.

4.4.2   Corporate Tax Planning and Tax Base Erosion

Once the contracts are signed, the Government has to make sure that all
due revenues are collected. This is especially difficult, given the prevalence
of aggressive tax-avoidance activities and base erosion and profit shifting in
the global extractive industries (African Union Commission/United Nations
Economic Commission for Africa, 2015). Once contracts are awarded, there
are many opportunities for companies to manipulate their accounting and
reporting to artificially maximise profit and deprive the State of revenues owed.

According to the International Monetary Fund, this is especially pertinent in countries with a legal regime operating through profit-sharing agreements whereby the company is contracted to extract the resource and is rewarded with a share of the production in return (International Monetary Fund [IMF], 2007). Thus, the oil is divided between 'cost oil retained by the contractor to cover cost and profit oil, which covers the remaining production and an agreed formula for dividing profit oil between the government (and/or NOC) and the contractor' (IMF, 2007, p.22).

One common form of manipulation under this regime is an inflation of cost oil figures or 'recoverable costs' by companies to misrepresent the costs of the project and therefore retain more revenue than the company is due. As described in a 2010 report by the Civil Society Coalition on Oil and Gas in Uganda:

> When the cost oil total is increased this reduces the quantity of oil remaining as 'profit oil' but as the profit oil is split between the companies and the state this only hurts the state because the cost of 'allowable expenditures' is passed onto the state in the form of reduced profit oil (Civil Society Coalition on Oil and Gas in Uganda, 2010, p.9).

As described by extractive industries economist Don Hubert (2016), this sort of cost manipulation is a form of tax base erosion. 'Because the bulk of government revenue normally comes from profit-based taxes—that is taxes that are assessed on net income- (after cost income-) inflated costs can significantly reduce the tax base' (Hubert, 2016, p.8). Companies can fraudulently inflate their costs using many tax planning tools such as transfer mispricing of transactions between associated entities, or thin capitalisation manipulation. Because of this sort of activity, the Government must diligently consider which types of costs to deem 'recoverable' to check that companies are not including expenses that should not be counted as recoverable.

In Uganda, such issues have arisen in past and current contracts. For instance, Heritage Oil attempted to submit voluntary corporate social responsibility initiatives as cost recoverable, although this is not an authorised recoverable cost. This type of misrepresentation occurred in Heritage Oil's reported cost recoverable figures. According to an Ernst & Young audit of the company's activities, the company over-claimed unauthorised cost recoverable expenditures of over US$ 500,000 (Civil Society Coalition on Oil and Gas in Uganda, 2010).

According to a 2014 analysis by Global Witness of the leaked 2012 PSAs signed between Government and the joint venture partners, many recoverable cost issues are also present in the current PSAs. According to the analysis, clauses in the PSAs to limit the artificial inflation of costs due to thin capitalisation and transfer mispricing are weak and put the Government at risk of undue revenue loss (Global Witness, 2014, p.37).

Outside recoverable costs, multinational companies employ aggressive tax-planning schemes to artificially reduce their general tax liability to the Government. In 2010, eleven days before Heritage Oil was to sell its oil shares in Uganda, the company deliberately re-domiciled its country of incorporation from Bahamas to Mauritius to avoid paying the Government of Uganda US\$ 400 million in capital gains tax (BBC News, 2016). Because Uganda has a double tax agreement with Mauritius, and Mauritius does not impose capital gains tax, the company decided to relocate to Mauritius in order to zero out its tax liability to the Government of Uganda (BBC News, 2016). The ensuing court case between the Government of Uganda and the company to recover the money from both Heritage and Tullow Oil dragged on for years and cost the Government additional money (BBC News, 2016). The aggressive tax avoidance scheme employed by the company was only fully uncovered in 2016 when emails surfaced during the massive 'Panama papers' leak. Other than information gleaned from this leak, it is very difficult to expose such practices by companies, despite the frequency of such acts.

In addition to these 'horizontal' risks, there are also many 'vertical' risks of revenue leakage in the intra-government management of oil revenues, as depicted in Figure 4.3. These types of leakages fall more in line with conventional notions of 'corruption' and are more commonly identified as such. Within the government revenue chain, it is very important that petroleum revenue is strictly managed with sufficient oversight in order to prevent embezzlement and malfeasance in the use of oil money. Given the potential for direct and immediate benefits to politicians from natural resource revenues, the principal-agent problem again arises wherein politicians as the agents become tempted to divert the newfound revenue stream for personal or political benefit, rather than for the benefit of the principal, in this case the citizens of Uganda.

In sum, oil revenues can incentivise and increase instances of political corruption. According to Robinson, Torvik and Verdier:

> In countries with institutions which limit the ability of politicians to use clientelism to bias elections, resource booms tend to raise national income. When such institutions are absent, the perverse political incentives may dominate and income can fall—there is a resource curse (Robinson, Torvik and Verdier, 2006, p.466).

Figure 4.3: **Risks for vertical revenue leakage in Uganda**

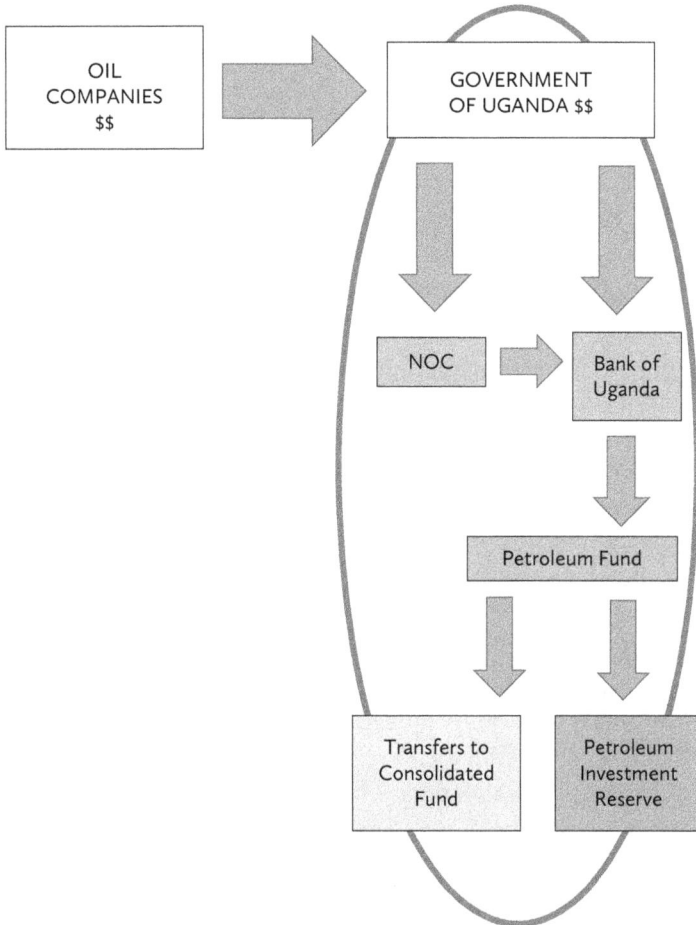

As the logic goes, resource rents simply present yet another opportunity, in the form of an additional revenue stream, for graft and embezzlement by politicians in resource-rich countries that politicians in resource-scarce countries do not have. According to Kiiza, Bategeka and Sswanyana, 'The "paradox of plenty" as the resource-curse is often termed, is embedded in the age-old maxim: Necessity is the Mother of Innovation. Resource-poor countries are forced to innovate and attain economic viability. By contrast, resource-rich countries suffer the paradox of plenty and remain poor' (Kiiza *et al.*, 2011, p.9).

4.4.3   Executive Capture

In countries with an overly dominant executive, oil revenues can 'leak' out of the public revenue chain by acts of executive interference. Simply put, if resource revenues can be easily called upon by a president or other powerful members of the dominant political party for instance, with no mechanisms to limit or regulate their usage, revenues risk becoming a slush fund for patronage and corruption. Importantly, because resource revenues are rent-based and not tax-based, there is often less accountability than with money that was earned or derived from citizens through taxation.

According to Robinson, Torvik and Verdier, oil can create perverse political incentives and entrench corruption.

> The existence of natural resources incentivizes the current political regime to over-extract regardless of the socially efficient rate of extraction because they cannot guarantee that they will have permanent access to the resource as they do now and thus due to political uncertainty, must reap maximum benefit they can in the short-term (Robinson *et al.*, 2006, p.466).

Therefore, the ruling regime feels pressure to take advantage of the benefits of extraction, uncertain whether power over the resource revenues will change hands in the near future. Often, regimes publicly exert their perception of control over the resource. It is common that the regime in power at the time of discovery will personalise possession of the oil, treating the resource as a possession of the ruling entity, abetting a transition into a kleptocratic State. This is most common in countries with an overly dominant executive, able to thwart protocols and regulations to limit political capture, as is certainly the case in Uganda.

In Equatorial Guinea, for instance, the Obiang regime exercises far-reaching control over all arms of government. Over more than two decades, the regime has managed to enshrine a fully functioning and intricate system of corruption to divert almost all of the country's natural resource revenues to the Obiang family and surrounding elite. Due to the degree of corruption, Open Society Foundation (2010, p.3) labelled the country 'an almost perfect kleptocracy' marked by 'a system of corruption unparalleled in its brazenness'. According to the report, the President and his son and nephew controlled the government oil account, and the three account signatories authorised the removal of US$ 34 million from the government oil account to shell corporations and accounts in tax havens all over the world to the benefit of the ruling family (Open Society Foundation, 2010, p.6).

In Uganda, President Museveni commonly refers to the oil as his direct possession, reinforcing suspicions of problematic personalisation of the national resource. According to Ugandan newspaper the Daily Monitor, at an international oil and gas summit in November 2016, the President 'accused the opposition of being after "my oil" and wanting him to quit leadership at time when the country is about to start oil production an earn revenues; which he said he won't leave in the hands of his opponents' (Musisi, 2016). During the 2016 campaigns, the President commonly referred to the oil as 'my oil' and vowed to maintain his control over the resource. According to the Guardian, Museveni made such statements several times, including at campaign rallies, quoting the President as saying, 'You hear people say "Museveni should go", but go and leave oil money?' (Mwesiga, 2016).

This is especially concerning, given that in Uganda the President can easily thwart almost all statutory limits to executive capture to call upon revenues whenever necessary. In 2011, the Government struck a deal with a Russian arms exporter for a US$ 740 million advance for the purchase of six fighter jets (Imaka, 2011). News of the purchase resulted in public outrage due to the negative impacts the sale had on the already stressed economy. During the subsequent parliamentary investigation into the purchase, the Governor of the Bank of Uganda explained that the President instructed the release of public funds without parliamentary authorisation for this purchase, on the condition that the money would be replenished by future oil revenues (Imaka, 2011). However, this is in contravention of the Government's position on oil revenue expenditure—that oil revenues will be used for infrastructure and development.

In January 2017, the President again decided to reward Shs six billion to 42 various government officials involved in the recovery of Shs 1.5 trillion in capital gains tax owed from Heritage Oil & Gas. This payment, which came to be known as the 'presidential handshake' was another disturbing example of the President's ability to make decisions in contravention of domestic laws. Not only was it revealed in subsequent investigations that many of the government officials, including high level Cabinet members, had absolutely no involvement in the case, all of the payments were in contravention of the Public Finance Management Act, 2015 (Musoke, 2017).

Contrary to the statement issued by the Uganda media centre after the scandal broke, asserting that the payments went through the 'necessary approval' process as mandated by the PFMA, the payments were explicitly contrary to the rules outlined in the Act, and without legal warrant. As revenues derived from 'the exploitation of petroleum reserves in Uganda', as outlined by the PFMA, the CGT award won in the case against Heritage falls under the designation of 'petroleum revenues'. According to the PFMA, all oil revenues are to be paid into a newly created Petroleum Fund, hosted by the Bank of Uganda (Public Finance Management Act [PFMA], 2015). The Annual Reports from the Bank of Uganda for 2014/2015 and 2015/2016 indeed confirm the partial payment of these monies into the Petroleum Fund in the past two years. Once money has been deposited into the Petroleum Fund, it may only be withdrawn

> Under authority granted by an Appropriation Act and a warrant of the Attorney General—(a) to the Consolidated Fund, to support the annual budget; and (b) to the Petroleum Revenue Investment Reserve, for investments to be undertaken in accordance with section 63 (PFMA, 2015, p.55).

Further still, the PFMA clearly restricts the use of oil revenues, stating that '[f]or avoidance of doubt, petroleum revenue shall be used for the financing of infrastructure and development projects of Government and not the recurrent expenditure of Government' (PFMA, 2015, p.56). The petroleum section of the PFMA, and the specific creation of a strictly managed Petroleum Fund, was written to prevent exactly this type of discretion and executive capture in the expenditure of oil revenues. This scandal demonstrated that, despite excessive posturing and rhetoric, the Government may have no interest in implementing the controls over oil revenue utilisation outlined in the PFMA. Lack of regard for such controls, coupled with little to no mechanisms for accountability or penalty for dubious actions, poses great risk for future corruption in Uganda's oil sector.

Based on Uganda's history with corruption, analysts project that politicians are likely to fall to the temptations of resource rents and engage in corrupt practices. According to Kiiza et al., 'If the systemic corruption in Uganda's public office is not disabled, oil discovery will beget a resource-curse' (Kiiza et al., 2011, p.12).

4.4.4 Institutional Mismanagement of Funds, Lacking Oversight and Accountability

The degree to which politicians can feasibly mismanage and embezzle resource rents depends on the level of agency and discretion allotted to the given actors. According to Robinson, Torvik and Verdier, institutions are the critical factor in determining the manner in which the extractive sector will ultimately be governed.

> The overall impact of resource booms on the economy depends critically on institutions since these can determine the extent to which political incentives map into policy outcomes. The relevant institutions here will be

political ones which promote the accountability of politicians, and generally develop state institutions away from patrimonial practices towards the use of rational and meritocratic criteria in allocating public sector resources (Robinson *et al.*, 2005, p.450).

The potential for corruption depends on the quality of institutions in a given country. As argued by Bategeka and Mawejje, 'low quality institutions … encourage non-productive policy choices (that is, policies that inhibit widespread engagement and growth in productive activities) by allowing politicians to plunder and engage in inefficient transfers of resources for purposes of buying votes and tightening their grip on power' (Bategeka and Mawejje, 2013, p.12). Kiiza, Bategeka and Ssewanyana also defend the importance of strong institutions. Illustratively:

> Why does some resource abundance deliver positive developmental outcomes in some countries and economic failure in others? The answer arguably lies in cross-national differences in the quality of domestic institutions. Resource-rich countries that have a malfunctioning bureaucracy and insecure property rights tend to attain lower growth outcomes and more violent conflicts than those that have high quality systems of public administration and predictable/reliable property rights institutions. In other words, institutions matter (Kiiza *et al.*, 2011, p.12).

According to Robinson, Torvik and Verdier, the resource curse proceeds in countries with 'grabber friendly' rather than 'producer friendly' institutions. 'Grabber friendly' institutions allow for rent-seeking activities and do not enforce adequate oversight or separation of powers to disable corrupt practices (Robinson *et al.*, 2006). 'Producer-friendly' institutions, on the other hand, enforce the efficient management of resource revenues through mechanisms for tracking and due diligence checks and balances. Therefore, the rents are able to penetrate the economy in productive ways and translate into positive economic benefits for the country.

In the case of Uganda, where use of public funds is always a controversial topic, the correct intra-government collection, transfer, management and dispersal of oil revenues is paramount. This type of corruption is made possible by weak regulations for sufficient oversight and protection of resource revenues. Revenues must be insulated and protected from such political interference through strict prohibitions on withdrawals and transfers as well as extensive oversight over foreign investment of oil revenues.

According to a 2013 public expenditure and financial accountability assessment performed in Uganda, the Government lacks fiscal discipline and adequate mechanisms for effective accountability with regard to intra-government revenue utilisation. The country received a failing score in multiple key areas including 'composition of expenditure out-turn compared to original approved budget, extent of unreported government operations, transparency of inter-government fiscal relations, and effectiveness of payroll controls' (Ministry of Finance, Planning and Economic Development, 2012). While the study reported adequate *budget transparency* mechanisms, the ineffective *budget control* mechanisms in Uganda present an opportunity for corruption.

In 2015, the Government passed the Public Finance Management Act, intended to strengthen and standardise public financial management and accountability protocols in the country. However, less than a year later, the Government pushed amendments through to undo some of the key mechanisms for financial accountability originally passed into law. Five months before the 2016 elections, Government successfully amended the Act to allow it to borrow money from the Central Bank without seeking prior parliamentary approval (Civil Society Budget Advocacy Group, 2015). According to local budget advocacy groups, 'This therefore means that Government can finance supplementary budgeting through re-allocation of funds of the annual budget without parliament approval' (Civil Society Budget Advocacy Group, 2015, p.2).

In the report findings of the 2013 parliamentary investigation into oil bribery and oil revenue mismanagement, the parliamentary committee identified numerous areas of concern. Primarily, the committee found that the reporting of monies between the Uganda Revenue Authority, the Ministry of Finance, the Ministry of Energy and the Bank of Uganda was inconsistent and required urgent harmonisation (Republic of Uganda, 2013, p.43). The committee also reported the presence of multiple petroleum accounts held in the Bank of Uganda opened by different government entities with little coordination (Republic of Uganda, 2013, p.50). Different government entities also reported conflicting narratives of utilisation for the same revenue streams. In sum, the report demonstrated many overlapping problems in the management of oil revenues to date, all of which could allow for revenue leakages for corrupt gain.

4.5   Preventing Oil Sector Corruption in Uganda

4.5.1   Anti-corruption Framework in Uganda

Uganda has instituted multiple government bodies and entities tasked with preventing and prosecuting corruption, including the Anti-Corruption Court, the Inspectorate of Government, the Auditor General, the Directorate of Public Prosecutions and other related bodies. However, due to lack of capacity, these entities continuously fail to fulfil their important tasks, bringing into question whether these bodies will provide the oversight necessary to prevent oil sector corruption.

According to a 2013 Human Rights Watch report, 'Uganda's current political system is built on patronage and that ultimately high-level corruption is rewarded rather than punished' (Human Rights Watch, 2013, p.2). In its report, Human Rights Watch explains that trends in Uganda's lacklustre anti-corruption responses are deliberate and political. Instead of prosecuting the highest government officials ultimately responsible for the numerous cases of 'grand theft of public resources', fledgling anti-corruption institutions penalise the technocrats under them as scapegoats for the kingpins. As the report rightfully asserts, during the entire tenure of Museveni's presidency, no minister has served prison time despite numerous cases of grand-scale corruption (Human Rights Watch, 2013, p.3).

This is also due to the chronic incapacitation of Uganda's many anti-corruption entities. As the report states:

> Most importantly, President Museveni and parliament, which is heavily dominated by ruling party members, have failed to empower key institutions, either by failing to fill key vacancies or by failing to establish institutions such as the Leadership Tribunal which could challenge inaccurate financial asset declarations (Human Rights Watch, 2013, p.3).

For instance, the position of Deputy Inspector General of Government, which legally must be filled in order for the office to prosecute cases, was left vacant from 1995 to 2013 and filled only after concerted donor pressure (Human Rights Watch, 2013, p.3). In 2015, Transparency International Uganda produced a report examining in closer detail the reasons for failure of these key institutions. Particularly, the report investigated the exact reasons for continuous failure to prosecute high-level corruption by the relevant bodies including the Anti-Corruption Division of the High Court, the Directorate of Public Prosecutions and other related government entities. While the report details many technical obstacles to prosecution in corruption cases, many of these technical issues arise out of lack of political will fully to operationalise and capacitate these corruption-focused prosecutorial bodies. Moreover, 'it is paradoxical that the government commits to the resource-demanding establishment of anti-corruption organs and legislation while simultaneously leaving these organs incapacitated' (Transparency International Uganda, 2015, p.36). This paradox brings into question the Government's intentions for the anti-corruption institutions themselves, as the report notes. 'It is up for debate whether Uganda's institutional framework in the fight against corruption is actually "meant" to be effective in curbing corruption, or whether it is intended to serve political purposes' (Transparency International Uganda, 2015, p.11). Such concerns are directly relevant to the country's ability to deter corruption in Uganda's burgeoning oil sector.

4.5.2   Uganda's Oil Legislation and Attempts to Stop the Leaks

The Government of Uganda has put in place multiple pieces of legislation to guide oil exploration, development and production. Most relevant to the topic of corruption are the Petroleum (Exploration, Development and Production) Act, 2013 and the Public Finance Management Act, 2015. These two pieces of legislation dictate how rights to extraction will be granted to companies and how the monies from the oil sector will be managed by government—addressing both the horizontal and vertical risks for corruption as depicted in Figure 4.4. With the exception of a few key provisions, the final laws contain many weak areas that could enable oil sector corruption.

The Petroleum (Exploration, Development and Production) Act, 2013, known as the Upstream Act, outlines how rights to extraction will be allocated and how each company's upstream activities will be regulated. According to the analysis above, this Act covers the scope of 'horizontal' transactions between companies and Government. The Act establishes a tripartite structure for oil sector management, dividing roles between a petroleum directorate, a petroleum authority, and the national oil company (NOC). The petroleum directorate is tasked with managing the sector headed by the Minister of Energy. The petroleum authority is tasked with providing independent oversight over the sector, while the NOC is tasked with managing Government's commercial interests in the sector.

While this tripartite structure does provide important *separation* of powers, due to an over-concentration of powers given to the Minister, it is unclear whether the system will provide effective *checks* on power. Neither the authority nor the NOC holds substantial powers compared to the Minister

Figure 4.4:   Addressing horizontal and vertical risks for corruption

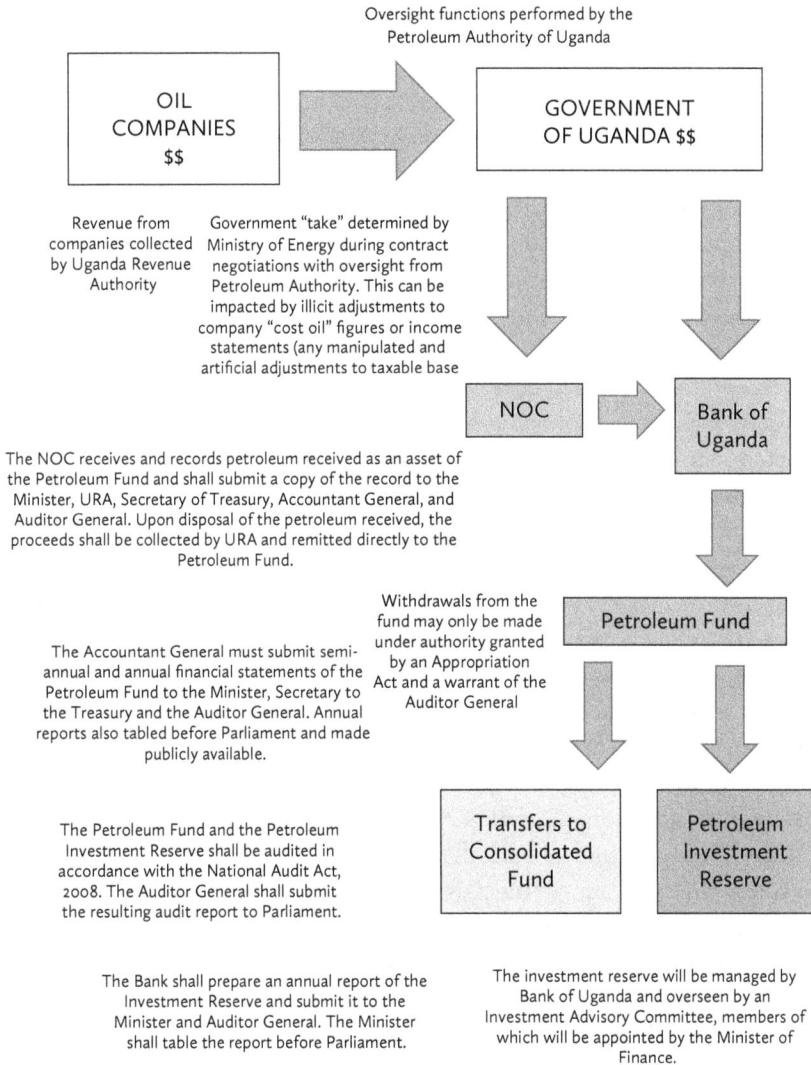

Oversight functions performed by the Petroleum Authority of Uganda

OIL COMPANIES $$

GOVERNMENT OF UGANDA $$

Revenue from companies collected by Uganda Revenue Authority

Government "take" determined by Ministry of Energy during contract negotiations with oversight from Petroleum Authority. This can be impacted by illicit adjustments to company "cost oil" figures or income statements (any manipulated and artificial adjustments to taxable base

NOC

Bank of Uganda

The NOC receives and records petroleum received as an asset of the Petroleum Fund and shall submit a copy of the record to the Minister, URA, Secretary of Treasury, Accountant General, and Auditor General. Upon disposal of the petroleum received, the proceeds shall be collected by URA and remitted directly to the Petroleum Fund.

Withdrawals from the fund may only be made under authority granted by an Appropriation Act and a warrant of the Auditor General

Petroleum Fund

The Accountant General must submit semi-annual and annual financial statements of the Petroleum Fund to the Minister, Secretary to the Treasury and the Auditor General. Annual reports also tabled before Parliament and made publicly available.

The Petroleum Fund and the Petroleum Investment Reserve shall be audited in accordance with the National Audit Act, 2008. The Auditor General shall submit the resulting audit report to Parliament.

Transfers to Consolidated Fund

Petroleum Investment Reserve

The Bank shall prepare an annual report of the Investment Reserve and submit it to the Minister and Auditor General. The Minister shall table the report before Parliament.

The investment reserve will be managed by Bank of Uganda and overseen by an Investment Advisory Committee, members of which will be appointed by the Minister of Finance.

(Petroleum Act, 2013, p.20). Although the petroleum authority is supposed to be independent, the Minister can send directives to the authority, and members of the Board of the authority can be removed directly by the President (Petroleum Act, 2013, pp.24–26).

Although the law was passed in 2013, the petroleum authority was not fully operationalised until 2016, which provides cause for concern since many important elements of the authority's stated mandate, including overseeing the licensing process, occurred prior to this without the authority in place. If the body is not fully capacitated and able to fulfil its mandate, it will represent yet another disingenuous attempt at oversight by the Government of Uganda. As explained in a 2011 Global Integrity Report, 'oversight institutions exist, but they operate under considerable restrictions. The executive branch inhibits their independence and often ignores or only partially implements the recommendations in their reports'.[2] The oil sector cannot afford to have such an inactive and unutilised oversight body.

With regard to the allocation of rights, the Upstream Act does establish processes of fair, open and competitive bidding to be followed. However, according to section 53 of the Act, the Minister may also receive direct bids in 'exceptional circumstances' (Petroleum Act, 2013, p.43). This provision, coupled with the sweeping powers allotted to the Minister in the Act, could be abused to allow for procurement-related corruption.

While the Act does establish standard content to be included in applications and licences, the law fails to mandate contract transparency. Although section 151 of the Act gives the Minister the right to share information with the public, section 152 weakens this assertion by establishing that all information shared between the licensee and Government will be kept confidential unless the licensee provides authorisation for disclosure. Despite repeated calls for public disclosure, the contents of the production-sharing agreements signed between Government and companies remain secret and are not accessible to the public, with the exception of two instances where PSAs have been leaked by civil society actors (Global Witness, 2014). This opacity limits citizens' ability to hold government officials accountable during contract negotiations, meaning that government officials are less incentivised to negotiate a good deal knowing that it will be scrutinised by the public.

In 2015, Government passed the Public Finance Management Act (PFMA) to establish the protocols for the 'vertical' or intra-governmental management of oil revenues. Importantly, the law establishes a Petroleum Fund into which all petroleum revenues will be deposited, separate from the rest of government revenues. Notably, the law introduces multiple forms of oversight over activities of the fund, including publication of the annual reports and audited accounts of the fund.

For instance, section 61 of the Act currently provides a strong foundation for critical information-sharing. According to section 61, semi-annual and

2   Global Integrity. Global Integrity Report: Uganda, 2011. Available at: https://www.globalintegrity.org/wp-content/uploads/2019/08/GIRScorecard2011_Uganda_comments.pdf.

annual reports, including such information as the inflows and outflows of the Petroleum Fund, the volumes and values of the petroleum produced and the source of the petroleum revenue, will be tabled before Parliament and made publicly available (PFMA, 2015, p.72). While these provisions for transparency must be applauded, all of the requirements for disclosure are ex post, meaning that the decision has been made and the money has already been utilised at the time of reporting. If, for instance, the money was embezzled, the Government could have significant difficulty recovering the stolen funds. It would be preferable for the procedures to be strengthened through provisions for more substantive multi-party involvement before the approval of key decisions.

Furthermore, the law offers no detailed provisions for petroleum revenue utilisation. The PFMA merely establishes that revenues from the Petroleum Fund will be put in a petroleum investment reserve or transferred to the Consolidated Fund 'to support the annual budget' and to 'be used for the financing of infrastructure and development projects of government' (PFMA, 2015, p.71). The legislation does note that the petroleum revenues will not be used for unplanned withdrawals or the collateralisation of loans. But there is no detailed information on spending. This represents a significant void in the legislation as Government should be required to publicly present a spending and allocation plan to inform the citizenry and allow for the monitoring of expenditures.

Apart from transfers to the Consolidated Fund, petroleum monies will also be put into a petroleum investment reserve (PFMA, 2015, p.66). The investment reserve serves many purposes and has an important mandate to help guarantee macroeconomic stability throughout the entire period of oil extraction through diversification of the oil revenue portfolio. Yet, protocols to ensure sound management of the investment reserve are relatively weak compared to the Petroleum Fund. Specifically, the protocols mandating transparency and sharing of information regarding the petroleum revenue investment reserve are largely absent (PFMA, 2015, p.76).

If details of the activity of the petroleum revenue investment reserve are not made public, this fund runs the risk of becoming a slush fund for corruption as petroleum monies could easily be invested into foreign assets and offshore accounts connected to politically exposed persons. Sovereign wealth funds have notoriously been linked to corruption in numerous countries around the world, so any sovereign wealth fund established in Uganda must be managed transparently with strong rules for investment and adequate protocols for effective oversight (Bauer et al., 2016, p.60).

4.5.3   Non-governmental Efforts to Promote Good Governance

Apart from government efforts, civil society actors, bilateral donors and other stakeholders have undertaken concerted efforts to prevent corruption and mismanagement in Uganda's oil sectors. Since the discovery of oil, a strong coalition of local and international civil society organisations has persistently engaged Government to ensure that a strong governance framework is put in place for oil sector management. In 2010, civil society organisations analysed the country's first ever leaked production-sharing agreements, providing critical feedback to Government on many problem areas in the initial agreements (Civil Society Coalition on Oil and Gas, 2010). Again in 2014, Global Witness leaked two of the current PSAs, providing in-depth analysis of the environmental, social and economic provisions of the agreements, to instruct the Government on how to improve future agreements truly to get the best 'deal' (Global Witness, 2014).

These leaks supplemented previously unsuccessful attempts to access petroleum contracts using Uganda's 2005 Access to Information Act. In 2009, two journalists from the Daily Monitor filed a case against Government after they were refused access to the country's production-sharing agreements signed with companies. The Solicitor-General in his response cited the confidentiality agreements in the contracts prohibiting public disclosure (Africa Freedom of Information Centre, 2011). The court acknowledged that mandatory disclosure was warranted in cases of public interest (Africa Freedom of Information Centre, 2011). However, the court ruled that the journalists had not duly demonstrated how they would use the information for public benefit, and thus struck down their request (Africa Freedom of Information Centre, 2011).

Civil society organisations, alongside Members of Parliament (MPs), were also very active in the debate on the upstream and midstream oil laws from 2011–2013. As stated, above, MPs went so far as to declare a moratorium on the issue of new licences until an adequate legislative framework was put in place to guide the processes. Although the executive did not heed this moratorium, MPs continued voicing adamant dissent to issues of corruption and executive interference in the oil sector. Such dissent resulted in the attempted suspension of a small number of MPs, labelled the 'oil MPs', from the ruling NRM party (Nalubega, 2013). President Museveni accused the dissident MPs and their civil society allies of 'trying to bypass the oil and gas experts in the ministry in the interest of their foreign backers' (Mugerwa, 2012).

The international donor community also provides another form of pressure on the Government of Uganda to adopt strong mechanisms for transparency and accountability in the extractive industries. Since 2009, the Government of Norway, through the bilateral NORAD Oil for Development Programme, has provided official assistance to the Government of Uganda in capacity and institutional development regarding the country's nascent oil sector. According to the stated outcomes of the partnership, the NORAD assistance aims to ensure government accountability in the management of the oil sector through the establishment of a strong policy, legal and regulatory framework 'for managing the petroleum sector in an economically, socially and environmentally sustainable way' (Ministry of Energy and Mineral Development [MEMD], 2015, p.22).

In this partnership, NORAD has achieved the intended outcomes in helping the Ugandan Government in formulating the country's national oil and gas policy as well as associated laws (MEMD, 2015, p.7). NORAD also assisted in the development of the Public Finance Management Act as well as the Oil and Gas Revenue Management Policy while the Norwegian Oil Taxation Office worked with the Uganda Revenue Authority to develop a petroleum tax manual (MEMD, 2015, p.15). These policies, formulated with NORAD assistance, prominently highlight the principles of accountability and transparency in oil revenue management.

Notably, the Oil and Gas Revenue Management Policy (2012, p.37) commits the Government of Uganda to 'observe the highest standards of transparency' by joining the Extractive Industries Transparency Initiative (EITI), an international initiative to promote good governance in the global extractive industries through payment transparency. Through EITI implementation, companies publish their payments to government while governments publish their payment receipts from companies, enabling reconciliation between the disclosures and reconnaissance of any discrepancy or 'missing funds' between the two.

Despite this assertion, the Government remained reticent to actually operationalise this commitment. However, in 2019, the Government publicly declared its intention to join the EITI. It is still too early to tell whether this intention will be carried out or whether this is empty rhetoric.

4.6   Conclusion

While this analysis has focused on the present opportunities for corruption in Uganda's oil sector, the potential for oil to entrench and catalyse new forms of corruption and the potential for democratic regression have been less examined. As described in the discussion of the 'resource curse' theory, scholarly research has determined an inverse relationship between oil extraction and democracy in countries around the world. As shown by political scientist Michael Ross (2001), 'oil and minerals have strong antidemocratic effects'.

Oil rents historically correlate with heightened vulnerability to corruption and a decline in democratic processes (Ross, 2001). Thus, the inflow of resource revenues can sometimes weaken the strength of democracy in oil-producing countries, particularly related to the relationship between the citizenry and government (Ross, 2001). Without organised and insistent demands from an informed public, the government-citizen relationship could become completely alienated in the process of resource extraction.

If democratic institutions are weakened in the wake of natural resource discovery, the country is at risk of developing into a 'rentier state'. In this scenario, such a great proportion of national wealth derives from oil rents that normal democratic processes become completely distorted. As researchers Anyanwu and Eriacho explain, 'a few political elites collect the revenues from the oil export and use the money for cementing their political, economic and social power by controlling government and its bureaucracy' (Anyanwu and Erhijakpor, 2012, p.5). This trend is especially worrying since democracy becomes even more important in the context of natural resource discovery. Given the temptations presented by natural resource windfalls, protecting domestic democratic institutions becomes essential to a continuously thriving democracy.

The challenge in Uganda and any evolving democracy is to incentivise political leadership continuously to work in good faith for the trust of the citizens in order to limit corruption and abuse of office. While the temptations of oil revenue may further incentivise corruption, discretion can be limited through mechanisms for oversight, accountability and continuous citizen engagement. Uganda's track record might lead some to predict continued corruption in the country's oil sector, but it should not be assumed that Uganda's oil is destined for graft. However, the interplay of corruption, oil and democracy in Uganda should continue to be analysed and monitored so that attempts can be made to ensure that oil strengthens, rather than erodes, Uganda's democracy through a strong governance framework that limits all opportunities for corruption in the oil revenue chain.

References

Africa Freedom of Information Centre (2011), 'Analysis of the Court Ruling in Charles Mwanguhya Mpagi and Angelo Izama vs. Attorney General (Miscellaneous Cause No. 751 or 2009) Against the Framework of the Uganda Access to Information Act, 2005 and International Access to Information Standards. Retrieved from: http://www.africafoicentre.org/index.php/ati-cases-africa/59-afic-analysis-of-ati-court-ruling/file.

African Union (AU) and United Nations Economic Commission for Africa (ECA) (2015), 'Illicit Financial Flows'. *Report of the High-Level Panel on Illicit Financial Flows from Africa.*

Retrieved from: https://www.uneca.org/sites/default/files/PublicationFiles/iff_main_report_26feb_en.pdf.

Bategeka, L., and J. Mawejje (2013), 'Accelerating Growth and Maintaining Intergenerational Equity Using Oil Resources in Uganda'. *Economic Policy Research Centre Research Series,*111.

BBC News (2016, 8 April), 'Panama Papers: How Jersey-based Oil Firm Avoided Taxes in Uganda', Retrieved from: http://www.bbc.com/news/world-africa-35985463.

Biryabarema, E., D. Jorgic, R. Lough and R. Pitchford (2012, 4 December), 'EU Joint National Donors in Freeze Aid to Uganda Over Graft', *Reuters*. Retrieved from: http://www.reuters.com/article/us-uganda-aid-idUSBRE8B30DA20121204.

Castel, V., and P. Ximena Meijia (2012), 'Could Oil Shine Like Diamonds? How Botswana Avoided the Resource Curse and its Implications for a New Libya'. *African Development Bank Chief Economist Complex.* Retrieved from: https://www.afdb.org/sites/default/files/documents/publications/could_oil_shine_like_diamonds_-_how_botswana_avoided_the_resource_curse_and_its_implications_for_a_new_libya.pdf.

Civil Society Budget Advocacy Group (2015), 'Parliament Approves Modified Public Finance Management (Amendments) Bill'. Retrieved from: http://csbag.org/wp-content/uploads/2015/11/Parliament-approves-modified-public-finance-management-amendments-bill.pdf.

Civil Society Coalition on Oil and Gas in Uganda (2010), 'Contracts Curse: Uganda's Oil Agreements Put Profits before People'. Retrieved from: http://www.acode-u.org/documents/oildocs/CSCO_oilcurse.pdf.

Global Witness (2010), 'Donor Engagement in Uganda's Oil and Gas Sector: An Agenda for Action'. Retrieved from: https://www.globalwitness.org/documents/uganda_final_low.

—— (2012), 'Rigged? The Scramble for Africa's Oil, Gas, and Minerals'. Retrieved from: https://www.globalwitness.org/en/reports/rigged/.

—— (2014), *A Good Deal Better? Uganda's Secret Oil Contracts Explained.* London: Global Witness Limited. Retrieved from: https://www.globalwitness.org/en/reports/good-deal-better/.

Hubert, D. (2016), 'Mapping Risks to Future Government Petroleum Revenues in Kenya'. *Oxfam Research Reports.* Retrieved from the Oxfam International website: https://www.oxfam.org/sites/www.oxfam.org/files/file_attachments/rr-mapping-risks-petroleum-revenues-kenya-060516-en.pdf.

Human Rights Watch (2013), 'Letting the Big Fish Swim: Failures to Prosecute high-level Corruption in Uganda'. Retrieved from; http://www.hrw.org/sites/default/files/reports/uganda1013_ForUpload_0.pdf.

Imaka, I. (2011, 6 November), 'Mutebile Reveals Oil Deal with Museveni', *The Daily Monitor.* Retrieved from: http://www.monitor.co.ug/News/National/688334-1273874-a2xo9wz/index.html.

International Monetary Fund (2007), *Guide on Resource Revenue Transparency.* Retrieved from: http://www.imf.org/external/np/pp/2007/eng/051507g.pdf.

Kathman, J., and M. Shannon (2011), 'Oil Extraction and the Potential for Domestic Instability in Uganda', *African Studies Quarterly*, 12(3), 23–45. Retrieved from: https://asq.africa.ufl.edu/kathman_shannon_summer11/.

Kiiza, J., L. Bategeka and S. Sswanyana (2011), 'Righting Resource-curse Wrongs in Uganda: The Case of Oil Discovery and the Management of Popular Expectations'. *Economic Policy Research Centre Research Series*, No.78. Retrieved from: http://ageconsearch.umn.edu/bitstream/150481/2/series78.pdf.

Larsen, A.R. (2014), 'Uganda Revenue Authority vs. Tullow'. Retrieved from the Action Aid website: http://www.actionaid.org/uganda/2014/07/uganda-revenue-authority-vs-tullow.

Ministry of Energy and Mineral Development (2015), *Strengthening the Management of the Oil and Gas Sector in Uganda: Phase II – 2015–2018*. Retrieved from: https://www.norad.no/co ntentassets/36585925a4814255bd1916fe9a4248b2/programme-document.pdf.

Ministry of Finance, Planning and Economic Development (2012a), 'Central Government Public Expenditure and Financial Accountability Assessment Report'. Retrieved from: https://pefa. org/sites/default/files/assements/comments/UG-Sep12-PFMPR-Public_0.pdf.

——— (2012b), *National Oil and Gas Revenue Management Policy*. Kampala: Government of Uganda.

Mugerwa, Y. (2012, 14 December), 'Museveni Hits Back at MPs in Oil Bill Row', *The Daily Monitor*. Retrieved from: http://www.monitor.co.ug/News/National/Museveni-hits-back-at-MPs-in-oil-Bill-row/688334-1643416-4yivwh/index.html.

——— (2015, 20 May), 'MPs Want Mutebile, Minister Sacked', *Daily Monitor*. Retrieved from: http://www.monitor.co.ug/News/National/MPs-want-Mutebile--minister-sacked/-/688334/2722692/-/bttrno/-/index.html.

Musisi, F. (2016, 23 November), 'I Am Not Excited about Oil – Museveni', *The Daily Monitor*. Retrieved from: http://allafrica.com/stories/201611240103.html.

Musoke, M. (2017, 16 January), 'Scandal over Museveni's Shs 6 billion "Handshake"'. *The Independent*. Retrieved from: http://allafrica.com/stories/201701160090.html.

Mwesiga, A. (2016, 13 January), 'Uganda Determined Not to Let Expected Oil Cash Trickle Away', *The Guardian*. Retrieved from: https://www.theguardian.com/global-development/2016/jan/13/uganda-oil-production-yoweri-museveni-agriculture.

Nalubega, F. (2013, 17 April), 'Ruling Party Expels Rebellious "Oil MPs"', *Oil in Uganda*. Retrieved from: http://www.oilinuganda.org/features/governance/ruling-party-expels-rebellious-oil-mps.html.

Open Society Justice Initiative (2010), 'Corruption and its Consequences in Equatorial Guinea'. *Briefing Paper*. Retrieved from: https://www.opensocietyfoundations.org/sites/default/files/equatorial-guinea-20100317.pdf.

Republic of Uganda (2011), Resolution of Parliament in Respect of Regularization of the Oil Sector and Other Matters Incidental Thereto. Kampala: Parliament of Uganda.

——— (2013a), Petroleum (Exploration, Development and Production) Act, 2013:   A c t s supplement to the Uganda Gazette No. 16 Volume CVI, 2013. Kampala: Republic of Uganda.

——— (2013b), *Draft Report on the Investigation into the Oil and Gas Sector by the Parliamentary Ad Hoc Committee in Respect of the Regularization of the Oil Sector and Other Matters Incidental Thereto*. Retrieved from: https://www.parliament.go.ug.

——— (2015), Public Finance Management Act, 2015. Kampala: Republic of Uganda.

Robinson, J., R. Torvik and T. Verdier (2006), 'Political Foundations of the Resource Curse', *Journal of Development Economics*, 79, 447–468. Retrieved from: https://scholar.harvard. edu/files/jrobinson/files/jr_polfoundations.pdf.

Ross, M. (2001), 'Does Oil Hinder Democracy?', *World Politics*, 53(3), 326–361. Retrieved from: http://www.jstor.org/stable/25054153.

Shepherd, B. (2013), 'Oil in Uganda: International Lessons for Success'. Retrieved from the Chatham House website: https://www.chathamhouse.org/publications/papers/view/188959.

Transparency International Uganda (2015), 'As Strong as its Weakest Link: Stakeholders' Perceptions of the Ugandan Legal and Institutional Anti-corruption Framework. Retrieved from: https://www.transparency.org/country/UGA.

——— (2018), 'Corruption: Anticorruption Glossary'. Retrieved from: http://www.transparency. org/glossary/term/corruption.

5
Closed but Ordered: How the Political Settlement Shapes Uganda's Deals with International Oil Companies

Badru Bukenya and Jaqueline Nakaiza

5.1   Introduction

In 2006 commercially viable quantities of oil and gas were announced in Uganda. It was estimated that the revenue from the country's oil reserves when production starts would be about US$ 2 billion per year, or around 12 per cent of GDP (Vokes, 2012), although later estimates downgraded this potential by one third, citing price volatility (Patey, 2015). Such oil quantities, if properly managed, can put Uganda on the world list of oil-producing and exporting countries with a real opportunity of fuelling the transition from a poor to a middle-income and perhaps even high-income country. For the benefits to emerge, however, numerous actors need to work collectively in the best interests of the country to transform oil resources into useable end products. The oil value chain is divided into three sub-sectors namely, upstream, middle stream and downstream (The World Bank, 2015).

While the upstream level includes activities related to oil reserve exploration and development, middle stream activities largely include oil and gas production, processing and refining into petrochemicals and natural gas. For their part, downstream activities are mainly dominated by products transportation, temporary storage, marketing and distribution to the middle and final consumers. It is generally understood that upstream and middle stream activities are complex and require huge sunk costs (Wamono, Kikabi and Mugisha, 2012). In the context of poor countries like Uganda, this makes such streams a preserve of the rich and experienced international oil companies (IOCs) and international companies that service the auxiliary functions of the oil industry. Wamono *et al.*'s (2012) analysis of Uganda's oil sector suggests that even downstream activities are likely to be dominated by foreign companies due to constraints on capital for many of Uganda's small and medium enterprises (SMEs) alongside the Government's interest in attracting foreign investors (despite the legal provisions for local content).

Given this background, therefore, the oil sector has attracted many foreign companies. Yet, the Government of Uganda (GoU) has been quite secretive in its dealings with these companies. Oversight bodies such as Parliament, the media and other civil society organisations (CSOs) are largely sidelined, not only from the negotiations between Government and the IOCs but also from accessing information about these negotiations (De Kock and Sturman, 2012). While such an opaque environment would predict a worse-off position for GoU in relation to the resultant deals with the usually experienced international players, available evidence so far indicates the opposite. For instance, the modelling report done by Global Witness showed that the Government of Uganda negotiated better deals in the production-sharing agreements (PSAs), the lack of important human rights and environmental safeguards notwithstanding.[1] In addition, the PSAs largely reflected the country's priorities with respect to guaranteeing the establishment of an oil refinery that the IOCs were initially reluctant to commit to (Hickey, Bukenya, Izama and Kizito, 2015; Patey, 2015).

The current chapter aims to investigate and analyse the dynamics of deal making between the Government of Uganda and foreign companies. Our discussion is anchored in the political settlement framework for, as one key informant rightly noted, 'it is the politics that is determining what the technocrat does and who gets what' in Uganda's oil sector. To explore how the interplay of Uganda's political settlement and the 'deals space' is influencing the Government's ability to protect national interests in negotiations with IOCs and its interactions with the other stakeholders involved in the oil sector, the chapter draws on both primary data and secondary sources. Primary data were collected from about 30 key informants with substantial knowledge of the oil sector in 2016. These included government officials, employees of IOCs, MPs, journalists and members of CSOs.

The rest of the chapter is organised as follows: the discussion proceeds with the mapping of the key actors in the oil sector, and thereafter conceptualises the political settlement and nature of state-business relations or the 'deals space'. The chapter then discusses the strategies employed by Government in its dealings with IOCs as well as the other local actors with an interest in the sector. The last section concludes.

---

1   Global Witness suggests that Uganda is likely to receive between 80 and well over 90 per cent of revenues after costs have been recovered, depending on the amount of oil which is discovered and its price.

5.2   Actors in Uganda's Oil Sector

Actors in Uganda's oil sector fall into two broad categories, namely, internal and external. The internal actors are mainly the President and key military figures (see the discussion of political settlement below). The list of internals also has some Cabinet Ministers and technocrats, especially those from the Ministry of Energy and Mineral Development (MEMD) and the Ministry of Finance Planning and Economic Development (MFPED), the Bank of Uganda (BoU) and the Uganda Revenue Authority (URA). Within MEMD, the primary agency is the Petroleum Exploration and Production Department (PEPD), to which the President has accorded relative protection to develop capabilities currently unparalleled by any other mainstream government agency (Hickey and Izama, 2016). The less powerful actors include the Parliament and the numerous CSOs with an interest in natural resources, governance or accountability issues.

On the external side it is international oil companies (IOCs) that dominate. The exact number of IOCs that are active in Uganda is difficult to ascertain, for the reason that some come and leave within a short time frame. However, a picture emerges when one examines documented deals between the Government of Uganda (GoU) and IOCs. It is reported that Uganda's first production-sharing agreement (PSA) under the national resistance movement (NRM) government was signed in 1991 with the Belgian company Petrofina. This was for the entire Albertine Graben region. Petrofina did little with its PSA as it pulled out of the country in 1993. In February 1995 the Government signed a similar PSA with a small US-based company called Uganda Works and General Engineering Company (Rwakakamba and Lukwago, 2013). Its operations were however suspended by GoU in March 1996 due to unsatisfactory progress. In January 1997 the country witnessed another PSA in which the Government gave Heritage Oil and Gas exploration rights in the Semiliki basin and the southern part of Lake Albert. Subsequent PSAs were signed with other companies, namely, Hardman in 2001, Neptune Petroleum-Uganda in 2005 and Dominium Petroleum in 2007.

In 2006 commercially viable oil deposits were announced in blocks jointly licensed to Heritage Oil (Canada) and Tullow Oil PLC (Ireland). Heritage sold its stake to Tullow for US$ 1.5 billion, after which Tullow brought in investment from two bigger players—Total E&P (French) and China National Offshore Oil Corporation (CNOOC)—each of which agreed to pay US$ 1.45 billion to split the area three ways (Vokes, 2012; Wass and Musiime, 2013). The farm-down was finalised in 2012 and it is regarded as 'one of the most impressive consortia in Africa' (Patey, 2015, p.15). By 2014, the Government estimated the country's petroleum reserve capacity at 6.5 billion barrels of oil while the projected recoverable stood at between 1.8 and 2.2 billion barrels. The Government claims that these estimates are based on only 40 per cent of the area expected to have oil[2] and, given the impressive 87 per cent success rate in encountering hydrocarbons (Van Alstine, Manyindo, Smith, Dixon and Aminga Ruhanga, 2014), some have predicted that Uganda is destined to become one of the oil giants in sub-Saharan Africa (Vokes, 2012).

Oil companies themselves need to hire firms to provide drilling and other expensive services, such as seismic surveying and transport. Halliburton, Schlumberger, Baker Hughes and Weatherford are some of the big companies in Uganda's oil services and drilling industry.

5.3   Uganda's Political Settlement

A political settlement (PS) is described as 'the balance or distribution of power between contending social groups and social classes, on which any state is based' (Di John and Putzel, 2009). It emerges through a process of struggle and bargaining between elite groups. According to Khan (2010) the political settlement shapes the capacity and commitment of Government and political elites to invest in building institutions and relationships that can underpin the development of countries. Khan identifies four types of PS namely: dominant leader/party, vulnerable authoritarian, weak dominant party and competitive clientelism. The dominant PSs, whose defining characteristics are a high degree of internal coherence and weak opposition from excluded elites, provide ruling coalitions with space to develop and implement longer term visions and invest in the development of state capabilities to realise these visions. Such conditions are likely to support the emergence of pro-reform coalitions. Conversely, the PS least likely to be developmental is competitive clientelism where the holding power of the ruling elites is under constant threat from their opponents in the opposition or internally within the party, thereby giving them no time to focus on long-term developmental projects. The preoccupation of ruling coalitions under competitive clientelism is on implementing short-term moves to retain power. In this respect, elites would be compelled to invest the oil revenues into regime maintaining areas as

---

2   Uganda's oil is potentially present in four basins, namely, Albertine Graben, the Hoima basin (to the east of Lake Albert), the Lake Kyoga basin (further east, in the centre of the country), and the Kadam-Moroto basin, still further east, in the Karamoja sub-region, but the main focus of the current exploration is in the first.

Figure 5.1:   **Uganda's Political Settlement**

		HORIZONTAL DISTRIBUTION OF POWER: *EXCLUDED ELITES*	
		WEAK ⟶ STRONG	
	WEAK	***DOMINANT***	***VULNERABLE AUTHORITARIAN***
VERTICAL DISTRIBUTION OF POWER: *LOWER LEVEL FACTIONS*		Longer-term horizons Implementation capabilities high **UGANDA (1986 to 2000)**	Initial implementation capabilities strong, vulnerable to being overthrown
		WEAK DOMINANT PARTY	***COMPETITIVE CLIENTELISM***
	STRONG	Implementation capabilities weakened by multiple demands and 'blockers' **UGANDA (2001 to present)**	Shorter-term horizons: threat of powerful excluded elitesImplementation capabilities weakened

Source: Bukenya & Muhumuza (2017, p. 6).

opposed to development programmes that benefit citizens more broadly (Bukenya and Hickey, 2018).

It is argued that political settlements are not static as countries can shed some of the defining characteristics of one category and increasingly take on those of another. As illustrated in Figure 5.1, for example, in 1986 Uganda started off as a dominant party PS but, since the early 2000s, it has increasingly adopted features of competitive clientelism. The defining characteristics of Uganda's current PS are that both the capacities of groups excluded from the coalition (horizontal power) and those of lower-level factions within the ruling coalition (vertical power) have increased.

Using PS lenses to look at Uganda we find that when President Museveni and his NRM party took power in 1986 a dominant party/leader form of political settlement emerged. Politics was by consensus via the movement system (no party/single party politics) with a broadly based ruling coalition that comprised key figures from the political and military wings of the NRM, members of other political parties who did not participate directly in the liberation struggle, and leaders of rebel groups who agreed to negotiate with the new government. The consensus principles of politics and governance remained until the early 2000s when elites increasingly challenged President Museveni's leadership and the NRM's hegemony (Golooba-Mutebi and Hickey, 2013). As elaborated below and in Figure 5.1, due to the increased agitation from within the ruling party (vertical power) and pressure from the opposition (horizontal power), the settlement has shifted to 'weak dominant' and tending towards competitive clientelism (Kjær, Ulriksen, Kangave and Katusiimeh, 2017, p.13). Today there is more resistance against President Museveni and the group around him from within the NRM party, particularly from younger party members who were not part of the National Resistance Army's guerrilla war in the early 1980s (Kjær et al., 2017, p.14). These developments have far-reaching implications for state capacity and the strategic vision of the ruling elite. Whereas it was easier to implement economic and fiscal reforms successfully while Uganda was in the *movement* political system, in which presumably 'everyone agreed on the basic principles' (Wang and Rakner, 2005), the heightened political competition seems to have caused compulsions of preserving political power by the ruling elite to take precedence over support for reform implementation.

Currently, the ruling coalition is comprised of three levels of elites as follows: an inner core, the inter-mediate circle and the outer circle (see Figure 5.2). At the centre of power—the inner core—is the President himself; his immediate family including the first son, wife and brother, all of whom hold influential positions in government; leading figures in the armed forces as well as the police force; and powerful regional political elites, most of whom were central in the liberation struggle (Golooba-Mutebi and Hickey 2013). The intermediate circle comprises Cabinet Ministers and some of the high-ranking bureaucrats positioned in key government agencies. These are 'display' elites carefully selected on the basis of region, ethnic origin, and/or religious background 'so that their constituencies can see that they are represented at the highest levels of government' (Golooba-Mutebi and Hickey, 2013, p.17). The broader outer circle has a more localised network that involves state ministers, local elites that occupy political and administrative positions in local governments, leaders within the NRM party, traditional authorities, religious leaders, and some of the leading business personalities.

Only the outer layer and, to some extent, the intermediate circle of the coalition change membership. Change mainly originates from party and general elections whose outcomes are used by the inner core as the basis for admitting or expelling members. However, there have been defections from the ruling coalition by high-ranking elites, mostly those with presidential ambitions who perceive Museveni as mopolising the position. Some formed their own political organisations while others joined existing ones—something that has seen the opposition raising a credible threat to NRM's hold on power during elections (Golooba-Mutebi and Hickey, 2013).

As the ruling coalition has become more fragmented and to some extent vulnerable, its sustainability now is dependent on the President's ability to

Figure 5.2:   **Uganda's ruling coalition**

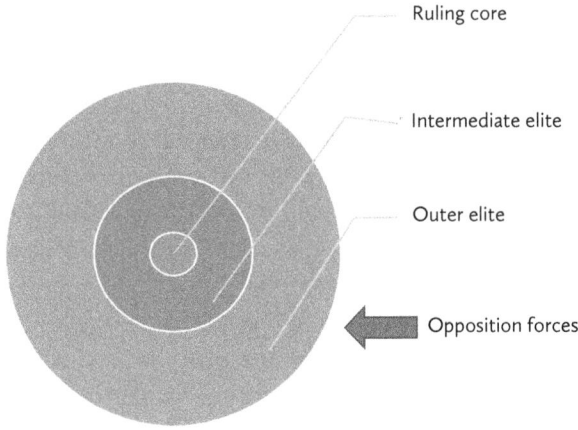

control the military and persuade the most powerful factions to remain within the coalition (Kjær *et al.*, 2017). The main strategy used by the ruling elite to maintain members within its fold and win the support of those outside the coalition 'has combined the use of patronage resources with coercion and informal socio-political networks' (Khisa, 2016, p.730). Securing the loyalty of the security apparatus has been useful for the ruling elite in deploying it to coerce dissenting voices into silence.

Another strategy is the personalisation of political power through a 'system organised around and fully dependent on decisions taken by the president' (Polus and Tycholiz, 2016). In this case the President presents himself as the solver of all challenges that citizens and investors face. This so-called Musev-enism avoids the use of public policies and political institutions to mediate official relationships between government and other entities (Rulekere, 2011). Interest groups like business owners, taxi drivers, teachers, and tribal leaders among others, have their concerns addressed after meeting the President, rather than the respective ministries (Rulekere, 2011). Such a strategy has clear political utility, 'it is a way of creating a private sector constituency that is grateful and loyal to the ruling party, particularly the President, and therefore most likely to become a source of campaign financing' (Mwenda, 2006). As discussed in the following sections, IOCs have learned the reality that everything starts and ends with the President, including awarding oil deals. The implications for public policy in the country are that official policies can easily be replaced with presidential directives (Bukenya and Muhumuza, 2017). Similarly, ministries cannot take major decisions without consulting the President, with those that do not heed to his will risk being embarrassed when he instructs them to reverse their decisions.

Lastly, the President needs resources to give to the numerous interest groups that flock to his residence for help. In the past, revenue from international development aid was a good source. It should be remembered that President Museveni from the early days of his rule established himself as a strategic ally of the West and a promising reformer. Thus, the international financial and donor community played a key role in funding Uganda's development programmes through bilateral budgetary support and development assistance (Khisa, 2016). However, Mwenda and Tangri (2005) argue that funds via donor-initiated programmes were captured and instrumentally deployed towards regime survival. In other words, donor interventions in Uganda inadvertently provided President Museveni with resources he used to entrench his rule. Meanwhile, since the mid-2000s donors have become disillusioned due to the continued misuse of their funding. Some unilaterally withdrew their support while others changed funding modality from budget support to project funding. The latter gives limited latitude to Government on how to spend the aid. As the international sources through donor agencies increasingly became unreliable, the country was blessed with oil discoveries in the Albertine Graben. If tightly controlled by the ruling elite, the sector promises a reliable source of revenue that can be deployed to serve political ends. This perhaps explains the high presidential interest in the sector. As observed by some, Uganda's oil sector is growing rapidly and will soon be one of the key organs of its economy and at the heart of its politics (Wass and Musiime, 2013).

5.4   Conceptualising State-Business Relations: The Politics of Deal Making in Uganda

In countries like Uganda that are characterised by a weak capability of government for policy implementation there are ubiquitous and widespread deviations of actual practice from 'rules that create winners and losers and prevent inclusive economic institutions from emerging' (Pritchett and Werker, 2012, p.39). Therefore, negotiations between business and government are defined by 'deals' as opposed to 'rules'. In the 'rules' environment, 'the stated "rules of the game" have near [full] predictive power for what will actually happen' (Pritchett and Werker, 2012, p.39). On the other hand, the 'deals' environment is where the *legal* or *de jure* policies are of only minimal relevance to business decisions. Indeed, within Uganda's oil sector, informal institutions and arrangements tend to prevail over rules-based approaches. As noted by a key informant, while Uganda on paper has very good laws and institutions, the political environment does not allow them to work:

> According to the law it's the directorate of the petroleum that is supposed to come up with policies, it's the petroleum authority that is supposed to regulate the oil companies both international and local, and parliament has its role of oversight. In actual sense it is the President who does all this (Oil Uganda, personal communication, November, 2016).

It is important to note that deals can be relatively ordered or disordered in terms of the likelihood of their being honoured and lasting ('ordered' vs. 'disordered'); and also relatively 'open' or 'closed', with reference to whether deals are widely available to all investors, large or small, as opposed to being captured by a smaller number of investors with strong political connections (Pritchett and Werker, 2012). As illustrated in Figure 5.3 a combination of these produces four types of business environment in which developing countries can be categorised.

Given Uganda's political settlement, it is clear that the deal space within which government and IOCs operate is closed but moderately ordered (Bukenya and Hickey, 2018). In other words, while it is mostly those with political connections that get to make deals, investors are confident that the deals will be honoured (seen in the huge capital investment of IOCs). However, as will become evident in the forthcoming discussion, the longevity of deals in the oil sector is linked to President Museveni's continuity in power. In the following sub-sections we expand on these observations with clear illustrations of the strategies employed by Uganda's ruling elite in their dealing with IOCs.

Figure 5.3: A Taxonomy of Informal Institutions: The Deals World

	Closed	Open
Disordered	Only those with political connections get to make deals, and even they can't be certain that officials will deliver	Anyone can make a deal, but no-one is certain that officials will deliver
Ordered	Only those with political connections get to make deals, but they can be confident that officials will deliver	Anyone can make a deal, and they can be confident that officials will deliver

Source: Authors' design based on Pritchett and Werker (2012, p. 46).

5.5   Personalisation of the Oil Resource by Uganda's 'Big Man'

President Museveni has personally supervised the developments in the oil sector since the 1980s. Many commentators believe that he takes oil in Uganda as his 'personal project', as seen in his assertions of 'my oil' and that 'I am the one who discovered oil' (Ssekikubo, 2013; Van Alstine *et al.*, 2014). To facilitate his firm grip, Cabinet passed a call to classify oil as a 'strategic resource'. According to Ugandan regulations, strategic resources are placed under the control of the presidency and the military high command (Hickey and Izama, 2016, p.12). As shown in the next sub-section, the military through the special oil protection unit have been deployed in the oil-producing regions to give security to IOC installations. The President also ensured that laws give the powers to negotiate and endorse petroleum agreements and to grant and revoke licences in the oil sector (to all main contracts and sub-contractors) to the Minister (who is directly answerable to him) instead of the more independent petroleum authority. Indeed, Parliament had granted such powers to the latter but this was changed on the President's orders.

In 2013, when Parliament was debating the legislative arrangements on oil, particularly the Petroleum Exploration, Development and Production Bill, the President ruthlessly fought to ensure that the executive branch maintained control over key aspects of oil governance through neutralising the most challenging actors from civil and political society (see later discussion). The President accused the groups which wanted the responsibility to go to the petroleum authority of trying to bypass the oil and gas experts in the Ministry of Energy and Mineral Development in the interest of their foreign backers (The Daily Monitor, 2012). However, activists insist that all that the 'big man' wanted was full control over the dealing process in the oil sector as he has absolute control over the politically appointed ministers (Key informant from a CSO, personal communication, 28 February 2014).[3] These political appointees act only after thorough consultations with their appointing authority. And where necessary he deals directly with IOCs:

> For most of the negotiations these companies go to the President directly. He is the one who accepts them or not; in 2012 we had made a law that powers belong to the Petroleum Authority, the President changed it. When parliament made resolutions in 2011 saying there should be no oil

3   Because of the worsened security situation of civil society people in Uganda, we need to ensure their absolute and complete anonymity.

transactions until laws have been put in place the President himself said no, those resolutions cannot be accepted! He went ahead to enter into transactions with Tullow in 2012, he allows Tullow to sell its assets to CNOOC and Total and in 2015 the government is made to lose $222M because of those transactions (Key informant from a CSO, personal communication, November, 2016).

Therefore, the President has been able to define his supreme position over the control and governance of oil, and with this has been able to identify suitable partners to work with, negotiate contracts with them, and influence the country's strategy for distributing oil revenue without much trouble. The sector is closed (i.e. only a few selected firms can participate) in the interest of the ruling elite. As noted by a key informant, 'there is no decision that is done without his consent'. While this appears to be a major strength in the bargaining process, it also seems to be the main weakness. According to one industry expert, 'we are too slow on everything, actually it is evident that Uganda is not ready to do business at an international level'. Another industry expert explained how the President's involvement is affecting the operations as follows:

It is the President who meets the investors and makes directives on who should be awarded licenses. The technocrat from the ministry, who knows the required procedure, only accepts the application from the company that the President wants. The rest of the applications you close your offices and go for a holiday. When the deadline passes you come back to evaluate the only application you received and award the license [sic] (Industry expert, personal communication, October, 2016).

Moreover, the President is the appointment authority for officers in senior government positions. Jobs are given to those of whom he is sure that they 'will more or less act in the interest of the appointing authority who is being looked at as a God father' (Industry expert, personal communication, October, 2016; also see Bukenya and Muhumuza 2017). This was evident in the appointment of three ruling party affiliated politicians, who had failed in their previous electoral campaigns, as board members of the national oil company. Their appointment was clearly patronage by the appointing authority.

There are both positive and negative implications arising from the big man syndrome of oil governance in Uganda. On the positive side, it has helped the Government to send a clear message to the IOCs that 'the companies are at the mercy of government not the other way round' (CSO activist, personal communication, July, 2016). One would have anticipated Government, given

Uganda's political settlement, to rush the process and strike deals with IOCs in order to obtain resources to deploy for patronage and other regime survival needs. However, the President has portrayed an image of a resilient government that can survive with or without the oil revenues. This is accurately captured by Polus and Tycholiz (2016) as follows, 'the Museveni regime can afford to present a tougher stance in licensing negotiations with oil companies, even at the expense of further delays, because oil revenues are not absolutely necessary for its survival'. Negotiations for the pipeline and refinery have also dragged and extended the production starting dates for the country. And even when formerly concluded deals collapse, for example the case of RT Global Resources for building the refinery, the Government is willing to return to the drawing board and start fresh negotiations without caving in to the demands of the oil companies.

On the negative side, Uganda's experience so far indicates that President Museveni is able to use the oil money in any way he wants, given the weak institutional safeguards. For example, Polus and Tycholiz (2017) report that in 2011 the President asked the Governor of the Bank of Uganda (BoU) to release US$ 741 million for the purchase of fighter jets from Russia. Despite the fact that such big amounts of public money should be approved by Parliament, the Governor 'released the funds on the verbal assurance that the money would be refunded when oil corporations begin paying tax' (Polus and Tycholiz, 2017, p.12). The authors conclude that, despite the theoretical independence of the BoU, President Museveni is not only able to withdraw funds from the national bank without Parliament's approval, but he can also collateralise future oil-related revenues. A related case arose from the 'golden handshake' scandal where the President allowed selected government officials to share millions of oil money for winning an oil tax dispute. While a parliamentary probe was instituted in January 2017 to investigate the implicated bureaucrats, the President shielded them from culpability. What this means for IOCs is that since the President is quite an influential figure in Uganda's oil sector, personal relations with his office are important not only in relation to sharing oil revenues but also in securing oil deals and the stability of the same.

5.6   Involvement of the Military

Given the importance that President Museveni attaches to the role played by the military in establishing security in Uganda and its continuing role in preserving the ruling coalition, it is not surprising that he has given them a central role in oil governance. Hickey *et al.* (2015) find that while there was no discussion of oil in the Cabinet until 2010, the military high command had been consulted and briefed about the discoveries and had had access to the first round of production-sharing agreements long before they were lodged in Parliament. The Government in 2012 announced the creation of a military unit called the Oil and Gas Protection Directorate to secure the Albertine Region. Until early 2017, the President's son commanded the Special Forces unit overseeing security in oil exploration areas. While oil companies employ additional private security companies to maintain security around their installations the company providing this service, Saracen, the main private security company, is associated with the President's brother.

However, and borrowing on Pritchett and Werker's (2012) deals terminologies, while IOCs can be assured that deals struck in such an environment can be relatively ordered, i.e. honoured in the short run, the likelihood of them being long-lasting is debatable, especially if President Museveni leaves office. The possibility of him losing power makes IOCs nervous. For instance, the president of Total was in Uganda at the peak of the 2016 election period and met the President. The suspicion was that he wanted reassurances from the President that his Government was in control of the political situation, although it was officially reported that he had come to negotiate the pipeline deal and to push for the production licences that had derailed (Journalist observer, personal communication, October, 2016). Similarly, every time the President travels to China he meets the president of CNOOC to discuss similar issues. Analysist argue that IOCs are aware that Museveni has managed to maintain control over the army, but the future of the army's loyalty with respect to another president is basically unknown (Polus and Tycholiz, 2017). In other words, the continuation of President Museveni's reign is key in the stability of the deals IOCs make with the Government of Uganda. According to our respondent, 'If you are an oil company your paramount interest is to have stability and make sure that the government that gave you a deal remains in power' (Journalist observer, personal communication, October, 2016).

5.7   Working Through Pockets of Effectiveness with Strong Presidential Backing

The primary agency responsible for Uganda's oil sector is the Petroleum Exploration and Production Department (PEPD) in the Ministry of Energy and Mineral Development (MEMD). PEPD was established in the mid-1980s with a mandate to establish and promote the country's petroleum potential.

Following NRM's power capture in 1986, the new Government cancelled the
negotiations with international oil companies, particularly with Shell and
Exxon, that had been started by its predecessors in the early 1980s. PEPD
received gradual and systematic capacity building sanctioned by President
Museveni. He is understood to have first wanted to work on the country's
capacity to manage the sector before moving ahead with exploration. According to key informant accounts,[4] corroborated by independent analysts
(for example, Patey, 2015; Polus and Tycholiz, 2017), the new Government
sponsored Ugandans to attend specialised oil-related training overseas,
for example as geologists. This was then followed by the establishment of
a petroleum unit in the Geological Survey and Mines Department in 1990
which was reorganised a year later into the PEPD. By this time, the PEPD had
capacity for 'data gathering/research; they did all the gravity surveys, airborne
surveys and exploration and did mapping' (Geologist Tullow, personal communication, November, 2016). At the time of writing, the PEPD has been
elevated into the Petroleum Directorate in MEMD. Apart from the formal
training, the PEPD also received technical support from bilateral agencies,
for example, the Norwegian Government, advice from Swiss oil consultants,
and legal support from American lawyers.

With such capacity, the Government, using its technical staff, has been in
a strong position to negotiate favourably with IOCs of all types and sizes. The
following example on negotiations over the oil refinery can help to substanti-
ate this claim. According to Hickey and Izama (2016) official discussions
about the refinery, which was part of the broader MoU with the Tullow-led
consortium, began in early 2013 and went on for almost a year (March 2013
to February 2014) with up to eight meetings and numerous letter exchanges
taking place between the IOCs and government officials. Meetings were
usually chaired by the Minister of Energy and Mineral Development, with
the support of the permanent secretary and the commissioner of PEPD, along
with senior representatives from the finance ministry, the Uganda Revenue
Authority, the Bank of Uganda, and the Uganda Investment Authority. More
significantly, half of these meetings involved the physical presence of the
President, usually for the entire duration of the meeting.

The IOCs are naturally interested in profit maximisation as early as possible.
For Uganda they intended to achieve this by constructing a pipeline to pump
crude oil out of the country to the coast. President Museveni saw the export
of oil in its crude form wasteful, describing it as 'sustain[ing] the good life
of outsiders' (as cited in Patey, 2015, p.15). Ugandan experts had advised

4   November 2016, interview with a geologist working with Tullow.

him that oil attracts better value when it is first processed. Therefore, he insisted that oil companies be obliged to first send oil to a domestic refinery for processing before being exported. On their part, IOCs were concerned that a refinery would leave insufficient reserves for export. To make matters worse, the Government pushed for a large refinery to produce quantities roughly the size of the entire East African oil consumption needs (Patey, 2015). In 2010, the Norwegian Government funded a feasibility study in which Foster Wheeler, a Swiss-based engineering company, reported that a 150,000 barrel-a-day (bpd) refinery (estimated to cost US$ 2 billion to set up) would be a viable option for Uganda. Tullow objected to this, suggesting that a 30,000 bpd refinery was adequate since Uganda's own market needed only 22,000 bpd. In the end, Government and IOCs agreed on a small refinery of 30,000 bpd, scalable up to 60,000 bpd. This was considered a concession on the part of Government as it dropped its ambition of satisfying the fuel demands across the entire East Africa region. It is important to note that the President emerges as a balancing force in these discussions, and he is the one who offers concessions to the oil companies in recognition of their motivations. Hickey and Izama (2016, p.182) observe that 'he does not want to be so hard on them, and on the other hand he does not want the country to be taken for a ride or to be exploited'.

Meanwhile the technocrats have also been keen to stamp their mark in these negotiations. In their analysis of the factors responsible for the delayed oil production in Uganda Polus and Tycholiz (2016) argue that technocrats who are keen on showing the Ugandan public that they take time to scrutinise all issues before making major administrative decisions and that they take no bribes to shortcut the long process perpetuate the delays. These dynamics have allowed Uganda to negotiate the best deals and perhaps, as confessed by a representative of the IOCs, 'one of the worst deals' for the oil companies (Polus and Tycholiz, 2017). Indeed, negotiations for PSAs between the Government and Tullow Oil and Total took over three years to finalise (Polus and Tycholiz, 2017). Such a protracted process, while closed to public scrutiny, instils confidence among investors in the stability of the resultant deal. The strategy has also worked to boost public confidence in Government despite the secrecy surrounding the negotiations. One key informant explained:

I applaud the government because they have tried everything to be pro-Ugandan. They have tried to negotiate the best deals in which they retain the higher percentage no matter what. That is why Tullow has been on and off but government doesn't care. At the moment it claims the PSAs don't favour them and the government says if they are not happy then they would rather sell out and leave. The government did very good training for the people in the petroleum sector. The staff employed at Uganda Petroleum Authority, are highly trained, they understand the sector laws, and what is best for Uganda… they bargain, advise government very well and the President listens to them (Tullow Oil Company employee, personal communication, September, 2016).

Therefore, in spite of the overwhelming experience of IOCs in the oil sector, the Ugandan technocrats with the backing of their President have managed to control them.

5.8   Keep the 'Enemies' Small

Following IOCs' and government's agreement over the terms of the refinery, government shrewdness came to the fore again during the awarding of the contract for constructing the refinery. Six companies, namely, Marubeni of Japan, Vitol, the China Petroleum Pipeline Bureau, Russia's Rostec Global Resources (RTGR), SK Energy, and Petrofac were interested. In a move seen as intended to limit the influence of IOCs, in particular the Chinese who already had a production licence, President Museveni and his team side-lined them from the refinery deal. This could be interpreted as a contingency plan for protecting government interests just in case relations with China degenerated in future. Out of the six, GoU shortlisted RT Global Resources and South Korea's SK Energy. The Russian firm was ultimately selected. However, just prior to the expected signature date at the beginning of June 2016, the RT-Global Resources Consortium made additional demands from the Government, seeking to reopen and renegotiate issues that had already been agreed between the two parties, which caused the deal to collapse.

Notwithstanding the mishaps with the RTGR deal, our point is that the Ugandan Government is wary of letting one player become too powerful for its capacity. As indicated by a key informant, 'this government does not allow monopoly' (Geologist Tullow Oil, personal communication, November, 2016). This can be seen in another incident. In 2009, when Heritage sought to sell its oil stakes to Italy's ENI, Tullow used its contractual rights to make the US$ 1.4 billion purchase itself. However, the Ugandan Government cautioned that it could veto the sale, as Tullow would hold a monopoly over the industry. It was not until Tullow made it known that it was bringing new partners, Total and CNOOC, on board with an equal 33.3 per cent share in the exploration areas that the Government relented. Otherwise the GoU is understood to have considered ENI. Our informants further noted that while Tullow, Total, and CNOOC are joint venture companies and expected to work together, they negotiate their contracts separately and have different levels of access to the President (Geologist Tullow Oil, personal communication, November, 2016). It is claimed that the Chinese, with their CNOOC, have easier access to the President compared to their counterparts and 'their things get done very fast... actually at the moment the Chinese are way ahead of the other companies' (Oil Uganda, personal communication, September, 2016).

5.9   Warding Off Competition from Alternative Centres of Power at Home

Following the Government's announcement of commercially viable deposits in 2006, a force of civil society emerged to influence the course of events in Uganda's oil sector. Their goal was to present Uganda with an opportunity to harness the oil resource underpinned by principles of justice and inclusive development. The late 2000s initially saw individual CSOs such as ACODE, International Alert, Publish What You Pay (PWYP) Uganda, and Oil Watch Network among others showing interest in the oil sector (Van Alstine *et al.*, 2014). Their approach was to work with Parliament, particularly through a pressure group called Parliamentary Forum on Oil and Gas (PFOG). CSOs aimed to support Parliament in making informed policy decisions on, and ensuring adequate oversight of, Uganda's nascent petroleum industry. They claimed that their advocacy was aligned with the intentions of the national oil and gas policy that guarantees optimum national participation in oil and gas exploration, production and decision making. However, as these hitherto bystanders (civil society and Parliament) piqued interest in the sector, tensions developed between them and the executive, whose monopoly of oil issues had historically gone unchallenged.

During the rewriting of section 9 of the Petroleum (Exploration, Development and Production) Act 2012,[5] about whether the Minister or the Petroleum Authority should have the power to license and revoke licences, President Museveni 'convened at least up to eight caucus meetings to be able to get

---

5   Parliament successfully passed section 9 whose essence was to give the negotiation and licensing powers to the Petroleum Authority instead of the Minister. Its reasoning was that 'the Minister is a political person and therefore could be influenced by the powers that be. ... Politicians are bound to be compromised by the appointing authority whereas the Petroleum Authority is accountable to the citizens' (Ssekikubo, 2013, p.2).

MPs accept to change what they had passed' (Key informant from a CSO, personal communication, February, 2014). This was unprecedented because, normally, it would take him one meeting to change the opinion of NRM legislators. This provoked the President's anger against CSOs because his informers told him that 'it is ACODE that have made these MPs stubborn' (Key informant from a CSO, personal communication, February, 2014). Indeed, on 13 December 2012, President Yoweri Museveni, during a special parliamentary sitting, accused some MPs and CSOs of 'working on behalf of foreign interests' to 'cripple and disorient the development of the oil sector' (Museveni, 2012, p.2). In his speech the President singled out the Advocates' Coalition for Development and Environment (ACODE), NAPE, Global Rights Alert, Centre for Constitutional Governance, AFIEGO and the Parliamentary Forum on Oil and Gas (PFOG) as some of the saboteur NGOs promoting the so-called foreign interests. He vowed to stop them 'by legal, political and media actions' (Museveni, 2012, p.15).

The ruling elite devised various strategies to keep CSOs in check. The critical ones, such as ACODE, were subjected to dubious government investigations. For example, in March 2012, the Bank of Uganda issued a memorandum requesting all financial institutions in the country to report on ACODE's financial transactions (Matsiko, 2012). This was to signal to other NGOs that '[i]f you don't check your ways, you are in trouble' (Matsiko, 2012). The Government also revised the NGO law to ensure that it has firm control over civil society advocacy and mobilisation activities. According to one KI 'they are planning to introduce a new arrangement where you must reveal to government where you get the money that supports your activities. They are borrowing this from Ethiopia' (CSCO, personal communication, February, 2014). Indeed, the activities of NGOs are now guided by the NGO Act 2016, which observers have noted to be targeting advocacy CSOs (Global Witness Alert, 2017). According to one respondent:

> the NGO law and the Public Order Management Act restrict freedom of association. What will happen when the people in Hoima, Buliisa [oil production areas] want to demonstrate against the oil companies, do they have to comply with the public order management act? Do they have to seek permission? And if police say they are not granting permission what do you do? Will you be enhancing accountability in the oil sector? (Ugandan Journalist, personal communication, October, 2016).

Similarly, Government indicated that since oil is a national resource, advocacy activities around it should be funded by resources mobilised nationally, from the people who have a stake in the sector. However, the Civil Society Coalition on Oil and Gas believes that this is likely to constrain CSO activities 'because very limited resources can be mobilised locally' (CSCO, personal communication, February, 2014). The President and senior NRM officials also launched verbal attacks on CSOs to undermine their credibility. They accused them of frustrating the activities of the NRM party and its caucus in Parliament by deliberately trying to misinform MPs on oil issues. In 2012 President Museveni (2012), who is also the NRM chairman, alleged that MPs who participated in the workshops organised by CSOs were paid huge honorariums as a way of bribing them. Similarly, in his submission in Uganda's daily, the New Vision, on 4 December 2012, Mr Ofwono Opondo, the vice spokesman of the NRM, suggested that 'it is necessary to examine who funds the noisy MPs and NGOs in the oil debate'. He accused CSOs of being 'agents of external forces' hostile to Uganda. He singled out one donor agency, USAID, as not wishing Uganda well on oil because an American firm, ExxonMobil, had lost out on acquiring oil deals in Uganda's petroleum sector so far.

Some outspoken parliamentarians were also persecuted by the NRM party for their stance on the control and governance of oil. In April 2013, the ruling NRM party expelled four of its Members of Parliament for indiscipline, accusing two of them of belonging to PFOG, a pressure group of legislators advocating for greater transparency in the oil and gas sector, but which the party said was 'opposed to the NRM position on oil' (Ssekikubo, 2013, p.3). The Constitutional Court later ruled that the expelled MPs should also lose their positions in the Parliament. The so-called 'rebel MPs' however successfully managed to challenge the ruling in the Supreme Court. Nonetheless the action sent a strong warning to other MPs. As a key industry watcher put it, 'many of them got scared of engaging in PFOG activities' (Key informant from a CSO, personal communication, October, 2016). The forum eventually lost steam. This was reflected in the poor attendance at PFOG's subsequent activities including general meetings. For example, out of the estimated membership of 200 MPs, only seven turned up for PFOG's 2013/2014 annual general meeting. With such strategies the ruling elite regained authority over 'its oil'. According to Hickey and Izama (2016, p.11) the President entreats citizens to entrust him, rather than government institutions, to manage the oil resource.

Meanwhile, IOCs have also deployed 'soft power' strategies to help the Government in demobilising opposition from civil society. Through their corporate social responsibility arrangements, they have given lucrative opportunities for employment and training to civil society activists. It is reported that the activists opt to undertake jobs and scholarship opportunities offered by oil companies and drop the advocacy work (Daily Monitor,

3 November 2012, p.6). For example, in 2012, beneficiaries of Tullow Oil group scholarships award included two outspoken civil society activists among the 20 recipients pursuing master's degrees (petroleum related) at selected universities in Britain (ibid.). One of the activists, the former chairperson of the Hoima NGO Forum, went on to pursue a degree in oil and gas management at the University of Coventry. The second one, the former treasurer of the Midwestern Regional Anti-Corruption Coalition, took a master's degree in management science and finance at the University of Manchester. The increased exodus of activists out of CSOs to join oil firms is said to weaken capacity and cohesion in local CSOs. Thus, CSOs are increasingly constrained to perform their watchdog roles over Government and its dealings with IOCs.

5.10   Conclusion

In 1986, when the NRM captured state power, the Government suspended all oil exploration activities that its predecessors had commissioned. Under the guidance of President Museveni, it was agreed that Uganda's capacity for petroleum exploration and production required development before any deals could be initiated with international oil companies. Indeed, the Government selected several of its technical staff and sent them overseas to attend specialised courses on petroleum. The country commenced the issue of PSAs in the early 1990s. The process was again halted following the discovery of commercially viable quantities in 2006. This time deal making was stopped to allow the setting-up of the necessary legal framework to guide the process. While these moves suggest a government that has foregone the short-term benefits of securing quick deals, the competitive character of the political settlement has meant that the governance of oil is informal and personalised by the President. President Museveni has a strong personal interest in the negotiations with oil companies and he has assigned a key role to the military. He has however restricted the participation of the other actors such as Parliament and civil society. As noted by Hickey *et al.*:

> ... The process is dominated by key actors from within the ruling coalition, who negotiate with rentier oil companies in a highly secretive manner, ... and adopt a repressive approach to those who oppose its plans and activities in the sector at both local or national levels (Hickey *et al.*, 2015, p.12).

Surprisingly, this 'close-ordered' deals environment has delivered, since the deals reached so far appear to be more in the national interest as they give few concessions to IOCs. The evidence presented shows that the President has proved capable of controlling rent-seeking activities in the sector and is willing to enable high-capacity oil technocrats to operate with significant levels of autonomy (Bukenya and Hickey, 2018). It seems unlikely, however, that these strategies will remain effective beyond the current President. As seen throughout this chapter, it appears that just one man has investors' confidence and holds Uganda's oil sector vision. The desire to maintain this stability could perhaps explain why processes including constitutional revisions to make Mr Museveni president for life have been vigorously pursued.

References

Bukenya, B., and W. Muhumuza (2017), 'The Politics of Core Public Sector Reform in Uganda: Behind the Façade'. *ESID Working Paper No. 85*. Manchester: The University of Manchester.
―――― and S. Hickey (2018), 'Dominance and Deals in Africa: How Politics Shapes Uganda's Transition from Growth to Transformation', in L. Pritchett, K. Sen and E. Werker (eds.), *Deals and Development: The Political Dynamics of Growth Episodes*. Oxford: Oxford University Press.
Daily Monitor (2012, 14 December), 'President Attacks MPS, Civil Society on Oil Bill', Daily Monitor.
De Kock, P., and K. Sturman (2012), 'The Power of Oil Charting Uganda's Transition to a Petro-State'. SAIIA Governance of Africa's Resource Programme, Research Report 10. Retrieved from: http://www.eisourcebook.org/cms/June%202013/Uganda,%20Charting%20its%20Transition%20to%20a%20Petro-State.pdf.
Di John, J., and J. Putzel (2009), 'Political Settlements: Issues Paper'. Discussion Papers. Birmingham: University of Birmingham.
Golooba-Mutebi, F., and S. Hickey (2013), 'Investigating the Links between Political Settlements and Inclusive Development in Uganda: Towards a Research Agenda'. *ESID Working Paper No. 20*. Retrieved from: http://www.effective-states.org/wp-content/uploads/working_papers/final-pdfs/esid_wp_20_goloobamutebi-hickey.pdf.
Hickey, S., and A. Izama (2016), 'The Politics of Governing Oil in Uganda: Going Against the Grain?', *African Affairs*, 163(463), 163–185. Retrieved from: https://doi.org/10.1093/afraf/adw048.
―――――, B. Bukenya, A. Izama and W. Kizito (2015), 'The Political Settlement and Oil in Uganda'. *ESID Working Paper No. 48*. Retrieved from: http://dx.doi.org/10.2139/ssrn.2587845.
Khan, M. (2010), 'Political Settlements and the Governance of Growth-enhancing Institutions'. Working Paper (unpublished). London: SOAS University of London. Retrieved from: https://eprints.soas.ac.uk/9968/1/Political_Settlements_internet.pdf
Khisa, M. (2016), 'Managing elite defection in Museveni's Uganda: the 2016 elections in perspective', Journal of Eastern African Studies, 10(4), 729–748. Retrieved from: https://www.tandfonline.com/doi/abs/10.1080/17531055.2016.1272288.
Kjaer, A.M., M.S. Ulriksen, J. Kangave and M.W. Katusiimeh (2017), 'A Political Economy Analysis of Domestic Resource Mobilization in Uganda'. *UNRISD Working Paper 2017–8*. Retrieved from: http://www.unrisd.org/unrisd/website/document.nsf/(httpPublications)/98FD9753BE1DA42BC1258144003622DE?OpenDocument.

Matsiko, H. (2012, 9 April), 'ACODE under Investigation: Mutebile Letter to Commercial Banks Upsets NGOs Involved in Oil Advocacy', *The Independent*. Retrieved from: https://www.independent.co.ug/acode-under-investigation/.

Museveni, Y.K. (2012), *Speech to Parliament of Uganda*. Kampala: President of the Republic of Uganda.

Mwenda, A. (2006), 'Redefining Uganda's Budget Priorities: A Critique of the 2006/07 Budget'. *ACODE Policy Briefing Paper*, No. 17.

—— and R. Tangri (2005), 'Patronage Politics, Donor Reforms, and Regime Consolidation in Uganda', *African Affairs, 104(416)*, 449–467.

Patey, L. (2015), 'Oil in Uganda: Hard Bargaining and Complex Politics in East Africa'. *OIES Working Paper* No. 60. Retrieved from: https://doi.org/10.26889/9781784670405.

Polus, A., and W. Tycholiz (2016), 'Why is It Taking so Long? Solving the Oil Extraction Equation in Uganda', 15 *African and Asian Studies* 77.

—— and ——(2017), 'The Norwegian Model of Oil Extraction and Revenues Management in Uganda', *African Studies Review*, 60(3), 181–201. Retrieved from: https://doi.org/10.1017/asr.2017.88.

Pritchett, L., and E. Werker (2012), 'Developing the Guts of a GUT (Grand Unified Theory): Elite Commitment and Inclusive Growth'. *(ESID) Working Paper No. 16/12*. Retrieved from: http://dx.doi.org/10.2139/ssrn.2386617.

Rulekere, G. (2011, 24 August), 'Musevenism: When the President has to Handle Every Issue', *UG Pulse*. Retrieved from: http://www.ugpulse.com/government/musevenism-when-the-president-has-to-handleevery-issue/1263/ug.aspx.

Rwakakamba, M., and D. Lukwago (2013), 'Farmers in Uganda's Oil Economy'. Retrieved from the Agency for Transformation website: https://agencyft.org/.

Ssekikubo, T. (2013), 'The Bells of Apprehension about the Oil are Already Ringing', *Black Monday Newsletter* (12), 2.

The World Bank (2015), *Leveraging Oil and Gas Industry for the Development of a Competitive Private Sector in Uganda*. Washington, DC: World Bank Group.

Van Alstine, J., J. Manyindo, L. Smith, J. Dixon and I. AmanigaRuhanga (2014), 'Resource Governance Dynamics: The Challenge of "New Oil" in Uganda', *Resources Policy, 40*, 48–58. Retrieved from: http://dx.doi.org/10.1016/j.resourpol.2014.01.002.

Vokes, R. (2012), 'The Politics of Oil in Uganda', *African Affairs*, 101(443), 303–314. Retrieved from: https://academic.oup.com/afraf/article/111/443/303/17334

Wamono, R.N., P. Kikabi and J. Mugisha (2012), *Constraints and Opportunities for SMEs Investment in Uganda's Oil and Gas Sector*. Retrieved from the Africa Portal website: https://www.africaportal.org/publications/constraints-and-opportunities-for-smes-investment-in-ugandas-oil-and-gas-sector/.

Wang, V., and L. Rakner (2005), 'The Accountability Function of Supreme Audit Institutions in Malawi, Uganda and Tanzania'. *CMI Report 2005:4*. Retrieved from the Chr. Michelsen Institute website: https://www.cmi.no/publications/2000-the-accountability-function-of-supreme-audit.

Wass, G., and C. Musiime (2013), *Business, Human Rights, and Uganda's Oil Part I: Uganda's Oil Sector and Potential Threats to Human Rights*. Retrieved from the IPIS website: http://ipisresearch.be/publication/business-human-rights-ugandas-oil-part-ugandas-oil-sector-potential-threats-human-rights/.

PART II

MACROECONOMIC AND FISCAL FRAMEWORK, POLICIES AND CHALLENGES

6
Oil Wealth in Uganda: Analysis of the Macroeconomic Policy Framework

Corti Paul Lakuma

6.1   Introduction

In 2006, Uganda discovered a large amount of recoverable oil deposits in the Albertine Graben (Energy International Agency [EIA], 2016). The discovery of oil in Uganda presents a unique opportunity to transform the economy through infrastructure development and poverty alleviation. Oil is expected to contribute an average net present value of US$ 2 billion (10 per cent of GDP) for at least 26 years. In this regard, oil and gas have been identified as an important building block to realising the long-term aspirations and objectives of Uganda's Vision 2040 of 'A Transformed Ugandan Society from a Peasant to a Modern and Prosperous Country within 30 Years' (Government of Uganda [GOU], 2015).

Uganda's oil sector is undergoing rapid development. Included in this development are upstream projects, such as the building of a refinery and the establishment of an export pipeline to the coast. The development of this sector will generate significant foreign direct investment in the country and is likely to bring windfall revenues to the national treasury. However, oil revenues also present significant macroeconomic challenges, especially in a low global oil prices environment. Oil can breed risk, leading to economic stagnation and wastage. These risks include Dutch disease, rent-seeking behaviour among political elites and corruption among others. In this chapter I will analyse Uganda's macroeconomic framework and policy approaches for dealing with these potential risks. In this regard the chapter has two specific objectives. First, it aims to document policies aimed at facilitating prudent macroeconomic management in order to mitigate the negative impact of the fluctuation of international oil prices. In this respect I will particularly focus on the following issues: the rate of extraction and welfare, inter-governmental revenue-sharing mechanisms, the relevance of a refinery, the effects of Dutch disease, the extent of local participation in the oil value chain and the tax code used to regulate the oil industry.

Second, the chapter also aims to discuss and analyse the fiscal rules the Government of Uganda has put in place to achieve a balance between spending and savings of the expected oil revenues. Where possible, the chapter will state the problems, their manifestation or likely manifestation, efforts to address them in the Ugandan context and possible outcomes/scenarios.

This chapter derives information from various government documents, contract information and past studies on Uganda's oil industry. The remainder of the chapter is organised as follows. Section 2 will discuss and analyse Uganda's macroeconomic management regime, while Section 3 will focus on Uganda's fiscal regime. Section 4 reviews how Uganda aims to achieve a balance between spending and saving its expected oil revenues. The last section concludes and offers some policy reflections.

6.2   Macroeconomic Management Regime

Oil and gas revenues are subject to volatility in volume and prices. Mitigation of such risks through fiscal policies is imperative. Prudent macroeconomic management policies are key to charting the sustainable path for production and revenue minimising the impact of Dutch disease and the boom and bust cycle. These and other issues are explored below in the context of Uganda.

6.2.1   Uganda's Production and Revenue Profiles

There are three clusters of 18 oilfields in the Lake Albert region known as Kingfisher, Kaiso Tonya, and Buliisa (Doshi, Joutz, Lakuma, Lwanga and Manzano, 2015). They are operated by Tullow Oil Company, Total and the Chinese National Offshore Oil Company (CNOOC). Excluding enhanced oil recovery (EOR), estimates suggest that close to 1.3 billion barrels will be recovered over 26 years with a peak of 230,000 bpd (Ibid.). Production is projected to start at a modest daily output of about 20,000 bpd (MFPED, 2015a). The Government's take will be 40 per cent of the first 5,000 barrels per day, rising to 65 per cent for production above 40,000 barrels per day (Doshi et al., 2015).[1] The Government's take includes a national oil company (NOC)

---

1   Information derived from public information on the oilfield characteristics and reserve estimates as well as existing upstream regulations and contract information on the fiscal regime. However, this could be adjusted.

Figure 6.1:   **Estimated Uganda's production profile**

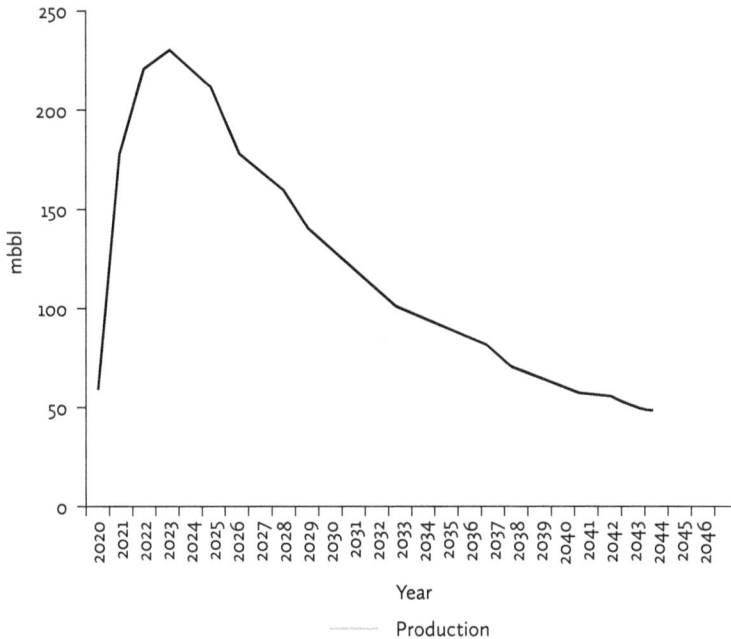

Source: Doshi et al. (2015, p. 25).

or state participating interest (estimated to be 15 per cent with exploration and production and development cost carried).

Figure 6.1 is bell-shaped, which suggest that Uganda's recoverable oil is finite and may last for only 26 years, which poses a challenge for transforming the resource into a permanent income, sustaining higher growth without overheating the economy and avoiding the Dutch disease. In this regard, the ministry responsible for energy and oil companies will decide on the amount of oil to be produced within a given period consistent with their development plans (MFPED, 2012). However, the extent to which the Government resists pressure, both political and from international oil companies (IOCs), will determine the rate of extraction. Given the need to recover costs faster, it is in the interest of the IOCs to exploit the resource at a faster rate, regardless of underlying national interest. However, a decision on the extraction rate should weigh the counterfactual evidence, which suggests that excess exploitation has a pass-through effect on the prices of products such as retail natural gas, retail electricity and commodity chemicals (Hausman and Kellogg, 2015).

Figure 6.2:   **Uganda revenue profile (Estimates)**

Oil revenues

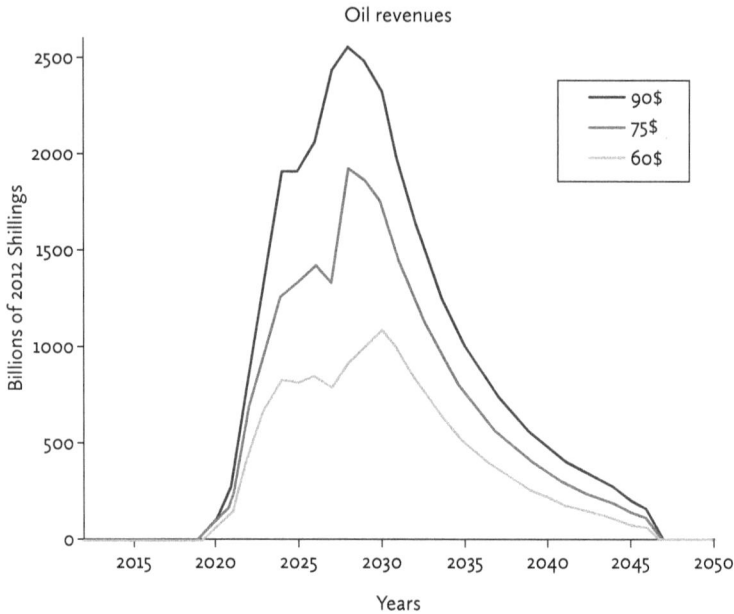

Source: Doshi et al. (2015, p. 26).

Owing to its waxy content, Ugandan crude oil may sell at a 30 per cent discount on benchmark crudes such as *Brent*. The discount is to account for its high viscosity that requires heating while in freight to export terminal(s) on the Indian Ocean (Doshi *et al.*, 2015). Figure 6.2 shows the expected profile of the oil revenues for different oil prices (US$ 60/bbl, US$ 75/bbl and US$ 90/bbl).[2] Industry estimates suggest that the marketability of Ugandan oil will depend on prices being above US$ 60. As such, protection of the budget from potentially large fluctuations in oil revenue as a result of price variability poses a challenge and must be managed in order to maintain macroeconomic stability. One alternative to cushion the budget from large variability is by sustaining the strengthening of non-oil domestic resource mobilisation through sustaining tax administration reforms and registration of the non-oil informal sector.

2   The revenues are expressed in 2012 real shillings by transforming nominal $ into real shillings by applying the average depreciation of the shilling and the average growth rate of the Ugandan GDP deflator.

The Government envisages a multi-institutional committee for the purpose of determining the price of oil. The committee will include officials from the Ministry of Finance, Planning and Economic Development (MFPED), the Ministry of Energy and Mineral Development (MEMD), the Uganda Revenue Authority (URA) and other specialised agencies. The committee will also set the price at which profit oil received in kind by the national oil company will be disposed of. However, the international price of oil is discovered in designated centres such as Singapore. Moreover, Uganda is a small producer and is effectively a price taker, and thus cannot influence world prices. This limits the relevance of the price-setting committee to setting domestic refined oil prices. Given this background, such a committee will be vulnerable to political pressure to discount the domestic price of refined oil to meet some political objectives. The committee's influence on regional prices may also be limited by the quality of fuel produced and the quantity demanded by the region. It is envisaged that the role of such a committee may be limited to setting benchmark prices.

6.2.2   Fiscal Decentralisation of Oil Revenues in Uganda

As provided for by various legal instruments including the Constitution, the management of natural resources is a responsibility of the central government. However, in the interest of social cohesion and a stable investment and production environment Uganda has a revenue-sharing mechanism. The Government will allocate 7 per cent of all royalty revenues to local governments located in the oil and gas-producing areas (MFPED, 2012). In this regard, 93 per cent will be retained at the centre. The criteria for allocation shall consider local governments within the oil resource rich region which may not produce oil themselves but are affected by oil activities and incur the social cost related to these activities. The criteria shall also consider each local jurisdiction level of production.[3] The transfer shall not exceed 100 per cent of the current non-oil fiscal transfer in order to encourage local tax mobilisation and mitigate dependence on oil revenue.

In absolute terms, each local government currently receives an average of UGX 15 billion per annum from the central government and mobilises 5 per cent of total transfers from central government out of local taxation (Lakuma, Marty and Kuteesa, 2016). Given that a local government cannot

3    $LGRS_i = R/2 *$ (Weighted LG population share$_i$ + Weighted LG production share$_i$), where: LGRS = individual local government royalty revenue share; LG = local government, R = total local government royalty share.

receive more than 100 per cent of its non-oil fiscal transfer, the paper estimates
that each local government will receive a maximum of UGX 30 billion. As for
local governments with absorptive constraint, any unspent balance will be
appropriated by the MFPED and reallocated to the same local government
in the next financial year (MFPED, 2016). However, this can lead to a race
to spend in a bid to prevent expropriation of unspent resources.

The aforementioned revenue-sharing criteria suggest that the Government
of Uganda model for revenue sharing favours a mix of the derivation principle
and those allocation principles that are similar to inter-governmental fiscal
transfer formulas.[4] The former ensures that each local government's share is
related to the oil revenue originating in its territory. The derivation principle
model has proven to be successful in preventing natural resource conflict risk
(Strachan, 2014). However, the model may promote or exacerbate already
existing horizontal inequality between local governments in producing areas
and those that have limited capacity for revenue collection. Certainly, older
oil-producing district such as Hoima have relatively better fiscal capacities
than newly created oil-producing districts like Buliisa and Nwoya or newly
created districts with no proven natural resources such as Ngora, Sironko
and Pader.

Given the poor standards of living and the infrastructural deficit in rural
areas, the revenue-sharing formula used by Uganda will provides a relatively
small proportion in transfers of oil proceeds to local government compare to
other reference countries. For example, sub-national governments in Bolivia
receive 60 per cent of the fiscal take (Aresti, 2016).[5] The Indonesian Government allocates 15.5 per cent of net oil revenues to sub-national governments
(Strachan, 2014). In Nigeria, Parliament revises the formula for oil revenue
sharing every five years, and a minimum of 13 per cent of oil revenue must be
reserved for oil-producing states (Haysom and Kane, 2009).

The extent to which the model will facilitate the improvement of living
standards could face significant challenges. While the revenue transferred
may be perceived to be inadequate, this may be in the best interest of local
government to prevent budget distortions in light of absorption constraints
and fluctuating oil prices. Fluctuating oil prices could also encourage local
governments to adopt shorter planning horizons in the face of fluctuating
prices due to uncertainty about future income. This could increase corruption

4   The inter-governmental fiscal transfer formula uses criteria such as population, needs or tax
capacity to determine revenue share.
5   Fiscal take is composed of direct tax, royalties, patents and any proceeds from fiscal
co-participation.

if local government officials have no confidence in the stability of government funds. This creates an incentive for local governments to appropriate as much as possible and as quickly as possible before oil revenues wane.

As mentioned earlier, one significant advantage with the Uganda's revenue-sharing model is that it explicitly specifies that the central government will regulate and govern hydrocarbon revenue sources and has the authority to issue licences for new explorations. While there is no ambiguity in the power relations between central government and local government with regard to policy guidance in matters of natural resources, the intra local government relationships and the relationship between local governments and cultural institutions are not clearly defined by the law and could prove to be a source of disagreement.[6]

6.2.3   Refining of Expected Crude Oil

Uganda plans to refine some or all of the expected oil production for domestic consumption and regional export. A feasibility study by Foster Wheeler (2011) found that a refinery was commercially viable with a net present value (NPV) of US$ 3.2 billion at a 10 per cent discount rate and an internal rate of return (IRR) of 33 per cent (MEMD, 2015). The proposed refinery will have an initial output of 30,000 bpd, growing to 60,000 bpd (Doshi *et al.*, 2015). Estimates suggest that a refinery will save Uganda US$ 1 billion annually in two ways: the first is self-sufficiency in petrol, diesel and kerosene with spill-over employment effects. The second is through supplying fuel to Rwanda, Burundi and parts of Kenya (Patey, 2015).[7]

A refinery also holds strategic importance for Uganda that cannot be discounted. Uganda is landlocked and imports its product through Kenya. On several occasions, Uganda has experienced supply disruption due to technical inefficiencies and political risk in Kenya (Patey, 2015).[8] If government plans do not change, the refinery will have the first call on crude. This suggest that over time all the crude produced in Uganda could be refined as production reaches

---

6   MFPED (2016) states that each local government may, in consultation with the Ministry responsible for culture and the other local governments, agree to allocate a share of its royalty grant to cultural institutions recognised by the Constitution in its locality. In addition, sub-counties within each of the eligible local government areas shall be entitled to share in the royalties received. However, the royalty shared with sub-counties shall be net of subventions to cultural institutions and will be on the basis of weighted population (MFPED).

7   Oil constitutes 10–15 per cent of Uganda's imports.

8   There were fuel shortages and price rises in Uganda following the post-election violence in Kenya.

peak and capacity to refine increases. Also, subject to domestic production capacity, the refinery may obtain crude oil or raw gas from outside Uganda (MEMD, 2012). This has been a point of contention among international oil companies participating in Uganda's oil sector (Patey, 2015).

What seems to be missing in the policy discussions is the fact that the operation of the refinery will be contingent on import cost and regional demand for crude refined in Uganda. In this regard, Patey (2015) notes that Uganda's refinery's product would have to compete for market share with imports from large and efficient refiners in the Middle East and India. There is also a possibility of new refineries emerging from Kenya, Tanzania and South Sudan. It is important for policy makers to consider that the performance of a refinery varies depending on region, demand for oil, market structure and price of oil. Foster Wheeler (2011) points out that the profitability of Uganda's refinery will depend on the international oil price not being below US$ 60.

Nevertheless, evidence also suggests that the profitability of refineries after the recent fall in crude oil prices has varied among refining countries. Refiners in Asia and Europe scored higher margins buoyed by heightened demand for oil to build inventories (Fitzgibbon, Kloskowska and Martin, 2015). North American margins fell sharply due to loss of some of the region's recent structural advantages versus the rest of the world (Fitzgibbon *et al.*, 2015). This calls for a comprehensive cost benefit analysis before embarking on financing a refinery. On that note, financing a refinery would cost around US$ 4 billion and the Government would probably use fuel subsidies to satisfy domestic demand, exacerbating public cost. Cost will also be incurred in transporting the crude to Rwanda, Burundi and parts of Kenya.

6.2.4 Mitigating the Risks of Dutch Disease

Empirical literature shows that the increase in profitability of the oil bids up the prices of factors of production, and draws such factors away from other sectors in the economy. The movement of factors of production into the oil sector contracts the non-oil tradeable sectors (manufacturing and agriculture) and bids up prices in the non-tradeable (services). In addition, large expenditure increases in public investments and transfers may also impede the competitiveness of the tradable sectors such as agriculture. The literature describes this as the Dutch disease. The impact of Dutch disease is worsened by volatility in oil prices and mostly harms the poor, exacerbating income inequality (Leamer, Maul, Rodriguez and Schott, 1999). Figure 6.3 shows a simulation by Doshi *et al.* (2015) that illustrates the impact of Dutch disease using Uganda's data. The first column of Figure 6.3 suggests that a

Figure 6.3:   Simulated Impact of Dutch Disease on Uganda's Economy

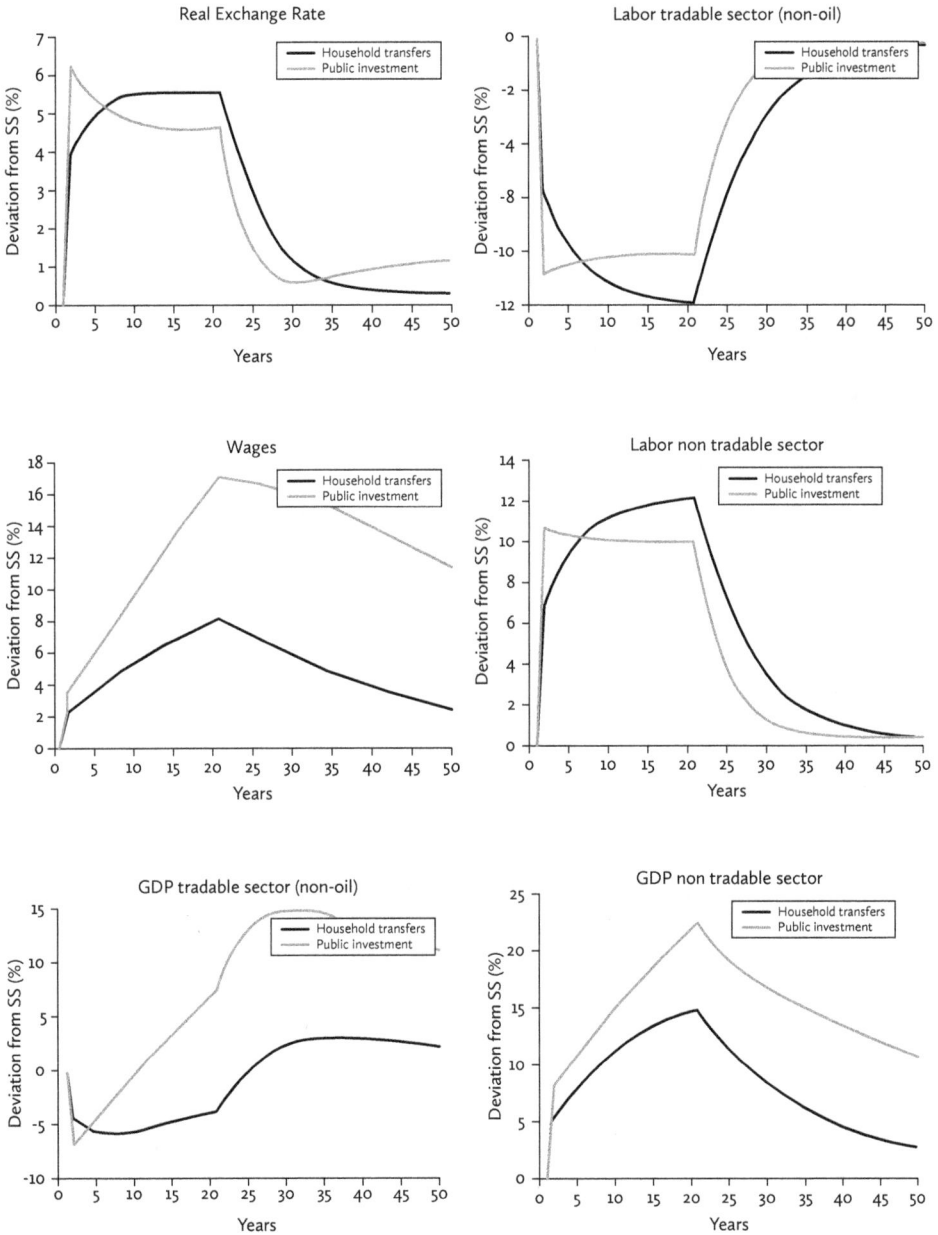

Source: Doshi et al. (2015, p. 25).

large increase in spending can push up relative prices (real effective exchange rates and wages) in favour of non-tradable sectors. This leads to a movement of labour and capital from the tradable (agriculture manufacturing) to non-tradable (services) sectors, as shown in the second column, reducing the contribution and competitiveness of the tradable sector (third column).

In relation to this, a large body of government of Uganda documents relating to oil governance points to the need for prudent macroeconomic management policies in the face of oil production. In particular, the Government has put in place a set of laws through the Public Finance Management Act (2015) to guide the resource-funded spending. The World Bank and many other civil societies have also pushed for prudent macroeconomic management of oil revenues in developing countries. However, alternative wisdom suggests that while revenue governance criteria are useful, they should not be overly strict or externally imposed for them to survive changing bargaining strengths and external conditions (Gérin and Houdin, 2010). Lessons from Chad and Cameroon are instructive: 'a country will develop its natural resources whether it is "institutionally ready" to administer the benefits or not' (Gérin and Houdin, 2010, p.2).

The extent to which Uganda strikes the right balance between resource and non-resource revenue generation will determine the degree of reliance on the former as the main source of budget financing. Empirical evidence suggest that the non-resource revenue sector is often neglected, which poses the risk of government over-relying on one commodity for its fiscal revenues. In this regard, the willingness of government to resist the pressure to draw from the petroleum fund to fund off-budget and unproductive activities will define the degree of the distortion caused by oil revenues. However, pressure to expand the non-oil budget deficit, given the level of infrastructural deficit and the rate of poverty could pose a challenge. The poverty rate was estimated to be at 20.7 per cent in 2012/2013 (Sewanyana and Kasirye, 2014).

6.2.5   Local Content Policy

Through the local content policy, the Government plans to address vocational skills and align them with the needs of the oil sector. The Government is also planning to expand and strengthen the delivery of oil and gas sector-related education and training through local institutions, and supporting capacity development of local private-sector players in the provision of ground handling and logistical services (MFPED, 2012). However, these are countable jobs, given that the oil and gas industry is an enclave activity that requires substantial skills that cannot be developed in the short run. In this regard, the direct mass participation of Ugandans and local enterprises may prove to be elusive.

Nevertheless, the idea of diversifying away from oil activities to mitigate dependence and excessive volatility, which hurts the poor, has also been proposed. In this regard, Uganda has taken a keen interest in lessons from resource-rich countries that have diversified their economies. For instance, Indonesia used much of her oil revenue to promote manufacturing and agriculture through public investment and market-friendly reforms (Ross, 2003). However, some policy makers have argued for development of the oil sector to be more pro-poor by creating employment through backward and forward linkage activities such as developing a petrochemical industry that ensures local participation (local content) in the oil value chain. Ravallion and Datt (1996) show that India has succeeded in building value chains by building the capacity of its citizens to participate in the intermediate petrochemical industry. Indeed, the expansion into petrochemicals has catalysed the diversification of countries in the Gulf Countries Cooperation (GCC) (Budde and Shah, 2014). The region's chemical industry currently supports an estimated 840,000 jobs. In 2011, chemicals represented 4.5 per cent of non-oil and gas GDP in Saudi Arabia (Budde and Shah, 2014).

Therefore, it is prudent for Uganda to consider the development of a petrochemical industry in its local content policy. A petrochemical industry would be not only be a source of employment, but also an avenue for exporting manufactures in plastics, mattress, pharmaceutical, fertilisers, chemicals, tyres and other intermediates that are used in other industries such as agriculture and manufacturing. This will integrate sectors such as agriculture and industry into the oil and gas industry. In general, the promotion of local content should strive to develop indirect participation in the industry as opposed to direct participation. As such, a refinery and the expected petroleum by-products such as naphtha could act as a feedstock and support the growth of a petrochemical industry.

6.3   Uganda's Fiscal Regime

The current fiscal regime for the petroleum sector is based on a production-sharing contract or agreement (PSA). Under this arrangement, the oil companies are contracted by Government and are rewarded with an agreed share in the production. Like Algeria's, Uganda's tax system tends to follow a tax on rent in the form of net cash flow. This requires firms to bid for the right to exploit the resource. Empirical research suggest that PSAs tend to perform better than a system that grant exemption to upstream activities, such as those in Ghana (EY, 2015). Nevertheless, countries' fiscal regimes vary depending on local political, economic and institutional conditions. Some countries treat extractive sectors more favourably than most other industries, through favourable treatment of such capital expenses as depletion, exploration and development, and the cost of acquiring resource properties (Broadway and Flatters, 1993).

The law imposes on the Uganda Revenue Authority (URA) in collaboration with other relevant technical departments under the Ministry responsible for Energy the responsibility to collect and administer taxes, dues, charges and levies on gas and oil-related activities. In its simplest form, the fiscal provisions of a production-sharing agreement have four main components: royalties, cost recovery oil, profit oil, and income tax (MEMD, 2012). The Government's total revenue is composed of royalties, which are payments made in lieu of resource extraction and are based on volume or value of the resource extracted. Royalties are made either in cash or in kind. Royalties are paid on the commencement of production. Percentages are provided in each PSA and depend on barrels of oil per day (bopd) (EY, 2015) Rough estimates suggest that royalties are between 7 and 12.5 per cent of production (MFPED, 2016). In some instance, a company in a PSA may decide to retain extracted oil to compensate for the costs associated with exploration, development and production. The PSA prescribes a ceiling for the amount of oil that can be retained to recover costs in a given period. Although a contractor can carry forward any costs that are not recovered for recovery in subsequent years, the Government must approve any cost recovery and, as such, unapproved costs are not recoverable. Profit oil refers to the share of production remaining after the contractor has retained the share attributed to cost recovery. This is split between the contractor and government according to an agreed formula. The share due to government is either paid in cash or taken in kind. The contractors' share of profit is subject to an income tax (30 per cent of profit).

Nevertheless, there is scope for transparency in Uganda's PSAs. Many of the obligations and requirements imposed on interested parties have been kept confidential (EY, 2015). The specific details such as financial obligations; health, safety and environment (HSE) requirements; and other data and reporting obligations are not known to the public (Ibid.). This can create room for corruption and backroom dealing. In addition, ambiguities in the tax code have led to several disputes between the Government of Uganda and international oil companies which have delayed the industry's development (Patey, 2015). First, contractors disputed Uganda's decision not to export all oil. Second, there was a dispute on what is taxable when transferring interest to a third party and capital gains tax on such interest. Lastly, long negotiations between the Government of Uganda and international oil companies on terms of production licences constrained the industry from further development. However, hard bargaining on infrastructure, tax, and contract demands is not unique to Uganda. It is common for resource-rich countries to have fairly flexible policies and laws due to political demands on the legislation and institutions running the sector.

Nevertheless, Ugandan policy makers need to note that instability in tax law may raise the discount rate that investors apply in evaluating projects. This can reduce the rent value of the resource, and therefore the amount of revenue that can be extracted without distorting investment. Frequent changes in taxation code may raise the supply price of the investors to investors to such an extent that low rates of taxation are required to attract investment. On the other hand, policy makers may need to note that low tax rates are counterproductive when high profitability is achieved. High profitability in turn generates pressure for change in the taxation arrangement and further increases the supply price of investment, thus yet again increasing the pressure for change in the tax arrangement.

In addition, Uganda's law is ambiguous about what happens when cash flow or production is negative. It is not clear whether the Government will provide a cash payment to the investor to compensate for the negative cash flows in such a case. In some practices, the Government depreciates the capital expenditure over a number of years as with standard income tax until such an investment is abandoned and assumed to be unsuccessful, or until there is an assessment of super profit against which it can be credited. There is also no clear law about undepreciated capital expenditure and unutilised tax credit. Normally, undepreciated capital expenditure and unutilised tax credit are accumulated at an interest rate equal to the government bond rate and carried forward. As mentioned earlier, it is not clear whether Uganda will treat undepreciated capital expenditure and unutilised tax credit as such. The URA needs to examine this clearly before the oil starts to flow to mitigate disputes.

There is also no clear guidance in the law on the taxation of downstream activities such as pipeline, refinery, storage and transport. While this is untestable, given that the midstream is currently a government monopoly, it is prudent to define the rules of engagement as the sector opens up to the private sector in the medium term. The fiscal regime also does not spell out how the IOC will transfer upstream knowledge and technology to the NOC. These impede the future capacity of NOC to explore and produce oil either solely or in a joint venture.

6.4   The Balance between Spending and Saving of the Expected Oil Revenues

This section analyses how and how far fiscal rules are being used to create a trade-off between saving and spending of expected oil revenues.

6.4.1   The Petroleum Fund and Front-loading of Public Investment

The Government of Uganda faces the challenge of transforming a finite resource (oil) into a permanent income. A permanent income is a sustainable constant consumption flow equal to the present value of the resource wealth. In this regard, a policy that encourages saving of the oil *windfall* provides fiscal sustainability, preserves the resource wealth for future generations, prevents intergenerational inequality and mitigates the real exchange appreciation associated with the Dutch disease (Doshi *et al.*, 2015). To address the above concern, the Government will establish a petroleum fund with a twin objective of financing the budget and saving for future generations (MFPED, 2012). The petroleum fund shall hold all revenues emanating from dues, charges, taxes, royalties and fines on oil and gas. This will include the proceeds from the sale of the Government's share of oil extracted that will be received in kind. The Government envisages quarterly reports from the Investment Advisory Committee on the performance of the fund. There is a possibility that in the future the fund could be invested in securities and equity outside Uganda. However, this aspect has not been considered in the current legal framework.

As earlier alluded to, savings in a petroleum fund may not be compatible with the social status (poverty, human and physical capital scarcity and credit constraints) of a developing country such as Uganda. This strengthens the argument for frontloading of public investments in the transport, education and health services. The infrastructural deficit notwithstanding, established fiscal prudence should be continued to ensure that oil and gas revenues are used productively to address the infrastructure and social needs of a fast-growing population.[9] However, high oil prices could produce unhealthy rates of expansion in the petroleum fund and pressure to expand the size of government, leading to a drop in efficiency. The Government of Uganda has a culture of creating new administrative jurisdictions (districts), some without the capacity to govern. It is possible that production of oil may encourage the creation of more administrative jurisdictions. In 2016, Uganda had 114

---

9   Uganda has a good reputation for fiscal prudence.

districts, more than double the number in 2002.[10] In the event of revenue volatility, the consequence would be unexpected interruptions in government programmes. Long-term projects in the transport sector that require years of sustained government funding and management will also be disrupted. In addition, people tend to invest in their future if government policies and institutions are stable. If citizens lose confidence in government policies and institutions, they will be less inclined to invest in their own future, hurting the poor.

Expected oil revenues have also incentivised a frontloading of public investment in Uganda. While this contributes to the closing of the infrastructure gap, it could lead to a fall in the quality of public investments, which can be harmful. The Government of Uganda needs to be observant because a rapid rise in revenues can lead to a desire to speed up economic growth or pressure from rent seekers leading to a relaxation of government standards for choosing investments, leading to a squandered windfall. High revenues can create a strong incentive to accumulate debt, given the perceived ability to service the debt. Nevertheless, many countries, and particularly those in Africa, have used oil revenues to finance infrastructure and deliver social services (Collier, van der Ploeg, Spence and Venables, 2009). Other countries have used the resource revenue to service external debt (Daban and Helis 2010). Yet others have used a mix of public investment, social service delivery and sovereign wealth fund (SWF) to address economic challenges and save resources for future generation (Berg, Portillo, Yangand and Zanna, 2013).

For illustration, the blue line in the left-hand panel of Figure 6.4 shows a simulation of oil revenues being spent in the form of transfers to households.[11] On the other hand, the red line shows an alternative policy in which the resource revenues are frontloaded in public infrastructure and the green line stand for gradual expenditure, which is equivalent to a SWF. Unlike transfers, frontloading public investments tend to have a longer lasting but lagged impact on poverty alleviation through an increase of productivity.[12] However, frontloading of investments and transfers can lead to Dutch disease. In the case of the SWF, expenditure is spread over a longer time span. A majority of the oil revenues are saved in the equity and investment funds. Gradual public investment further delays the consumption increase, but it is more sustained

10   There were 56 districts in 2002.

11   The rationale for household transfers in developing countries is immediate poverty alleviation by increasing present consumption (and thus welfare). However, financial transfers can lead to rent-seeking and dependency.

12   The productivity effect applies only to public investment policies, either front-loaded or gradual.

Figure 6.4:   **Simulated Impact of Fiscal Rules on Welfare and Growth**

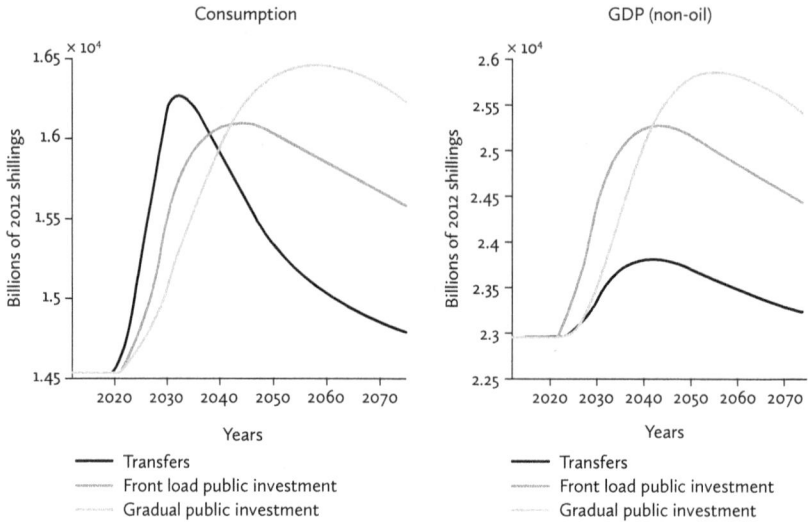

Source: Doshi et al. (2015, p. 25).

and higher over time than both transfers and frontloading investment. On the other hand, the right-hand panel of Figure 6.4 shows that the increase in the efficiency of the utilisation of labour and capital in production of GDP is much lower under the gradual policy but lasts longer.[13] The transfers policy produces the lowest and most short-lived impact on GDP.

6.4.2   Public Debt

Uganda can maintain its debt at the current rate (35 per cent) by servicing new contracted (accumulated) debt with oil revenues. This however will come at a cost to service delivery. This calls for strengthening of the debt rules. There is also a perception that Uganda's engagement with traditional development partners in Europe and North America will be limited, given the new oil find and emergence of new lending partners, especially China. However, estimates suggest that Uganda's oil output will not be sufficient to meet all its financing needs. Therefore, engagement with development partners may be sustained in the medium term.

---

13   GDP is a product of labour and capital (and technology). Since resource wealth is spent much more slowly, the substitutability between money and capital is much slower.

Figure 6.5:   **Simulated impact of efficiency of public investment on Uganda's economy**

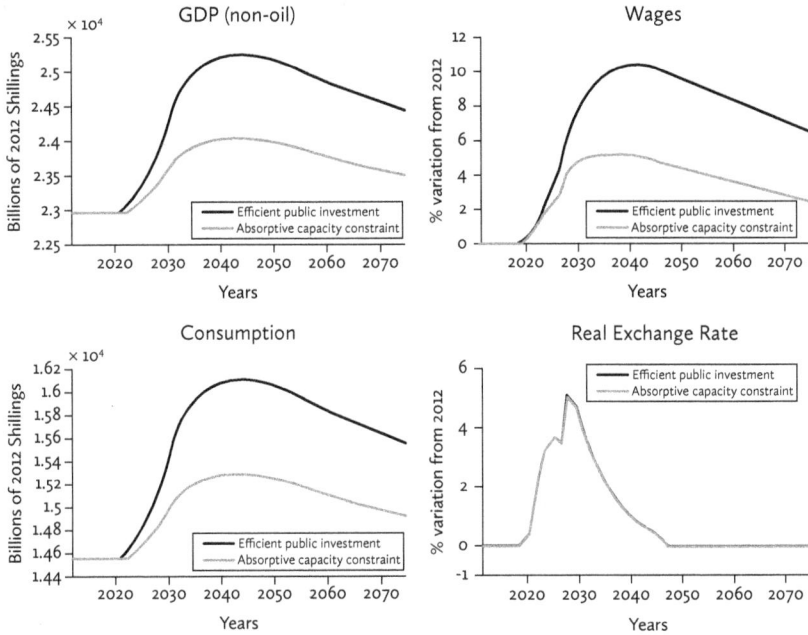

Source: Doshi et al (2015, p. 26).

6.4.3   Efficiency of Public Investments

While oil and gas present an opportunity for Uganda to accelerate its development process, utilisation of these resources is subject to the absorptive capacity of the economy. More often, many developing countries face absorptive constraints where (high) investment rates lead to large cost overruns, leading to low capital accumulation (Van der Ploeg, 2012). On average, sub-Saharan projects cost 74 per cent more than initial investment estimates (International Monetary Fund [IMF], 2012). To mitigate misuse of natural resource revenues, Uganda plans to integrate oil and gas revenues into the overall macro economy and the fiscal framework (MFPED, 2012). In the short to medium term, the Government will limit the growth in government expenditure by linking overall expenditure to the non-oil-related revenues rather than to total revenues (MFPED, 2012).[14] However, the Government

14   Total revenues include oil revenue.

plans to allow for flexibility to adjust government spending to a level that is consistent with the economy's needs and absorptive capacity in the medium term. In the long-term, the Government envisages that expenditure will be restored to a level that is equivalent to interest earned on the petroleum fund. This will ensure that the principal of the petroleum fund is saved for future generations (MFPED, 2012).

However, the issue is whether Uganda can select the *right* projects subject to its institutional capacity to appraise, implement and monitor those projects. As mentioned earlier, public investment effectiveness will be subject to institutional capacity. Figure 6.5 simulates two different scenarios of front-loaded public investment policies in Uganda's economy. The blue line represents the case where the country can fully absorb investment. The red line represents the case where the country wastes half of public investment. The red line suggests that absorptive constraint significantly impacts on GDP, consumption and wages by reducing the productivity of public capital. However, absorptive constraint has no impact on the real exchange rate. This suggest that the spending effect of public investment, whether absorbed or not, will trigger Dutch disease.

6.5   Conclusion and Policy Options

Oil production will generate significant additional revenues for Uganda. However, the emergence of a natural resource windfall is usually accompanied by several challenges. These challenges are mainly of a macroeconomic, budgetary and governance nature. The impact of these additional revenues on Uganda's competitiveness and economic transformation will critically depend on the prudent management of these oil resources. On the basis of the above analysis, we can formulate a number of policy recommendations which could contribute to this goal.

First, on the basis of the estimated production profile, the best strategy is to smooth production to spread the revenue over time. A sequenced development of oilfields will facilitate a smooth distribution of the resources over a longer period of time. This policy would also help in mitigating the impact of price volatility by enabling the smoothing of price shocks over time. Production should be focused on the first third of the production lifecycle contingent on prices. Ideally the highest production should be achieved when prices are the highest and have a very high impact on the overall economics.

Second, intergovernmental fiscal transfers may promote equity, but may also undermine efforts to mobilise resources at the local level. As such, political commitment to fiscal rules is imperative. The fiscal rules should emphasise counter-cyclicality, should ensure a sustainable debt path and should be consistent with the medium-term expenditure objectives.

Third, there is a strong case for the Ugandan Government to commit to making realistic and relatively conservative projections of future oil prices in order to mitigate unaffordable expenditure commitments in the event of oil revenues falling short of the forecasted levels. Related to this, the streamlining of the collection of oil revenues is key to ensuring transparency and account-ability. In particular, the petroleum fund should support fiscal policy and a policy of inter-generational equity. As such, the fund should be separated from the reserve bank's exchange reserves.

Fourth, more information needs to be generated on the refinery before it is actually built. The refinery would benefit from more research on the cost of transporting refined oil to the region, market structure, regional demand for oil and the price of oil. Furthermore, there is scope for sharing information on the value and future prospects of natural resources to ensure that all parties are equally well informed.

Fifth, frontloading investment has a positive impact on public capital through the productivity channel. Transfer to household has a positive impact on welfare through the spending channel. However, both of these polices may have a Dutch disease effect. Gradual investment has a positive impact on public investment, but the impact is delayed. Moreover, importantly, the Government should build the institutional capacity to resist pressure to increase the annual allocations above the level budgeted. Any amendments should be orderly and fully justified. In this case, parliamentary oversight and involvement of the civil society will be imperative.

References

Aresti, M.L. (2016), 'Oil and Gas Revenue Sharing in Bolivia'. Retrieved from the Natural Resource Governance Institute website: https://resourcegovernance.org/sites/default/files/documents/oil-and-gas-revenue-sharing-in-bolivia_0.pdf.

Berg, A., R. Portillo, S. Yanganda and L.F. Zanna (2013), 'Public Investment in Resource-Abundant Developing Countries', *IMF Economic Review* WP/12/274. Washington, DC: International Monetary Fund (IMF). Retrieved from: https://www.imf.org/external/pubs/ft/wp/2012/wp12274.pdf

Broadway, R., and F. Flatters (1993), 'The Taxation of Natural Resources: Principles and Policy Issues', *World Bank Policy Research Working Paper No. 1210*. Washington, DC: World Bank Group.

Budde, F., C. Günther and M. Shah (2014), 'When Gas Gets Tight: Next Steps for the Middle East Petrochemical Industry'. Retrieved from the McKinsey & Company website: http://www.

mckinsey.com/industries/oil-and-gas/our-insights/when-gas-gets-tight-next-steps-for-the-middle-east-petrochemical-industry.

Collier, P., F. van der Ploeg, M. Spence and A.J, Venables (2009), 'Managing Resource Revenues in Developing Economies', *OxCarre Working Papers 015*. Oxford, UK: Oxford Centre for the Analysis of Resource Rich Economies, University of Oxford.

Daban, T., and J.L. Helis (2010), 'A Public Financial Management Framework for Resource Producing Countries'. *IMF Working Paper*, 72(10).

Doshi, T., F. Joutz, P. Lakuma, M.M. Lwanga and B. Manzano (2015), 'The Challenges of Macroeconomic Management of Natural Resource Revenues in Developing Countries: The Case of Uganda'. *EPCR Research Series No. 124*.

Energy International Agency (EIA) (2016), Country Profile: Uganda. Retrieved from: https://www.eia.gov/beta/international/analysis.php?iso=UGA

EY (2015), 'Global Oil and Gas Tax Guide'. Retrieved from the EYGM Limited website: https://www.ey.com/Publication/vwLUAssets/ey-global-oil-and-gas-tax-guide-2019/$FILE/ey-global-oil-and-gas-tax-guide-2019.pdf.

Fitzgibbon, T., A. Kloskowska and A. Martin (2015), 'Impact of Low Crude Prices on Refining', *Energy Insights*. Retrieved from the McKinsey and Company website: https://www.mckinsey.com/industries/oil-and-gas/our-insights/impact-of-low-crude-prices-on-refining.

Foster Wheeler (2011), 'Uganda Refinery Study: Summary Report'. Retrieved from: http://www.ugandaoil.co/2011/12/26/download-of-fosterwheeler-report-on-uganda-oil-industry-refinery/

Gérin, J., and C. Houdin (2010), 'Chad, the Challenge of Development: Policy Implications of the Chad-Cameroon Petroleum Project'. *The North-South Institute Working Paper*. Ottawa, Canada: The North-South Institute. Retrieved from: http://www.nsi-ins.ca/publications/chad-cameroon-petroleum-policy/.

Government of Uganda (GoU) (2015), 'The National Development Plan 2010/2011–2014/2015'. Kampala: Government of Uganda.

Hausman, C., and R. Kellogg (2015), 'Welfare and Distributional Implications of Shale Gas'. *NBER Working Paper No. 21115*. Retrieved from: https://www.nber.org/papers/w21115

Haysom, N., and S. Kane (2009), *Negotiating Natural Resources for Peace: Ownership, Control and Wealth Sharing*. Geneva: Henry Dunant Centre for Humanitarian Dialogue. Retrieved from: http://comparativeconstitutionsproject.org/files/resources_peace.pdf.

International Monetary Fund (2012), 'Senegal: Staff Report for the 2012 Article IV Consultation, Fourth Review'. Retrieved from the International Monetary Fund (IMF) website: https://www.imf.org/external/pubs/ft/dsa/pdf/2012/dsacr12337.pdf.

Lakuma, C.P., R. Marty and A. Kuteesa (2016), 'Survival Analysis of Regional Unemployment in Uganda: Evidence from the Uganda National Panel Survey (UNPS)', *African Development Review*, 28(1), 140–154.

Leamer, E.E., H. Maul, S. Rodriguez and P.K. Schott (1999), 'Does Natural Resource Abundance Increase Latin American Income Inequality?', *Journal of Development Economics*, 59(1), 3–42.

Ministry of Energy and Minerals Development (MEMD) (2012), The Petroleum (Exploration, Development and Production) Bill. Kampala: Republic of Uganda.

——— (2015), 'Uganda's Oil Refinery: An Opportunity for Transformation'. *Press briefing*. Retrieved from: http://www.energyandminerals.go.ug/downloads/UGANDAOILREFINERY.pdf.

Ministry of Finance Planning and Economic Development (MFPED) (2012), 'Oil and Gas Revenue Management Policy'. Kampala: Republic of Uganda.

——— (2016), The National Budget Framework Paper 2016/2017. Kampala: Republic of Uganda.

Patey, L. (2015), 'Oil in Uganda: Hard Bargaining and Complex Politics in East Africa'. *OIES Working Paper 60*. Retrieved from: https://www.oxfordenergy.org/wpcms/wp-content/uploads/2015/10/WPM-601.pdf.

Ravallion, M., and G. Datt (1996), 'How Important to India's Poor Is the Sectoral Composition of Economic Growth?', 10 *The World Bank Economic Review* 1. Retrieved from: https://elibrary.worldbank.org/doi/abs/10.1093/wber/10.1.1.

Ross, M.L. (2003), 'Nigeria's Oil Sector and the Poor'. *Position Paper for DFID-Nigeria*. Retrieved from: https://www.sscnet.ucla.edu/polisci/faculty/ross/papers/other/NigeriaOil.pdf.

Ssewanyana, S.N., and I. Kasirye (2014), 'Uganda's Progress Towards Poverty Reduction During the Last Decade 2002/3–2012/13:   Is the Gap Between Leading and Lagging Areas Widening or Narrowing?'. *EPCR Research Series No. 118*, 1–40.

Strachan, A.L. (2014), 'Oil and Gas Revenue Sharing'. *GSDRC Helpdesk Research Report 1123*. Retrieved from the University of Birmingham website: http://www.gsdrc.org/docs/open/hdq1123.pdf.

Van der Ploeg, F. (2012), 'Bottlenecks in Ramping Up Public Investment', *International Tax and Public Finance*, 19(4), 508–538.

7
Oil Revenues and Social Development in Uganda

Joseph Mawejje

7.1   Introduction

Uganda has set ambitious targets aimed at propelling the country to upper middle-income status by 2040. The ability of Uganda to transform from a largely low-income agrarian economy to a modern diversified economy depends, in part, upon available avenues for revenue mobilisation and the ability of government to transform such revenues into prudent investments. Given Uganda's demographic structure, with more than 50 per cent of the population aged less than 16 years, it makes sense to prioritise investments that can unlock such human capital potential to ensure a sustainable and inclusive growth path.

The emergence of the oil sector provides a timely opportunity to generate the necessary means to finance the social and economic transformation of society, including for the marginalised groups such as women, rural inhabitants and the urban poor. In addition, the population has formed strong expectations about improvements in service delivery that could potentially arise from development of the oil sector (Tumusiime, Mawejje and Byakagaba, 2016; Mawejje, 2019). Managing such expectations, while putting in place developmental institutions to minimise leakages and rent-seeking, will be critical in deriving maximum benefit from oil resources.

A key feature of the oil and gas sectors is that they are enclave activities with minimal links to the rest of the economy. Aside from generating significant revenues that can be used to strategically invest in other sectors, the direct development impact of oil and gas sectors is limited. Given that oil development is highly capital-intensive, only a few thousand jobs can be expected to be generated, mostly for technical and highly-skilled personnel. It is estimated that at peak production the oil and gas sector will require 15,000 direct jobs and 35,000 indirect jobs, with an additional 100,000 jobs created through the redistribution of oil revenues in the local economy. Even then most jobs will be shed after the development phase, with only about 25 per cent of the direct jobs retained during the operations phase (SBC, 2013). This therefore implies that the social development outcomes arising out of the direct and indirect employment will be limited.

Dutch disease and resource curse literature has shown potentially detrimental effects of natural resource sectors on social sectors, including agriculture (Apergis, El-Montasser, Sekyere, Ajmi and Gupta, 2014), education (Cockx and Francken, 2016) and health spending (Cockx and Francken, 2014). Therefore, it is crucial to ensure that the development of the oil and gas sector provides a springboard for agricultural transformation and improves service delivery in the social sectors, particularly health and education. Recent discussions have explored the risks and opportunities that the oil sector presents for accelerating sustained development in Uganda (Mawejje and Bategeka, 2013). Gelb and Majerowicz (2011) highlighted the potentially large effects of using oil revenues to roll out cash transfer programmes as a way of ensuring social protection, particularly for the elderly and other vulnerable categories of people. Wiebelt, Paw, Martov, Twimukye and Benson (2011) analysed the potential poverty reduction impacts of spending oil revenues for agricultural transformation.

In addition, opportunities can be created if local content opportunities are exploited. In this regard, investments that improve the business environment, skills development, and support the capacity development of the local entrepreneurial class to engage in the supply of local content by exploiting backward linkages are critical (Tordo, Warner, Manzano and Anouti, 2013). The Government of Uganda has taken the strategic decision to invest in the development of a refinery in the Albertine Region near the oil exploration areas. This creates opportunities for private-sector engagement in the development of forward links in other spin-off industries that straddle the oil and gas value chain. Such investments that diversify the economic benefits from natural resources can generate sustained employment creation beyond the life cycle of the resource.

This chapter explores the opportunities that the oil sector presents with regard to social development. We advance the argument that oil revenues can support social development if a people-centred approach is taken that prioritises investments in agricultural sector transformation, human capital development, social protection, and harnesses the demographic dividend by focusing on interventions that can lead to sustainable improvements in mortality and fertility outcomes. While oil revenues can advance social and economic development in Uganda, it should be emphasised that other factors such as inefficiencies due to rent-seeking, elite capture and fraud could derail the anticipated positive impacts. Therefore, strengthening the governance structures across the board is required to ensure that the opportunities for social development are not missed.

The remainder of the chapter is organised as follows. First, Section 2 sets out the economic and social context of Uganda. Section 3 then discusses the development of the oil sector in Uganda, while Section 4 discusses the options for scaling up social development with the help of the anticipated oil revenues. Section 5 concludes.

7.2   Uganda's Economic and Social Context

Uganda's growth and social development patterns were disrupted by the political mismanagement that followed independence. Specifically, the economy was marred by economic crises resulting from extreme political instability during 1971–1986. Most productive sectors were badly damaged during that period, and real growth rates were effectively negative during 1980–1987. The infrastructure stock was virtually wiped out during the post-independence period as political unrest led to neglect and limited investment. The restoration of peace and stability, starting in 1986 with President Museveni's new government, coupled with policy reforms that mostly focused on promoting macroeconomic stability, liberalisation, and privatisation formed the basis for economic recovery in the post-conflict years (Kuteesa, Tumusiime-Mutebile, Whitworth and Williamson, 2010). Subsequently the economy recorded impressive growth rates in the post-crisis era. Real economic growth averaged 6.9 per cent during the 1990–1999 period and reached 7.2 per cent during the 2000–2010 period.

The growth attained over the years has led to significant headcount poverty reduction. Based on the proportion of the population living on less than a dollar per day, poverty declined to 20.7 per cent in 2013 from 56 per cent in 1992 (see Figure 7.1). Consequently, the number of poor people dropped from 9.8 to 7 million in the last decade alone, signifying the robust poverty reduction effects of economic growth (Ssewanyana and Kasirye, 2014). However, the benefits of growth were not shared equally among the various regions. For example, the Northern region did not benefit much from this recovery owing to a protracted and brutal armed conflict during 1986–2006, the cost of which was estimated at 3 per cent of GDP (Okidi, Ssewanyana, Bategeka and Muhumuza, 2007).

The strong growth trajectory, however, has not been sustained during the period following the global financial crisis. During the five fiscal years from 20011/2012–2016/2017 the economy grew by an average of 4.5 per cent

Figure 7.1:   **Growth and poverty in Uganda**

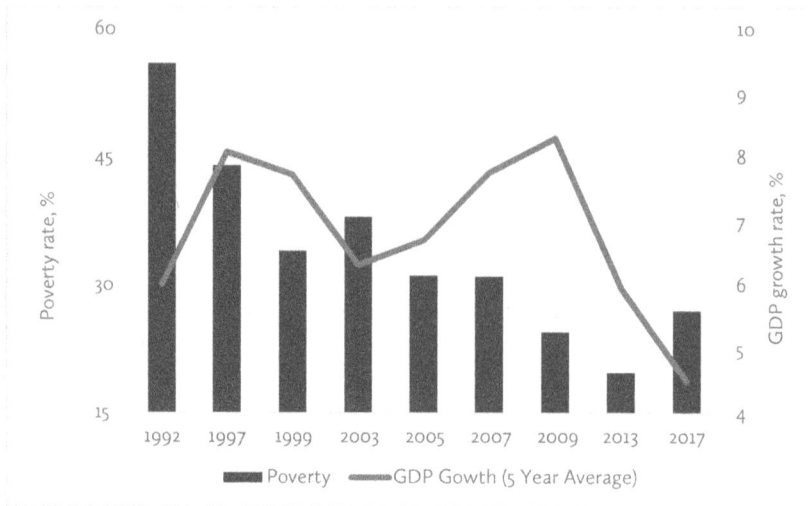

Source: Author's computations based on data drawn from Uganda Bureau of Statistics (2017).

less than during any other period since 1990. The slow-down in economic performance during this period has been occasioned by the large global imbalances, unfavourable domestic demand and supply factors and challenging geopolitical situations such the re-emergence of instability in South Sudan. Moreover, the latest Uganda poverty assessment shows that more Ugandans are slipping into poverty with the number of poor people increasing to 10 million in 2016/2017. With these developments, income poverty levels have increased to 27 per cent, signifying a significant reversal of trends after a sustained poverty reduction period.

Uganda's recent growth experiences reflect some fundamental challenges for long-term economic growth. While the share of agriculture in total GDP has remarkably declined, the contribution of industry has largely stagnated at about 18 per cent of GDP. Rather tellingly, the share of labour in agriculture has not declined as would be expected if growth were structurally transformative (Brownbridge and Bwire, 2016). This points to challenges emanating from low productivity growth in the agricultural sector leading to weak forward linkages to industrial development. Thus, the major source of growth continues to be in the services sectors. However, these have not created many employment opportunities because a large proportion of the services sector is still dominated by low-productivity micro and small informal businesses with limited opportunities for growth (Brownbridge and Bwire, 2016).

Moreover, people continue to grapple with other forms of non-monetary facets of poverty, particularly due to constrained service delivery in critical areas such as education, health, nutrition, access to electricity and sanitation. The recent discovery of oil reserves promises alternative pathways for accelerating the growth and performance of the economy. It is expected that oil revenues will generate government revenues equivalent to about 10 per cent of GDP at peak production and that the lifetime cumulative revenues from oil and gas sector are expected to be approximately 250 per cent of 2013 GDP (Adam, Bevan and Ohlenburg, 2014). The oil sector thus presents an enormous opportunity for accelerating growth, scaling up social development and poverty reduction.

7.3   The Development of the Oil Sector in Uganda

Uganda is among a list of African countries that have discovered significant natural resource wealth in the last decade. Exploration efforts so far have largely been concentrated in the Albertine districts and have confirmed the existence of oil reserves estimated at 6.5 billion barrels with approximately 1.4 billion barrels believed to be recoverable. This has placed Uganda among the top owners of proven oil reserves in Sub-Saharan Africa (see Figure 7.2). However, the exact oil potential is unknown, considering that exploration efforts have so far covered only about 40 per cent of the region confirmed to have oil deposits. Production is not expected before 2022 (Verma and Mukherjee, 2019). The Government is going ahead with plans to have a small/medium-sized refinery that will process 30,000–60,000 barrels per day. The expectation is that this refinery will service the local and regional markets. In addition, the Government is finalising plans for an oil pipeline for the export of the excess crude oil via Tanzania's Tanga port. It is expected that oil production will peak at 225,000 barrels/day around the year 2025 and, barring any further discoveries, decline until 2044. However, the current slow-down and uncertainty in the international oil prices will probably affect the timing of the project.

The expectation is that oil prices will hover within the US$ 50–60 range per barrel over the medium term. Annual revenues are, therefore, expected to peak at around US$ 600 million around the year 2025 if prices rise to within the US$ 60 range per barrel (see Figure 7.3). Cumulative government revenues are therefore expected to be in the range of US$ 5,000–9,000 million. Annual revenues are expected to be in the range of 5 to 10 per cent of GDP. To put this in context, Uganda collects the equivalent of about 14 per cent of GDP in

Figure 7.2:   **Proven oil reserves in selected Sub-Saharan African countries,**
2015

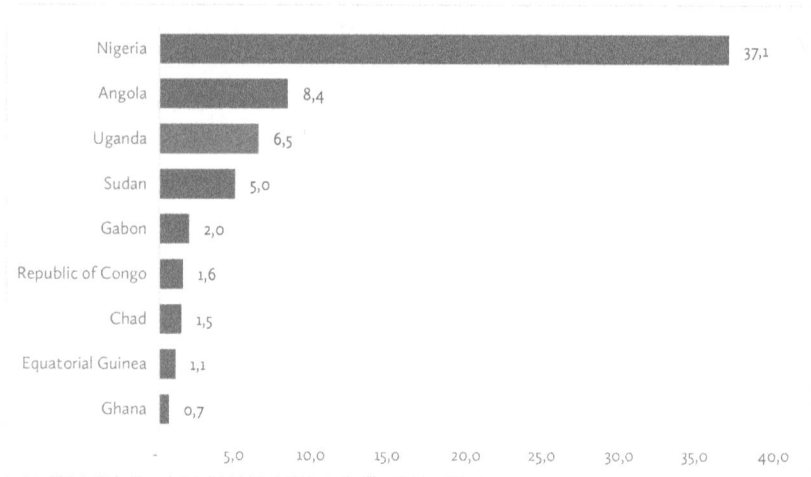

Country	Value
Nigeria	37,1
Angola	8,4
Uganda	6,5
Sudan	5,0
Gabon	2,0
Republic of Congo	1,6
Chad	1,5
Equatorial Guinea	1,1
Ghana	0,7

Axis: 5,0 10,0 15,0 20,0 25,0 30,0 35,0 40,0

Source: Author's computations based on data drawn from ENI Energy Statistics.

Figure 7.3:   **Expected government revenues**

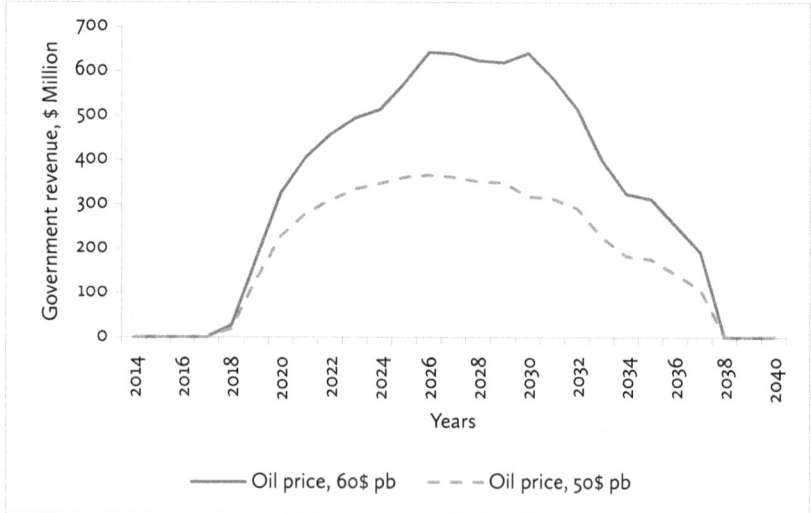

Government revenue, $ Million — Years (2014–2040)

——— Oil price, 60$ pb   – – – Oil price, 50$ pb

Source: Author's computations using Global Witness oil models for Uganda.

annual taxes. Clearly, oil will bring a modest contribution to the economy. If well managed, such revenues can achieve improved socio-economic outcomes, but are potentially disruptive if badly handled.

7.4   Options for Scaling Up Social Development Using Oil Resources

Uganda has the opportunity to achieve high growth levels leading to social and economic transformation through the prudent use of natural resource revenues from the oil and gas sectors. To achieve this, adequate consideration must be accorded to expenditures that are inclusive and socially transformative. Improving the productivity of agriculture will have the largest potential for social transformation considering the ubiquity of the sector. In addition, prioritising social protection and improved service delivery in the education and health sectors will ensure a labour force that is skilled, healthy and productive. In equal measure, adequate attention must be paid to interventions that will lead to employment creation. In this regard, enterprise development by leveraging local content possibilities will doubtless harness the potentially large benefits of the large young population. In particular, oil can lead a diversification drive, enabling the development of other non-oil primary sectors. These issues are discussed in the subsections that follow.

7.4.1   Improving the Productivity of Agriculture

The narrative on improving the social and economic conditions of Ugandans should be cognizant of the fact that most households in Uganda are still based in the primary sectors, notably in agriculture. Indeed, agriculture remains the dominant sector, employing some 72 per cent of Uganda's working population (Uganda Bureau of Statistics [UBOS], 2016). However, as shown in Figure 7.4, the agricultural sector's productivity as measured by value added per work has been steadily declining since the early 2000s. This implies that real wages in the agricultural sector are declining. This decline in productivity is worrying because the sector continues to provide the most employment opportunities and provides the lowest hanging fruits for poverty reduction and the realisation of superior social outcomes (World Bank, 2016).

The declining productivity in the agricultural sector is due to a number of factors, including falling soil fertility and limited use of modern inputs; dependence on rain-fed production; limited innovations due to low levels of research and development; more frequent climate shocks; and limited commercialisation in the sector leading to weak links with limited value addition.

There are a number of ways through which well-thought-out utilisation of oil revenues can support improved productivity in the agricultural sector. First, oil revenues can be used to finance research and development to ensure

Figure 7.4:   **Agriculture value added per worker (constant 2010 US$)**

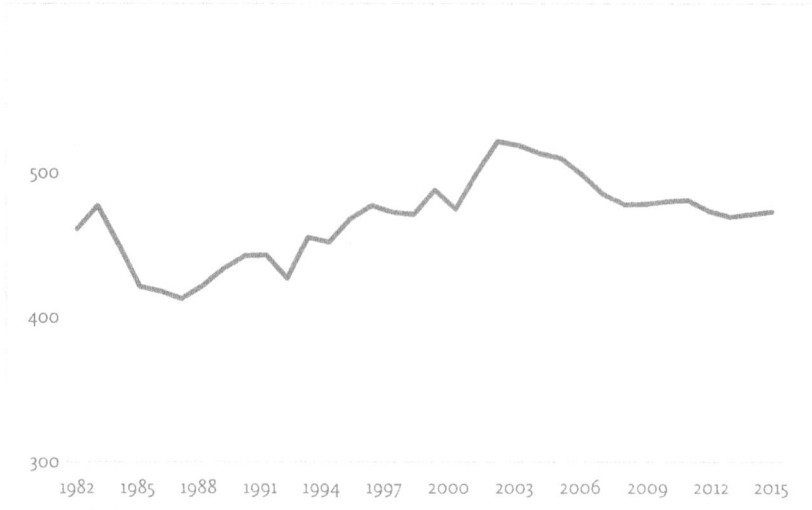

Source: Author's computations based on data drawn from World Development Indicators, The World Bank, 2017. Available at: https://datacatalog.worldbank.org/dataset/world-development-indicators.

the development of appropriate technologies and innovations in the sector. Second, oil revenues can be used to finance water for production and to promote the development of climate-smart agriculture. Third, oil revenues can be used to finance the development of warehouse receipt systems with a view to facilitating agricultural commercialisation and developing value added links to manufacturing and agro-processing. Fourth, oil revenues can be strategically used to improve access to financing in the sector, for example, through an agricultural bank, or any other special-purpose vehicle to bridge the financing challenges that are specific to the sector. We will now explore each of these policy options in more detail.

Research and Development for Agriculture
The agricultural research system in Uganda is centrally managed through the National Agricultural Research Organisation (NARO). The organisation coordinates a system of six sector-specific research institutions in crops, livestock, fisheries and forestry. These include: the National Crops Resources Research Institute, the National Fisheries Resources Research Institute, the National Forestry Resources Research Institute, the National Livestock Resources Research Institute, the National Semi Arid Agricultural Research

Institute and the National Coffee Research Institute. These institutes have done well, particularly in the generation of new technologies. However, they continue to face constraints and cannot keep pace with the growing demands of the sector. For example, in the year 2014/2015 only 49 production technologies were generated out of a planned 90. This represents a performance rate of 54 per cent compared to 113 per cent (80 planned, 90 delivered) in 2012/2013. In addition, NARO is grappling with non-performance with regard to the completion of research studies, ostensibly due to insufficient, delayed and non-release of funds (Ministry of Finance Planning and Economic Development [MFPED], 2016).

Agriculture research is particularly constrained by two issues that oil revenues could help to resolve. First is the issue of financing. It is reported that the high cost of laboratory analyses and equipment, limited funding for supervision, delayed procurements and inadequate technical staff are some of the most crippling challenges affecting the performance of agricultural research in Uganda. Second is the issue of weak research-extension-farmer links. Uganda does not have an effective agricultural extension system, having restructured the National Agricultural Advisory Services (NAADS) in July 2014 to focus on input procurement and distribution. The role of extension has since been re-incorporated into the greater Ministry of Agriculture Animal Industry and Fisheries (MAAIF) under the single-spine system. However, the current state of the extension system is challenged by huge human resource gaps that have undermined agricultural productivity. The revenues from the oil sector could, therefore, be strategically used to solve some of the challenges of agricultural research and extension by enabling more reasonable resource allocations.

Water for Production and Climate-smart Agriculture

Another area where oil revenues could be used to transform the agricultural sector in Uganda is through investments in water for production. Increased episodes of climate variability mean that Uganda faces frequent and sometimes prolonged periods of drought and floods that result in losses of agricultural output. Mwaura, Katunze, Muhumuza and Shinyekwa (2014) estimate that such losses cost up to 8 per cent of gross domestic product in Uganda in the year 2010 alone. These losses could be avoided with adequate investment in water for production and climate-smart agricultural technologies. Unfortunately, the adoption of irrigation technology is low in Uganda. Only 0.59 per cent of farming households applied modern irrigation techniques on their plots in 2014 (see Figure 7.5), fewer than in 2011 when the adoption rate was 2.59 per cent.

Figure 7.5:   **Water for production technologies**

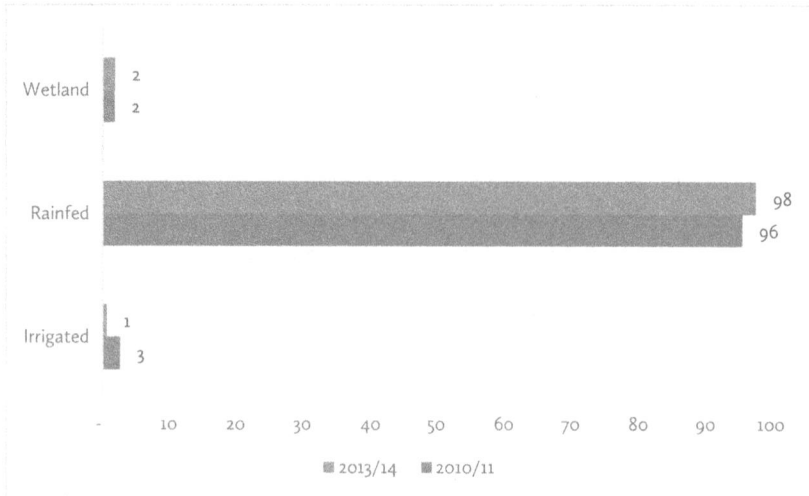

Source: Author's computations based on data from the 2011 and 2014 Uganda National Household Survey (UNHS) datasets. Available at: http://www.ubos.org/unda/index.php/catalog

This low adoption of water for production techniques poses risks to food security, poverty traps and missed opportunities to enhance human development outcomes and social and economic transformation. These risks provide compelling evidence of the potential gains from investing in appropriate irrigation technologies to improve agricultural productivity for social development. Earlier efforts to improve water for production by investing in valley dams in some of the country's most vulnerable districts were patterned with political capture, rent seeking and allegations of fraud. If governance issues around expenditure and the selection of projects can be resolved, the oil revenues could be used to scale up investments in water for production and irrigation, especially for smallholder farmers who are most vulnerable.

Investing in Warehouse Receipt Systems
Productivity in the agricultural sector has remained low on account of limited opportunities for value addition, commercialisation, trade, and the weak links to manufacturing. In many ways, investing in warehouse receipt systems can alleviate some of these challenges by minimising, among others, post-harvest losses, and encouraging agriculture commercialisation and trade through bulking and collective marketing (Katunze, Kuteesa, Mijumbi and Mahebe, 2017). In addition, investments in agricultural technologies can be encouraged when farmers know that prices are protected and markets guaranteed. With

Figure 7.6:   **Private sector credit distribution, 3-year average 2013- 2016**

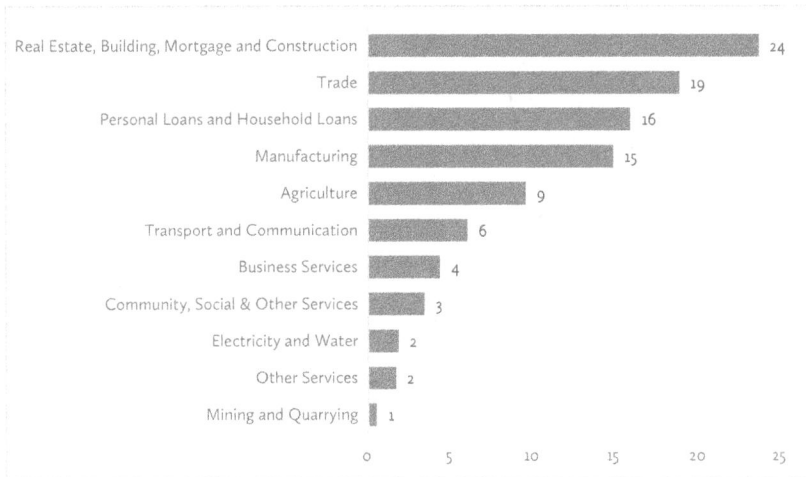

Source: Author's computations based on data drawn from the Bank of Uganda.

such systems in place barriers to innovations in agricultural insurance and climate-smart technologies can be greatly reduced. Moreover, warehouse house receipts can be traded or even used as collateral, thus facilitating access to credit. Thus, they have the capacity to transform and drive efficiency in agricultural markets. Therefore, using part of the oil resources to fast track the development of the warehouse receipt system is one way in which oil revenues could be used to drive agricultural transformation.

Agricultural Financing

Lastly, a major constraint that oil revenues could help to ease in order to support growth in agricultural productivity is the challenge of access to financing. There have been a number of interventions that have tried to improve access to credit, especially by smallholder farmers. These include interventions through the microfinance support centre, the prosperity for all programme and the agricultural credit facility. However, the impact of these interventions has been minimal for a number of reasons. First the interventions were scattered across ministries and departments, thus enlisting weak implementation and coordination. Financing of agriculture is also inhibited by the various risks, particularly the lack of bankable agricultural projects that are attractive to commercial lenders and the inherent climate risk that many insurance companies are not willing to pick up. The result is that financing of agriculture has averaged less than 10 per cent of total private-sector credit over the past three years (see Figure 7.6).

Some of these challenges can be overcome through measures to improve governance in the sector to ensure that any additional financing to the sector yields the expected results. One way through which oil revenues can support agricultural financing is by expanding the available financing, particularly the Agricultural Credit Facility which is operationalised through participating commercial banks and subsidised by the State to provide cheaper loans.

7.4.2   Human Capital Development

Uganda has one of the fastest growing populations in the world. Population growth rates are estimated at about 3.2 per cent, meaning that the population can potentially double every 20–23 years. Indeed, according to some projections, the population will grow to more than 80 million by 2040. The high population growth rate has persisted because of the high fertility rate, estimated at about 5.9 children per woman. Because of this high fertility rate, the population is guaranteed to continue growing even if the fertility rate drops to 2 births per woman in accordance with the Vision 2040 aspirations. Indeed, the population would continue to grow and only stabilise at about 170 million people by about the year 2100 (Uganda National Planning Authority [NPA], 2014). With such high fertility rates, investments in education and health have not kept pace with the growing population, with deleterious consequences for human development. Consequently, the potentially transformative effects of a demographic dividend might not be realised (United Nations Development Programme [UNDP], 2015).

Uganda can ensure sustained social and economic transformation if oil resources are used to ramp up investments in human capital so as to improve the capabilities and productivity of the population. In particular, focus should be on improving the outcomes in education and ensuring that the labour force, particularly the youth, is adequately skilled; and focusing on health outcomes, including efforts to reduce child and maternal mortality.

Improving the Quality of Education and Skills Development
The education sector in Uganda introduced reforms targeted at increasing literacy and numeracy by encouraging increased school enrolment. Universal primary education was introduced in 1997, and later a universal post-primary education and training (UPPET) programme was introduced in 2007. As a direct result of these reforms, school enrolment rates initially rose quickly. However, gains in enrolment were not matched by commensurate

Figure 7.7:   **Education expenditure**

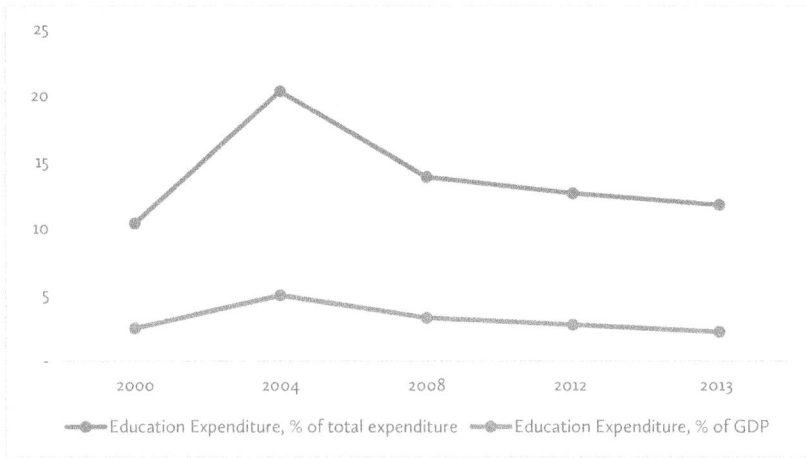

Source: Data drawn from World Development Indicators, The World Bank, 2017. Available at:
https://datacatalog.worldbank.org/dataset/world-development-indicators

improvements in attainment and the overall progress has not been sustained:
school enrolment rates have stagnated, completion rates are low and literacy
rates have not improved much. This has been due to a combination of limited
funding that has constrained investments in infrastructure and training to
improve the quality of teachers to keep pace with the growing population.
These challenges have affected teacher motivation leading to absenteeism.
In addition, the situation reflects a much larger problem of underfunding to
the education sector.

In effect, government expenditure on education as a percentage of both
total expenditure and total GDP has been falling since the early 2000s. For
example, education expenditure as a percentage of total expenditure has
declined from 20 per cent in 2004 to 12 per cent in 2011 (see Figure 7.7). Thus,
improvements in education infrastructure and spending have not kept pace
with the increasing population. In addition, the quality of such expenditure
has been poor with many schools and laboratories poorly constructed and
maintained. At the school level, the central government transfers approximately UGX 50,000 (US$ 14) for each pupil over the primary cycle of seven
years. Unfortunately, this amount has not been adjusted for price changes
since the inception of UPE.

The challenges in Uganda's education system, particularly at the primary
level, have been highlighted by a recent World Bank evaluation of service
delivery in the sector. The World Bank service delivery indicators (SDI)

Table 7.1: Education Service Delivery in Selected East African Countries

	Uganda (2013)	Kenya (2012)	Tanzania (2014)
Teacher ability			
Minimum knowledge (% teachers)	19.5	40.4	21.5
Test scores (out of 100)	45.3	57.1	48.3
Teacher effort			
School absence rate (% of teachers)	26.0	14.1	14.4
Classroom absence rate (% of teachers)	52.8	42.1	46.7
Scheduled teaching time	7h 18min	5h 37min	5h 54min
Time spent teaching	3h 18min	2h 49min	2h 46min
Availability of inputs			
Observed pupil-teacher ratio	47.9	35.2	43.5
Textbook availability (% pupils)	5.0	48.0	25.3
Minimum equipment availability (% classrooms)	80.6	78.8	61.4
Minimum infrastructure availability	53.7	59.5	40.4
Pupil learning			
Language test score (out of 100)	47.1	75.4	36.5
Mathematics test score (out of 100)	43.4	59.0	58.2

Source: Wane and Martin (2015a, p.10).

study in education showed that only 19.5 per cent of teachers have the minimum expected knowledge and mastery of the curriculum they teach; teacher school absenteeism was estimated at 26.0 per cent, and textbooks were available to only 5.0 per cent of the pupils. These results show that service delivery in Uganda's education sector is lagging behind that of other East African countries for which comparable data is available. In particular, teacher ability, effort, knowledge and availability of inputs are lower in Uganda (see Table 7.1). In addition, Uganda has relatively crowded classrooms, as observed through the pupil-teacher ratio of 47.9 compared to 35.2 in Kenya and 43.5 in Tanzania. Consequently, survival rates to primary seven, primary seven completion rates, numeracy and literacy rates are very low (Uwezo, 2016).

The universal primary education programme has helped to keep the primary school enrolment rate high, mainly due to free primary education. Unfortunately, more than half of the pupils drop out of school before completing primary school. Keeping children in school by creating a conducive study environment and investing in both teachers and infrastructure is one way through which the oil resources could contribute to the education of Uganda. Equally worrying is that enrolment in secondary schools has remained low, occasioned by the rather high drop-out rates during primary school and the low progression rate from primary to secondary level. These challenges have made skilling the population a challenge because the primary and secondary schools have not been effective in imparting the necessary pedagogical bases necessary for onward skilling. Improving service delivery and skilling the youth, therefore, is one area where oil revenues can support the education sector to improve the social and economic outcomes.

There are ongoing efforts to improve the skilling of the youth. The Uganda Petroleum Institute Kigumba has been revamped with a special focus on providing skills for the oil and gas sector. However, given that government policy is looking to diversify the economy to support also the non-oil sectors, oil revenues can support the development of skilling centres in other non-oil activities in line with the diversification strategy. Improving service delivery using additional resources from the oil sector should be done in the awareness of the likely rent seeking and fraud that usually undermine the performance of expenditures in Uganda. Circumventing these challenges requires that funding is conditioned upon specific outcomes.

Improving the Quality of Health Service Delivery

The health sector in Uganda attracted increasing funding during the early 1990s through to the 2000s. This increased funding, however, was driven mainly by external actors. During 1995–2010 external resources for health increased from 12 per cent and reached 51 per cent. The increase in external development financing, which was usually targeted at specific projects, has led to phenomenal improvements in health sector outcomes over the past years. For instance, births attended by skilled workers have increased from 38 per cent during 1990–1995 to 60 per cent during 2011–2015. Likewise, improvements have been recorded in various measures of mortality and access to basic healthcare including for HIV/AIDS and malaria.

Fertility rates have also started declining and averaged 5.92 during 2011–2015, down from 7.06 children per woman during 1990–1995. Consequently,

Table 7.2: Health Sector Outcomes 1990–2015

	1990–1995	1996–2000	2000–2005	2006–2010	2011–2015
Births attended by skilled health staff (% of total)	37.80	36.90	41.90	58.00	60
Maternal mortality ratio (national estimate, per 100,000 live births)	529.00	524.00	418.00	432.00	-
Mortality rate, infant (per 1,000 live births)	105.92	95.42	76.86	55.96	41.44
Mortality rate, under-5 (per 1,000 live births)	177.95	158.78	124.20	86.68	61.14
Fertility rate, total (births per woman)	7.06	6.93	6.71	6.33	5.92
Antiretroviral therapy coverage (% of people living with HIV)	-	-	3.60	15.00	38.50
Prevalence of HIV, total (% of population ages 15–49)	12.62	9.12	6.80	6.76	7.15
Under 5 children with fever receiving antimalarial drugs, %	-	-	61.00	64.50	-
Life expectancy	44.20	45.02	49.60	54.40	63.3

Source: Author's computations based on data from the World Development Indicators, The World Bank, 2017. Available at: https://datacatalog.worldbank.org/dataset/world-development-indicators.

life expectancy has increased from an average of 44.2 during 1990–1995 to 63 in 2014, as indicated in Table 7.2.

However, external financing started declining in 2011. By 2013 external financing to the health sector reached 35 per cent and is set to continue declining due to changing landscapes for external development finance (see Figure 7.8). Therefore, the authorities in Uganda ought to start looking for innovative and alternative sources of financing to sustain the improvements in health outcome indicators. Oil revenues could play an important role here by helping to plug the financing deficits in the health sector. In addition, service delivery in the health sector has been deteriorating on account of reduced funding, increasing population, and reduced motivation of health workers. In particular, like in many departments, the health sector has suffered from low budgeting for operations and maintenance, meaning that much of the infrastructural stock has been deteriorating with minimum provisions for repair.

Figure 7.8:   **Health expenditure patterns**

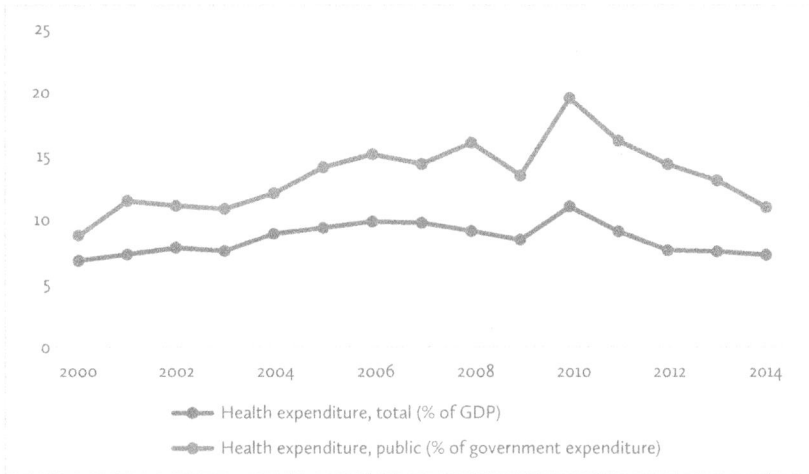

Source: Author's computations based on data drawn from the World Development Indicators, The World Bank, 2017. Available at: https://datacatalog.worldbank.org/dataset/world-development-indicators.

A service delivery survey of health facilities in Uganda by the World Bank indicated that Ugandan health service providers have relatively lower caseloads per day (6.0) compared to providers in Kenya (15.2) and Tanzania (7.3) (see Table 7.3). This might be attributed to lower demand for health services in Uganda. Despite this lower caseload, Uganda's score on service delivery indicators such as absence from a health facility (46.7 per cent), diagnostic accuracy (58.1 per cent), adherence to clinical guidelines (41.4 per cent), management of maternal and neonatal complications (19.3 per cent), drug availability (47.2 per cent) and equipment availability (21.9 per cent) are all low and worse than in Kenya and Tanzania.

These poor service delivery outcomes are obtained despite Uganda having better health infrastructure availability (63.5 per cent) than both Kenya (46.8 per cent) and Tanzania (50.0 per cent). While achieving improvements in some of the indicators does not require increases in budget allocations, others, particularly equipment and drugs availability, require budgetary increments. In addition, many social workers in Uganda, including in the health sector, are de-motivated owing to poor working conditions, the unavailability of equipment and drugs, and poor pay. Some of these challenges might explain the poor efficiency within health service delivery. Oil revenues can provide the financing necessary to ensure that drugs, equipment and infrastructure

Table 7.3: Health Service Delivery in Selected East African Countries

Indicators	Uganda (2013)	Kenya (2013)	Tanzania (2014)
Caseload (per provider per day)	6.0	15.2	7.3
Absence from facility (% providers)	46.7	27.5	14.3
Diagnostic accuracy (% providers)	58.1	72.2	60.2
Adherence to clinical guidelines (% clinical cases)	41.4	43.7	43.8
Management of maternal and neonatal complications (% clinical guidelines)	19.3	44.6	30.4
Drug availability (% drugs)	47.2	54.2	60.3
Equipment availability (% facilities)	21.9	76.4	83.5
Infrastructure availability (% facilities)	63.5	46.8	50.0

Source: Wane and Martin (2015b, p.10).

are in place. In addition, improving the remuneration of health workers and investing in the logistics management systems to ensure efficient drug distribution and delivery would improve outcomes in the health sector. But the complete overhaul of the health systems will require improving the institutional set-up in which the different actors operate. In other words, oil revenues alone cannot solve some of the service delivery challenges; interventions are required to tackle the governance issues surrounding service delivery in the health sector.

Expanding Social Protection

In addition to investments in education and health, oil revenues could be spent on ensuring social protection, particularly for the elderly and vulnerable. Uganda is already piloting a social protection grant under the Expanding Social Protection Programme (ESPP) with funding from DFID. The major objective of the programme is to reduce material deprivation, increase economic security, reduce social exclusion and increase access to services. While the programme has registered positive outcomes such as reduced poverty and increased demand for social services, there are concerns over its sustainability and scalability (Oxford Policy Management *et al.*, 2013). These challenges can be overcome if a proportion of oil and gas revenues is invested and a part of the proceeds is used each year to offer social security for the vulnerable in Uganda.

7.4.3 Harnessing the Demographic Dividend

One possible area that will facilitate the sustained attainment of both social and economic goals from the use of oil resources pertains to investments that will harness the demographic dividend. Capturing the demographic dividend will entail pursuing investments that will increase labour productivity by taking advantage of a changing demographic structure and population dynamics. Uganda's population is fairly young: 82 per cent of the population is below the age of 35, with 60 per cent below the age of 20 and 18 per cent below the age of 5. With this very young population structure, the dependency ratios are very high. Results from the 2014 Census showed that for every 100 economically active people, there are 103 dependants (UBOS, 2014). Such high dependency ratios stifle social and economic progress because they alter savings and investment decisions and perpetuate poverty to a significant degree.

There are a number of ways through which oil revenues could be invested in ways that can fast-track capturing the demographic dividend. Some of these investments, such as interventions in health, education, and skilling, have been discussed earlier. Accelerating the demographic transition requires sustained investment to reduce mortality and fertility, while improving the skills sets and productivity of the population. With falling fertility and mortality rates, the country can quickly transit into a period of rapidly falling dependence ratios. With fewer dependants, a larger share of working age population can then lead to improved standards of living if the right mix of supportive policies is implemented.

One such policy should be aimed at ending child marriages. Uganda's fertility rate has not declined fast enough and is estimated at 5.9 children per woman, significantly higher than the Sub-Saharan average of about 4.8 children per woman. With these high fertility rates, population growth rates have remained high, stabilising at around 3 per cent per annum, significantly straining improvements in service delivery. Child marriage is commonplace in Uganda. The World Bank (2017) estimates that three in ten girls have their first child before their eighteenth birthday, and more than one in three marry before the age of 18. As a consequence, both child marriage and early child-bearing account for 25 per cent of school drop-outs for girls aged 10–18 years, exacerbating low educational attainment.

Ending child marriage would reduce fertility by up to 8 per cent nationally, and potentially lower the overall population growth rate by close to 0.2 per cent. Moreover, child marriage is associated with other agency costs that include higher risks for stillbirths, stunting, child mortality and gender-based violence. Moreover, ending child marriage improves labour participation rates for women with significant knock-on effects for lifetime earnings and welfare (Wodon, Nguyen and Tsimpo, 2016). Overall, the economic and social costs of child marriage are large. Therefore, using oil resources to invest in girls' education, end child marriage and prevent early childbearing would significantly contribute to efforts that would harness the demographic dividend and lead to better social and economic outcomes.

7.5   Conclusions

The development of the oil sector presents enormous opportunities for the social and economic development of Uganda. However, the realisation of these opportunities partly depends on the quality of investments that the Government chooses to undertake. In this chapter we have examined the investments that would probably have the largest positive impact on social and economic outcomes in Uganda. The development of the oil and gas sector comes at a time when Uganda's economy is experiencing multiple domestic and external shocks. There is a risk that the current periods of low growth might reverse the gains in poverty reduction and socio-economic development. The Government has made it clear that oil resources will be used above all for the development of the country's infrastructures, particularly in the transport and energy sectors. This position is understandable, given the huge infrastructural deficits the country is facing.

However, using oil resources to ensure sustainable growth requires following a people-centred approach in which the capabilities of the people are enhanced so that they can participate better in the growth processes. This requires interventions that will promote and support human capital development, in particular by improving people's health, education and skills outcomes. Transforming the sectors that provide the most livelihood opportunities is also key. In Uganda's case, investments that would improve agricultural productivity, health and education systems, as well as deepening social protection systems, should therefore be prioritised. In addition, supporting young girls to achieve their full potential by addressing the social, cultural and economic issues that perpetuate early child marriages, early childbearing, and eventually leading to low educational attainments is critical.

This chapter has discussed how these issues can be approached. In the agricultural sector, oil revenues can be used to improve productivity by funding research and development, water for production, agricultural financing and the development of warehouse receipt systems to facilitate value addition and commercialisation. With regard to human capital development and improving the capabilities of the population, focus should be on skilling the labour force through the prioritisation of technical and vocation education away from the current policy that has favoured universities. In addition, improving service delivery in both the education and health sectors and deepening social protection are key interventions that could be financed with oil revenues. Particular attention should be placed on governance by scrutinising all planned expenditures to avoid instances of rent-seeking, fraud and/or corruption. Lastly, better social outcomes can be forged through harnessing the demographic dividend by improving schooling outcomes, especially for girls. Higher educational outcomes will positively affect people's lifetime earnings and overall welfare.

References

Adam, C., D. Bevan and T. Ohlenburg (2014), 'Public Investment and Growth in Uganda'. Retrieved from the International Growth Centre website: https://www.theigc.org/publication/public-investment-and-growth-in-uganda-working-paper/.

Apergis, N., G. El-Montasser, E. Sekyere, A.N. Ajmi and R. Gupta (2014), 'Dutch Disease Effect of Oil Rents on Agriculture Value Added in Middle East and North African (MENA) Countries', *Energy Economics*, 45, 485–490.

Brownbridge, M., and T. Bwire (2016), 'Structural Change and Economic Growth in Uganda'. *Bank of Uganda Working Paper No. 03/2016*, 1–18.

Cockx, L., and N. Francken (2014), 'Extending the Concept of the Resource Curse: Natural Resources and Public Spending on Health', *Ecological Economics*, 108, 136–149.

—— and —— (2016), 'Natural Resources: A Curse on Education Spending?', *Energy Policy*, 92, 394–408.

ENI (2015), *World Oil and Gas Review 2015*. Rome: ENI. Retrieved from: https://www.eni.com/docs/en_IT/enicom/publications-archive/publications/wogr/2015/WOGR-2015-unico.pdf.

Gelb, A., and S. Majerowicz (2011), 'Oil for Uganda – or Ugandans? Can Cash Transfers Prevent the Resource Curse?'. *Centre for Global Development Working Paper No. 261*. Retrieved from: https://www.cgdev.org/publication/oil-uganda-%E2%80%93-or-ugandans-can-cash-transfers-prevent-resource-curse-working-paper-261.

Global Witness (2017), 'Economic Modelling Tool Guide — Global Witness (Undated). Retrieved from: https://www.globalwitness.org/documents/17829/economic_model_guide_uganda.pdf

Katunze, M., A. Kuteesa, D. Mijumbi and D. Mahebe (2017), 'Uganda Warehousing Receipt System: Improving Market Performance and Productivity', *African Development Review*, 29(2), 135–146.

Kuteesa, F., E. Tumusiime-Mutebile, A. Whitworth and T. Williamson (2010), *Uganda's Economic Reforms: Insider Accounts*. Oxford: Oxford University Press.

Mawejje, J. (2019), 'The Oil Discovery in Uganda's Albertine Region: Local Expectations, Involvement, and Impacts', *The Extractive Industries and Society*, 6(1), 129–135.

—— and L. Bategeka (2013), 'Accelerating Growth and Maintaining Intergenerational Equity Using Oil Resources in Uganda'. *EPCR Research Series No. 111*, 1–64.

Ministry of Energy and Minerals Development (MEMD) (2016), 'Capacity Needs Analysis for Oil and Gas Sector skills in Uganda: Demand and Supply Assessment Report'. Kampala: Republic of Uganda.

Ministry of Finance Planning and Economic Development (MFPED) (2016), 'Key Constraints to Agriculture Research in Uganda: The Case of NARO Institutions'. *BMAU briefing paper No. 3/16*. Kampala: Republic of Uganda.

Mwaura, F., M. Katunze, T. Muhumuza and I. Shinyekwa (2014), 'Budget Analysis and Assessment of Investments in Water Smart Agriculture for Smallholders in Uganda and East Africa'. *Economic Policy Research Centre Occasional Paper No.36*, 1–50.

Okidi, J.A., s. Ssewanyana, L. Bategeka and F. Muhumuza (2007), 'Uganda's Experience with Operationalising Pro-poor Growth, 1992 to 2003', in T. Besley and L. Cord (eds.), *Delivering on the Promise of Pro-poor Growth: Insights and Lessons from Country Experiences* (pp.169–198). London: Palgrave MacMillan and Washington, DC: The World Bank.

Oxford Policy Management, Economic Policy Research Centre, Department of Anthropology and Sociology (2013), 'Valuation of the Uganda Social Assistance Grants for Empowerment (SAGE) Programme: Baseline Report'. Retrieved from: https://www.opml.co.uk/files/Publications/7265-uganda-sage/sage-baseline-report.pdf?noredirect=1.

SBC (2013), Industrial Baseline Survey Report. Prepared for Total E&P, Tullow Oil and CNOOC. Kampala, Uganda: Schlumberger Business Consulting.

Ssewanyana, N.S., and I. Kasirye (2014), 'Uganda's Progress Towards Poverty Reduction during the Last Decade 2002/3–2012/13:   Is the Gap between Leading and Lagging Areas Widening or Narrowing?'. *EPCR Research Series*, 118, 1–31.

Tordo, S., M. Warner, O.E. Manzano and Y. Anouti (2013), *Local Content in the Oil and Gas Sector*: A World Bank study. Washington, DC: The World Bank.

Tumusiime, D.M., J. Mawejje and P. Byakagaba (2016), 'Discovery of Oil: Community Perceptions and Expectations in Uganda's Albertine Region', *Journal of Sustainable Development*, 9(6), 1–14.

Uganda Bureau of Statistics (UBOS) (2016), *Statistical Abstract*. Kampala: Uganda Bureau of Statistics.

—— (2017), *Statistical Abstract*. Kampala: Uganda Bureau of Statistics.

Uganda National Planning Authority (NPA) (2014), 'Harnessing the Demographic Dividend: Accelerating Socioeconomic Transformation in Uganda'. Kampala: Uganda National Planning Authority.

United Nations Development Programme (UNDP) (2015), 'Uganda Human Development Report: Unlocking the Development Potential of Northern Uganda'. Kampala: United Nations Development Programme.

UWEZO (2015), 'Are Our Children Learning? Five Stories on the State of Education in Uganda in 2015 and Beyond'. Kampala: Twaweza East Africa.

Verma, N., and P. Mukherjee (2019, 13 February), 'Uganda Expects First Oil Production to be Delayed to 2022 – Minister', *Reuters*. Retrieved from: https://www.reuters.com/article/oil-uganda-tanzania/uganda-expects-first-oil-production-to-be-delayed-to-2022-minister-idUSL3N20833P.

Wane, W., and G. Martin (2015a), *Education Service Delivery in Tanzania*. Washington, DC: The World Bank Group. Retrieved from: http://documents.worldbank.org/curated/en/415111468179674045/Education-service-delivery-in-Tanzania.

—— and ——(2015b), *Health Service Delivery in Tanzania*. Washington, DC: The World Bank Group. Retrieved from: http://documents.worldbank.org/curated/en/520361468185934337/Health-service-delivery-in-Tanzania.

Wiebelt, M., K. Paw, J.M. Martov, E. Twimukye and T. Benson (2011), 'Managing Future Oil Revenue in Uganda for Agricultural Development and Poverty Reduction: A CGE Analysis of Challenges and Options'. *International Food Policy Research Institute Discussion Paper 01122*, 1–46.

Wodon, Q., M.C. Nguyen and C. Tsimpo (2016), 'Child Marriage, education, and Agency in Uganda', *Feminist Economics*, 22(1), 54–79.

World Bank (2016), 'Farms, Cities and Good Fortune: Assessing Poverty Reduction in Uganda from 2006 to 2016'. *The Uganda Poverty Assessment Report*. Washington, DC: The World Bank.

——— (2017), 'Educating Girls: A Way of Ending Child Marriage and Teenage Pregnancy'. *Uganda Economic Update 10th Edition*. Washington, DC, and Kampala, Uganda: The World Bank.

8

Getting a Good Deal? An Analysis of Uganda's Oil Fiscal Regime

Wilson Bahati Kazi

8.1   Introduction

Uganda has discovered large quantities of recoverable oil reserves since 2006. In August 2016, Uganda granted eight production licences to a range of joint venture partners, including Tullow Uganda Limited (TUL), China National Offshore Oil Corporation (CNOOC) and Total E&P Uganda Limited (Kazi and Beyeza, 2017). The revenues from these licences are estimated to be in the region of US\$ 1.5 billion a year for the duration of the different oil fields (Kazi and Beyeza, 2017). The relationship between the Ugandan government and the different international oil companies is governed by so-called production-sharing agreements (PSAs). PSAs stipulate precisely what proportion the Government gets, and how much of production will be retained by the oil company (Global Witness, 2014). PSAs regulate the relationship between governments and the oil companies. The oil companies need licences to operate. The Government uses the licensing system to grant exclusive rights to companies to explore for and extract the oil. Licences are therefore a key element of PSAs, which are at the heart of the oil fiscal regime.[1]

The key issue to be addressed in the design of fiscal terms is how the investment costs are recovered and the profits shared (Kazi and Beyeza, 2017). The fiscal terms must enable Government to maximise returns from its oil resources by encouraging the appropriate levels of exploration and development activities, as well as enabling oil companies to build equity while maximising returns on investment by finding and producing oil in the most cost-effective way (Kazi and Beyeza, 2017). The Centre for Energy Economics (2007) posited that the fiscal terms which deliver a fair return to

---

1   Exploration licences give the exclusive right to companies to explore for oil within a given timeframe and specific area, while production licences give oil companies that have discovered oil the exclusive right to extract the oil in a specific area (see Global Witness, 2014).

both a government and an investing oil company must discourage unnecessary speculation, limit excessive administrative and compliance costs, and should be flexible enough to ensure healthy competition and market efficiency. The most common oil sector fiscal regime consists of production-sharing, income tax, royalties, annual surface rentals and bonus payments (Sunley, Baunsgaard and Simard, 2002).

In this chapter we will analyse the basic fiscal instruments being used or developed by Uganda for oil revenue generation and collection. We will also examine the returns from the fiscal regime in terms of realised and unrealised revenues and critically evaluate and assess the main strengths and weaknesses of Uganda's oil fiscal regime in terms of sustainability, effectiveness and expected revenue returns. The chapter will proceed as follows. Section 2 covers Uganda's legal-institutional framework for oil revenue administration. Section 3 provides a systematic overview of the main fiscal instruments and issues associated with oil revenue generation and collection. Section 4 then contains an analysis of the revenues collected so far and also reviews the anticipated oil revenues. Section 5 subsequently analyses the main strengths and weaknesses of Uganda's fiscal oil regime. Section 6 concludes and offers some policy reflections.

8.2   Legal-Institutional Framework for Oil Revenue Administration

The legal framework for Uganda's oil revenue administration is derived from the PSAs,[2] the revenue laws,[3] the upstream law,[4] the midstream law,[5] the Public Finance Management Act, 2015,[6] the National Oil and Gas Policy and the Oil and Gas Revenue Management Policy. These laws define the scope of oil revenues[7] and how the revenue will be collected, reported and accounted

---

2   These can be classified into pre-2008 PSA and the 2012 PSAs. This is because Uganda signed its first PSAs before 2008 and others in 2012.
3   These include the Income Tax Act, Stamp Act, Customs Management Act, VAT Act, and Traffic and Road Safety Act.
4   Petroleum (Exploration, Development and Production) Act, 2013.
5   Petroleum (Refining, Conversion, Transmission and Midstream Storage) Act, 2013.
6   See Ministry of Finance, Planning and Economic Development, Uganda Public Finance Management Act 2015, retrieved from: https://finance.go.ug/test/services/uganda-public-finance-management-act-2015/.
7   The royalties, taxes, bonus payments, dividends, premiums, and in-kind revenues will be reported on a gross basis, indicating all adjustments required in official fiscal documents (oil and gas revenue management policy, 2012).

for. The Uganda Revenue Authority (URA) and the Directorate of Petroleum (DOP) are responsible for the assessment and collection of the tax and non-tax revenues respectively from the oil industry. The Uganda national oil company (UNOC) will be responsible for receiving and marketing the Government's share of profit oil and the UNOC, as government nominee, has elected to take the Government's participating interest in all the production licences so far issued at a level of 15 per cent, as provided for in the respective PSAs. The Bank of Uganda (BoU) will manage the petroleum fund on behalf of the Government. The Auditor-General's Office is responsible for ensuring that the petroleum fund is prudently managed and there is value for money in its application. The Petroleum Authority of Uganda (PAU) will monitor and regulate the exploration, development and production activities. All these institutions are mandated with the collection and prudent management of the oil revenues.

8.3 Overview of Fiscal Instruments

The oil sector is characterised by substantial economic rents, perverse price uncertainty, information asymmetry, high sunk costs with long production periods and extensive involvement of international oil companies (Kazi and Beyeza, 2017). Gudmestad, Zolotukhin and Jarlsby (2010) postulated that oil and gas resources provide an extraordinary rate of resource rent. For these reasons, a special tax regime rooted in the rent theory is needed for the oil sector, taking into account these peculiarities (Mazee, 2010). The tax handles for Uganda's upstream oil are royalties,[8] cost recovery, production sharing, corporate tax, ring-fencing, capital gains tax (CGT),[9] windfall profits tax, non-tax revenues[10] and indirect taxes (Kazi and Sarker, 2012). In this chapter the authors concentrate mainly on upstream taxes and not the indirect taxes which are more associated with the midstream and downstream oil operations. The regime delivers 67.5 per cent of 'profit oil' to Government and 32.5 per cent to oil companies. Uganda's oil fiscal regime emphasises fiscal responsibility and sustainability (Kazi and Sarker, 2012). The African

8   In addition to the daily production royalty, the 2012 PSAs introduced a new cumulative production royalty (see article 10 of the 2012 PSAs).

9   The ITA of Uganda imposes CGT on gain from the direct or indirect transfer of an interest in a petroleum agreement, and share disposals in a company whose property principally consists directly or indirectly of an interest or interests in immovable property located in Uganda.

10   Annual surface rentals, signature and discovery bonuses, training fees, and stamp duty are among the non-tax revenues provided for in Uganda's PSAs.

Development Bank (2009) states that proxies for profit, the internal rate of return and the Government's take determine which oil fiscal regime a country should adopt. Sunley *et al.* (2012) pointed out that evidence suggests that oil fiscal terms endogenously respond to global oil prices.

The Government can benefit from oil production through royalties, profit oil share and corporate taxes on the oil company's profits. This implies that if a project fails the Government does not suffer any loss but the contractor does. The recoverable costs from production net of royalties are reduced by the value of cost oil received, with any unrecovered costs carried forward to later years until full recovery is made. It should be noted that this is not a tax or any kind of relief like indemnity, but is simply the recovery of expenditure incurred by the oil company. PSAs are contractual in nature, with the Government retaining resource ownership and the approvals of the oil company budgets, work programmes, expenditure, procurement and employment, while the oil company provides finance, equipment and technology required for the exploitation of the oil resource (Kazi and Beyeza, 2017). Thus, the oil produced is shared between Government and the company at negotiated production-sharing percentages (Kazi and Beyeza, 2017).

8.3.1   Royalty and Additional Royalty

In addition to the single royalty in the pre-2008 PSAs[11] that is based on daily production, the 2012 PSAs contain an additional royalty based on cumulative production which, according to Global Witness (2014), is an unusual PSA revenue provision in favour of Uganda. With the additional royalty, revenue will continue to accrue even when oil extraction starts declining because the cumulative royalty is assessed based on the amount of oil extracted from the time production started. This implies that, with an increased rate of oil production, the rate of royalty due to Government increases. Royalties will be collected on a monthly basis.[12] The PSAs of Uganda provide for incremental royalties. Because royalties are deducted from production before cost recovery, they guarantee upfront revenue for Government soon after production begins. The royalty on gross daily production will be charged at rates of between 5 and 12.5 per cent (see Figure 8.1 below), depending on the level of production, while additional royalty on cumulative production will be charged at rates of between 2.5 and 5per cent (see Figure 8.2 below). Thus, Uganda's royalty

---

11   For the purposes of this chapter, all PSAs signed in 2008 and before are referred to as 'pre-2008 PSAs' while those PSAs signed in 2012 are referred to as 'the 2012 PSAs'.
12   See article 10 of the 2012 PSAs, p.26.

Figure 8.1:   Royalty rates versus gross daily production

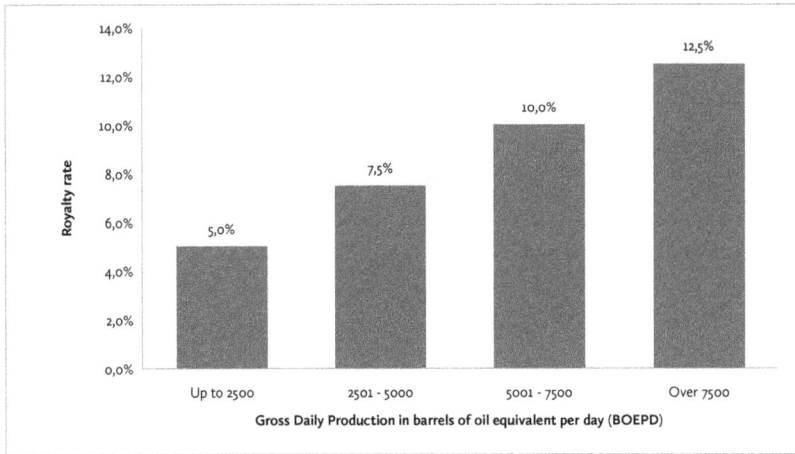

Source: Author's calculations using PSAs data.

Figure 8.2:   Additional rates on cumulative production

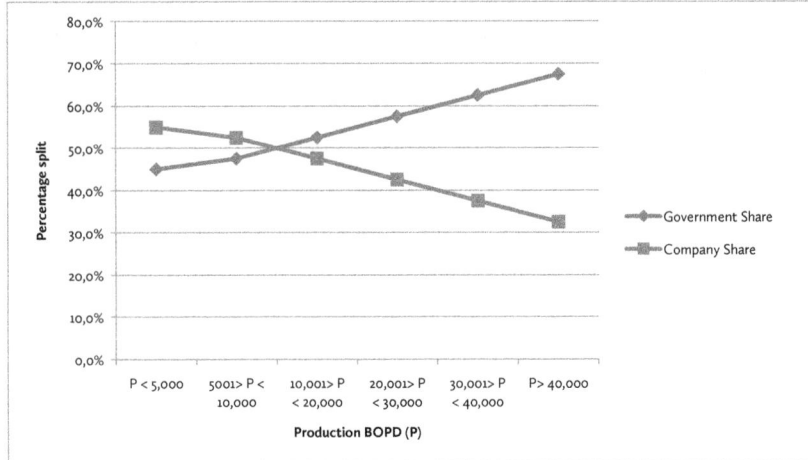

Source: Author's calculations using PSAs data.

regime has an in-built profit element.[13] Royalty payments are tiered, so if daily production was 6,000 barrels then the company would pay 5 per cent on the first 2,500, 7.5 per cent on the next 2,500 and 10 per cent on the remaining 1,000 (Global Witness, 2014).

8.3.2   Cost Recovery

The recoverable costs are pooled together each year and reduced by the cost oil received. In other words, cost oil refers to an oil company's entitlement to production as cost recovery under a PSA. This means that an oil company gets cost oil from which it deducts recoverable cost when commercial oil production has commenced. The Uganda PSAs provide that the amount to be retained as cost oil is 60 per cent of total oil production after deducting royalty. If cost oil is less than the costs available for recovery, any unrecovered costs are carried forward to subsequent years until their full recovery.is completed. However, if cost oil is more than the recoverable costs, the excess of the cost oil forms part of the profit oil. It is worth noting here that recoverable costs incurred in respect of licence area can only be offset against oil produced from that area. This practice, called 'ring-fencing', prevents companies from recovering costs for areas where no commercially viable oil reserves are found. Therefore, such costs are borne by the company. The Government must approve recoverable costs before they can be reduced from cost oil. This is likely to raise governance issues such as rent seeking and corruption, which might ultimately pose a risk of revenue leakage.

8.3.3   Production-sharing

Once the company deducts 60 per cent from total production as cost recovery after royalty, what remains is profit oil. The size of profit oil depends on the international price of crude oil, the project's internal rate of return and also the size of any surplus of cost oil over the amount needed for cost recovery. According to the 2012 PSAs, the Government's share of profit oil will be 67.5 per cent and 32.5 per cent for the company at peak production. The share of profit oil due to the Government will be received and marketed by UNOC. The profit oil split will depend on the level of production; for example, as production increases so will the Government's share, while the company share will decline (see Figure 8.3 below). The negotiated profit split ratios

---

13   See Chile, Thailand, etc for details of royalty regimes with some profit element (Sunley *et al.*, 2002).

Figure 8.3:   **Oil profit distribution between the Government and oil companies**

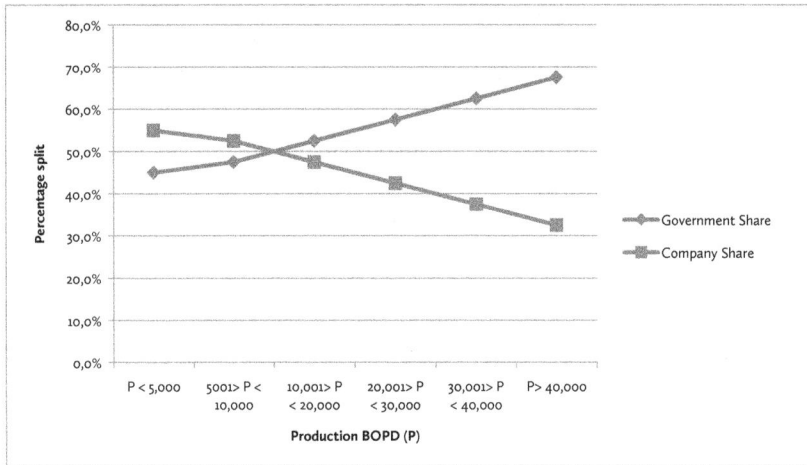

Source: Compiled by author using percentages in 2012 PSAs, p. 32.

between Government and the oil companies give PSAs a built-in flexibility which helps to offset differences between basins and licensed areas (Kazi and Beyeza, 2017).

8.3.4   Income Tax

Prior to 2008, there was no specific taxation regime provision for oil operations in ITA, though the PSAs contained some tax provisions. In 2008, Part IXA, containing a specific tax code in relation to petroleum operations, was inserted in the 1997 ITA through the Income Tax (Amendment) Act of 2008.[14] This issue of whether the ITA or PSA was the one applicable in the context of taxes was prominent during the CGT disputes, as oil companies urged that the tax clauses of the PSA took precedence over the ITA when it came to the taxation of oil operations, including the transfer of an interest in an oil licence (see Uganda Legal Information Institute, 2014). The amendment was meant to clarify the ambiguity as well as plug the potential tax loopholes in the taxation of oil operations. In the provisions it is stated that in the event

14   In addition to providing for the taxation of upstream petroleum operations, this part of ITA also has special provisions dealing with the taxation of mining operations.

of an inconsistency between Part IXA of ITA and PSAs, as well as other provisions of the ITA, Part IXA takes precedence.

The profit oil share of the company attracts 30 per cent corporation tax in accordance with the ITA. And any distributions of company profits (dividends) after corporation tax will attract 15 per cent withholding tax in the hands of the shareholder. The ITA thus provides for a comprehensive set of income tax rules that accords with the commercial principles under which the oil sector operates. These provisions clarify and provide certainty on how oil sector activities will be treated for income tax purposes.

8.3.5   Ring-fencing

Corporation tax is a key element of an oil PSA imposed on the 'taxable income' of a contractor computed on a block-by-block basis. The costs incurred in respect of one block cannot be used to reduce income from other blocks (see 1.3.2 Cost recovery. above). Ring-fencing bars consolidation of income and deductions for tax purposes across various oil activities and projects undertaken by the same taxpayer. 'Ring-fence' applies to both income and expenditures. By ring-fencing tax accounts of individual blocks in accordance with the provisions of the PSAs, corporate tax deferral is effectively curtailed (Kazi and Beyeza, 2017). This measure helps to streamline oil taxation in order to secure government revenues.

8.3.6   International Tax Issues in the Oil Sector

In the context of the oil sector, the size of the corporate tax base depends on the amount of contract costs incurred and any profit-shifting practices adopted by the multinational oil companies (MNCs) (Kazi and Beyeza, 2017). In this section we focus on the practices used by MNCs to shift profits and reduce their corporation tax base in order to minimise their tax liabilities.

Thin Capitalisation

Thin capitalisation rules prevent financing structures with high debt-equity ratios. Interest expense is tax deductible while dividend is not, so high debt to equity can reduce taxable profits and hence tax payable. Sunley *et al.* (2002) stated that thin capitalisation affects interest deductibility and corporation tax base. Under this rule, interest payments of thinly capitalised companies are disallowed and taxed as constructive dividends in some countries. In Uganda, interest deductible is restricted to the foreign debt to foreign equity ratio of 1.5:1 (Kazi and Beyeza, 2017). The excess amount of interest is disallowed for corporation tax purposes. However, unlike in the UK and other countries, Uganda does not treat the disallowed interest portion as a constructive dividend, and therefore does not impose withholding tax on it. Note that if interest deductibility were not restricted, MNCs would use excessive loan finance in order to utilise the interest thereon to shift profits to associated companies domiciled in tax havens. The measure therefore limits tax avoidance through the use of low-taxed interest payments in line with the base erosion and profit shifting (BEPS) project of the Group of 20 countries (G20) and the Organisation of Economic Co-operation and Development (OECD).

It should be noted, however, that effective from 1 July 2018, this thin capitalisation rule under section 89 of the ITA was repealed by the Income Tax (Amendment) Act, 2018 and replaced with a new interest deductibility limitation provision under section 25 of the same Act. The new rule requires that the amount of deductible interest in respect of all debts owed by a taxpayer who is a member of a group shall not exceed 30 per cent of the tax earnings before interest, tax, depreciation and amortisation (EBITDA). Any interest amount that exceeds 30 per cent of the EBITDA shall be carried forward for a maximum period of three years. The excess interest is treated as incurred during the following year of income. This implies that deductible interest in a year of income is capped at 30 per cent of EBITDA and excess interest, if any, is deferred for deduction in the next three years of income, beyond which the excess interest cannot be claimed as deductible expense for income tax purposes. In other words, after three years of income, if there is still any excess interest it will be disallowed and taxed.

Transfer Pricing

Companies seek to minimise taxable profits through transfer pricing (Sunley et al., 2002). Transfer pricing can be used to shift profits between tax jurisdictions in related party oil transactions.[15] Baunsgaard (2014) stated that transfer-pricing risks in the oil sector can be minimised through the use of joint venture structures, standard output measures and prices. Observable physical operations, standardised measurements and benchmarking using international prices can assist in mitigating the transfer-pricing risk (Kazi and Beyeza, 2017). Uganda's transfer-pricing regulations enacted in 2011 and the information exchange provisions in the DTAs are means designed to address

---

15   Such transactions may involve the use of hedging instruments, leasing of equipment, plant and machinery, intra-group loans, high technical service fees and high management fee pay-outs (see Kazi and Beyeza, 2017).

tax avoidance using cross-border transactions.[16] The transfer-pricing regulations, like the 2012 PSAs, require that related party transactions be reported at arm's length price (i.e. the price that would be charged to an independent company for the same services or goods under similar conditions). They call for a comparability analysis to ensure that technical service fees paid to an associated company are at arm's length. Global Witness (2014) observed that comparability analysis may be difficult to make in practice because there are relatively few comparable providers of technical services in East Africa, besides it being hard to determine the services rendered.

Treaty Shopping

Treaty shopping allows the unintended use of tax treaties by third country residents. This practice leads to loss of tax revenues in the source State; hence the anti-treaty shopping domestic law provisions. The anti-treaty shopping provision is contained in section 88(5) of ITA, but it is only section 88(5) that overrides any provisions of DTAs.[17] This section was restructured following Heritage's attempt to re-domicile from the Dominican Republic to Mauritius in order to avoid CGT on the sale of its oil interests to TUL because the DTA between Mauritius and Uganda exempts capital gains from tax. The domestic tax law criteria non-resident entities must fulfil in order to access DTA benefits such as reduced tax rate or an exemption were clarified to put limits to treaty shopping and curtail revenue leakage. Non-resident entities other than publicly listed companies will not access Ugandan treaty benefits unless: (a) they receive the income in a capacity other than that of a beneficial owner; (b) they do not have a full and unrestricted ability to enjoy that income and to determine its future uses; and (c) they do not possess economic substance in the country of residence (EY Global Tax Alert Library, 2017).

The above is a radical departure from the earlier limitation of benefit (LoB) rule that restricted the DTA benefits application in Uganda only to resident persons of the other contracting state where 50 per cent or more of the underlying ownership of that person was held by resident individuals of that other contracting State for purposes of the DTA. The anti-abuse provisions cannot operate effectively if not supplemented by the exchange

16   These regulations are yet to be updated to bring them into line with the 2017 OECD TP regulations which take into account the BEPS action points 8–10 and 13 of the G20/OECD project.
17   Uganda has DTAs with Denmark, UK, South Africa, Mauritius, India, Zambia, the Netherlands, Norway and Italy. In the case of inconsistencies between the DTA provisions and those of the ITA, the DTA provisions will prevail over the provisions of the ITA except in cases of tax avoidance.

of information[18] with other tax jurisdictions. Uganda is a signatory to the OECD Convention on Mutual Administrative Assistance in Tax Matters (MAAC). This means it can now request for information about taxpayer operating in 104 countries to facilitate audits and investigations of MNCs, including those involved in oil sector.

8.3.7 State participation

Under the 2012 PSAs, Uganda will get 15% of the oil company's share of profit oil under state participation provisions should government opt to exercise its right to participate in oil development and production. Indeed, through the UNOC, government elected to take its participating interest in all the eight production licences so far issued at a level of 15% in accordance with the PSAs (Kazi & Beyeza, 2017). The oil companies will meet Government's costs but the companies are entitled to recover these costs, including interest at the London Inter-Bank Offer Rate (LIBOR), out of the cost oil.

The government is therefore entitled to a proportion of the oil produced and saved from each contract area equal to its 15% interest in the joint venture assets (The 2012 PSAs). UNOC will dispose of the state's share of profit oil at a price determined by the Multi-institutional committee[19] and remit the sales proceeds to the Petroleum Fund operated and managed by BoU.[20] Uganda will be responsible for paying any taxes arising out of its share in the Joint Venture, and it will get its share of its participating interest directly or indirectly in the form of dividends taxable at 15% withholding tax. The government's role as a regulator and shareholder (owner) in these oil licenses raises governance issues of conflicts of interest and corruption which may lead to revenue leakage. Given the level of institutional maturity in Uganda, it might be wise for government to focus on taxing and regulating oil activities for now and leave the oil operations to companies.

18   On 4 November 2015 Uganda became the 95th country to sign the Convention on Mutual Administrative Assistance in Tax Matters (MAAC). The deposit of the instrument of ratification was done on 25 May 2016 and the MAAC came into force in Uganda as law on 1 September 2016. Uganda also ratified the African Tax Administration Forum (ATAF) Agreement on Mutual Assistance in Tax Matters

19   The committee includes officials from the MFPED, MEMD, URA, and any other specialised agencies to be determined by the Finance Minister; the value of oil produced is a function of a price and the quantities. The quantities to be produced within a given period will be agreed between the Energy Ministry and the oil companies.

20   See Ministry of Finance, Planning and Economic Development, Uganda Public Finance Management Act, 2015, retrieved from: https://finance.go.ug/test/services/uganda-public-finance-management-act-2015/.

8.3.8   Capital Gains Tax (CGT)

Capital gains tax (CGT) is imposed on a gain made on the assignment or transfer of an interest in an oil licence from one contractor to another (see section 89G(a) of the ITA).[21] The determination of a gain on disposal of an interest in an oil licence is governed by the provisions of the ITA. Taxable gains arise on the disposal of business assets such as company shares or commercial property and an interest in an oil licence either directly or indirectly.[22] An indirect transfer takes the form of the sale of shares in a company whose assets are principally immovable property[23] located in Uganda. It often involves non-resident shareholders selling their interests to a resident company. Because of the difficulty of collecting taxes from non-residents, the CGT is paid by the resident oil company acting as an agent of the non-resident company. For example, the CGT of US$ 449 million on Heritage's transfer of its assets to TUL was paid by TUL acting as the agent of Heritage.

CGT may also be triggered on a person[24] (including oil companies) located in Uganda whose assets and liabilities are deemed to have been realised and re-acquired or re-stated through a direct or indirect change in its ownership by 50 per cent or more within a three-year period (section 75 of the ITA, as amended by the Income Tax (Amendment) Act, 2018). The direct and indirect change of ownership of an entity located in Uganda gives rise to income (capital gains) sourced in Uganda.

It should be noted that CGT is not a reliable revenue source because it arises only when a business asset is transferred or assigned. Besides, it is difficult to determine the cost base of an oil interest where the interest in question is being transferred to a third owner. For instance, one of the issues contested when TUL disposed of the interest it had acquired from Heritage to Total E&P and CNOOC was the determination of the cost base. In practice, the cost base is the base price paid for the interest plus incidental costs of the disposal. The incidental costs include contingent, guarantee and commitment fees, stamp duty on acquisition, legal fees and signature bonuses. Should the costs not yet recovered by the transferor under the cost recovery clauses be part of the cost

---

21   This includes the transfer of the whole or part of the interest in a petroleum agreement.

22   'Business asset' means an asset which is used or held ready for use in a business, and includes any asset held for sale in a business and any asset of a partnership or company. For capital gains purposes business asset excludes trading stock and a depreciable asset (see the ITA);

23   Improvable property is defined to include 'any intangible asset which is a business asset or any part of the business' (see Income Tax (Amendment) Act, 2018).

24   Person excludes an individual, a government, a political subdivision of government and a listed institution.

base of the asset? These are pertinent issues that must be clearly addressed if Government is to get its fair share of revenue on any transfer of an oil interest.

As a result of the CGT disputes, the current PSAs clearly provide that the transfer of an oil interest shall attract CGT in accordance with the ITA, and that tax disputes in relation to the PSAs shall be handled in accordance with the dispute resolution mechanisms stipulated under the Laws of Uganda (see the 2012 PSAs). Global Witness (2014) maintains that the Uganda-Heritage arbitration in London over the CGT assessment relating to the 2010 farm-down to TUL was far from settled.

8.3.9   Oil-related Non-tax Revenues (NTRs)

Non-Tax Revenues (NTRs) are an important source of revenue for government during the pre-production phase of oil. These NTRs include bonuses, annual surface rentals, training and development fees, proceeds from the sale of oil data and of the oil refinery feasibility study report. The NTRs are assessed and collected by the DOP of the Energy Ministry. The 2012 PSAs provide for the collection of US$ 300,000 in signature bonuses and US$ 2,000,000 as discovery bonus. The annual surface rental of US$ 7.50 per square kilometre for an area under an exploration licence is collectable, while it is US$ 500 per square kilometre for an area under a production licence. The company exploring for oil is required to pay US$ 37,500 half yearly, and on the grant of a production licence US$ 200,000 annually to cater for oil-related training and development of Ugandans.[25] Stamp duty is also collectable on the registration of oil contracts and performance security (for example, insurance bonds and bank guarantees) and on transfers of oil interests at the rate of between 0.5 and 1.5 per cent. NTRs motivate oil companies to explore and develop oil in a licensed block rapidly and they are easy for Government to administer and for companies to comply with.[26]

8.4   An Analysis of Uganda's Oil Revenues: Looking Back and Looking Ahead

The oil sector will generate a significant number of revenue streams for Uganda. Oil revenues will be collected either in cash or in kind (Kazi and

---

25   The government personnel that have so far benefited from this training are officials of BoU, URA, the Energy Ministry, the Finance Ministry and officials of any other government agency concerned with oil exploitation.
26   W.B. Kazi and B. Beyeza, *supra* n. 3.

Beyeza, 2017). The organs mandated to assess and collect oil-sector revenues in Uganda are URA, DOP and UNOC.[27] The in-kind revenues will be collected by UNOC and disposed of in the manner provided for under the PFMA, 2015. The revenues must be transparently collected in a coordinated manner using streamlined revenue collection and reporting systems. Oil receipts collected by each organ shall be transmitted to the petroleum fund under the BoU. In the next two sub-sections we will examine how much oil revenue has been collected since 2001, and how much revenue can be realistically expected to flow to the Government in the future.

8.4.1 Revenues Collected

There are currently 40,385 barrels of the non-flared crude oil from well testing in stock.[28] The Government plans to sell this crude oil on a competitive basis. Taking the June 2017 international crude oil price of US$ 60.43 per barrel as the benchmark, then the Government would earn US$ 2,440,466 from selling this stock of oil. Even before Uganda's oil begins to flow, the country has collected substantial revenue from capital gains on transfers of interests in oil licences. For instance, CGT of US$ 449 million was collected when TUL bought out Heritage's interest, while the CGT of US$ 467 million[29] payable arose when TUL sold 66.67 per cent of its interests to Total E&P and CNOOC (Kazi and Sarker, 2012). But the CGT amounts sparked off tax disputes between the Government and the oil companies, partly because of the interpretation and application of the provisions of PSAs in the context of the ITA. In particular the interpretation of article 23 of the pre-2008 PSAs was disputed. TUL claimed that article 23 exempted them from CGT, a claim which was disputed by the Government (see Uganda Legal Information Institute, 2014). The amount excludes corporate tax and royalty which will start flowing in when commercial production starts.

The total revenues received over the 2001/2002–2013/2014 period amount to US$ 630,068,004 (see Table 8.1). The amount comprises CGT on transfer of Heritage's interest to TUL, stamp duty on the farm-down of part of the interest of TUL to Total E&P and CNOOC and oil-related NTRs and interest income

27 See Ministry of Finance, Planning and Economic Development, Uganda Public Finance Management Act, 2015, retrieved from: https://finance.go.ug/test/services/uganda-public-finance-management-act-2015/.

28 It is stored at Ngiri-2 and Kasamene-1 well sites as well as Tangi camp (see MEMD annual report 2014).

29 The figure was arrived at after the TUL took URA to TAT on the grounds that the transaction was exempt from CGT under article 23.5 of the model PSA of 1993.

Table 8.1: Oil Revenues Collected

Revenue handle	Amount (in USD)	Percent of gross revenue
CGT	449,424,960	71%
Stamp duty	171,000,000	27%
Interest (in 2013 & 2014)	403,044	0%
Oil related NTRs (FY2001/02–FY2013/14)	9,339,625	1%
Total	630,167,629	100%

Source: Data drawn from: 1) Bank of Uganda (BoU). Annual Reports 2011–2016. Available at: https://www.bou.or.ug/bou/publications_research/annual_reports.html; 2) Ministry of Energy and Mineral Development (MEMD). Statistical Abstracts 2013 & 2014. Available at: https://www.energyandminerals.go.ug/.

from investing stamp duty monies in short-term money market deposits.[30] The table indicates that oil-related NTRs form a small portion (1 per cent) of the revenues, while CGT forms a bigger part (71 per cent) followed by stamp duty at 21 per cent. This serves to indicate that the tax administration systems and procedures and the tax laws must be streamlined and strengthened, and staff should be well equipped with skills in the valuation of oil, cost audits, cost monitoring and apportionment to avert the possible loss of revenues due to inflation of costs by the oil companies. The CGT revenue balances were deposited in the oil tax fund at the Bank of Uganda.[31]

8.4.2   Anticipated Revenues from the Oil Sector

The upstream oil revenue sources are royalties, 'profit oil', corporate tax, bonuses, annual surface rentals and other fees. The 2012 PSAs provide for the possibility of collecting windfall profits taxes in cases of a rise in oil prices, which adds to the amount of revenues potentially collectable from the oil sector. However, no environment taxes are provided for under the PSAs. Asymmetric information, volatile prices, massive sunk costs and the long production periods make the forecasting of oil revenues very difficult. Nonetheless, the authors attempt to make forecasts of the revenues expected

---

30   Oil-related NTRs comprise signature bonuses, annual surface rentals, sales of oil data, sales of the oil refinery feasibility study report, training fees and permit fees.

31   The oil tax fund was renamed the petroleum fund following the enactment of the PFMA, 2015.

from Uganda's oil project. Below, we first review the oil revenue forecasts for Uganda so far made by analysts in order to inform our choice of model to use to make our oil revenue estimates for the purposes of this chapter.

Global Witness (2014) reported that the cumulative royalty would bring in an additional 1–2 per cent of government take. This could translate to between US$ 27 million and US$ 190 million with a 10 per cent 'discount rate'[32] for one licence area alone, depending on oil prices and field size, and potentially far more if larger oilfields are discovered or long-term oil prices rise. The Global Witness forecasts were based on the two PSAs for EA1 and Kawabata Prospect Area that TUL and Uganda made in February 2012. Global Witness (2014) used a conservative starting oil price of US$ 80 per barrel[33] and estimated that Uganda would receive between 80 and well over 90 per cent of revenues. In their analysis, they compared the fiscal terms in the 2012 PSAs[34]with those in the pre-2008 PSAs to conclude that improved 2012 PSA fiscal terms would increase government take by around 1–2 per cent. It also estimated that oil production from blocks EA1, 2 and 3A would earn Uganda roughly between US$ 15 billion and US$ 21billion with a 10 per cent discount rate in revenues over the lifetime of the project: about US$ 3.3bn per year over a 20-year period based on the oil volumes and changes in oil prices.

Henstridge and Page (2012) used oil prices and the production time horizon assumptions to make the first forecasts for Uganda's oil revenues and estimated that between 86 and 99 per cent of the net present value of the combined investments would accrue to the Government from various revenue streams.[35] The Oxford Policy Management (OPM) (2013) study estimates that oil revenue is expected to account for 17 per cent of baseline government revenue over the 30-year oil-production period. These findings reflect both the significant project size and Uganda's current low tax collection rates.[36] Over the first ten years of production, new oil revenues are expected to account for 2 per cent of GDP if prices decline by 25 per cent, and 6.9 per

32   Investors and governments value money now more than money in the future. They therefore apply a 'discount rate' to projected future revenues in order to calculate the value of those returns to them at the present time. This does not affect the actual revenues received. A 10 per cent discount rate is fairly standard for the industry.

33   This price is inflated at a very standard rate of 2.5 per cent and the prices quoted in the various studies as reference points also use standard inflation methodologies.

34   These PSAs were signed in February 2012 between TUL and Uganda and the Kanywataba Prospect Area located in EA 3A; these licensed areas are jointly owned by TUL, CNOOC and Total.

35   W.B. Kazi and B. Beyeza, *supra* n. 3.

36   In 2009 Uganda's total revenue expressed as a share of GDP was only 12.5 per cent (IMF 2013a).

cent of GDP if prices increased by 25 per cent. In absolute terms, Uganda's oil revenues would be US$ 2.6 billion over the first ten years of production. This will represent 31 per cent of GDP, reflecting the country's relatively narrow tax base and low tax collection rates.

Global Witness (2014) quoted the World Bank's predicted revenue of US$ 3billion per year near oil peak production for Uganda while the Oxford Centre for the Analysis of Resource Rich Economies (Oxcarre) predicted that the Government would receive US$ 20 billion for its oil over the life of the project with a 7 per cent discount rate. According to Global Witness, these estimates were most likely based on lower rates of production that reflected the smaller finds at the time. While putting their estimates in perspective, Global Witness reported that in 2013 GDP was about US$ 21 billion, while the government budget was about US$ 4.4 billion. Using the World Bank's Commodity Market Review Report which quoted a crude oil price of US$ 60.43 per barrel (June 2017) and 1.4 billion barrels of recoverable reserves, the authors estimated that Uganda's oil revenues from the Albertine Graben project would amount to US$ 43.4 billion (not discounted) over a 30-year period (see World Bank, 2017).[37] Clearly with the production of oil, Uganda's GDP, budget and revenues will potentially increase and socio-economic infrastructures will be provided to the people of Uganda absent corruption.

8.5   Uganda's Oil Fiscal Regime: Strengths and Weaknesses

According to Global Witness (2014), it is not possible to ascertain if a PSA presents a good or bad deal simply by reading it. The oil fiscal terms must be modelled to determine the revenues that government will reap, assuming the PSAs are publicly available. Platform *et al.* (2010) analysed the fiscal terms of some PSAs signed by Uganda with oil companies before February 2008 (hereafter the pre-2008 PSAs) and greatly criticised the deals Uganda had signed, stating that the PSA represented a bad financial deal for Uganda. In contrast, Global Witness (2014), based on an analysis of two PSAs signed by Uganda and oil companies in February 2012 (hereafter the 2012 contracts), said

---

37   The authors also assumed an average royalty rate of 8 per cent, cost oil of 60 per cent, the State's share of profit oil of 65 per cent and corporation tax at 30 per cent. We also assumed that the amount of oil produced throughout the 30-year period would be uniform. This revenue comprises royalty, additional royalty, the State's share of profit oil and corporation tax, but excludes the dividend on 15 per cent of equity share, NTRs and CGT.

that Uganda had achieved a better financial deal in the 2012 PSAs compared with the ones in the pre-2008 PSAs. In what follows we examine the main strengths and weaknesses of Uganda's oil fiscal regime.

8.5.1   Strengths of Uganda's Oil Fiscal Regime

The 2012 PSAs provide that Uganda will resolve any tax disputes through either the court system or arbitration within Uganda. The 2012 PSAs provide for 'joint and several liability', implying that all joint venture partners in a licensed area will be liable in the case of contractual breaches by any one of them. For instance, any taxes due from a partner can be recovered from other joint venture partners. This safeguards government revenues and also indemnifies the paying partners from potential court actions by the partner that is liable for paying the taxes. For instance, Heritage's CGT liability was recovered from TUL after a protracted and costly legal battle, but Heritage later sued TUL for non-settlement of its debt.

Stabilisation clauses insulate companies against regulatory changes that impact on project profitability and thus provide assurance to the oil companies which meet upfront costs and risks that they will recoup their investment without Government having to impose undue regulatory burdens on them by encouraging companies to undertake oil sector investments. For instance, the pre-2008 PSAs' stabilisation clauses provided that in the event of changes in the financial terms resulting in extra compliance costs, Uganda would compensate the oil companies. However, the 2012 PSAs' stabilisation clauses are limited to taxes and stipulate that any ITA changes that impact on the oil company's profitability substantially and adversely will call for an 'in good faith' renegotiation of PSA terms so as to restore and/or maintain the company's profitability prior to the change. The clauses also permit Government to impose windfall taxes on additional profits resulting from increased global oil prices. Thus, Uganda's fiscal regime for oil is responsive to macroeconomic changes and will thus generate additional revenues from windfall profits taxes for the State.

Given Uganda's experience with tax disputes, the 2012 PSAs provide in clear terms that companies will pay CGT on transfer of their interests in oil licences, thereby providing certainty on CGT.[38] These PSAs also provide for

---

38   The Government of Uganda is involved in two tax disputes with Tullow Oil; one over VAT and another over the capital gains tax assessment for the sale to Total and CNOOC. Tullow maintains that its PSA for EA 2 exempts it from capital gains tax, a point which the Government disputes. The Government of Uganda–Heritage Oil arbitration in London over the capital gains

settlement, in Ugandan courts and/or using local arbitration mechanisms, of any tax disputes relating to the PSAs. The CGT clause will help Uganda avoid the kinds of costs and difficulties encountered during the previous tax disputes and preserve future revenue from transfer of interests. Note, however, that CGT is payable only when a company sells a part, or all, of its interests in a licensed area, making it hard to rely on CGT as a predictable revenue source, since it is difficult to predict if and when companies will transfer their interests. The fiscal regime provides for daily and cumulative production royalties. Thus, as overall cumulative production rises, so will government revenue from this additional royalty. The cumulative production royalty is a rare revenue clause of PSAs which will generate more revenue for Uganda based on the amount of oil produced in a given licensed area. Royalties can secure an upfront revenue stream[39] from day one of production and have an element of progressivity, i.e. the rate increases as production increases.

Bonuses are a one-off payment to the State by the company. A signature bonus payment is made to Government on the signing of a PSA, while discovery bonuses are paid when oil has been found. The signature bonuses due to Uganda are US$ 0.3 million[40] and US$ 0.2 million,[41] and the discovery bonus is US$ 2 million for both licensed areas. Bonuses contribute a small portion of government revenues but they motivate companies to speed up oil exploration. To put this in perspective, a total of US$ 500,000 was collected in signature bonuses when the 2012 PSAs were signed in February 2012 and US$ 2 million in discovery bonus when oil was found in February 2013, thereby guaranteeing the Government upfront revenue.

Under the PSAs, oil companies meet exploration and development costs, but they begin to recoup these costs when oil begins to flow. While the cost oil of 60 per cent of production is high by international standards, it will help companies to recoup their investments faster, and thus encourage investments in the oil sector in Uganda (Global Witness, 2014). The 'ring-fencing' bars companies from recovering costs incurred in licensed areas where neither oil has yet been found or commercially exploitable oil has not been found, and thus it enables the Government to generate revenues from those areas where oil has been discovered and production is taking place. Ring-fencing

tax assessment relating to the 2010 farm down to Tullow oil is still ongoing (see Global Witness, 2014).

39   Royalties generate revenue for government as soon as production commences,

40   See clause 9 of PSA between Uganda and TUL for the Kanywataba Prospect Area February, 2012

41   See clause 9 of PSA between Uganda and TUL for Exploration Area 1 (EA1) February, 2012

therefore helps the Government to counter tax avoidance and evasion through manipulating transfer prices.

In view of the foregoing, Uganda's oil fiscal regime encourages investments, guarantees government revenues and ensures sustainability. The royalty and production-sharing regimes have an element of progressivity, making the fiscal regime responsive to current prices and the inherent risks of the oil industry. The implementation of PSAs is simple since they consolidate all fiscal elements of oil exploration and development in a single document. Through corporate tax both the Government and the oil companies share the risks of oil production and development. The oil company pays tax when it has taxable profits and any carried-forward tax losses are offset against future taxable income as a deduction. The corporation tax paid in Uganda will be available to offset against tax payable to the home country of the oil company. However, the corporate tax base can easily be decreased through transfer pricing, thin capitalisation and treat shopping.

8.5.2   Weaknesses of Uganda's Oil Fiscal Regime

Cumulative royalty may lead companies to opt out of the project early because it may reduce the profit that the company expects as companies pay higher royalty rates even while production is falling. Royalties enable companies to make minimum payments for the oil extracted. Kazi and Beyeza (2017) observe that developing countries find it hard to cope with mundane processing and reporting, thereby hindering effective filing and payment enforcement, while the IMF (2012) indicated that the administration of royalties involves frequent assessments, no annual tax returns and no reconciliation to corporation tax returns, making it inefficient. Annual surface rentals generate minimal revenues, but they can encourage companies to explore and develop contract areas and/or to relinquish their rights in a contract area. These would help to isolate the incompetent investors.

Royalties discourage investments by increasing the marginal cost of oil extraction. Royalties are never claimed as foreign tax credits against the home country income tax assessed. The corporate income tax and the PSAs are hard to administer, since they require specialised skills in cost audits and valuation and experience in negotiating PSAs respectively, which are lacking in Uganda. Uganda's fiscal regime offer is loaded with exemptions, such as VAT on imports, which are hard to administer and may aid tax evasion and avoidance.

8.6   Conclusion and Policy Options

Uganda's fiscal regime is very competitive and ensures certainty and stability, and there will not be need for frequent revisions in fiscal terms. Uganda's PSAs have clauses on taxation, royalty and additional royalty, cost recovery, signature and discovery bonuses, annual surface rentals, CGT and windfall profits tax. This kind of fiscal regime generates government revenues both in the pre-production stage and in the production stage. International oil companies will be able to recoup their investments and make profits in the production stage. Uganda's oil fiscal regime combines upfront government revenue with a sufficiently high return on capital for the oil companies. A combination of corporation tax, royalty regime and production-sharing regimes generates government revenues without distorting incentives to invest in oil exploration and development.

Uganda secured significant additional revenues in the 2012 PSAs with the adoption of a new cumulative production royalty in addition to the existing daily production royalty. In 2014, Global Witness analysed the fiscal terms in both the pre-2008 PSAs and 2012 PSAs and concluded that the Government of Uganda would potentially receive additional revenues from the cumulative production royalty and the levying of windfall taxes, if global oil prices increased over and above what was expected (see Global Witness, 2014). Unlike corporation tax and PSAs, the oil-related NTRs are easy to administer since they do not require specialised skills in oil valuation, cost audits, cost allocations and apportionment (Kazi and Beyeza, 2017). The oil production is yet to start, but oil revenues from both NTRs and CGT have already flowed into the Government's account.[42]

We could not empirically ascertain the effectiveness and sustainability of key fiscal instruments for the oil sector such as corporation tax, royalties and production-sharing tax the collection of which is dependent on oil flow. The tax regime in place remains a work in progress. However, it is clear that Uganda has successfully negotiated more favourable fiscal terms by securing a higher share of revenue. The fiscal regime presents a good deal for Uganda because, if the Government opts to introduce a new windfall tax, government revenue will go up without eating into the anticipated company profits. If oil prices rise above what is expected or project costs are significantly less

---

42   Petroleum revenues means tax charged on income derived by a person from petroleum operations, the Government's share of production, signature bonus, surface rentals, royalties, proceeds from the sale of a government share of production, and any other duties or fees payable to the Government from contract revenues under the terms of a petroleum agreement.

than predicted, then Uganda would receive significant additional revenues through royalties (Global Witness, 2014).

Based on the information available, it appears that the Government has done enough preparatory work in terms of putting in place the necessary legal and institutional framework, including staff training, and enhancing the capacity to deal with the intricacies of assessing, collecting and managing oil revenues. Moreover, Uganda's oil fiscal regime appears to be flexible and progressive enough to allow lessons learned during its implementation to further help in refining it without the regime having to be renegotiated as the profitability of oil companies increases.

Uganda should however optimise production recovery rates through the oil licensing regime. Uganda should publish the oil PSAs' fiscal terms to assist in tracking state revenues and in making reliable and accurate forecasts of expected revenue from the sector. TUL, CNOOC and Total are registered and listed on the stock market in the US, EU and Norway, whose new rules will require the publishing of detailed breakdowns of the payments they make to governments, and so it will be much more difficult for Uganda to hide under the national and corporate confidentiality veil. Uganda's Government should start publishing disaggregated oil sector data to promote good governance and avert white collar crimes in the sector.

References

African Development Bank (2009), 'Managing Oil Revenue in Uganda: A Policy Note'. *OREA Knowledge Series No. 1*, 1–28. Retrieved from: https://www.afdb.org/fileadmin/uploads/afdb/Documents/Project-and-Operations/Managing%20Oil%20Revenue_in%20Uganda%20ENG%20version_01.pdf.

Bank of Uganda (BoU) (2011), Annual Report. Retrieved from: http://Bou.go.ug/annualreports.

—— (2012), Annual Report. Retrieved from: http://Bou.go.ug/annualreports.

—— (2013), Annual Report. Retrieved from: http://Bou.go.ug/annualreports.

—— (2014), Annual Report. Retrieved from: http://Bou.go.ug/annualreports.

—— (2015), Annual Report. Retrieved from: http://Bou.go.ug/annualreports.

—— (2016), Annual Report. Retrieved from: http://Bou.go.ug/annualreports.

Baunsgaard, T. (2014), 'Fiscal Regimes for Extractive Industries: Policy Design and Implementation'. *Paper presented at the Africa Tax Dialogue in Arusha, July 2014*. Retrieved from: http://www.imf.org/external/np/pp/eng/2012/081512.pdf.

Centre for Energy Economics (2007), 'Fiscal Terms for Upstream Projects: An Overview'. Retrieved from: https://www.ffe.de/en/the-ffe.

Civil Society Coalition for Oil in Uganda (2010), 'Contracts Curse: Uganda's Oil Agreements Place Profit before People. Retrieved from: http://www.platformlondon.org/carbonweb/documents/uganda/Cursed_Contracts_Uganda_PLATFORM_CSCO_Tullow_Heritage_2010_February.pdf.

EY Global Tax Alert Library (2017, 6 March), 'Uganda Enacts Income Tax Amendments Impacting Carry Forward of Losses and Withholding Tax on Rental Income'. *EY Tax Alerts*. Retrieved from: www.ey.com/taxalerts.

Global Witness (2014), *A Good Deal Better? Uganda's Secret Oil Contracts Explained*. London: Global Witness Limited. Retrieved from: https://www.globalwitness.org/en/reports/good-deal-better/.

——— (2017), 'Economic Modelling Tool Guide'. Global Witness. Retrieved from: https://www.globalwitness.org/documents/17829/economic_model_guide_uganda.pdf

Gudmestad, O.T., A. Zolotukhin and E.T. Jarlsby (2010), *Development of Petroleum Resources with Emphasis on Offshore Fields.* Southampton: WIT Press.

Henstridge, M., and J. Page (2012), 'Managing a Modest Boom: Oil Revenues in Uganda'. *OxCarre Research Paper 90*, 1–35. Retrieved from: https://www.economics.ox.ac.uk/materials/working_papers/4870/oxcarrerp201290.pdf.

IMF (2012, 12 August), 'Fiscal Regimes for Extractive Industries: Design and Implementation'. IMF Policy Papers Series. Retrieved from: https://www.imf.org/en/Publications/Policy-Papers/Issues/2016/12/31/Fiscal-Regimes-for-Extractive-Industries-Design-and-Implementation-PP4701.

Kazi, W.B., and T.K. Sarker (2012), 'Fiscal Sustainability and the Natural Resource Curse in Resource-rich African Countries: A Case Study of Uganda', *Bulletin for International Taxation IBFD*, 66(8). Retrieved from: https://www.ibfd.org/IBFD-Products/Journal-Articles/Bulletin-for-International-Taxation/collections/bit/html/bit_2012_08_int_2.html.

——— and Beyeza, B. (2017), 'Analysis of the Oil Fiscal Regime of Uganda', *Bulletin for International Taxation IBFD*, 71(11). Retrieved from: https://www.ibfd.org/IBFD-Products/Journal-Articles/Bulletin-for-International-Taxation/collections/bit/html/bit_2017_11_int_1.html.

———, T.K. Sarker and D. Tumuhirwe (2013), 'Fiscal Sustainability and Natural Resource Endowment in Uganda: Is an Effective Tax Administration the Answer?', *Bulletin for International Taxation IBFD*, 67(6). Retrieved from: https://www.ibfd.org/IBFD-Products/Journal-Articles/Bulletin-for-International-Taxation/collections/bit/html/bit_2013_06_int_3.html.

Mazeel, M. (2010), *Petroleum Fiscal Systems and Contracts*. Hamburg: Diplomica Verlag.

Ministry of Energy and Mineral Development (MEMD) (2013), Statistical Abstract. Retrieved from: http://www.energyandminerals.go.ug/downloads/statisticalabstracts2013.

——— (2014), Statistical Abstract. Retrieved from: http://www.energyandminerals.go.ug/downloads/statisticalabstracts2014.

Ministry of Finance, Planning and Economic Development (2012), Oil and Gas Revenue Management Policy. Kampala: Republic of Uganda.

Oxford Policy Management (OPM) (2013), 'DFID PEAKS Topic Guide: Extractive Industries, Development and the Role of Donors', September 2013. Retrieved from: https://www.gov.uk/dfid-research-outputs/topic-guide-extractive-industries-development-and-the-role-of-donors.

Sunley, E.M., T. Baunsgaard and D. Simard (2002), Background paper prepared for the IMF Conference on Fiscal Policy Formulation and Implementation in Oil-producing Countries, 5–6 June 2002. Retrieved from: http://citeseerx.ist.psu.edu/viewdoc/download?doi=10.1.1.202.7408&rep=rep1&type=pdf.

Uganda Legal Information Institute (2014), 'Tullow Oil v Uganda Revenue Authority (TAT APPLICATION NO. 4 OF 2011) [2011] UGTAT 1 (16 June 2014)'. Retrieved from: https://ulii.org/ug/judgment/tax-appeals-tribunal/2014/1.

World Bank (2017), Commodity Market Review Report. Washington, DC: The World Bank. Retrieved from: http://econ.worldbank.org/wbsite/external/extdec/extdecprospects.

9
Human Resources and Oil in Uganda: An Analysis of Uganda's Human Resource Development for the Oil Sector

Jackson A. Mwakali and Jackson N.M. Byaruhanga

9.1 Introduction

In 1992 the Government of Uganda issued the first petroleum exploration licence, followed by the second one in 1997. Since then significant and commercially exploitable hydrocarbons have been discovered in the Albertine Graben. It is expected that many direct and indirect employment and business opportunities will be available in the midstream and downstream phases of the petroleum value chain, when oil field development, production, refining and evacuation will go full blast. However, the extent to which Ugandans will be able to take advantage of these opportunities will crucially depend on the preceding human resources development.

In this chapter we aim to analyse the human resource challenges and opportunities facing Uganda's emerging oil sector. We will start by tracing the evolution of Uganda's education and skills development sector from the British colonial era in the early twentieth century to the post- oil discovery years in the twenty-first century. We will then analyse the impact of oil discovery on the human resource development dynamics. Subsequently, we will examine the reciprocal influence of the country's human resource profile on the development of the fledgling oil and gas industry. Subsequently, Uganda's human resource supply side is compared and contrasted with the oil and gas sector's demand side in the upstream, midstream and downstream segments of the entire value chain during the country's anticipated 40-year-or-so oil boom epoch. In the last section we will conclude and provide some policy reflections.

9.2   A Brief History of Business, Technical and Vocational Education and Training (BTVET) in Uganda

9.2.1   Colonial Era

Vocational or occupational education is a type of education that aims at imparting practical skills to learners. It is productive education or education for job creators. It is skill-based as opposed to general education, which is an academic type of education (Rauner and Maclean, 2009). In Uganda, business, technical, vocational education and training (BTVET) are put together as separate, but all of them can conveniently be called vocational education. The system of formal vocational skills training or education in Uganda dates way back in the colonial period, especially in the late 1940s when the World War II former camps were converted into skills training centres to re-train demobilised soldiers and younger children to acquire skills for survival. During that time, the general practice of most organisations was to employ a youth as a helper or a cleaner under the name of 'spanner boy'. In this way, the boy picked up a smattering of skills without proper guidance. In 1952, the Artisan Training Organisation was established in the Ministry of Labour, headed by a director, to train artisans in various trades. It was particularly put in place for the resettlement of World War II veterans. Later on, in 1953, the trade testing and guidance section was established to assess the skills competences of persons being trained.

During the colonial times, Uganda's education system was developed largely by voluntary organisations, especially Christian missionaries. Good educational facilities were available to only a small group of elites and oriented towards white-collar jobs, while the majority of the people remained illiterate or poorly educated. This system produced mainly clerical and administrative personnel required by religious foundation bodies and the colonial administration. The colonial education produced people with a general education devoid of technical or vocational skills, and these products—the educated workers—were to serve as clerks, chiefs and administrators. Such jobs as those of clerks, interpreters, chiefs and administrators attracted heftier benefits in monetary terms than vocational jobs. The high cost of vocational education therefore made missionaries think more of general education, an irony which has not changed at all in Uganda's education system. As a start to exercising control, the Government of Uganda (GOU) established the Directorate of Education in 1925. Thereafter in the 1950s and 1960s the education sector expanded rapidly.

The negative attitude towards technical vocational education was aggra-vated by the British popular notion in Uganda that 'the rulership' of the world was in the hands not of technicians but of those who studied humanities. There is a little regard for technical and commercial studies; physical work is not necessarily considered as an essential part of education. The general practice is for the 'brighter' pupils to go on and on with theoretical studies and for the less talented to branch off into technical or vocational courses. Cleverness is still judged only on the basis of ability to memorise and regurgitate theoretical information, and practical people are automatically regarded as less bright. Despite repeated criticisms of the inherited colonial system of education as anachronistic and irrelevant and the efforts of successive governments to change it, no fundamental transformation has occurred over the years of independence in relating education to the social and cultural realities of Uganda.

9.2.2   Post-independence

Note must be taken of the fact that the colonial government in Uganda tried its best to give vocational education to the people in Uganda but it was not a success story, unlike the general education system. Government through the selection system in the country promoted the inferior tendencies of technical education; the selection system for academic and technical schools played an adverse role in the success of technical schools. It was the students who were scoring low marks at the end of primary or secondary school education that were being channelled into technical schools. Students with high marks were being selected for higher levels of education. As much as there is an upsurge in the demand for the vocational education system, people's attitude towards it has not been corrected fully. The enrolment of technical and vocational institutions is still low. For example, in 2007 there were only about 30,000 students in all the technical, vocational education and training institutions. Largely the stigma and negative attitude attached to BTVET courses hinders the sub-sector from getting good learners. Because enrolment is very low, most of these institutions are operating below capacity (Okinyal, 2006). Whereas most BTVET subjects are science-related, students who pass sciences do not easily opt for BTVET and so the sub-sector continues to admit low grade students into its institutions. Currently, BTVET institutions can admit students only after the universities have selected the best students. In terms of selection at the national level, candidates for the Uganda Advanced Cer-tificate of Education (UACE) are selected first, and then technical vocational institutions grab the remnants. Yet, as the National Council for Higher Education (NCHE) notes in this respect:

> Besides the over-emphasis that students and parents put on university education at the expense of other tertiary programmes, the sad trend [has been] the continuing neglect of technical education as well as of the Hotel/ Tourism sectors. Unless this country changes its attitudes, we shall continue importing skilled labour to work on our roads, in our factories, hotels and tourist resorts (National Council for Higher Education, 2007, p.14).

> The current skills capacity bottlenecks … can partly be attributed to the inability of tertiary institutions to produce skilled human resources as a result of under-funding and probably the over-emphasis on universities at the expense of Other Tertiary Institutions. By concentrating on technical, diploma in health, veterinary, agriculture and vocational training, the chances are that certificate and diploma holders are less likely to go abroad for greener pastures than university graduates (Ibid., pp.36–37).

However, the status of vocational education is beginning to change now that the academic education system can take one nowhere in the job market.

As observed in the preceding section, the BTVET as we know it today was a small sub-sector designed to produce manual labourers, mainly the underprivileged and uneducated sections of society. This was the beginning of the social stigmatisation of BTVET. No focused policy existed specifically to guide the development of BTVET until 1972 when the Directorate of Industrial Training (DIT) was established as the first deliberate move by GoU to accord skills training legal and therefore due attention, although implementation faced challenges for a long time thereafter. With the enactment of the National Curriculum Development Centre Act in 1976, committees were formed to address the specific BTVET curricula requirements. Earlier in 1967, the Japanese Government offered the Uganda Government the building of a modern vocational training institute at Nakawa to increase the production of craftsmen and women and retraining the same to meet the industrial demands. In 1968, GoU came up with a strategy of strengthening the industrial vocational training schemes. The idea did not take off until 1972, when the Employment Act was repealed and the Industrial Training Decree No. 2 of 1972 together with the Industrial Apprenticeship Training Regulations was promulgated. This made apprenticeship training more prominent than ever before, especially among the manufacturing and repair industries and organisations.

In 1987, GoU appointed the Education Review Commission to inquire into policies governing education in Uganda and recommend how to make education relevant to the development needs of the country, embrace modern curricula and pedagogic trends and developments, assess the role of the private sector in providing education and make the education system as a whole cost effective. With regard to technical and vocational education training, the Commission categorised it in three levels, in particular:

– Stage 1:   Vocational education primary school: emphasis was laid on the need for attitudinal change at this level and mastering fundamental knowledge and skills with much focus on teaching agriculture.
– Stage 2:   Vocational education ordinary level: according technical education the status of other traditional subjects and adequately equipping technical and commercial schools and converting them into vocational secondary schools with students at these choosing one vocational subject for specialisation.
– Stage 3:   Vocational education advanced level: further specialisation was recommended and the creation of regional polytechnics through the merger of five Uganda Technical Colleges (UTCs) and Uganda Colleges of Commerce (UCCs). The establishment of one polytechnic per district with adequate facilities for girls was also recommended, but this seems to have remained on paper (Okinyal, 2012, p.7).

In 2002 the first ever BTVET strategic plan was produced and the BTVET Act came into being in 2008. In addition, the First and Second National Development Plans emphasise public-private partnerships (PPPs) on skills development covering formal, non-formal and informal avenues of acquiring skills and competences (The Republic of Uganda, 2010; 2015). Relevance, equitable access, efficiency and effectiveness are underscored as core themes in education development.

Generally, Uganda's education system is not practically oriented. The current BTVET system is not in a position to cater for the present and future skills requirements of the economy. Most BTVET providers do not refine their students to the required current and future skills needs. The training contains too much theory and too little hands-on experience. Even practical skills are theoretically explained with gestures and pictures. Looking at the outdated curriculum as a contradiction to the development of the vocational education system, there has been no serious policy put in place to try to review the curriculum of the TVET institutions. Although some attempts to review the curriculum were made in 1998 by both the Curriculum Development Centre and the former Uganda Polytechnic Kyambogo, no changes were affected, leaving the TVET institutions to continue with the outdated curricula. Technology rapidly changes with time. To match the job market requirements the training curricula must be up to date. Effective curriculum planning and development in this area should be a dynamic process (Okinyal, 2006).

9.3   Manpower Demands of the Oil and Gas Sector

According to Industrial Base Line Survey findings, the Lake Albert basin development projects will generate thousands of direct jobs in Uganda, with a peak of about 13,000 workers in the construction phase and a plateau of 3,000 people in the operation phase. Out of the total manpower required 15 per cent are engineers and managers, 60 per cent are technicians and craftsmen and 25 per cent are people without any educational background ('unskilled'). Education focus should be on civil construction, electrical and mechanical fields. Beyond direct jobs that will be created on site, oil and gas (O&G) activity will also have the potential to generate 100,000 to 150,000 indirect and induced jobs. Out of the total newly created jobs, 80 per cent will be short-term for the peak of construction and will have to be transferred to other sectors of the industry or to the neighbouring countries to remain sustainable.

The survey highlights industries whose capacity or compliance with O&G standards requires future support in order to avoid massive imports. All sectors will need to upgrade the quality of their overall management standards and quality of delivery to align with oil and gas expectations. Some sectors will need a complete transformation to be able to cope with future needs as the gap between future demand and current supply is at the range of the multiplier, like transport and logistics (goods) or hazardous waste management and hazardous waste disposal. Transport and logistics (goods) include freight transport by road, warehousing and storage, lifting services, and other transportation support activities (clearing, customs, and forwarding) and hazardous waste disposal. The survey reveals that a few industries should be able to absorb the peak of demand, like cement or structural steel.

Ugandan companies call for more visibility of the future needs of the O&G projects and support from large companies, banks and public authorities. Emphasis should be put on the training of skilled people, the reinforcement of the oil and gas certification process and supporting the educational system by reinforcing the best academic institutions already in place and by founding a training centre to develop qualified technicians.

Some specific sectors should be supported by O&G partners in Uganda. Specific industries to support include hazardous waste management, operations and maintenance services, light equipment manufacturing, work safety products (PPE), agriculture, metal scaffolding and road safety.

9.4   The Government of Uganda's Petroleum Sector Skilling Programme

Recognising the weaknesses and opportunities in the current BTVET system, the Government of Uganda (GoU)'s strategy to improve the BTVET system and provide training for the skills needed by the petroleum sector has two main components: the Skilling Uganda programme and the development of Uganda Petroleum Institute Kigumba (UPIK) as a benchmark for other technical colleges.

9.4.1   Uganda Petroleum Institute Kigumba (UPIK)

The GoU realises that it must help to provide manpower for the petroleum industry. In 2009, it established UPIK in north-western Uganda envisaged to be a centre of excellence (CoE) for the training of technicians, craftsmen and professionals in the petroleum sector. The UPIK institutional development plan (IDP) 2014/2019 outlines the strategies and actions to be undertaken to address the institutional weaknesses and gaps (Ongode and Nalubega, 2014). To be relevant, UPIK aims to adopt a demand-driven programme development and delivery to ensure that industry representatives play a major role in identifying curriculum standards, training programmes design, equipment specifications and training programme delivery. The first UPIK intake programme was at times too broad and not developed in close collaboration with the local industry. However, UPIK has established relations with Rogaland Training and Education Centre (RKK) and the Stavanger Offshore Technical College of Norway to obtain support for curriculum development, management development and staff skills development to offer a two-year diploma in petroleum studies with options in drilling, electrical installation, instrumentation and welding. Upon completion of the diploma at UPIK, students undertake an additional six month apprenticeship programme at Kenson School of Production Technology in Trinidad and Tobago, which provides graduates with City and Guilds of London international vocational qualifications in electrical installation, instrumentation, welding and pipe fitting and fabrication. UPIK should also support other BTVET institutes to deliver basic-level training in the above-mentioned disciplines.

To be relevant, UPIK will have to ensure that the international oil companies (IOCs), the national oil company (NOC) and petroleum industry service companies and other development partners are effectively represented on its Governing Council for policy making, planning and development and delivery of its programmes. The institute is in the process of developing and delivering certificate and diploma courses for skilled technicians in petroleum upstream operations, petroleum downstream operations, mechanical and electrical maintenance, instrumentation maintenance and other disciplines that may be required for IOCs, NOC and petroleum industry service companies and refinery operations. By 2018/2019, UPIK will start graduating approximately 224 students annually in the foregoing disciplines. The two-year upstream operations in petroleum engineering diploma course content will include petroleum industry service companies' and exploration and production companies' field production techniques and equipment, reservoir engineering including enhanced recovery, gas processing, drilling, petroleum chemistry, technical communications, petroleum engineering, geosciences, petroleum safety fundamentals and geology. For downstream operations, a two-year diploma in either chemical or engineering technology which covers most downstream equipment or processes that turn raw petroleum resources into final products, gas processing, refining and petroleum production programme will include oil and gas chemistry, process equipment, unit operations, material and energy balances, plant processes and pipelining.

According to UPIK IDP 2014/2019, the current UPIK instructors have acceptable academic qualifications with some exposure in oil and gas industry operations and technical training at Stavanger, Norway, and from Trinidad and Tobago. However, they lack hands-on practical workplace experience and have little or no knowledge of competence-based training (CBT) and assessment. Up to August 2013, 88 students had benefited. With support from DFID, UPIK established an instructor development programme in Trinidad and Tobago for CBT to provide them with on-the-job training placements in chosen fields starting in January 2014. UPIK is implementing technical conversion courses with the University of Trinidad and Tobago (UTT) to reorient scientists and engineers trained in non-petroleum fields to become managers in the petroleum sector. A long-term approach to Ugandan instructor development should be established at UPIK in partnership with an internationally recognised training organisation in the petroleum sector which can mobilise its own expatriate instructors over a three- to four-year period to deliver training programmes to students and Ugandan instructors as well.

In the short to medium term, UPIK should emphasise artisanal and technical skills and conduct studies for degrees later after it has attained acceptable standards in the former. It is envisaged that UPIK will graduate 460 students between 2017 and 2019. UPIK intends to expand access through recognition of prior learning and recruit students with either A or O level prerequisites for selected short courses and also develop clear pathways for UPIK graduates to continue on to university degree-level programmes. Twinning institution instructors along with UPIK national instructors was to begin teaching the five targeted programmes in July 2016, graduating its first batch of instrumentation, electrical and mechanical maintenance students in June 2017. Upstream operations students should complete their two-year diploma programme and graduate in June 2018. CNOOC, Total and Tullow Oil have indicated that the UPIK graduation schedule synchronised well with field development plans and that they look forward to hiring certified graduates. UPIK has a programme through its Student Job Placement Unit and the Petroleum Sector Skills Council (SCC) to place its graduates in the three major petroleum and service companies such as Schlumberger (UPIK IDP, 2014–2019). All expatriate instructors are expected to leave in July 2017 and turn over all programmes to UPIK national instructors.

For effective governance, UPIK will seek increased autonomy to determine its own curriculum, set its own fees, and budget, hire and fire teaching staff, determine remuneration, and adjust its training programmes and content to respond flexibly to petroleum needs while at the same time being accountable to its supervising ministry. UPIK should continuously lobby for the introduction of a petroleum skills training fund and supporting legislative reforms to allow it to generate additional revenue by selling services or courses on a fees-for-service basis. A UPIK governing council with considerable autonomy has been appointed by GoU with significant representation from the private sector and the oil industry. The challenge the council has is to put in place a competent and dedicated management team with an in-depth understanding of the labour needs of the petroleum industry. UPIK needs to develop a sustainable financing model for both operating and capital expenses that has contributions from GoU, students, donors, and the petroleum industry.

A key success factor of a petroleum training institute is the organisation that supports the education and training facilities. All the elements of a CoE for petroleum education such as effective organisation and governance arrangement with autonomy, high calibre chief executive officer, administrative staff and instructors, relevant curriculum development and programming, quality instruction and delivery, sustainable financing and strong industrial linkages and support are missing at UPIK and should be introduced as soon as possible. According to the UPIK campus' master development plan (September 2013), equipment purchased should support the new operations and maintenance. More practical curriculum training facilities and equipment specific to oil and gas industry applications are needed. There is currently no location for a well pad in the master plan. A small drilling rig or service rig is a common component of oil and gas technical training facilities with a fully cased 1,000-metre directional well. There is no location for a typical oilfield production facility that would include a common training pilot plant/ simulator used at petroleum technical institutions throughout the world. The ratio of classroom space to workshop training laboratory appears to be too high. DFID is assisting UPIK with initial purchases of workshop equipment.

Large-scale training equipment possessing industrial characteristics should be used in the practical workshops and laboratories, and if possible UPIK should work out an arrangement to use some of the equipment from petroleum contactors or service companies (such as Schlumberger, Baker and Hughes, and Halliburton). Pilot plants and simulators ordered by UPIK should have full data acquisition and automation systems comparable to those used by the oil and gas industry in Uganda. The training equipment specified should be state-of-the-practice, not state-of-the-art, equipment often used for undergraduate engineering training. Among key performance indicators of UPIK are training cost per graduate, the employment rate of graduates within the oil and gas sector and the completion rate of graduates. Unfortunately, the majority of UPIK graduates are unemployable by the petroleum sector due to lack of quality relevant skills (The Observer, 2013).

9.4.2 Skilling Uganda Programme

As indicated in the "Industrial Base Line Survey" findings referred to above, most of the jobs to be created by the O&G activity will be indirect and induced jobs in the non-oil sectors that will also mainly supply low risk low technology and some high-risk low technology inputs to the O&G sector. It is therefore imperative that Uganda develops strong and dynamic BTVET as a key sector to train and supply skills to the O&G activity and the economy in general. This effort requires enormous resources, technical training and expertise. Therefore, it will have to be a well-coordinated and collaborative intervention by Government of Uganda, International Oil Companies, the private sector, development partners and other non-state actors.

Uganda's Vision 2025 and the National Development Plan (NDP) 2010/2011–2014/2015 identify BTVET skills shortages based on which the BTVET (2012/2013 to 2021/2022) Strategic Plan for Skilling Uganda was developed (The Republic of Uganda, 2015). The plan incorporates activities by the BTVET Department and DIT under the Ministry of Education and Sports, and its strategies go beyond the traditional formal BTVET under the education sector to serve development interests of other sectors, notably agriculture, health, trade, tourism and industry. Part of the total costs will therefore be borne by government sectors other than education. The Strategic Plan provides for establishment of a Skills Development Authority (SDA) reflecting the broadened mandate of the BTVET sector and the need for broader partnerships. Under the Strategic Plan, the BTVET system will be transformed from an educational sub-sector into a comprehensive system of skills development for employment, enhanced productivity and growth to create employable skills and competences relevant in the labour market instead of educational certificates. It will embrace all Ugandans in need of skills, not relegated to (low achieving) primary and secondary school leavers as in the past. At its final transition, the proposed SDA will be a private sector-led institution that will provide the mechanism to promote a demand-driven BTVET in the country. While delivery of BTVET content has been largely through the school system, the shift aims at a flexible, modular workplace-oriented environment.

On 23 October 2012 the Minister of Education and Sports established the Reform Task Force (RTF) for Skilling Uganda chaired by Uganda Federation of Employers and composed of 26 members drawn from the private sector, the Ministry of Education and Sports and other key ministries, civil society and trade unions. The purpose of the RTF is to spearhead reform of the system of BTVET and to oversee and manage the Skilling Uganda reforms until a permanent, integrated SDA is established. The strategic plan has five objectives, namely: 1) to make BTVET relevant to productivity development and economic growth; 2) to increase the quality of skills provision; 3) to increase equitable access to skills development; 4) to improve the effectiveness in BTVET management and organisation; and 5) to increase internal efficiency and resources available to BTVET. To achieve economic relevance, it is envisaged that by 2020, 70 per cent of employers will be satisfied by the competences of BTVET graduates and 80 per cent of BTVET graduates will have found employment or be self-employed generating sufficient income. The coverage of a legally recognised and implemented Uganda Vocational Qualifications Framework (UVQF) will be expanded and accelerated.

The share of Uganda Technical Colleges graduates of all tertiary BTVET graduates is to be increased to 40 per cent by 2020 (baseline: 15 per cent in 2008). At least 50 per cent of all post-secondary BTVET enrolment covers defined priority areas. Agriculture training will be expanded and improved. By 2020, at least 70 per cent of informal sector and medium scale enterprises utilising BTVET graduates should confirm that upgraded skills contribute to higher productivity and the raising of product quality. A labour market information system (LMIS) will be established to regularly produce data and information for BTVET. To increase the quality of skills provision, UVQF assessment pass rates should have increased to 90 per cent by 2020. The institutional capacities of BTVET providers will be strengthened by upgrading at least 250 public and private institutions. The aim is to increase enrolment in BTVET instructor training by 10 per cent annually and widen the range of occupational areas in line with labour market priorities. Major efforts will also be undertaken to upgrade the existing corps of BTVET instructors to make them fit for competence-based education and training (CBET). The target is to upgrade up to 500 existing BTVET instructors annually by 2015. Funds have been set aside to kick-start incentive schemes for BTVET instructors to increase attractiveness. A quality assurance system for both public and private BTVET providers in line with regional standards and practices will be put in place.

At least 40 public BTVET institutions will undergo comprehensive institutional strengthening. Development of the oil industry in Uganda will be given immediate priority. In view of limited capacities in Uganda, the Government of Uganda will seek partnership arrangements with leading vocational and technical institutions in other countries. In addition, a BTVET investment fund will be set up to provide resources for private and public BTVET providers on a competitive basis for expansion or rehabilitation, for human resource development and the introduction of new programmes based on labour market needs in accordance with institutional development plans. Centres of excellence, where possible, managed by or in cooperation with industry or industry associations will be developed for particular occupations. All public and several private BTVET institutions will receive support during the plan period to upgrade their ICT facilities in order to introduce ICT-based training and improve training management. This will be based on a strategy to introduce 'E-BTVET' in Uganda.

GoU has a comprehensive policy and strategy for the support of private BTVET providers in cooperation with the Association of Uganda Private Vocation Institutions (UGAPRIVI). Towards that end, an inventory of formal and non-formal private training providers will be made. This will include the reduction of regulatory barriers for private training providers and simplifying registration/accreditation procedures, the provision of incentives for initiating and expanding private provision, e.g. through matching investment grants, and the introduction of redeemable vouchers and access to all support schemes offered to BTVET institutions.

The implementation of the envisaged key reforms in skills development requires strong organisation and management of BTVET. At presently, the BTVET management is fragmented under various government agencies. It lacks focused direction and incentives to increase performance. The strategic plan therefore foresees the establishment of an integrated management body (SDA) for BTVET, the devolution of administrative power to training institutions while introducing accountability, and building an effective management information and monitoring system dedicated to skills development. Together with stakeholders, especially employers, the SDA will be responsible for policy-making, standard-setting, assessment and certification and other quality assurance functions, information, monitoring and evaluation, accreditation of training providers, financing and possibly the management of public training institutions. In addition, independent status could help to raise the image of skills development and counter the prevailing negative attitude towards technical-vocational training. Ultimately, BTVET institutions will be self-governed, able to set their own fees and budgets, receive funds and subsidies from the centre, hire and fire teaching and other staff within some flexible national norms, and introduce or change training programmes in response to market needs. Devolution of authority will be linked to the establishment of an internal quality management (IQM) system and the creation of a new accreditation system.

To increase the efficiency of BTVET provision through results-oriented transfer mechanisms, budget allocation to BTVET institutions will be linked to performance results. Currently, institutional base-funding is provided through payment of staff salaries. This funding mode is not related to the actual number of trainees enrolled or to other indicators of institutional performance. It furthermore discriminates against those institutions that encounter difficulties in attracting teachers, for instance because the institution is located in a remote area. A new funding formula will therefore be developed and gradually implemented based on actual performance, thus stimulating institutional initiatives to improve results. As a starting point, allocations should be based on the number of trainees enrolled. More outcome-oriented indicators may be introduced at a later stage, for example trainee completion rates, exam pass rates and the success of graduates in securing employment.

The resources available for BTVET will be increased through the upscaling of income-generating activities of public BTVET institutions such as the sale of items produced during training, services such as car repair or running a restaurant, contract work such as construction, the sale of agricultural produce, the renting of facilities, the organisation of special courses, and the introduction of a training levy through a consultative process with employers and the business community to ensure that it is appropriate and efficiently managed. Currently, based on Education Management Information System (EMIS) data, income generated from the sale of BTVET products and services accounts for only 0.2–2.1 per cent of total expenditure. Experience in other countries such as Botswana suggests that up to about one quarter of total training costs can be recovered from income-generating activities. Apart from financial returns, income-generating activities can also link the institution better with local markets and stimulate a business culture. The resource base of the BTVET system needs to be increased and diversified. Depending on the type and level of training, annual unit costs of between 1.5 and 3.5 million UGX have to be calculated to deliver training at acceptable standards. Costs involved in non-formal basic level skills development are estimated at around 350,000 UGX for a three-month programme. A skills development fund (SDF) will be established to pool all public resources available for BTVET in Uganda including the income from the training levy, allocations from the public budget, contributions from development partners and other income. The fund will cover training, special support and development programmes and the new organisational set-up costs for BTVET management.

Development Costs

The major share of the development expenditure, 35 per cent during the first and 82 per cent during the second phase of the plan period, is earmarked for rehabilitating and strengthening the existing network of BTVET institutions (without agriculture), both public and private, preferably in partnership with leading technical institutes abroad and with the support of considerable international technical assistance. Development costs include the establishment of centres of excellence, the rehabilitation and expansion of physical facilities, the modernisation of equipment and workshops, staff development including overseas training of instructors, support to curriculum development and the development of training and learning materials, and management capacity building. The estimated costs also include the BTVET investment fund, which will allocate grants for institutional strengthening to public and private BTVET institutions on a competitive basis. It is expected that up to 40 institutions will receive grant support under the investment fund every year.

Funding Gap and Options for Closing It

Public resources to implement the BTVET strategic plan are estimated at 2,001 billion UGX or US$ 870 million divided into recurrent costs (55 per cent) and development costs (45 per cent). The bulk of development expenditure is earmarked for rehabilitating and strengthening existing BTVET institutions, both public and private, and for agriculture training (much of which will be borne by the Ministry of Agriculture, Animal Industry and Fisheries). About 40 per cent of the recurrent budget is earmarked for raising access and quality. About 433 billion UGX would be spent on capitation grants/bursaries to support school leavers attending formal BTVET programmes. Enrolment in formal BTVET is projected to increase from 42,000 to 103,000 trainees in 2019/2020, an annual growth of 10 per cent. Per capita funding will be raised gradually to ensure that training is provided at good standards. About 40 per cent of the formal BTVET trainees will receive public scholarships. Non-formal BTVET will be integrated permanently into the public BTVET portfolio. The plan allocates 160 billion UGX for non-formal BTVET. This is projected to increase enrolment in publicly sponsored non-formal training from 20,000 people in 2010/2011 to 40,000 in 2015 and 60,000 by 2016.

A substantial funding gap exists between requirements of the strategic plan and currently projected public expenditure under the revised ESSP (2010 Revision). For the first four years, corresponding to the current medium-term expenditure framework (MTEF), the funding gap amounts to 60 per cent of total estimated costs, 424 billion UGX. Options for closing the funding gap include increased public allocation to BTVET, an increased engagement of development partners, co-funding by other government sectors, and development of more cost-effective training delivery. Further, the strategic plan envisages the introduction of a training levy, which may become a significant additional revenue source for the BTVET system from 2015/2016 onwards. The current calculations exclude any potential proceeds from a levy. Priorities will have to be defined within the strategy should any gaps remain.

Options for closing the funding gap include increasing public budget allocation to BTVET through domestic and external borrowing and seeking grants from development partners and a contribution from international oil companies. Just over half of the estimated recurrent expenditure is required to expand enrolments in formal BTVET programmes (capitation grants, teacher salaries). Enrolment at fixed levels of public expenditure may be increased by channelling more funds through private BTVET providers, and by shifting parts of the BTVET supply towards cooperative (dual) training and enterprise-based training. The latter would require a dedicated approach to the policy of strengthening employer-based and dual training. The Strategic Plan envisages the introduction of a training levy, which may become a significant additional revenue source for the BTVET system from 2015/2016 onwards. Assuming that during the first phase of the plan period the post-primary seven (P7) programmes will gradually be converted into modular courses of one year's duration on average, the total intake at this level is expected to rise by 540 per cent. The expected increase is 220 per cent for BTVET at post-secondary (S4) levels and 185 per cent at post S6.

Monitoring and Evaluation

BTVET sub-sector monitoring has been weak. Yet thorough monitoring is an essential management tool to strengthen skills development. Systematic monitoring of BTVET outcomes will be introduced for the first time. A number of baseline studies will be carried out in the set-up of the monitoring system.

The Skilling Uganda interpretations of what the reform is about and where to go are widespread, and there is still a gap between the perceptions on the part of employers and the business community on the one hand, and the other hand with the officials in the Ministry of Education and Sports departments concerned, such as the BTVET Department and the Directorate of Industrial Training as the leading entities (Ministry of Education and Sports, 2011a). The perception is that training providers, companies and local authorities on the ground have had little voice in the process. If the two BTVET systems, the existing one and the new system laid out as a blueprint in the Skilling Uganda Strategic Plan, are compared, the key differences are as presented in the table below.

Table 9.1: Comparison of Old and New BTVET Systems

	Characteristics of the old model	Characteristics of the new model
1.	Supply-driven	Demand-driven
2.	No public-private partnership	Public-private partnership
3.	Policy and implementation are concentrated in the same hands/departments.	Policy and implementation are separated.
4.	The voice of the private sector, employers and trades unions is not systematically heard.	The private sector participates on all levels: 1) Policy formulation 2) Development of instruments and tools (programme development, training of trainers, certification, quality improvement, innovation) 3) Governance of public and private training providers
5.	Government funding, input financing	Government and private sector funding, output based financing

Universities and Technical Colleges

Since 1999, the Department of Geology and Petroleum Studies, Makerere University, has been offering a Master of Science degree in Geology by coursework and thesis. However, the ongoing Master's programme was started before the discovery of commercial petroleum reserves in the Albertine Graben and therefore does not adequately cover this discipline. In response, two years ago, a new undergraduate programme was launched, titled Bachelor of Science in Petroleum Geosciences and Production. The Department of Geology and Petroleum Studies also proposes to introduce a new Master of Science degree programme in petroleum geosciences by coursework and thesis the emphasis of which will be laid on various aspects of petroleum geology. This programme is intended to train geoscientists in Uganda and from the region to work in the emerging petroleum sector, taking into consideration the current global challenges. The areas of emphasis will include stratigraphy, structural geology, geophysics, geochemistry, sedimentology, environmental geology and fieldwork. Funding for teaching, learning and research costs will come from student tuition fees. The energy and petroleum (EnPe) scholarships fund supported by the Norwegian Agency for Development Cooperation (NORAD) is expected to provide start-up (seed) funds by sponsoring students (the first cohort of five students for two years and another cohort of five students for one year), equipping laboratories and library, and providing expatriate staff. The programme will be taught by the existing members of staff from other departments such as physics and MUIENR, as well as external sources such as the Directorate of Petroleum of the Ministry of Energy and Mineral Development and expatriates from the University of Bergen, Norway. As part of the EnPe project, a number of academic and technical Staff will undertake refresher courses in Norway to enhance their ability to offer some of the courses in the programme.

The Norwegian Petroleum Academy (NPA) has launched training programmes in Makerere University aimed at beefing up services to support the oil and gas industry when production starts. In 2015, Makerere University in association with New College at Nottingham University, United Kingdom, established the Cormac Vocational Training Institute to produce as many as 2,000 artisans and craftsmen annually. Mbarara University of Science and Technology under its Faculty of Applied Sciences and Technology has established the Department of Energy, Mineral and Petroleum Studies to offer Bachelor of Chemical Engineering, Bachelor of Petroleum Engineering, Bachelor of Energy in Petroleum Studies and Bachelor of Mineral and Mining Engineering courses. Ndejje University offers basic engineering skills, while Makerere University Business School (MUBS) BTVET Department offers certificate, diploma and degree programmes. However, at the present level of oil and gas industry development in Uganda, the petroleum contractors have advised that practical skills are vital rather than undergraduate/graduate university engineering and other programmes which focus on design and are not being absorbed by the industry.

9.5   Private Sector Contribution to the Provision of Relevant Skills Development in Uganda

The private sector is at the forefront of skills development in Uganda, the core framework of which consists of:
1.   Formal, private skills education and training institutions
2.   Internship training
3.   Non-formal sector skills development
4.   Corporate investment in employee skills development
5.   Private sector associations training programmes

9.5.1   Private Sector Role in Formal Skills Training

The mainstream skills development in Uganda is through the BTVET formal education system beginning with post-primary education and training (PPET) and includes tertiary institutions awarding certificates and diplomas as an alternative for school leavers who do not proceed on the main academic pathway through secondary school to university. A significant number of BTVET institutions are owned by private providers, and include private commercial training institutions, faith-based training institutions, training institutions run by NGOs, CBOs and projects. According to the Ministry of Education and Sports' Statistical Abstract (2011b), of the 189 PPET institutions 96 (51 per cent) are privately run. Indeed, of all the PPET enrolment, about 36 per cent is in private institutions. At the tertiary level, according to the National Council for Higher Education (NCHE), 86 of the 141 institutions are private and at university level, 31 of the 37 universities are private, enrolling 55,000 students (42 per cent).

9.5.2   Internship Training in Private Sector Enterprises

In the formal training system of skills development, internship is critical in providing an opportunity for hands-on experience in an authentic workplace environment and it is a compulsory requirement. Internship opportunities are sought in both public and private enterprises across the whole education system. Private primary and secondary schools support teacher training programmes through school practice placements. To illustrate this point, a review of internship placements for the Bachelor of Industrial Chemistry at Makerere University for the last two years reveals that 79 per cent of students did their internship in private companies.

9.5.3   Skills Development in the Informal Sector

The informal sector has a dominant share of economic activities in Uganda, covering mining, manufacturing, and commerce and finance sectors, among others. The specific activities include:
1.   the processing and vending of food,
2.   health care by traditional healers,
3.   the tailoring of garments,
4.   the manufacturing of furniture, and
5.   the repair of automobiles.

The size of the sector is estimated to account for about 42 per cent of gross domestic product (GDP). About 80 per cent of those employed in the informal sector are self-employed and less than 5 per cent of these have a post-secondary education. The common approach to developing skills in the informal sector is through non-formal training, largely by apprenticeship. Over 90 per cent of the officially recognised non-formal training institutions are government-run (Ministry of Education and Sports, 2011b). However, there is a large number of privately run, unregistered, small-scale non-formal training outfits which are part of the informal sector themselves. These are for short duration to fit the 'just-in-time' learning needs of trainees; the programmes offered often require limited investment in equipment and facilities and provide easy market entry and exit for the providers. The lack of standardisation and quality controls in this kind of training, the inadequate number of skilled craftspersons available to train apprentices, the fragmented and undocumented nature of the training that does not follow any qualifications and certification framework makes informal training ineffective.

Technical/vocational education in Uganda is very popular in non-formal settings. Non-formal and out-of-school technical and vocational education is taken to be an organised education activity outside the formal system. Many NGOs have vocational programmes for youth and adult learners throughout the country. They also have specific skill development programmes which are available through a number of delivery mechanisms. These non-formal training centres have been very effective in establishing links with employers, especially in the areas of financing and labour market information. By design they are inherently better able to offer short courses based upon occupational analysis, and to use part-time instructors from industry from well managed non-formal training centres, which have the demonstrated capacity for flexible response to a changing labour market. Private training providers of technical/vocational education are over 400, about three times the number of the government-aided technical/vocational institutions, and they provide short and long courses to the public. The informal sector consists of small entrepreneurs and casual workers involved in a wide variety of activities, such as craftwork, workshop production, service activities and commercial ventures.

9.5.4   Corporate Investment in Employee Skills Development

Corporate firms in petroleum and mining, manufacturing and service industries provide needed skills training for their employees to promote efficiency in their operations to achieve their goals. The training offered tends to be short-term and uses the firm's own skilled workers or engages external training consultants. In many cases, it is offered on-site in the form of apprenticeship, or offsite in instructional institutions. The focus is on key aspects in the development and management of businesses, corporate tax services, supply chain management, and marketing of their products.

9.5.5   Private Sector Associations' Training Programmes

The private sector is also contributing to skills development through their agencies and associations. This is in a bid to provide specialised skills to address the gap in skills availability, especially in managerial and technical areas. Examples of such agencies are enterprise and industry associations serving the formal sector, for example, the Uganda Manufacturers' Association (UMA) and Uganda Small Scale Industries Association (USSIA). USSIA's enterprise-based skills development programme (ESDP) in partnership with the Chamber of Skilled Crafts and Small Businesses Cologne is focusing on strengthening the entrepreneurial and technical capacity of its members, while the USSIA Vocational Qualification Programme (UVQP) – Worker's PAS is a programme implemented in partnership with the Chamber of Skilled Crafts and Small Businesses, Directorate of Industrial Training (DIT) and The Association of Uganda Private Vocational Institutions (UGAPRIVI) to validate the skills of the informal and formal sectors in Uganda through skills assessments which result in acquiring a Worker's PAS (Practically Acquired Skills) document. UVQP touches all the sectors of USSIA. USSIA is carrying out a programme for cottage training for business start-ups in all sectors. The associations' training departments offer short-term courses that develop critical skills in business management, including business plan development, strategic management, customer care, marketing and export management by their members (Uganda Small Scale Industries Association, n.d.).

The Private Sector Foundation Uganda (PSFU) and other business skills development and mentoring organisations such as TECHNOSERVE Uganda and the NEW VISION PAKASA initiative through which business training and advice to SMEs in entrepreneurship development is given need to be harmonised, standardised and certified by an internationally recognised arrangement. On the other hand, the Uganda National Chamber of Commerce and Industry (UNCCI) should be revived to execute its mandate.

9.5.6   Oil Companies' Contribution to BTEVT

Industrial Baseline Survey Findings
The 2013 Industrial Baseline Survey findings indicate that training in oilfield construction is best left to the Firm Foundations programme proposed by Tullow Oil (SBC, 2013). This programme is to set up a massive apprenticeship training scheme in association with the construction industry in Uganda to be conducted at Nakawa Vocational Training Institute and other selected Uganda Technical Colleges. The contribution of IOCs to BTVET seems to be fragmented and based on their corporate social responsibility (CSR) policies and strategies. They include sponsorship for BTVET, graduate and postgraduate training. International Oil Companies Tullow Oil, Total E&P, and CNOOC, the three oil majors in Uganda, in partnership with their governments, are all providing scholarships to Ugandans from all backgrounds for training locally and abroad in order to build the capacity of relevant government departments to handle oil and gas issues. There is a need to centrally coordinate and monitor oil company contribution to BTVET training in accordance with the Skilling Uganda programme, production sharing agreements (PSAs) and the Petroleum Act supervised by the Petroleum Authority of Uganda (PAU).

Policy Issues for Private Sector Contribution to Skills Development
In Uganda today there is no comprehensive, multi-sectoral government policy or consistent programme to encourage the private sector to invest in skills development. The Public-Private Partnership (PPP) for Universal

Post O'Level Education and Training (UPOLET) implementation is such an attempt, but it needs to be strengthened and focused. In the Skilling Uganda programme, as articulated in BTVET Strategic Plan 2012/2013–2021/22, there are plans to engage the private sector in skills development by supporting skills development centres and groups in terms of technical advice and access to funding. Through DIT, the Ministry of Education and Sports is also supporting skills development in the non-formal sector, which is largely private, under the Uganda Vocational Qualifications Framework (UVQF) for non-formal training. However, the impact of all these efforts is reduced by the absence of an articulated and comprehensive policy framework to encourage, direct and coordinate private sector participation in skills development. It is expected that the planned Skills Development Authority will provide for articulation of such a framework that cuts across sectors of social service provision, including education, labour, agriculture and trade. The other policy issue relates to the need for Government to recognise the cost of skills training as a legitimate social responsibility expense by companies, which should qualify for tax rebates. A policy that allows companies to deduct eligible training costs from their income for tax purposes or that provides tax credits for proven training expenses would go a long way in encouraging the private sector to invest more in skills development. Under such a policy, Government may come up with feasible incentives that subsidise the cost of companies investing in skills development.

The envisaged loss of tax revenue by such incentives could be recovered through a complementary measure that introduces skills training levies. Like in a number of Sub-Saharan African countries, a national skills training fund could be established from levies on business and personal incomes to finance the provision of skills training in both public and private institutions and to reimburse enterprises for the cost of skills training undertaken.

9.6   Conclusions and Policy Recommendations

The Government of Uganda has supported vocational education since independence in 1962, but until recently the proportion of expenditure has been extremely low, and thus the quality of vocational education has also been greatly affected. With significant attention now being given to education, the country faces enormous challenges from various aspects of the sub-sector, and because all these are being addressed simultaneously, the impact is slower than many people would like to see. Today, education is ranked amongst the top priority sectors of government. The mission of the Ministry of Education and Sports is to provide quality education, to eradicate illiteracy and to equip individuals with basic knowledge, skills and attitudes to exploit the environment for self and national development. With very strong political support, vocational/technical education faces an uphill task of developing the nation's workforce. It is blatantly clear that there is a dearth of skilled human resource in the Ugandan economy to meet the demands of the fledgling oil and gas industry. For many years during the production phase of the oil and gas industry, it is going to be difficult to satisfy the local content requirements of the petroleum laws and agreements.

Generally, Uganda's education system is not practically oriented. It is apparent that the BTVET system's capacity to deliver its intended objectives is lamentably weak. The current BTVET system is not in a position to cater for the present and future skills requirements of the petroleum industry in particular and the economy in general. Most BTVET providers do not refine their students to the required current and future skills needs. The training contains too much theory and too little hands-on experience. Reforming the BTVET system is an onerous task which must be handled seriously by all stakeholders through ongoing wide consultations.

In view of the fact that technical and vocational training is very dynamic and expensive, there is a need for strong institutional co-operation. Partnership with the private sector and all beneficiaries of education, especially joint strategic planning, will inevitably improve on problem identification, prioritisation of activities and, above all, achieve optimum utilisation of scarce resources. There is also a need to develop a vocational teacher development and management plan to address the current problem of both shortage and quality of vocational teachers. The quality of education and training depends a great deal on the ability of institutions to adjust the content of training to meet changing skills needs. This is especially important in training for strategic occupations that are rapidly changing under the impact of new technology. A multi-disciplinary approach is necessary, involving professional groups and representatives of industry and general educators as well as the teachers of technical and vocational education.

Furthermore, there is a need to continuously sensitise the population about the importance of technical and vocational education and attract not just leftovers from academic education but first-class students who can impact on technological innovations and economic development. In addition, the public needs to be made aware that not everyone can go to college and that university education is not the only way to success in life. There are other ways to win (Gray and Herr, 2006). And, finally, there is serious need to assist institutions practically to integrate business and entrepreneurship skills into technical and vocational education and build their capacity for income generation. Institutions should operate units to supplement their incomes. The excessive dependence on central government funds stifles the initiative of students, teachers and school administrators and they do not take advantage of their local communities and local talents to generate income to supplement government funding (Okou and Humphrey, 2002).

Uganda is a nascent oil nation. The education system therefore needs to be strengthened in terms of compliance with oil and gas certification requirements and on-the-job practical training. The existing institutions need to be more oriented on O&G qualifications in order to match the oil industries' requirements. Focus should be on the technicians and not the engineers available in number. Emphasis should be put on the training of skilled people, the reinforcement of the oil and gas certification process and supporting the educational system by reinforcing the best academic institutions already in place and by founding a training centre to develop qualified technicians. The Government of Uganda and the oil and gas operators need to support the educational system in Uganda since most institutions are too far from international O&G standards in terms of skills required. Oil and gas operators should target their support to the best existing institutions in Uganda. Yet, given that Uganda's development approach is private-sector led, it is pertinent that the role of the private sector in skills development is adequately recognised, coherently planned for and deliberately promoted in the development of national policies and programmes. The contribution of IOCs to BTVET seems to be fragmented and based on their corporate social responsibility policies and strategies. There is a need centrally to coordinate and monitor oil company contributions to BTVET training in accordance with the Skilling Uganda programme, Production-sharing agreements and the Petroleum Acts supervised by the Petroleum Authority.

References

Gray, K., and E. Herr (2006), *Other Ways to Win: Creating Alternatives for High School Graduates*. Thousand Oaks, California: Corwin Press.

Ministry of Education and Sports (2011a), 'Skilling Uganda – BTVET Strategic Plan 2012/3–2021/2'. Kampala: Republic of Uganda.

———— (2011b), 'Uganda Education Statistical Abstract 2011'. Kampala: Republic of Uganda.

National Council for Higher Education (2007), 'The State of Higher Education and Training in Uganda 2006:   A Report on Higher Education Delivery and Institutions'. Kampala: Republic of Uganda.

Okinyal, H.F. (2006), *Status of BTVET in Uganda*. Lilongwe: UNESCO.

——— (2012), 'Reforming the Business, Technical, Vocational Education and Training (BTVET). Sub-sector: Challenges, Opportunities and Prospects'. Paper Presented at the Uganda Vice-Chancellors' Forum (UVCF). Retrieved from: http://trustafrica.org/en/publications-trust/ workshops-and-convenings?download=262:reforming-the-business-technical-vocational-education-and-training-btvet-sub-sector-challenges-opportunities-and-prospects.

Okou, J. E., and H. Humphrey (2002), *Meeting the Challenges of Technical/Vocational Education: The Ugandan Experience*. Pennsylvania: Penn State University.

Ongode, B., and F. Nalubega (2014, 5 August), 'Petroleum Institute Receives Third Intake, Introduces New Courses'. *Oil in Uganda*. Retrieved from: http://www.oilinuganda.org/ features/social-impacts/petroleum-institute admits-third-intake-introduces-new-courses.html.

Rauner, F., and R. Maclean (2008), *Handbook of Technical and Vocational Education and Training Research* (Vol. 1). Dordrecht: Springer.

SBC (2013), Industrial Baseline Survey Report. Prepared for Total E&P, Tullow Oil and CNOOC. Kampala, Uganda: Schlumberger Business Consulting.

Ssekika, E. (2013, 14 May), 'Kigumba Graduates Can't Find Oil Jobs'. *The Observer*. Retrieved from: https://observer.ug/business/79-businesstopstories/25279-kigumba-graduates-cant-find-oil-jobs.

The Republic of Uganda (2010), National Development Plan (2010/2011–2014/2015). Kampala: Republic of Uganda.

——— (2015), Second National Development Plan (NDPII) 2015/2016 –2019/2020. Kampala: Republic of Uganda.

Uganda Small Scale Industries Association (2019), 'Technical Skills Upgrade'. Retrieved from: http://www.ussia.or.ug/index.php?page&i=58.

PART III

OTHER MAJOR GOVERNANCE POLICES AND CHALLENGES

10
Environmental Sustainability: An Afterthought or a Key Objective for Uganda's Oil Sector?

Moses Isabirye

10.1   Introduction

Oil discovery in Uganda, now ranked the fourth largest crude oil reserve in sub-Saharan Africa (IMF), presents not only an opportunity to fix the country's economic deficiencies but also the need to manage pollution challenges. Recovering 1.2–1.7 billion barrels of oil from crude oil deposits of 6.5 billion barrels will require considerable infrastructural developments that among others include: the construction of roads, railway and pipeline network, an air field, a refinery, and a 1444 km pipeline with a capacity of 200,000 barrels per day to Tanzania. Consequently, the oil sector presents an environmental challenge in the areas of chemical pollution, climate change, resource and energy depletion, and the loss of biodiversity and ecosystem integrity.

Focusing on the environment, Uganda's regulatory system is well documented with good intentions to sustain the environment, albeit with the occurrence of gaps and weaknesses that limit the citizenry in fully exercising its informal hand in getting the regulatory system to work where environmental challenges exist. Section 52(3) of the National Environment Act, 1995 stipulates that waste originators shall minimise waste through the treatment, reclamation and recycling of waste materials. As reflected in the various policies, regulatory systems and planning documents, the national desire is to create fundamental changes that prevent pollution and promote sustainable development.

The challenges faced by state agencies like the National Environmental Management Authorities (NEMA), the Uganda Wildlife Authority (UWA), the National Forestry Authority (NFA) and Fisheries in implementing environmental regulations are a pointer to inadequacies in existing regulatory systems to regulate potential environmental problems associated with the petroleum industry. The objective of the current chapter is to assess the adequacy of the existing environmental regulatory systems in regulating potential problems associated with the upstream oil and gas activities in Uganda.

10.2   Environmental Factors Related to Upstream Petroleum Activities

The Albertine Rift area is biodiversity rich and recognised globally as a bio-diversity hotspot with a variety of birds, mammals, amphibians and reptiles accommodated in protected areas such as forest reserves, community wildlife reserves, wildlife reserves and national parks (National Environmental Management Authorities [NEMA], 2010; 2012). The soils in the Albertine Rift are highly permeable and fragile with low resilience when exposed to agents of soil degradation including buffering against oil spills. The advent of petroleum activities has been described by UNESCO as incompatible with the Albertine Rift, also home to a quarter of the World's mountain gorillas (Vision Reporter, 2015).

It is evident that petroleum-related issues are generally increasing over the years, with business issues leading and closely followed by societal interest that largely focuses on welfare (see Table 10.1). It is noteworthy that although the focus on environmental issues is currently low in importance they remain key determinants of sustainable development of the oil and gas sector.

Seismic reflection techniques used in hydrocarbon exploration are associated with dynamite explosion that may disrupt animal patterns of feeding, breeding and communication, including relocation to other areas. Furthermore, exploration activities clear vegetation cover with consequent habitat disturbance, species loss, and accelerated soil loss with consequent long periods of plant recovery (NEMA, 2012). The oil development and production phase will be associated with vegetation clearing, earth movement, the influx of both vehicle and human traffic and subsequent urbanisation with likely devastation of the environment. Moreover, in the production phase, oil spills destroy ecosystems and kill biodiversity that includes birds, mammals, fish; the relocation of birds, destruction of breeding sites, disruption of migratory birds, destruction of their natural waterproofing and insulation against bad weather and sometimes death are the disasters faced by birds (NEMA, 2010).

In Nigeria, oil spill contamination of the topsoil has rendered the soil in the surrounding areas 'unsuitable for plant growth by reducing the availability of nutrients or by increasing toxic contents in the soil'. Gas flaring has also been associated with reduced crop yields and plant growth on nearby farms,

Table 10.1:   Petroleum Issues in Newspapers (2000–2016)

Issue	Valued Ecosystem Component (NEMA, 2012)				
	Aquatic Ecosystems [17]	Terrestrial Ecosystems [11]	Pollution Issues [9]	Society [76]	Business [112]
Legislation	10	3	2	10	8
Environment	5	6	5	3	2
Capacity	1	1	1	29	3
Equity	1	1	1	13	4
Business				8	87
Compensation				4	
Food production				2	
Private sector				3	
Recruitment				1	
Revenue				2	

Source: Author's analysis data on data drawn from *The New Vision* archives. Available at: www.newvision.co.ug.

and disruption of wildlife in the immediate vicinity (Trade Environmental Databases [TED], n.d.). Oil spills are also associated with poisoning by lead and barium through contamination of drinking water by oil spills triggered by political instability and civil wars (New Vision, 2016). In addition to causing lung cancer, gas flaring is also known to cause global warming and acid rain with the consequent destruction of trees and fish in acidified lakes.

10.3 Environmental Regulation Within the Framework of Petroleum Activities: The Stakeholders

The provisions for sustainable management of the environment are enshrined in a range of environmental acts, including most notably the 1995 National Environmental Act; the 1998 Land Act,; the 2003 National Forestry and Tree Planting Act, the 1997 Water Act; the 2001 Uganda Wildlife Act, the 1951 Fish Act and the 2013 Petroleum Act. The environmental Acts are operationalised through related regulations and guidelines supported by a legal framework and institutional structures (see Table 10.2). Working through a harmonised system, environmental Acts, regulations and institutions are expected to ensure a clean and healthy environment which is every citizen's responsibility.

Table 10.2:   An Overview of Stakeholders in the Oil and Gas Framework

Institution	Category	Levels	Interests	Who influences them?	What do they want?	What motivates them?
Parliament	Legislature	National	Good governance	Executive Citizenry	Sustainable oil extraction	Inadequate regulatory system
Cabinet	Govern-ance	National	Money in the treasury	Citizenry	Business model mgt	Inadequate development
Court	Judiciary	National	Functional regulatory system	Executive	Arbitration	Inadequate interpretation of the laws
NEMA	Agency	National	Healthy environ-ment	Executive Parliament	Compliance to regulations	violation of the environmental statute
Petroleum Authority	Agency	National	Blessed & Equitable oil	Executive Parliament	Sustain-able oil production	Unsustainable oil production
Citizenry	Citizen	National	Income; Royalties	Executive Parliament	Equitable oil benefits	Evictions, misappropriation of funds
Companies	Business	National	Profit	Executive Parliament	Fair investment	Peace, good prices and tax holidays
Academia	Academics	National	Teaching, Research	Executive Parliament Companies	Opportu-nity to do research	Contribute to sustain-able petroleum development
Civil Society Organiza-tions	Watch dog	National	Blessed & Equitable oil	Citizenry Executive	Equitable oil benefits	Evictions, misappropriation of funds

Oil is a highly valued resource with the potential to create resource management-related conflicts that cut across social, economic, administrative and political boundaries. The responsibility for the management of the oil resource is shared between the Government, the Petroleum Authority, the national oil company and the oil refinery company. The institutional arrangement is complex with conflicting roles and responsibilities that may hinder the effective implementation of stakeholders at local, district and national levels. Since conflict of interest is likely to affect the effectiveness of the regulatory system, stakeholder analysis that will identify areas of conflict and suggest mitigation measures is necessary. By delineating what agencies do and interactions among them, it will be possible to minimise conflicts that might impede the functioning of environmental regulatory systems.

The working of government through the administrative law has a major influence on the environmental regulatory system, and therefore the sustainability of the environment in relation to petroleum activities. It is therefore important to understand how the tripartite model of Ugandan government works in relation to environmental regulations, i.e. originating, regulating, implementing and financing. The Government of Uganda works through Parliament, the executive and the judiciary.

10.3.1 The Parliament

The Parliament of Uganda, in view of its mandates and functions, has a major influence on the environmental regulatory system, and therefore the sustainability of petroleum activities. Parliament, by working through the committees on natural resources, has the opportunity to influence agencies to operate according to their statutory mandate. Parliament has powers to amend the statute and perform oversight for agencies and agency officials, and apply sanctions such as the reduction of budgets. Furthermore, parliamentary appropriation of more funds to address an environmental concern at hand can greatly motivate the performance of agencies.

10.3.2 The Executive

The power of the executive is vested in the President of Uganda, who is responsible for implementing and enforcing the laws written by Parliament and also appoints the Cabinet. The implementation of the laws is done by ministries and related agencies. The executive controls the appointment process wherein a relevant minister appoints the top agency official. The budget is largely shaped within the executive before moving to Parliament for approval.

10.3.3 The Judiciary

Headed by the Chief Justice, appointed by the President, the judiciary is one of the three arms of the Government of Uganda charged with the responsibility to oversee justice in the country. The Constitution of the Republic of Uganda, Article 126(1), spells out the mandate of the judiciary: 'Judicial Power is derived from the people and shall be exercised by the Courts established under this Constitution in the name of the people and in conformity with the law and with the values, norms and aspirations of the people' (see Republic of Uganda, 1995). The judiciary has the core role of promoting the rule of law and contributing to the maintenance of order in society in Uganda. Its functions focus on administering justice through resolving disputes between individuals, and between the State and individuals.

The courts are the arbiters of the meaning of a particular statute or constitutional provision (see Republic of Uganda, 1995). What an agency can or must do is what the courts in interpreting the statutory or constitutional provisions say it can or must do. The judiciary may reverse an agency's decision or remand it to the agency for further consideration if it finds that the agency has violated any of these sources of the law, including adherence to the originating statutory mandate, adherence to its own rules and procedure, and adherence to the Constitution.

10.3.4 The National Environment Management Authority

The National Environment Management Authority (NEMA), a creation of the National Environmental Act, 1995, has a statutory mandate to manage the environment through coordination, monitoring and supervision of environmental activities. While it is everyone's duty to maintain and enhance the environment, NEMA has a statutory responsibility to enforce environmental regulations that may involve court actions. An Environmental Police Force unit was established to consolidate the enforcement mandate. NEMA, a leading environmental agency, spearheads environmental sustainability initiatives in the oil and gas sector. Section 10 of the Petroleum Act provides for the authority's cooperation with ministries, departments and agencies of government with related duties, aims or functions. This provision facilitates the consistent implementation of all regulatory systems related to environmental management. As such environmental activity gaps arising from orphaned mandates or roles will be minimised or avoided altogether.

NEMA uses established environmental protection standards to monitor changes in environmental quality by comparing with data from waste originators who are obliged to publish relevant data on environmental quality and resource use. The polluter pays principle is upheld where there is need for compensation and the covering of costs related to pollution by waste originators. Furthermore, a refundable performance deposit bond is levied to act as security for good environmental practice. The refund is made where

Table 10.3: Stakeholder Analysis of Power in the Context of Environmental Impact

Institutions	Parliament	Cabinet	Court	Agencies	Citizenry	Companies	Academia	CSO
Goals	3	4	0	7	3	3	3	5
Direction of influence	5	5	3	2	0	6	2	5
Legal mandate	5	6	4	7	3	2	0	1
Human resources	3	3	1	7	0	5	4	5
Technical know how	3	2	1	7	0	6	5	4
Management capacities	5	3	0	7	0	5	2	4
Acceptance by population	4	3	5	2	7	0	1	6
Financial resources	5	7	4	2	0	6	1	3
Logistics	3	2	1	5	0	7	4	6
Commitment	5	4	1	7	2	2	1	6
Power/capacity	41	39	20	53	15	42	23	45

the operator has observed good environmental practice to the satisfaction of the authority.

NEMA is recognised as the principal agency responsible for environmental management within the petroleum sector. Therefore, NEMA has a statutory mandate to issue licences in consultation with the Petroleum Authority of Uganda. Accordingly, NEMA originates (NEA, section 107) regulations that are statutory instruments to the operationalisation section, section 52(3), that would manage and minimise waste during the production, transport, storage, treatment and disposal of waste arising out of petroleum activities.

10.3.5 The Citizenry and CSOs

While the Government holds petroleum rights on behalf of and for the benefit of the people of Uganda, it is everyone's duty to protect and improve the environment. The citizenry has the responsibility to ensure that petroleum activities do not violate their rights to a clean and safe environment with

Table 10.4:   Government Institutional Roles and Conflict Identification

Institution	Ministry	Oil unit	Mandate
Parliament	Justice	Absent	Originator of agencies; grant new powers and responsibilities; performance review; do amendments; budget control; makes regulations
Cabinet	Justice	Absent	Exercise control over agency decision making; control the appointment process; possibility of interference where interest differ; budget control; regulate the use of land; hold in trust and protect natural resources;
Supreme Court	Justice	Absent	Interpretation and arbitration of the statute, enforcement of regulations; supervisory jurisdiction
NEMA	Water & Envt.	Present	Manage the environment; coordinate, monitor and supervise activities in the field of environment; evaluate EIA; clear EIA expert; protect resources; make regulations and policies; coordinate policy implementation; originate legislative proposals, standards and guidelines; promote public awareness about environmental issues
UWA	Water & Envt.	Present	Make regulations and policies
NFA	Water & Envt.	Present	Control and monitor industrial and mining developments in Central Forest Reserves; authorise industrial and mining activities in forest reserves; make regulations and policies
Fisheries Dept.	MAAIF	Absent	Make regulations and policies;
UIA	Finance	Present	Management and control of investment related activities
Oil Companies	Finance	Present	Oil and gas production
Universities	Education & Sports	Present	Capacity building in the oil and gas sector
Local Govt.		Absent	Delegated custody of natural resources;
Citizen			Manage and use land according to the Forest Act, the Mining Act, the National Environment Act, the Water Act, the Uganda Wildlife Act;
Petroleum Authority	Ministry of Energy and Mineral Development	Present	Monitor and regulate petroleum activities including reserve estimation and measurement of the produced oil and gas
Uganda oil refinery company	Ministry of Energy and Mineral Development	Present	Subsidiary of national oil company

Institution	Ministry	Oil unit	Mandate
National oil company	Ministry of Energy and Mineral Development	Present	Manage Uganda's commercial aspects of petroleum activities and the participating interests of the State in the petroleum agreements
Uganda Petroleum Institute	Ministry of Education	Present	Capacity building in the oil and gas sector
Uganda National Bureau of Standards (UNBS)		Present	Development of standards for the petroleum sector
The Civil Society Coalition on Oil and Gas (CSCO)		Watch-dog	A platform where organisations working in the petroleum sector can share information, work together for synergy and strategise for joint advocacy on oil and gas matters

functional ecological and aesthetic services. As primary beneficiaries, all efforts should be focused on satisfying the needs of the citizenry. The citizenry should ensure that petroleum activities are sustainable, to the benefit of the public. The right of oil workers and the citizens in general to know the environmental hazards associated with oil production should be protected. Combined with the agency's effort, their voice forms a political and legislative social pressure that can trigger legislative decisions to the benefit of the workers and citizenry.

10.4 Stakeholder Analysis of Power in the Context of Environmental Impact

The analysis of power for institutions affected by the petroleum activities was based on a pair-wise matrix comparison of the institutions for each of the following elements of power: goals, direction of influence, legal mandate, human resources, technical knowhow, management capacities, acceptance by the population, financial resources, logistics and commitment. It is clear from Table 10.3 that government agencies are the most 'powerful' institutions, closely followed by CSOs, Parliament, companies, and the Cabinet. Courts and academia are trailing the list with the citizenry at the tail end. The citizenry is the key beneficiary in environmental regulation and should therefore be at the forefront of checking the performance of the other stakeholders. Government agencies derive their power from their legal mandate, availability of human resources, technical knowhow, management capacity and commitment. Ideally, these government agencies are viewed as watchdogs and are highly respected by the citizenry. However, their autonomy and effectiveness are undermined by the fact that cabinet can control them through budget controls.

10.5   Government Institutional Roles and Conflict Identification

The legislation provides for the authority's cooperation with ministries, departments and agencies of government with related duties, aims or functions (see Table 10.4). This provision enables consistent implementation of all regulatory systems related to environmental management. As such environmental activity gaps arising from orphaned mandates or roles will be minimised or avoided altogether. However, there is a need to monitor closely the functional relationships between NEMA and the petroleum authority, and the petroleum authority and its subsidiary companies, the national oil company and the oil refinery company.

10.6   Challenges of Uganda's Regulatory System

Statutory agencies are created to operate as independent entities and therefore expected to make environmental decisions independently. However, this independence is vulnerable to interference and eventual conflict, as there are cases where agencies' directions will differ from the executive's position. The executive asserts considerable control over agency decision making and much of the influence is likely to stem from the appointment and budgeting process. The top agency officials are appointed by the Minister. Occasionally, the executive also makes informal directives that restrain technical agency officials from enforcing regulations. Consequently, this erodes the citizenry's confidence in the working of the agencies. It further curtails the enforcement of regulations meant to ensure sustainability.

The independence of Parliament is also doubted as the executive, who are members of the ruling party, can influence parliamentarians to make decisions that favour the government position which may be against the integrity of the environment. Further, the courts are expected to operate independently and shall not be subject to the control or direction of any person or authority. The judiciary focuses on administering justice by resolving disputes between individuals and between the State and individuals. The courts are the arbiters of the meaning of a particular statute or constitutional provision. Yet, the courts are also vulnerable to interference by the executive which appoints the top judicial officials. Therefore, courts may not arbitrate fairly in an environmental case where the executive has interest with a direction that puts environmental integrity at stake.

A court can correct an agency's action only when the case is taken through the judicial system to an appropriate court. In a situation where both the executive and Parliament are adamant, justice is limited as an inadequately empowered disgruntled citizenry has a fear of courts, let alone the dreaded legal liabilities that come when a defendant loses a case. It also requires time and effort for a case to go through the judicial system to an appropriate court, say a Constitutional or Supreme Court.

While the citizenry is largely ignorant and not empowered to seek court redress against violators of the environmental statute, the critical citizenry mass may not be realised as areas where the drilling for petroleum is carried out are desolate because of migrated families and the occurrence of the national game parks. Furthermore, the citizenry's voice must rise above the short-term political imperatives and therefore the need to ensure that strong social actors emerge (Kasita, 2013). Who can stand in the gap and become a citizenry voice in a situation where state agencies, the judiciary and even Parliament are not independent and liable to political interference? These interferences are at all levels of governance.

According to Karkkainen (2001), a knowledgeable community is necessary for risk reduction. The citizenry can deploy a variety of costly, disruptive and, therefore, frequent countermeasures, including boycotts, adverse publicity, court actions or the threat of them, and political pressure on regulators and elected officials to enforce existing regulatory standards, enact new requirements, or exercise discretionary governmental authority against the offending firm. But there is a hurdle to achieving Karkkainen's observation in Uganda as the social divide between the lower- and middle-class citizens does not enable the use of costly measures to have their demands met.

Civil society organisations (CSOs), either individually or as a consortium, have pressured the authorities in various ways to act positively, but their effort has not yielded much. CSOs cannot achieve much as their very existence, including registration, monitoring and renewal of registrations, is owing to the executive, making them a vulnerable lot too. As such, CSOs exert limited pressure compared to the citizenry who, given their voting power, can wield tremendous political and legislative pressure on elected officials and regulators to enforce standards or enact new regulations. Largely uneducated, poor and ignorant of its rights, the citizenry is powerless and not likely to act. By empowering the citizenry, CSOs strengthen the community's informal hand to cause enforcement of regulations and relevant legislative amendments by the authorities.

Information management is a key element of environmental management wherein the obligations of the licensee, worker and citizenry are spelt out to ensure safety, health, environment and welfare. Whereas the polluter is obliged immediately to inform NEMA of the discharge of hazardous substances, chemicals, oil, etc. into the environment, information submitted about activities for which a pollution licence is required is proprietary in nature and treated as confidential. It is doubtful, given the current secret nature of managing petroleum activities, that the freedom to access this information can be exercised in situations where extensive pollution threatens environmental integrity.

10.7   Conclusions and Policy Recommendations

According to the 1995 Constitution of Uganda, every Ugandan has a right to a clean and healthy environment (see Republic of Uganda, 1995). The 1995 National Environment Act further empowers and encourages Ugandans to participate in the development of policies, plans and processes for the management of the environment. The Ugandan Parliament also has a crucial role to play in this regard. Although the Ugandan Parliament has on paper an influential position with respect to the development of environmental legislation, it is nonetheless dependent on the executive (in particular the President), which controls a lot of resources and can greatly influence the performance of individual members, and hence their re-election chances. It is further a sobering observation that so far, from an environmental point of view, the Ugandan Parliament has not been effective in legislating and monitoring the oil and gas sector. Similarly, statutory environmental agencies are vulnerable to interference and eventual conflict, as in most cases the direction favoured by the executive has differed from the position of the environmental agency. Moreover, the executive is known to make informal directives that restrain technical agency officials from enforcing regulations. Consequently, this erodes the citizenry's confidence in the agencies and further curtails the enforcement of regulations meant to ensure environmental sustainability.

Although environmental challenges are currently low in importance, they remain key determinants of sustainable development of the oil and gas sector. It is, therefore, vital to explore ways in which these challenges can be addressed before oil exploitation and production really takes off. A crucial policy recommendation to ensure that environmental laws and regulations are effectively monitored and upheld is the establishment of a legal non-partisan body of stakeholders, who will ensure that the oil sector will develop in a transparent and environmentally responsible way. Such a body could be constituted by representatives of academia, the religious sector, the traditional leaders, the elders' forum and NGOs. Such arrangements to ensure transparency have positively contributed to the effective monitoring of the oil sector in countries such as Ghana, Chad and Alaska among others (Shepherd, 2013). The envisaged body could promote the right to know and be informed to an extent where communities are empowered enough to challenge pollution originators in and outside courts. The independence and non-partisan nature of this body will also enable close monitoring of the effectiveness of the multi-institutional management of oil resources. Furthermore, the body can promote the establishment of a statutory institution that certifies waste management plans, access to waste production inventories and supervision of waste management. Such institutions, semi-voluntary or voluntary in nature, must be able to solicit support from Government or other key stakeholders, be specialised, focused and independent and be able to do impact research and also verify records of 'source' facilities.

References

American University (2019), TED (Trade Environmental Databases) case studies. Retrieved from: http://www1.american.edu/ted/ogoni.htm.

Government of Uganda (1995), The National Environmental Act, Cap 153. Retrieved from: https://www.wipo.int/edocs/lexdocs/laws/en/ug/ug019en.pdf.

––––––– (2013), The Petroleum (Exploration, Development and Production) Act, 2013 Acts Supplement No. 3, Acts Supplement to The Uganda Gazette No. 16 Volume CVI dated 4 April 2013. Entebbe: Uganda Printing and Publishing Corporation.

Karkkainen, B.C. (2001), 'Information as Environmental Regulation: TRI and Performance Bench-marking, Precursor to a New Paradigm?', Georgetown Law Journal, 89, 259.

Kasita, I. (2013, 12 February), 'Debate on Oil Must Move Beyond Politics', The New Vision. Retrieved from: https://www.newvision.co.ug/new_vision/news/1314139/debate-oil-politics-uk-report.

Ministry of Energy and Mineral Development (2008), National Gas and Oil Policy for Uganda. Kampala: Republic of Uganda.

National Environment Management Authority (NEMA) (2010), Environmental Sensitivity Atlas for the Albertine Graben. Kampala: NEMA.

——— (2012), *The Environmental Monitoring Plan for the Albertine Graben 2012–2017*. Kampala: Republic of Uganda.

New Vision (2016, 4 March), 'S. Sudan Oil Production Pollution "Threatens Thousands"'. Retrieved from: http://www.newvision.co.ug/new_vision/news/1418694/ssudan-oil-production-pollution-threatens-thousands#sthash.RQA6aUVN.dpuf.

Republic of Uganda (1995). Constitution of the Republic of Uganda. Kampala: Republic of Uganda.

Shepherd, B. (2013), *Oil in Uganda: International Lessons for Success*. London: Chatham House, The Royal Institute of International Affairs.

The New Vision (2015, 15 March), 'Gorillas vs Oil: DR Congo Seeking Way to Explore at Virunga Park, 2015'. *The New Vision*. Retrieved from: https://www.newvision.co.ug/new_vision/news/1322371/gorillas-vs-oil-dr-congo-seeking-explore-virunga-park.

11

Land Grabbing in the Albertine Graben: Implications for Women's Land Rights and the Oil Industry in Uganda

Roberts K. Muriisa and Specioza Twinamasiko

11.1   Introduction

The discovery of commercially viable oil deposits in Uganda in 2006 brought a lot of optimism about the contribution of this new discovery to the development of the country. Optimistic voices have claimed that the discovery of oil will transform Uganda from a low into a middle-income country by 2030, and into a high-income country by 2040. Moreover, some people have even claimed that 'Uganda is on the verge of becoming an OPEC powerhouse' (Bategeka *et al.*, 2013). According to Bategeka *et al.* (2013), these predictions are especially promoted by politicians who have a populist's approach to politics, where leaders want to maintain themselves in power by overselling the expected benefits of the country's oil wealth. The popular argument is that oil proceeds will finance the national budget, liberate Uganda from donor dependency and boost investment in the development of infrastructure such as roads, health, education and recreation. At the local level, the argument is that oil revenues will boost the districts and free them from dependence on the central government.

However, the optimism with which this discovery was associated fell short of reality when people in the oil-rich region of the Albertine Graben began facing evictions from their land. Some of them were even forced to live in internally displaced people's camp (IDP)-like conditions.[1] With more than 200 people evicted from their land to pave the way for an oil refinery in Kabaale, the initial hope and optimism of getting employment and a decent life from the oil industry quickly dissipated among local communities. In

---

1   http://www.observer.ug/business/38-business/38987-oil-rich-hoima-struggles-to-solve-the-land-question.

addition to land being lost to oil exploration and development, there are reports that speculative land acquisitions have increased sharply. This also affects people's livelihoods and may transform into conflicts which in turn may affect the oil industry in the long run.

Little academic work has examined the land-grabbing phenomenon in Uganda and its consequences. Much of the land-grabbing literature is on the 'green grab' (see, for example. Fairhead, Leach and Scoones, 2012), with justifications of the 'green', food and biofuels as necessitating land grabbing because of the expanse of land involved in agriculture and less focus on 'black grabbing'. We argue that the manner in which the Government acquired the land for oil exploration as well as the speculative investments and land acquisitions by individuals in the Albertine Graben after the discovery of oil in 2006 needs to be studied.

Since 2006, the Government has embarked on the construction of the oil refinery which is expected to sit on approximately 29 square kilometers. Because of the oil refinery and the preparation for this refinery, which involves extensive infrastructure development, there is a lot of oil-related activities, which have affected the livelihoods of many people in the Albertine Graben. Apart from the oil-related developments, there is competition for land in this region by speculators who hope to gain from appreciations in land prices.

In this chapter, we explore the processes of land grabbing as a result of oil exploration and exploitation in Uganda in the districts of Buliisa and Hoima. We examine the nature of land grabbing related to oil discovery, the drivers of land grabbing, and the resultant outcomes of land grabbing. In this regard key questions raised and answered in this chapter are as follows: what is the nature and the process of land acquisitions? What are the resultant conflicts in the oil rich region of Uganda? How has land grabbing impacted on women's rights? What are the implications for the oil industry?

11.2   Methodology and Theoretical Framework

The discussion in this chapter is based on data collected in Buliisa and Hoima, existing literature and government reports.[2] We carried out field research in the villages of Bukona, Nyamasoga and Kyapolani, all in the Hoima district.

---

2   Data for this chapter were gathered as part of a VLIR project entitled 'Oil Wealth and Development in Uganda: Prospects, Opportunities and Challenges' and the preliminary findings of the Baseline Survey for the PhD project by Specioza Twinamasiko, entitled 'Oil Discovery and Compensation: Conceptualizing the Risks and Vulnerabilities for Women'.

These villages were purposely selected because of their close proximity to Kabaale Parish, where most people, especially those still awaiting compensation/relocation, lived. It is also the area where speculative land grabbing has taken place on a large scale and where the prospective oil refinery is planned to be constructed. We conducted a large number of in-depth interviews with local residents—a majority of whom were women—in order to understand the contestations over land and how their lives have been affected by the oil discovery in their region. Interviews were also held with civil society organisations as well as community leaders. In-depth interviewing was preferred because of the flexibility it allowed in getting more data through the detailed probing of respondents.

In this chapter we are guided by a political economy approach to understand land grabbing. Further, land grabbing in the Albertine Graben can be positioned in the wider debates about land grabbing where capital accumulation and capital gain for economic development are called upon to justify appropriations of land. Appropriation involves the transfer of ownership, user rights and control over resources that were once publicly or privately owned (Fairhead *et al.*, 2012), by expelling the existing claimants (presumably a small investment) in the interest of large investment.

Using a political economy approach, one is able to understand the complex mix of formal and informal institutions that shape individual and group behaviours and State responses to these behaviours. The approach helps us to understand the policy processes and how they have shaped the land question in the Albertine Graben. The nature of legislation on oil and gas, land laws and how they evolved, and how they have impacted on land ownership, acquisition and compensation are all understood within this framework. The African Union observes that the colonial legacy of land-acquisition processes combined with the rush for land for energy and food production opened Africa to a new form of scramble for Africa, and recommends that countries must put in place policies and legislation for the avoidance of risks of losses of land by the poor, or at least to get proper compensation for land in case it is taken away (Wisborg, 2014). In addition, the political economy framework helps us to understand how different groups and individuals exploit policy weaknesses for their own benefit. We argue that the land question in the oil-rich region has largely been shaped by the weaknesses in the enforcement of the land law, weaknesses that have been exploited by land grabbers. The masses who hold customary land for example are insufficiently informed about the formal process of owning land. And those who grab land from people are not prosecuted.

11.3   Conceptualising Land Grabbing

Land grabbing connotes a process in which land is acquired using fraudulent means. The process may be direct; i.e. a situation where previous landowners are forced to sell their rights and are evicted with little or no compensation (Muriisa, Mbabazi and Twinamatsiko, 2014). It may also be in the form of restricted access to land on which community livelihoods depend as a source of food (such as farming and grazing lands), fuel wood and water. These lands, which Willy (2010) argues the community holds an undivided share in due to their nature as woodlands/forests, rangelands/pasturelands and marshlands, are most at risk of involuntary loss to land grabbing. Land grabbing may also take an indirect form, where people are made to sell their land rights without actually realising that they have sold their rights to the land. Here people are made to sign documents which are drawn up to support the claim to the land by the land grabber. This may take place when people agree to the terms of the land sale or to move from land upon promises of compensation and benefits such as employment, service access and revenue/profit-sharing (Muriisa *et al*, 2014). Critics such as Kachika (2010) argue that such deals cannot amount to land grabbing, because such deals are legal and negotiated between people who consent to being compensated for their land and/or decide to voluntarily leave their land. It has to be noted, however, that a lot still remains unanswered with regard to the information people possess, the size of the compensation, the process of compensation, the value of the land and property on it, and the level of involvement in negotiating the compensation. Article 237 of Uganda's Constitution vests land ownership in the hands of the people and Article 26b(i) of the Constitution stipulates that the compulsory taking of possession or acquisition of property is done under the guidance of law and requires prompt payment of fair and adequate compensation prior to the taking of possession or acquisition of the property.[3]

It has to be noted that land negotiations in the current period are often made secretly between the Government and investors without allowing local people to participate in the negotiations, not even to negotiate their right to continued access and utilisation. In some instances, negotiations are made between middlemen who purport to represent certain people. In all cases,

---

3   The Government of Uganda is proposing to amend this Article by proposing to compulsorily take over land before compensating owners by depositing the amount of money it presumes to be fair for land it wishes to acquire in the event that there is contention over the adequacy of compensation by the land owner.

whether indirect or direct, land grabbing affects people's land ownership and livelihoods.

11.4   History of Oil Discovery in Uganda

Land grabbing in the Albertine Graben can be placed in the history and the process of exploration of this natural resource. The commercial oil exploration in Uganda started in the early 2000s, although the discovery of oil goes as far back as the early 1900s (Miriima, 2008). Following the confirmation of the presence of oil in early 1980s, Uganda introduced legislation regarding oil exploration and exploitation. What is important in these explorations and legislation for this paper is the manner in which exploration and legislation were carried out, and the influence on land grabbing.

The exploration lacked the transparency it deserved. It was largely 'underground' and hidden, with no popular discussions and limited provision of information to people in the region. With the confirmation of the existence of oil in the region, the Government enacted the Petroleum Exploration Act in 1985 which made petroleum and oil recognised by Government as special minerals different from other minerals. Miirima (2008) claims that the investment code created in 1991 was crafted to attract foreign investors to invest in the oil sector since it required heavy investment. The 1985 legislation was followed by the Petroleum and Oil Exploration Act,[4] which became the first formal and institutionalised way of looking at oil in Uganda, by gazzeting this important resource and other minerals as solely owned by the Government, although the land above these minerals belonged to the people. We argue that the discovery of oil opened the doors to large investments and a rush for land acquisitions by speculators who hoped to benefit from compensations for land. All these factors promoted land grabbing in the Albertine Graben region, which in turn made many residents lose their land.

11.5   The Nature of Land Grabbing in the Albertine Graben

Exploring the nature of land grabbing in the Albertine Graben indicates that land grabbing takes various forms and the process of land acquisition fulfils almost all the conditions for land grabbing. There are outright violations of

4   http://www.ulii.org/ug/legislation/consolidated-act/150 29/09/2016 [what does this date signify?].

land rights, there is limited information on the land acquisition and takeover, and there was limited participation in the process of land deals by local people. In addition, the forms included forcible take-overs followed by evictions, dubious dealings, and 'compulsory acquisition' – appropriations of public lands by Government in the public interest, as provided for under Articles 237(26) of the Constitution. The different forms of land grabbing are discussed below.

11.5.1 Appropriation of Public Lands

Most of the land where oil reserves are held in Hoima and Buliisa is public land. Mainly it is the national park, and along the shores of Lake Albert, and therefore protected public land. People evicted from these lands were illegal occupants (the Balalo) and migrant Congolese who had also settled in Buliisa. Land grabbing also involves public lands which may be given out by Government to foreigners at a give-away price or no price at all. Most lands in Buliisa was acquired through lease of land to oil, but in a special way by paying compensation for actual properties on site using district compensation rates (Muriisa et al., 2014). Most of the lands acquired are in national parks where people have been depending for survival on pasturelands and sources of fuel wood and medicinal plants.

11.5.2 Fraudulent/Dubious Land Deals

In Buliisa, the claim by land grabbers is that they bought the land. But investigations show that the people land grabbers claimed to have bought from either do not exist or never owned land. In an interview with the local council chairman of Kasenyi where the Kasemene oil well belonging to Tullow oil company is located, it was revealed that when the community land was sold there was no involvement of the community, but people who had previously settled on the land are said to have sold the land, and attempts to investigate the sale by communities were met with hostility and violence since land grabbers, who were mostly absent landlords, were supported by government operatives to prevent the repossession of land by local residents (Muriisa et al., 2014).

11.5.3 Forceful Evictions

Since 2006, the Government has been preparing the ground for the oil refinery to be located in Kabaale parish, Hoima district. In order to pave the way for the construction of the refinery, people were to vacate the land. The Government was responsible for compensating them for their property to enable them get another decent living. People were to choose either money and to look for their own place to go to, or to be relocated to a place chosen by the Government. In this case there emerged four groups; those people who refused the compensation because they felt the compensation process was not fair and their property was not given its true value and so they refused to move; those who agreed to be relocated and were waiting to be relocated; those who agreed to be compensated and had not yet been compensated; and those who were compensated and had vacated the land. Importantly, many people were dissatisfied with the amount as well as the procedure for obtaining compensation for their land. The compensation was often delayed and, in the meantime, people were not allowed to use their land for agriculture; i.e. their main source of livelihood. The Africa Institute for Energy Governance (AFIEGO) helped to lodge a case in the High Court of Uganda on behalf of the people waiting for their compensation. Even with a court case pending the Government was not moved and AFFIEGO had to step in and assist those who accepted the meagre compensation to acquire land and establish themselves in decent housing. As noted by AFIEGO (2014) in this respect:

> ... in addition to the case, we supported those who accepted the inadequate compensation to use it to begin a new life. We sensitized them on how to utilize their compensation and also provided legal protection to women who were being denied by their husbands to be signatories to the bank accounts in which the compensation funds were to be paid (AFIEGO, 2014, p.12).

11.5.4 Drivers of Land Grabbing in the Albertine Region

Unlike the green grab, which is driven by land for agriculture and carbon control, the 'black grab' is largely influenced by large capital gain from investment. In both cases, however, the facilitators of land grabbing are local economic and social conditions. In what follows we discuss facilitating conditions for land grabbing.

11.5.5 Land Tenure System

Land tenure refers to the complex relationship among people with respect to land and its resources. According to Rugadya (1999) land tenure security is the individual's perception of his/her rights to a piece of land on a continual basis, free from imposition or interference from outside sources, as well as the ability to reap the benefits of labour or capital invested in land, either in use or upon alienation. The tenure system defines how land rights are assigned and who has access to the land or the rights of use. Uganda's 1995 Constitution recognises four types of land tenure systems in Uganda: i.e. Mailo, leasehold (public), freehold and customary land tenure systems, and the Land Act, 2010, as amended, provides how tenure, particularly the customary system, can be secured. Interestingly, a majority of Ugandans are ignorant about how the land tenure system operates. It is this ignorance that land grabbers have exploited (Muriisa *et al.*, 2014).

The majority of the land in the oil-rich region of the Buliisa and Hoima districts is customarily owned. This may not be surprising as customary land accounts for 85 per cent of land in the country (Government of Uganda, 2001, p.34). This is because the 1995 Constitution repealed extant legislature, notably the 1975 decree, which had vested ownership of all land on the state.[5] Land holding in Albertine Graben in Buliisa and Bunyoro is customary. Control and distribution are vested in the hands of local council chiefs and elders in the area (Byakagaba and Twesigye, 2015), unlike the areas in the northern region where the control of land, although individualised, lies in the hands of the clan heads (Mabike, 2011). The Land Acts, 1998 and 2010 (as amended) provide that proof of ownership of land under the customary land tenure system shall be the possession of a certificate of registration. The Constitution of Uganda, Article 237(4a), provides that people may apply for a certificate of ownership of land but does not oblige them to do so, and this makes them vulnerable to land grabbing. Indeed, much of the land grabbing, especially by speculators, has been a result of this individualised land ownership in the region and lack of registration of customary tenure.

It has long been thought that customary tenure and authorities are inadequate in protecting tenure. In the Albertine Graben the distribution of power and wealth is affected by the land-holding position of community members. On the one hand the long-time settlers in the Albertine Graben have depended on the customary land tenure holding system with limited control, since no one has formally registered his/her customary rights. On the other hand, the elite group who are now driving out the former residents of the Albertine Graben region are able to do so because they have registered land in their names and acquired title to land. Possession of a land title is the only legal claim that one can show as evidence of owning land since titling and privatising guarantee land security and the protection of rights to land (Cousins, 2002).[6] Cousins' arguments resonate well with World Bank arguments for promoting agrarian

---

5   The 1975 land decree which had declared all land to be public land was largely denounced by the Constitution, and this returned land in Bunyoro and Buliisa to customary holding.

6   This can, however, be challenged depending on how the title was acquired. In the Albertine Graben region, land titling has been largely fraudulent. Recently 14 titles to land in the oil-rich region were cancelled

reforms and the formalisation of property rights (Deininger, 2003). It should however be noted that titling might contribute to inequality and exclusion, decrease security of tenure for women, and disregard communal rights as well as the variety of rights of different people to the same property. In a system where pursuing land rights is expensive and the poor dominate, the poor are on the losing side even when law supports their claim. The Constitution allows the conversion of customary land into freehold. But, besides a lack of knowledge not only of the process of conversion but also the Constitution, the process itself is expensive and unaffordable by most people (Muriisa *et al.*, 2014), and therefore most of the lands in the Bunyoro region remain predominantly customary.

With the increased rush for land in the Albertine region for speculative purposes, the existing land tenure has clearly contributed to land grabbing. The region has been affected by land grabbing because the tenure system is weak and does not provide proper ways of formal individual ownership. As indicated earlier, the current legislation (see, for example, Article 237(1) of the Constitution of Uganda as well as the Land Act of 1998) provides for the existence of four types of land tenure in Uganda. Among the four types of tenure ownership and the claim of ownership of land is proven by possession of land title, except for customary tenure where ownership is acquired by simple registration.

The aim of making it possible for customary rights to be acquired by 'simple' registration was to make land ownership a less complicated procedure, and it was envisaged that it would enable customary landowners to acquire secure land rights without having to follow the cumbersome procedure of land titling as in the other three alternatives. Moreover, the legal requirements of surveying and stone marks were not a requirement for this. However, the law does not provide proper channels through which the certificate may be acquired, and people are not sensitised to the process of registering their customary rights. It is worth noting in this respect that both the Constitution of Uganda and the 1998 Land Act have not been widely disseminated to the people of Uganda (Stickler, 2012).

The powerful elites including government officials (Kwesiga, 2016), the Government and large investment farms have illegally taken over land which formerly belonged to people in some parts of the Bunyoro and Buliisa districts where most oilfields are found, leaving people who formerly occupied these lands without land.[7] The land taken over is not well compensated for because of the lack of land titles and where it is located. The cancellation of 14 land

---

7   According to this reporter, one of the 14 land titles which had been acquired illegally belonged to a former First Deputy Prime Minister in the NRM government.

titles acquired illegally in the Albertine Graben is testament to this assertion (Kwesiga, 2016).

In Buliisa, most oil exploration sites are located in the national park and its surrounding areas and many local residents have already been evicted from these areas. Buliisa residents have petitioned the Government to allow them access to the 56-square mile piece of land from which pastoralists were evicted (Mugerwa, 2012). This land comprises block 2 in the Albertine Graben where Tullow Oil Uganda has registered oil discoveries. The land, which was fertile for cotton and food crop production, belonged to the native Bagungu who no longer have access to the land since it was sealed off by police (Mugerwa 2012).

11.6   Land Governance, State, State Institutions and Land Grabbing

Land governance considers policies, processes and institutions by which land, property and natural resources are managed. It involves putting in place the most efficient ways of administering land issues, and includes decisions on access, land rights, land use and planning, making investment decisions as well as legislation on land, land management, secure tenure and the transfer of land rights. It is the processes and structures through which decisions are made about the use of and control over land, the manner in which the decisions are implemented and enforced, and the way that competing interests in land are managed (Deininger, 2003). Legislation on land defines ownership rights and creates means through which land can be transferred. Central to land legislation is the role of the State and state institutions responsible for implementing the legislation. In what follows we discuss the manner in which legislation has aggravated land grabbing in the Albertine Graben. The manner in which land legislation is implemented, including sensitisation, providing for possible conflict resolution and quick response to conflict, influences land grabbing. Lack of legislation and poor implementation of legislation aggravate land grabbing. Land grabbing may thus be aggravated by state institutions either directly or indirectly. As Borras *et al.* (2011, p.30) have noted:

> Stepping back, and looking at the bigger picture, there emerge three broadly distinct but interlinked areas of state actions that are relevant in understanding contemporary land grabs, namely, 'state simplification process', assertion of sovereignty and authority over territory, coercion through police and (para) military force to enforce compliance, extend territorialisation, and broker for private capital accumulation. First, in

order to administer and govern, states engage in simplification process to render complex social processes legible to the state. The creation of Cadastre, land records and titles are attempts at simplifying land-based social relations that are otherwise too complex for state administration (Borras *et al.*, 2011, p.30).

The institutionalisation of land ownership is a first step that enables land grabbing. This is largely seen through poor/weak land laws or poor implementation of the would-be good land laws. Weak land laws facilitate grabbing by providing loopholes which land grabbers exploit to grab land. In essence the law provides an enabling environment for land grabbing. In Uganda, while it is stated by the Constitution that land belongs to people, there are other legislations such as the Acts for mineral and oil exploration and exploitation which indirectly indicate that the people after all have limited control of land.

In consideration that the exploration and mining of oil would require land, there has been legislation to guide exploration for and exploitation of oil. While care has been taken to minimise the impact of oil exploration and mining on the people resident on land, there is no doubt that licensing these companies to explore oil lead to mass displacement of people.[8] This is either indirectly by oil spills and the pollution that is generated by oil drilling or directly by acquiring land for exploration. Direct displacement takes place through either buying or forced displacement. It should be noted that it was not envisaged that oil exploration would generate related land conflicts and land grabbing and human rights challenges (the subject of this chapter), and therefore there was no proper preparation for addressing these challenges. This is evidenced by various pieces of legislation that were drawn up to guide petroleum exploration in the pre-colonial and post-colonial period until 2014. For example, it is an irony that the Petroleum Act of 2013 stipulates that people shall continue using the land surface for grazing and cultivation. How can this be if oil is exploited underneath and oil infrastructure has to be developed without interfering with exploitation? It should be emphasised that the legislation concerning oil exploration was

8   The national oil and gas policy for Uganda 2008 (6.1.1) provides that people should be compensated for land acquired for oil exploration, infrastructure development and mining. The Petroleum Act, 2013 (135) restricts the licensed oil companies from exploiting people and undermining people's rights, and directs that people's interests should be taken care of in the process of oil exploitation and development. Cap 136(1) of the same Act provides that people shall continue using land for grazing and stocking and cultivation as long as the activities do not interfere with oil exploitation and mining.

more concerned with oil-petroleum 'theft'[9] rather than human rights, and thus the legislation lacked a human face. The concentration was on the protection of oil as a national resource rather than the effects that the oil would have. Moreover, the legislation of the time considered only land title as granted by Government and Government was given express control of land where oil resource would be discovered. For example, Chapter 48 of the 1949 Mining Act (section 2), states

> The entire property in and control of all minerals and petroleum in, under or upon any lands or waters in Uganda are and shall be vested in the Government, except insofar as the property and control may in any case be limited by any recognition of title or express grant (Republic of Uganda, 1949).

And the 1985 Petroleum and Oil Exploration Act states that:

> Without prejudice to the exercise of any right under this Act, the property in, and the control of, petroleum in its natural condition in or upon any land in Uganda is vested in the Government on behalf of the Republic of Uganda (Republic of Uganda, 1985).

And defines who will explore oil thus:

> No person shall carry on any exploration or development operations on petroleum in or upon any land in Uganda except under, and in accordance with, a license issued under this Act (Republic of Uganda, 1985).

It should be noted however that the later legislation and policies including Uganda's 1995 Constitution and the oil and gas policy 2014 put the human face into mineral and land dealings. Ironically, the human face in the legislation is eroded as has been alluded to and as will be shown in later discussions, since the legislation that is supposed to protect people is used to advance land grabbing. The 1995 Constitution and the national oil and gas policy created optimism over land ownership. Chapter 15 of Uganda's Constitution is dedicated to land and the environment, and in its opening statement it states that land belongs to the people (Article 237(1)). Uganda's Constitution places ownership of land in the hands of Ugandans and recognises four

---

9   There are outcries that the mining and exploration of oil in Uganda has remained secretive and largely less than transparent.

land tenure systems under which land is held. The Constitution defines the rights and powers of a lawful occupant and *bona fide* occupants. The Constitution further defines the Government's position on land ownership and shows that the Government's ownership of land is limited to the rivers, lakes, wetlands, forest reserves, game reserves, national parks and any land to be reserved for ecological and touristic purposes for the common good of all citizens. Article 244 of the Constitution provides that all minerals and petroleum on or under any land or waters in Uganda are vested in the Government on behalf of the people of Uganda. This Article does not in any way contradict Article 237; rather it reinforces the fact that for Government to own this resource people who formerly owned land (Article 237) should be compensated before Government can mine its minerals and oil from land where it is found.

The 1998 Land Act also provides for easy access for everyone interested in land (including Government), provided that the landowner is adequately compensated for his/her land or the use of it. Ironically a law that is supposed to allow easy access has made it impossible for everyone to have equal and protected access. Instead the loophole in the law opens up vast lands for direct or indirect grabs (Muriisa *et al.*, 2014; Rugadya, Nsamba-Gayiiya and Kamusime, 2008). It is these loopholes that open up the Albertine Graben for grabs. Moreover, Sticker (2012) and Deininger *et al.* (2011) argue that countries with weak land laws open up land for grabs.

11.7   State Organs and Operatives

The role of the State is to serve and protect the citizens. This is made possible by the use of state organs, the police, the judiciary, and the military and other state institutions. The other role of the State is to invest and to attract investment. In essence, serving and protecting citizens and attracting state or private or foreign investment in the country are aimed at sustaining the lives of the people, which is one of the cardinal goals of development (Goulet, 1995). The two goals, however, have produced different outcomes which have negatively impacted on the lives of the people they are supposed to sustain.

With regard to state institutions, instead of protecting citizens there is increasing evidence from studies such as Muriisa *et al.*, 2014 and Rugadya *et al.*, 2008 that institutions of the State such as the police and the military, and in some cases the judiciary, have instead served the interests of land grabbers and not protected people. In Mubende District, it is alleged that state agencies including the military evicted 401 families to clear land for the occupancy of Kaweri Coffee Co. Ltd to start its operations in 2001.[10] In Buliisa, where this study is positioned, it is alleged that the police were instrumental in facilitating land grabbing by harassing and beating up people who protested at land takeovers by investors (see Muriisa, *et al.*, 2014).

With regard to investment, the increasing role of the State in attracting foreign investors partly opens up land for potential land grabbers as a result of the positive provisions for the 'investors' to access land easily. According to the Uganda land policy:

> The Government of Uganda has a duty to attract private investment both domestic and foreign, into productive sectors of the economy. The duties include creating an enabling investment climate, as well as facilitating investors to access land (Ministry of Lands, Housing and Urban Development 2011, p.7).

As already mentioned, the legislation over oil and the creation of an investment code allowed the attraction into the oil sector of investment by foreigners due to the heavy capital investment required in this industry.

11.8   Impact of Land Grabbing on the People of Buliisa and Hoima

When we interviewed people on what was compensated and how compensation for land was determined, it was indicated that if one had a land title the compensation was higher compared to when there was no land title. In other cases, some people were not compensated because of the lack of titles and because the land occupied was considered public land (national park and water bodies). In one of the villages on the shores of Lake Albert, a respondent interviewed said thus;

> I was made to leave my land together with my family so as to give way for oil drilling I received compensation for the crops on land, my house, but not for the land because I held no land title and certificate of ownership

---

10   See in particular 'Complaint against Neumann Kaffee Gruppe under the OECD Guidelines for Multinational Enterprises (2000)–Request to the German National Contact Point (Federal Ministry of Economics and Technology) to initiate the procedures for the solution of conflicts and problems in the implementation of the Guidelines'. See also: https://www.business-humanrights. org/en/kaweri-coffee-part-of-neumann-gruppe-lawsuit-re-forced-eviction-in-uganda.

and in the process someone came with a land tittle claiming it was his land. Therefore, the compensation I received was not enough to enable me construct a new home (Key informant in Kasenyi, personal communication, November 2015).

In other areas such as Rwamutonga where oil waste is managed, people were evicted without compensation (Paulat, 2014).[11] The matter is with court and people live in camp-like conditions.

When the matter was taken to court, it was ruled that we negotiate with government, we are doing that but the matter is not being settled. Our people have been frustrated and they are living a hopeless life (Local leader in Kabaale, Hoima, personal communication, November 2015).

There are claims that residents felt that they were made to sign agreements which they did not understand since they were written in English, and there were no mechanisms for interpreting the contents of the agreements. Some women claimed they did not know what they were signing, while others thought they were signing land use and access agreements, yet they were sign-ing for compensation for destroyed crops (Uganda Human Rights Commis-sion – UHRC, 2013). The Government and the compensation-implementing agency deny the claim and that people have not received compensation and are directing them to vacate without further notice.[12]

In other areas people were compensated for land and property taken away, although this compensation was not enough for the property, since the valu-ation of property and assets was done by a government-appointed valuer who in some instances overlooked some property. Moreover, compensation took too long to arrive. For instance, by 2014 people had not received compensation even though the valuation exercise had ended in June 2012 (Uganda Human Rights Commission – UHRC, 2013). It was against this background that the Africa Institute for Energy Governance (AFIEGO) advised residents to file

---

11   Evictions were conducted by a McAlester company, having paid a rich man who owned a land tittle and was the one who received compensation. About 1,000 hectares previously occupied by about 700 residents were cordoned off and residents were denied access to their gardens (https://reliefweb.int/report/uganda/land-eviction-breeds-violence-oil-rich-hoima-uganda, accessed on 9 September 2019). The Land Act stipulates that before evictions or transactions on land, the *Bona fide* occupants must be adequately compensated.

12   http://ugandaoil.co/2014/10/refinery-site-residents-abandon-farming-as-they-await-oil-compensation-money/, accessed on 17 November 2016.

a case against the Government in the High Court of Uganda demanding immediate and adequate compensation:

> ... on 28th March 2014, led by AFIEGO, some residents of Kabaale parish, Buseruka sub-county, Hoima district affected by the refinery sued government for violating their right to timely, fair and adequate compensation for the loss of their property (AFFIEGO, 2014, p.10).

It should be noted however that the Government denied any wrongdoing including unfair compensation and denying people access to and use of land before compensation (Ssekika, 2016). The Government's denial of wrongdoing contradicts many media reports of the poor compensation and other injustices suffered by people in the oil-rich Buliisa (see, for example, AFIEGO, 2016a). The media reports are further supported by AFIEGO (2016c) which notes thus:

> Families which refused compensation in the refinery project on grounds that it was low have not received compensation yet. Additionally, 93 families with over 465 members which opted for relocation have not been relocated yet despite the cut-off date for use of land in the refinery area having been put on June 2, 2012 (AFIEGO, 2016c, p.3).

It should also be noted that for those who were compensated, the compensation was neither a negotiated nor a bargaining process. What was to be compensated for was predetermined by the contracted organisation (Strategic Friends International) and the government valuer. Many properties were not compensated for according to their owners' expectations; there was no compensation for animals, some pieces of land were left out of the compensation, not all crops were compensated for as expected. A respondent who settled in Kigaga parish, when asked whether all her properties were compensated for, had this to say:

> No. there are three pieces of land that were left out (approximately three hectares). When I asked, they told me for us we have already finished the work and we cannot go back; some crops were left out, these people came already determined to pay what they wanted not what we had, we were asked to show our gardens and for them they picked what they wanted, some mango trees were not counted, for example if one had 5 trees, they counted 3 and 2 left out; I had a garden of sugarcane but only for trees were

counted and not the whole garden (Key informant, personal communication, November 2015).

UHRC (2013) also found similar complaints that people were never consulted in the process of valuation to determine the true worth of their properties. The appointed government valuer never considered what residents were getting from mango trees and cabbages were undervalued at shillings 200 compared to the market value of 2000 shillings. Indeed, an interview with one former resident of Kyapoloni now residing in Buseruka Trading Centre awaiting relocation, when asked to say what was compensated for and the value of the compensation, revealed:

> Banana plantations, pineapples, maize and bean gardens, but they never paid for my fruit trees. Each banana plant was valued at 4000, maize garden 120,000 and pineapple 500 (Key informant, personal communication, November 2015).

Asked about the adequacy of the compensation, it was indicated that this was not enough and that there was a lot of inequality in the compensation:

> How can you compensate someone's garden of beans, maize at just 120,000 irrespective of the size the garden? This was unfair (Key informant in Buliisa, personal communication, November 2015).

In addition to the disappointment with compensation for the physical land, people felt that the compensation for land could not be worth the attachment they had to the land. Moreover, the value was based on land as a physical asset, but often the social implication of relocation was not determined. The importance of land is recognised by the Government. It is considered a basic resource in terms of the space it provides, the environmental resources it contains, and the capital it generates. It is an asset that can be traded and is important for national identity as it provides symbolic meaning for the nation and the people living on the land. It also 'influences spirituality and aesthetic values of all ... societies' (Ministry of Lands, Housing and Urban Development, 2011). Given this huge importance accorded to land, taking it away from people in any form creates insecurity, not only in terms of food but also pride, and psychological stress. Land is used as a burial ground, and people when relocating leave these grounds behind. The attachment to burial grounds and abandoning them cause psychological distress and emotional stress since memories and remembrance are part of human life which cannot be erased. Moreover, in cases where people were given money to transfer graves, exhume and transport the remains of their loved ones, they claimed that the Uganda shillings 200,000 which was paid was not enough (UHRC, 2013).

11.9   Land Grabbing and Land Disputes

Disputes over land use and access continue to escalate in the Albertine Graben. The land tribunals which had been put in place to assist the justice system were suspended in 2006, leaving a big gap in the land conflict resolution system, especially as the formal justice system lacks the capacity to handle a large number of cases. The court system is expensive for most local people and this has also undermined the justice system as regards land dispute resolution. It should be noted that while the State is supposed to protect its citizens, the State has delegated its responsibility; for example, the Government hired a consultant—Strategic Friends International Ltd—to take over the valuation of and payment of compensation for land, and the relocation process of people affected by the oil refinery. The organisation has not done much to educate people on the land compensation process, and land that is eligible and ineligible for compensation. The situation has culminated in a number of land-related disputes ranging from contestation over compensation to outright confrontation between locals and the Government (in the form of mass protests), and between locals and the investors.

The other dispute over oil discovery is related to revenue-sharing between the Bunyoro kingdom and Government. The relations between Bunyoro kingdom and the central Government over revenue-sharing are souring day by day. The policy that considers revenue-sharing ignores the traditional leadership in the area. According to the Oil and Gas Revenue Management Policy (MFPED, 2012), 7 per cent of all royalty revenues are to be set aside for sharing between local governments and the communities directly affected by the oil and gas mining. It is not clear what 'communities' mean here. Moreover, it was not specified beforehand how the sharing between communities and local government would be done. The assumption could be that the 7 per cent share is used by local communities to develop themselves by way of the construction of community infrastructure such as roads, health centres and schools, to mention just a few. However, it should be noted that the people of Bunyoro, especially the kingdom, expect more. That the kingdom should benefit from oil is a matter that should not be ignored. Uganda, although not having a federal system of governance, respects the functioning of local cultural institutions as long as they do not engage in partisan politics, as provided for in Chapter 246 (3e) of the Constitution of Uganda.

11.10   Land Grabbing, Land Rights and Women's Livelihoods

Land grabbing has a negative impact on all people, but for the vulnerable groups such as women and children, who largely depend on land for their livelihood, the situation is worse. Land is a source of women's livelihoods and survival; they grow food and it is a means through which they can provide for their families. These common lands have the most insecure tenure; they are often considered by Government to be wastelands, and therefore are given away to outside investors (Behrman, Meinzen-Dick, and Quisumbing, 2011). Giving away or limiting access to these lands undermines women's source of livelihood and their welfare. Women depend on these lands for collecting firewood, water, fodder and medicinal plants necessary for a healthy living for them and their families.

Apart from common lands, women derive their livelihoods from family land to which, although having no rights of control and disposal (Jacobs, 2009), they have access rights and from which they can produce food and get vegetables. In the African tradition, the woman should provide food for the family. Having rights over land increases women's economic strength and ability to bargain, both in and outside the household. In addition, women can access services such as financial, maternal and family planning and maternal health care services. Jacobs (2009) provides three basic reasons why land rights are important for women: equity, welfare and efficiency. Taking rights to land away from women denies them the ability to be efficient in decision making and the right to welfare. The 1998 Land Act states that any decision made on customary land according to the customs or traditions that denies women access to ownership, occupation or use of any land, violates the rights of women. Section 39 of the Act give all spouses the right to security of occupancy of family land and requires the consent of the spouse for transactions in family land (Republic of Uganda, 1998). In spite of these provisions, it should be noted that, as in most African countries, in Uganda women's rights are largely limited to access, and other rights such as control, as well as disposal and use, are held by men. As a result, women were never fully involved in the process of negotiating land deals and compensation for land. Most women, when asked about their involvement in the negotiation and valuation of property, intimated that the men were the ones involved and that they were never consulted. The compensation money was deposited in men's accounts and they could do anything with it, including taking on second families (marrying new wives, often abandoning the old one) without involving women.

Reports indicate that the involvement of women in compensation negotiations was minimal (AFFIEGO, 2014), a situation that put women at a risk of losing their husbands to young women. Media reports indicated that women have not been involved in the compensation process and that some men, after getting compensation, had to marry other wives while others left their families completely.

> Our men were ok when they were still poor but after getting money, they forgot about us, my husband married another woman whom we have to share everything we have… I have lost everything including my husband who was like a brother to me before oil discovery (Key informant, personal communication, November 2015).

A key informant corroborated the above evidence and said, 'some women are still here, they have nowhere to go, their husbands left them' (Local Council Chairman, Nyamasoga, personal communication, November 2015). It was found that the welfare of many women was affected by the oil discovery and exploration most especially after the compensation was received. In the first instance there was family unity with strong relationships between men and women before compensation was paid. Men and women used to work together, even on the farm. But as the compensation was paid out to men, this was followed by social disunity in many households. Many men either left their wives or married others and became polygamous. Many women were affected because they were not given opportunities to be part of the agreement when receiving compensation. According to available sources, there was no provision for spousal consent in documents to be filed before compensation was paid out, and bank accounts opened for the compensation process were largely registered in the names of men (Ongode, 2015). It should be noted that the compensation was to be either in the form of cash or to buy and relocate people to the new places. Those who received cash, especially in Kabaale where the oil refinery was to be built, have already left the place. Those who were to be relocated have waited for relocation and the matter is taking too long. Some women have been abandoned by their husbands in this process and have remained behind. For those women who are abandoned by their husbands and not yet relocated, the challenges are many, ranging from failure to tend their gardens as they are not allowed to plant to fear of being raped by strangers since the place they live is almost abandoned, many people having left. In Kabaale Kitengwa, an interview with a respondent who is a woman village leader revealed:

> When the exercise was just starting they promised to care for the vulnerable like women, children and disabled. They also promised to train women with hands on skills to help them use the money from compensation very well, none of these came as promised. Men have married other women and have left us with children alone. We are not progressing in any way, nobody cared about us. We are being raped by strangers because the area is empty and bushy. Girls and other children no longer go to school because of fear to let them move alone. Our children have no future because they are not being educated (Woman Village Leader, Kitengwa village, Personal communication, November 2015).

The above is supported by Global Rights Alert (2015) which reports that many people awaiting compensation are faced with the challenge of broken-down institutions such as schools and water systems, surroundings of bush as many people have left the area and a threatening future for them and their children. Some of the parents withdrew their children from school awaiting compensation, while others forced them into early marriage (Uganda Human Rights Commission-UHRC, 2013; AFIEGO, 2016b).

11.11 Implications for the Oil Industry

The immediate implication of the above for the oil industry in Uganda is delayed oil exploitation and mining. As indicated above, people have resisted moving from the land where the refinery is to be located. Until these people move, the mining of oil cannot start. The implication of not giving a specific share of oil proceeds to the kingdom of Bunyoro is that a conflict between the kingdom and the Government of Uganda can cause paralysis in the mining and exploitation of oil. Throughout the world there are a number of examples; Sudan, and now southern Sudan and Nigeria, where control of oil resource has resulted in civil war and/or armed conflicts leading to a halt in mining the resource. Ross (2004) posits that discontent among local communities about the extraction of oil leads to civil war. This hypothesis postulates that grievances among local communities over land appropriation, the failure to provide jobs, social disruptions and environmental hazards lead to civil war. In the previous discussion, we have already indicated that the people of Bunyoro are discontented about their land, and in Muriisa, Mbabazi and

Twinamastiko (2014) it is argued that there is limited contribution to creating job opportunities by way of the oil extraction. While Ross (2004) found no evidence linking grievance and civil war, it is not unlikely that grievance may lead to political crisis. Uganda recently experienced a political crisis in the Kasese region where the King of Rwenzulu expressed discontent and wanted to secede from the republic of Uganda.[13]

The last expected implication of land grabbing for the oil industry is the disruption of the flow of oil in the pipeline. As already discussed, oil exploration and exploitation in the Albertine Grabben have led to the internal displacement of people from the lands on which their livelihood depends. The likely implication of this is that the people, especially the youth, will probably start looting the oil in order to survive by disrupting the pipeline once it has been laid to carry unprocessed crude oil to the refinery. In Nigeria, oil theft and vandalism are the biggest crimes the oil industry is facing, and these result in massive loss of both crude oil and revenue (Ogunleye, 2016). It is further indicated that many of these crimes began as economic crimes. With the oil displacements in the Albertine Graben with no immediate economic benefits it is likely that once the pipeline is finally laid it will face vandalism.

11.12 Conclusions

The discovery of oil in Uganda brought a lot of optimism that oil would bring development. Ironically the initial stages of oil exploration and preparation for its extraction and processing has led to desperation and despair among the highly optimistic and expectant Ugandans. In particular, the discovery has led to land takeovers and the displacement of people brings the phenomenon into the discourse of land grabbing. This paper has examined how Uganda's oil discovery has led to land grabbing with particular emphasis on the nature of land grabbing related to oil discovery, the drivers of land grabbing, the impact of land grabbing on people's land rights, particularly women's, and the implications for the oil industry in Uganda.

From the discussions presented, the paper concludes that land grabbing in the Albertine Graben is real and is manifested through government takeover and the grant of concessions of public lands to investors through forceful evictions and dubious dealings. The drivers are many, but given their manifestations we conclude that the drivers of land grabbing in the Albertine

---

13   This matter is in court and it cannot be discussed any further in this paper until the courts resolve the matter.

Graben are the result of institutional failure, ranging from poor institutions and laws to the failure of institutions to protect people. Uganda's move to amend Article 26b(i) of the Constitution will do nothing but will aggravate land grabbing, and this is likely to be seen more in the Albertine Graben. With regard to the impact on women, it is concluded that land grabbing has affected women negatively since the source of livelihoods for them has been taken away. Given the fact that oil exploration and mining have been met with contention and resistance, we conclude that this is likely to affect the oil industry by interfering with mining and tampering with the oil lines, and to a minimal level it may lead to civil war resulting from discontent about sharing the oil proceeds.

References

AFIEGO (2014), Annual Report 2014. Kampala: Africa Institute for Energy Governance (AFIEGO). Retrieve from: https://www.afiego.org.

—— (2016a), Annual Report 2016. Kampala: Africa Institute for Energy Governance (AFIEGO). Retrieved from: https://www.afiego.org.

—— (2016b), 'Help Us: Refinery-Affected People in yet more Efforts for Justice'. Retrieved from: https://www.afiego.org/download/refinery-affected-people-in-yet-more-efforts-for-us tice/?wpdmdl=1048&refresh=5d75bf8fd2ec61567997839.

—— (2016c), 'The Role of Social Impact Assessments in Promoting Human Rights'. *Policy Briefing,* Paper no 2, January 2016, Kampala: Africa Institute for Energy Governance (AFIEGO). Retrieved from: http://idf.co.ug/wp-content/uploads/2016/04/Issue-1-AFIEGO-newsletter.pdf.

Bategeka, L., J. Kiiza and S. Ssewanyana (2013), 'Oil Discovery in Uganda: Managing Expectations'. Kampala: Economic Policy Research Centre and Makerere University. Retrieved from: https://www.mak.ac.ug/documents/EPRCUDICPaper.pdf.

Bainomugisha, A., H. Kivengyere and B. Tusasirwe (2006), 'Escaping the Oil Curse and Making Poverty History: A Review of the Oil and Gas Policy and Legal Framework for Uganda'. ACODE Policy Research Series, No. 20, 2006, Kampla: ACODE.

Behrman, J., R. Meinzen-Dick and R.A. Quisumbing (2011), ,The Gender Implications of Large-Scale Land Deals', *The Journal of Peasant Studies,* 39(1), 49–79. Retrieved from: https://doi.or g/10.1080/03066150.2011.652621.

Borras, J., M. Saturnino, J. Franco, C. Kay and M. Spoor (2011), *Land Grabbing in Latin America and the Caribbean Viewed from Broader International Perspective.* Santiago: FAO.

Byakagaba, P., and B. Twesigye (2015), *Securing Communal Land and Resource Rights in the Albertine Region of Uganda: The Case of Hoima and Buliisa Districts.* Kampala: CRED. Retrieved from: http://creduganda.org/wp-content/uploads/2019/05/Securing-communal-tenure-and-resource-rights-in-the-Albertine-graben-of-Uganda.pdf.

Cousins, B. (2002), 'Legislating Negotiability: Tenure Reform in Post-apartheid South Africa', in K. Juul and C. Lund (eds.), *Negotiating Property in Africa.* Portsmouth, New Hampshire: Heinemann Educational Books.

Deininger, K. (2003), *Land Policies for Growth and Poverty Reduction: A World Bank Policy Research Report*. Oxford: Oxford University Press.

————, D. Byerlee, J. Lindsay, A. Norton, H. Selod and M. Stickler (2011), *Rising Global Interest in Farmland: Can it Yield Sustainable Benefits*. Washington, DC: World Bank.

————— and R. Castagnini (2004), *Incidence and Impact of land Conflict in Uganda*. Washington, DC: World Bank.

de Soysa, I. (2000), 'The Resource Curse: Are Civil Wars Driven by Rapacity or Paucity?', in M. Berdal and D.M. Malone (eds.). *Greed and Grievance: Economic Agendas in Civil Wars*, Boulder, Colorado: Lynne Rienner Publishers.

FAO (2007), *Good Governance in Land Tenure and Administration*, Rome: FAO.

Fairhead, James, Melissa Leach and Ian Scoones (2012), 'Green Grabbing: A New Appropriation of Nature?', *The Journal of Peasant Studies*, 39(2), 237–261. Retrieved from; http://dx.doi.or g/10.1080/03066150.2012.671770 19/11/16.

Gary, I., and K.L. Terry (2003), *Bottom of the Barrel: Africa's Oil Boom and the Poor*. Baltimore, Maryland: Catholic Relief Service. Retrieved from: https://www.internationalbudget.org/ wp-content/uploads/Bottom-of-the-Barrel-Africas-Oil-Boom-and-the-Poor.pdf.

Global Rights Alert (2015), *Acquisition of Land for the Oil Refinery: Tracking Progress in Resettling Project Affected Persons who opted for land for land Compensation*. Kampala: Global Rights Alert. Retrieved from: https://www.globalrightsalert.org/sites/default/files/GRA_Reset-tlement_Report.pdf.

Goulet, D. (1995), *Development Ethics: A Guide to Theory and Practice*. New York: Zed Books.

Government of Uganda (2001), *Land Sector Strategic Plan: Utilising Uganda's Land Resources for Sustainable Development*. Kampala: Government of Uganda.

Hallam, D. (2009), 'International Investment in Agriculture', in M. Kugelman and L.S. Levenstein (eds.), *Land Grab? The Race for the World's Farmland*. Washington, DC: Woodrow Wilson International Center for Scholars.

Jacobs, S. (2009), 'Land reforms, Land Titling and Gender Dilemmas in Africa: An Explora-tion of Issues', in M. Ndulo and M. Grieco (eds.), *Power, Gender and Social Change in Africa*. Newcastle-upon-Tyne: Cambridge Scholars Publishing.

Kachika, T. (2010), *Land Grabbing in Africa: A Review of the Impacts and Possible Policy Responses*. Oxford: Oxfam International Pan African Programme. Retrieved from: https://www.oxfam-blogs.org/eastafrica/wp-content/uploads/2010/11/Land-Grabbing-in-Africa.-Final.pdf.

Kwesiga, P. (2016), 'Government Cancels Oil Field Land Titles Illegally Acquired', *New Vision*, 31(97), 3–10.

Mabikke, B.S. (2011), *Escalating Land Grabbing in Post-conflict Regions of Northern Uganda: A Need for Strengthening Good Land Governance in Acholi Region*. Brighton, UK: Institute of Development Studies, University of Sussex.

Matsiko, H. (2012, 3 January), The Great Land Grab', *The Independent*. Retrieved from: https:// www.independent.co.ug/great-land-grab/.

Mbabazi, P. (2013), *The Oil Industry in Uganda: A Blessing in Disguise or an all Too Familiar Curse?* Uppsala: Nordiska Afrikainstitutet. Retrieved from: https://www.pcr.uu.se/ digitalAssets/654/c_654442-l_1-k_fulltext01.pdf.

Miirima, F.H. (2008), *Demystifying Oil Exploration in Uganda: Simplified Facts and Terminologies Related to Oil Exploration in Uganda*. Kampala: Henry Ford Miirima.

Ministry of Lands, Housing and Urban Development (2011), *The Uganda National Land Policy Final Draft*. Kampala: Government of Uganda.

MFPED (2012), *Oil and Gas Revenue Management Policy*, Kampala: Ministry of Finance, Planning and Economic Development (MFPED).

Mugerwa, F. (2012, 9 November), 'Buliisa Locals Petition Government over Oil-rich Land', *Daily Monitor*. Kampala: Monitor Publications. Retrieved from: http://www.monitor.co.ug/News/National/Buliisa+locals+petition+govt+over+oil+rich+land/-/688334/1514034/-/c062syz/-/index.html 10/11/2012.

Muriisa, K.R., P. Mbabazi and M. Twinamatsiko (2014), 'Land Deals in Uganda: An Invisible Hand into Land Grabbing and Rural Development', in P. Mihyo (ed.), *International Land Deals in Eastern and Southern Africa*, Addis Ababa: Organization for Social Science Research in Eastern and Southern Africa (OSSREA).

Ongode, B. (2015, 27 May), 'Oil Compensation Exposes Abuse of Women in Hoima', *The Observer*. Retrieved from: https://observer.ug/business/38-business/38035-oil-compensation-exposes-abuse-of-women-in-hoima.

Ogunleye, T.A. (2016), 'Establishing Oil Theft and Other Related Crimes Tribunal for Speedy Trial: Legal Issues and Challenges', *IOSR Journal of Humanities and Social Science (IOSR-JHSS)*, Issue 4, 20–27.

Oxfam (2011), 'Land and Power: The Growing Scandal Surrounding a New Wave of Investing in Land'. *Oxfam Briefing Paper*, No.151, Oxford: Oxfam. Retrieved from: http://www.oxfam.org/sites/www.oxfam.org/files/bp151-land-power-rights-acquisitions-220911-en.pdf.

Paulat, L. (2014, 24 September), 'Land Evictions Breed Violence in Oil Rich Hoima Uganda', *Voice of America*. Retrieved from: https://reliefweb.int/report/uganda/land-eviction-breeds-violence-oil-rich-hoima-uganda.

Republic of Uganda (1949), The Mining Act, 1949. Retrieved from: http://www.ulii.org/ug/legislation/consolidated-act/148.

———— (1985), The Petroleum and Oil Exploration Act, 1985. Retrieved from: http://www.ulii.org/ug/legislation/consolidated-act/150.

———— (1998), The Land Act, 1998. Retrieved from: https://ulii.org/ug/legislation/consolidated-act/227.

Ross, L.M. (2004), 'How Do Natural Resources Influence Civil War? Evidence from Thirteen Cases', *International Organization*, 58(1), 35–67. Retrieved from: https://doi.org/10.1017/S002081830458102X.

Rugadya, M. (1999), *Land Reform: The Ugandan Experience*. Paper presented at Land Use and Villagization Workshop, Hotel de Mille Collines in Kigali, Rwanda, 20–21 September 1999. Retrieved from: http://citeseerx.ist.psu.edu/viewdoc/download?doi=10.1.1.433.9383&rep=rep1&type=pdf.

————, E. Nsamba-Gayiiya and E. Kamusime (2008), *Northern Uganda Land Study: Analysis of Post Conflict Land Policy and Land Administration: A Survey of IDP Return and Resettlement Issues and Lesson: Acholi and Lango regions*. Kampala: The World Bank. Retrieve from: https://www.landcoalition.org/sites/default/files/documents/resources/northern_uganda_land_study_acholi_lango.pdf.

Sachs, J., and A. Warner (1995), 'Natural Resource Abundance and Economic Growth'. *NBER Working Paper*, No. 5398. Retrieved from: http://ideas.repec.org/p/nbr/nberwo/5398.html.

Ssekika, E. (2016, 18 May), 'Government Declines to Back Down in Oil Refinery Compensation Case', *The Observer*. Retrieved from: https://www.observer.ug/business/38-business/44293-govt-declines-to-back-down-in-oil-refinery-compensation-case.

Stickler, N. (2012), *Governance of Large-Scale Land Acquisitions in Uganda: The Role of the Uganda Investment Authority*. Paper presented at the International Conference on Global Land Grabbing II, 17-19 October 2012, organised by the Land Deals Politics Initiative (LDPI) and hosted by the Department of Development Sociology at Cornell University, Ithaca, NY.

Uganda Human Rights Commission (UHRC) (2013), *Oil in Uganda: Emerging Human Rights Issues Special Focus on Selected Districts in the Albertine Graben*. Kampala: Human Rights Commission.

Unsworth, S., and G. Williams (2011), 'Using Political Economy Analysis to Improve EU Development Effectiveness: A DEVCO Background Note'. Retrieved from: https://europa. eu/capacity4dev/political-economy/blog/using-political-economy-analysis-improve-eu-development-effectivenessdraft.

Willy, L.A. (2010), 'Whose Land are You Giving Away Mr. President?'. Paper presented to the Annual World Bank Land Policy and Administration Conference, Washington, DC, 26 –27 April 2010. Retrieved from: http://citeseerx.ist.psu.edu/viewdoc/download?doi=10.1. 1.370.5763&rep=rep1&type=pdf.

Wisbor, P. (2014), 'Transnational Land Deals and Gender Equality: Utilitarian and Human Rights Approaches', *Feminist Economics*, 20(1), 24–51. Retrieved from: http://dx.doi.org/1 0.1080/13545701.2013.862341.

12

Expecting Eldorado? An Analysis of Ugandans' Expectations of Their Country's Oil Wealth

Byaruhanga Musiime Chris

12.1   Introduction

When Uganda found oil in 2006, President Yoweri Museveni held national thanksgiving prayers to celebrate the historic discovery. Just like the President, the majority of Ugandans then were very excited that the country would soon start reaping billions from its oil and gas resources and join the likes of Nigeria and Libya in the prestigious ranks of Africa's oil producers at the time. Shortly after that discovery, the Ugandan Government endorsed a proposal for an early production scheme[1] (EPS) that would see the country start producing oil in the shortest time possible. This was perhaps the biggest indicator then of how urgently the Government needed to start pumping and earning from the country's petroleum resources.

The discovery was perceived as a great win for all Ugandans, and the media were awash with stories about how oil would significantly alter the country's development trajectory for the better. Some doubted that the NRM government, which had been in power for over two decades, would be inclined to manage the country's oil resources for the benefit of all Ugandans. They pointed to early signs of elite capture, an overbearing presidency and increasing militarisation of the oil producing areas as warning signs of what might come (Global Witness, 2010).

Ugandan civil society, known for too often being in bed with the 'other side', quickly jumped on the oil bandwagon and cautioned Government against misusing oil money. They brought into this discourse terms like the

---

1   The EPS was planned to start in 2009 with production of 4,000–5,000 barrels of oil per day.

'resource curse'[2] and 'Dutch disease'[3] and went into the oil-producing areas to sensitise people about the wealth beneath their soil. There was talk in civil society circles about some NGOs revising their strategic plans to justify funding from donors to enable them 'work on oil'.

Communities in oil-producing areas were convinced that they could earn from oil either by way of providing goods and services to the industry or by their children obtaining employment in the oil camps. Politicians took it a notch higher and started making demands for what they believed should be their region's fair share of oil proceeds. In an unprecedented move, the King of Bunyoro stormed Parliament demanding that his kingdom receive 12.5 per cent of oil royalties (Ssekanjako, 2012). Young professionals sniffed out an opportunity to cash in, and those who could afford it sought post-graduate qualifications in oil and gas disciplines, most of them in fairly expensive universities in Europe (Ongode, 2013). The business community was perhaps the most excited of all, with many local businessmen rushing to banks to acquire loans to set up a facility or service to feed the oil and gas industry. This was generally the mood across Uganda in the first few years that followed the historic announcement that the country had oil and gas in commercial quantities.

Almost 13 years later, Uganda is yet to see its first oil, despite an impressive exploration programme that has confirmed that the country possesses in excess of 6.5 billion barrels of oil in the ground, with only a fraction of the mapped oil basins explored (Ministry of Energy and Mineral Development, 2016). The Government insists that it deliberately decided to take its time in mapping its oil future because it wanted everything to be done right for the benefit of the country, specifically defending what the oil companies perceived as slow action in approving production licences to enable commencement of the production phase. There has been some progress on the development of infrastructure, with the Government finally agreeing on the route for the crude pipeline to the export terminal at Tanga, Tanzania. However, beyond announcements that the international oil companies (IOCs) had been granted

2   The resource curse, also known as the paradox of plenty, refers to the paradox that countries with an abundance of natural resources, specifically non-renewable resources like minerals and fuels, tend to have less economic growth, less democracy and worse development outcomes than countries with fewer natural resources.

3   'Dutch disease' refers to a situation where growth in income from natural resources damages other sectors of a country's economy. This happens because increased revenues from natural resource exports tend to increase the value of the exporting nation's currency. That makes the country's other exports, such as agricultural products and manufactured goods, more expensive and therefore less competitive in world markets. The economy thus becomes over-reliant on the natural resources that it is exporting—and this can be particularly damaging if, for any reason, there is a drop in world price for those natural resources.

additional production licences, Ugandan citizens remain largely uninformed of developments in the oil industry.

In fact, the past five years have been confusing. First was the slump in global crude oil prices that led some to question the viability of Uganda's oil and gas projects; then Government and the IOCs disagreed on how to proceed with development of the country's oil and gas resources, initially about the refinery and later the route of the pipeline (Aching, 2016). The businesspeople who borrowed heavily from commercial banks have been unable to repay their loans and the Government has faced difficulty getting a viable investor to build its refinery (Matsiko, 2016). Many of the young people who invested in acquiring an oil education cannot find jobs. In the oil-bearing areas there has been a surge of land conflicts and some communities have been dispossessed of their land, losing lives and property in violent confrontations with those interested in the land.

This chapter will, in the context of the background sketched above, analyse the expectations Ugandans have concerning their country's oil and gas resources, and whether the Government and the oil companies are managing those expectations adequately. The chapter will systematically examine the roles of the different key players in the oil and gas sector, in particular the Presidency, politicians, the media, civil society and academia, with specific focus on how they have helped to shape the public's expectations either positively or otherwise over the past decade. The information presented in this chapter is based on a critical review of the published literature, press reports, government documents, oil company statements and reports from civil society groups. These were augmented with additional data collected by the author in the course of his work as a writer and editor of an oil and gas sector publication, which included interviewing key stakeholders in the oil and gas industry over a period of five years.[4]

12.2   Understanding Ugandans' Expectations

The average Ugandan adult is aware that Uganda has oil and gas resources and expects that exploitation of those resources will have an impact on them either directly or indirectly, positively or negatively. For the purposes of this chapter, the Ugandan population has been divided into three different groups: the hosts, the poachers and the spectators. Each group has different expectations from the oil and gas industry. The degree of expectation varies depending on

4   See www.oilinuganda.org.

several factors that include the person's proximity (in geographical terms) to the oil-producing areas, and their involvement politically, economically, culturally or professionally in the oil and gas sector. The three groups are discussed in more detail below.

12.2.1 The Hosts

These are the people in the eye of the storm. They are inhabitants of the oil-rich Albertine Region and perceive the oil and gas as being beneath 'their' land. Although Ugandan law grants ownership of natural resources to the State,[5] these people still claim ownership of the oil resources and feel they deserve more benefits from its extraction than the rest of the country. They argue that they will face the brunt of its exploitation either socially or environmentally, and hence need to be adequately compensated. Indeed, the Government recognises this and even made a provision in the Public Finance Management Act, 2015 returning some of the revenues earned from oil production to the hosts. Section 75(1) of that Act therefore explicitly states: 'Government shall retain 94% of the revenue from royalties arising from petroleum production and the remaining 6% shall be shared among local governments within the petroleum exploration and production areas of Uganda'.[6]

The law further makes provision for the cultural institutions that may exist in those oil-producing areas by granting them 1 per cent of the royalties due to the Central Government.[7] The Bunyoro Kingdom, the most prominent cultural institution in the Albertine Region, had initially made demands to Parliament seeking to be allocated much more of the revenue from royalties. The King of Bunyoro, Solomon Gafabusa Iguru, presented those demands to the parliamentary Committee on Natural Resources in 2012. He demanded that his Kingdom,[8] which includes the seven districts of Hoima, Masindi, Buliisa, Kiryandongo, Kagadi, Kakumiro and Kibaale, should be given 12.5

---

5   See the Petroleum (Exploration, Development and Production) Act, 2013, Part II Section 4: Vesting of petroleum rights: (1) in accordance with Article 244 of the Constitution, the entire property in, and the control of, petroleum in its natural condition in, on or under any land or waters in Uganda is vested in the Government on behalf of the Republic of Uganda. (2) For the avoidance of doubt, the Government of Uganda shall hold petroleum rights on behalf of and for the benefit of the people of Uganda.

6   Ministry of Finance, Planning and Economic Development, Uganda Public Finance Management Act, 2015, retrieved from: https://finance.go.ug/test/services/uganda-public-finance-management-act-2015/.

7   Section 75(8) of the Public Finance Management Act, 2015.

8   Of the seven districts that comprise Bunyoro Kingdom, only Hoima and Buliisa have proven oil reserves.

per cent of royalties when oil production commences. He reminded the Committee that he was the valid trustee of the Bunyoro customary lands and natural resources, and therefore needed a fair share of the royalties so that he could develop the kingdom.

In a separate interview in 2012, the Bunyoro King justified his kingdom's demands as follows:

> All the kings and cultural leaders must be given a percentage so that they can continue doing something good for the people. For example, building schools, hospitals, roads—and culture and behaviour will be addressed using the resources. HIV/AIDS is spreading fast, so how do we stop it? We need that money to teach our youth how to behave well. Young people must also have skills to address issues of poverty that are spreading like a wild bush fire. We need money for this (cited in Young, 2012).

The King's claims are entrenched in a colonial agreement his father, Tito Gafabusa Winyi IV, signed with the British in 1955.[9] In particular, Article 36 of that agreement stipulated the following: 'In the event of any mineral development taking place, a substantial part of the mineral royalties and revenues from the mining leases shall be paid to the native government of Bunyoro-Kitara'.

In other parts of the Albertine Region some leaders have formed lobby groups to advocate for the interests of their people. An example is the Acholi Technical Working Committee on Oil and Gas (ATWCOG) in Northern Uganda. This particular group has repeatedly expressed concern at what it considers its deliberate exclusion by Government from the oil discourse. Its sentiments arise from a belief that its Region is contributing most of the oil and hence deserves to be involved in the planning processes.[10] In a 2014 interview, Prof. Morris Ogenga-Latigo, a leading politician and Chairman of ATWCOG at the time, said:

> The basic story you hear is that oil is in Bunyoro. It turns out that the refinery in Hoima will get its crude oil largely from the Jobi oil field in Acholi. That the refinery in Hoima will get literally more than ninety percent of its oil from one oil field in Acholi. Yet the other entire (planned) oil infrastructure

---

9   See for more information the Bunyoro-Kitara Kingdom website, retrieved from: https://bunyorokitarakingdom.org/.

10   This is an unverified claim by Acholi leaders that most of the oil discovered so far lies in basins located in Northern Uganda (Nwoya and Nebbi Districts) and not in Hoima and Buliisa as reported by the Ugandan Government.

like the Refinery, Central Processing Facilities and the pipelines and pump stations are not in Acholi. Other than just piping of the oil for refining in Hoima and export, there is nothing planned for Acholi (cited in Nalubega and Ongode, 2014).

Both Government and the oil companies deny those claims and insist that their decisions are purely technical, not political, and are based on assessments of least-cost options. They point out that the oil in northern Uganda is found in the Murchison Falls National Park which makes it impossible to set up infrastructure. That does not stop the negative sentiments within communities in Northern Uganda from growing nonetheless. Even in areas where exploration efforts yielded no oil, the residents there still feel a strong sense of ownership and look forward to becoming oil producers. In Rhino Camp, Arua District, Neptune Petroleum drilled three wells but was not lucky, forcing it to abandon the area. However, the residents remain hopeful that the company will return and find oil. They believe that a tree species, known locally as 'Tiika' and relatively abundant in the area, is a sign of oil lying beneath the surface (Oil in Uganda, 2013a).

At the southern tip of the Albertine Graben is Ntoroko District. One of the prospective areas, Kanywataba, was leased out to the Chinese National Offshore Oil Corporation (CNOOC) (Tullow Oil plc, 2011). The company did some drilling there in 2012 but did not find oil. The Chinese packed up and left the area and their licence consequently expired and reverted to the Uganda Government for possible re-licensing. It was eventually awarded to Armour Energy, an Australian Company, in 2017 (Acomai, 2017). However, residents remain confused about the status of 'their' oil resources, but many are optimistic that their area has oil. They seem unprepared to accept that perhaps they may not be as lucky as their countrymen further north.

12.2.2 The Poachers

This category includes people who are mainly driven by their personal desire to gain individually from the oil sector, through deals, career development, employment, consultancies, business opportunities, etc. Many of these people do not hail from the oil-producing areas but are merely taking advantage of a nascent, potentially lucrative oil and gas sector. Many of them are part of or are in some way associated with the business, professional or political class. A classic example is the select group of 42 people who received a combined pay-out of 6 billion shillings (US$ 1.8 million) from the Government as appreciation for their efforts in winning a tax case against British oil firms,

Heritage Oil and Gas and Tullow Oil. Heritage Oil was instructed to pay US$ 434 million to Uganda in capital gains tax, from which award 6 billion shillings was retained and split amongst staff of the Uganda Revenue Authority (URA), officials from the Ministries of Justice and Constitutional Affairs, Finance, Planning and Economic Development, Energy and Mineral Development and others. Media reports indicate that this scheme was initiated and coordinated by the head of the URA, who convinced the President that the officials concerned needed to be rewarded for their effort in salvaging billions of Uganda's tax money (Musisi, 2017).

That case demonstrates how poachers typically operate. For them, the oil and gas sector is a cash cow that must be milked dry irrespective of what other members of the public stand to lose. The expectations of poachers tend to lean more towards personal needs because they have made some investments and expect returns from the sector. For example, career people may have invested in a postgraduate education abroad, or the business community may have borrowed heavily from commercial banks to set up oil-related facilities or politicians may have spent heavily to be elected into office. Whatever the case may be, all these people expect a return.

12.2.3 The Spectators

This group of Ugandans is somewhat detached from developments in the oil and gas sector because they do not see how they can benefit directly. They hail from outside the Albertine Region and are not associated with the business, professional or political class. They perceive oil as the preserve of a minority group of people close to the political establishment. They are aware of the potential of the sector but do not have any point of entry because they lack the connections. These people will wait for whatever Government apportions to them, preferably by way of improved service delivery. They are the majority of Ugandans. In 2013, *Oil in Uganda*, a Ugandan oil and gas publication, carried out a survey that set out to establish the interest of a cross-section of Ugandans in Kampala and Luwero Districts (Central Region) in oil issues. The survey discovered that most people regard oil as a preserve of the Government and connected 'big people'. Below are some of the quotations from a few of the respondents who were interviewed:

> 'I don't know much and I don't need to know much because we will not benefit much. We are in Luwero, oil is in Hoima. I don't think we shall benefit so much like the people in Hoima. If they decrease transport costs, that is all we need.'

'I have heard about Uganda's oil. I think extraction started some time back. People like me who are not so much into oil only get information when we stumble upon it. I do not know how I am going to benefit; truth be told. Everything is going to the big guys up there.'

'I hear they are going to drill oil from Hoima but the big people are the owners of this oil. President Museveni and his cabinet own the oil, they will be the major beneficiaries. We shall benefit little, we the people at the ground. They will earn the big money—like 99 per cent of the oil money and us the little ones will get 1 per cent' (Nalubega and Ongode, 2013).

These quotations demonstrate that there is a section of Ugandans that does not anticipate any tangible benefit from oil revenues. They also bring up the issue of the 'big men' in government and the private sector—the poachers, who are connected to the political establishment and have positioned themselves to reap big from the sector. One may argue that the spectators are disinterested in oil because the country has not commenced production and they do not know what difference oil revenues will make. That is a possibility. But the underlying reason for their lack of interest is simply because they see nothing in it for them.

12.3   Oil Expectations: Realistic or Not?

The people of Uganda in general, and in other areas where the discoveries have been made in particular, expect quick revenues, jobs and businesses, among other things.[11]

The above quotation was picked from the 2013 Annual Report of the Ministry of Energy and Mineral Development. It demonstrates that the Government is aware that many Ugandans indeed expect Eldorado from the exploitation of oil and gas resources. The quotation distinguishes between the 'people of Uganda in general', i.e. 'the spectators', and those in 'areas where discoveries have been made', i.e. the hosts. Indeed, the expectations of the 'people of Uganda in general' and those in 'areas where discoveries have been made' are quite different. The former tend to have general-type demands like better public services, while the latter have personal and community-based demands like jobs and a share of the oil money in cash.

11   See Ministry of Energy and Mineral Development (2013), Annual Report, retrieved from: https://www.energyandminerals.go.ug/resources/topics-and-issues/.

The survey mentioned above, which was carried out in non-oil-producing districts in Western and Central Uganda revealed that a bigger percentage of Ugandans there would like the Government to invest oil proceeds in improving roads and other transport infrastructure. Out of a total of 595 respondents who were randomly interviewed in the three districts, 21 per cent said they would like the Government to spend oil money on improving feeder roads in the rural areas. 14 per cent said they wanted to see improvements in the health sector, 12 per cent vouched for education, while 11.6 per cent revealed that they would prefer it if the oil money were used to create more jobs and employment for Ugandans. 11 per cent of the people spoken to suggested that Government should take advantage of the additional revenue from oil to institute subsidies that would reduce the cost of living for Ugandans, including through cheaper fuel (Oil in Uganda, 2015).

These expectations are generalist in nature and, if realised, would benefit all of Uganda. Expectations of the 'hosts' tend to be more localised and more provincial than generalist. They tend to focus on communal benefits for the people living in that particular area where the oil activity is taking place. Common demands are communal infrastructure facilities like roads and health centres. However, mainly due to the work of some NGOs and politicians, some community members are seeking individual benefits like employment (especially for their children), direct cash transfers and business opportunities. One of the biggest expectations is employment, because people generally assume that oil brings with it a massive job bonanza. The reality is not as rosy. A three-month survey commissioned by the joint venture partners (Total, CNOOC and Tullow) gave some figures on jobs that will be generated by the sector, reporting that at production stage only 13,000 people will be directly employed by the sector, although it has the potential to generate up to 150,000 new jobs through 'indirect and induced' opportunities in other sectors that will be feeding off it (Hamman, 2014).

The report analyses the labour demand in the sector in the run-up to production as well as the potential of the market to meet this demand. Out of the total manpower required, 15 per cent are engineers and managers, 60 per cent are technicians while 25 per cent are unskilled labourers with no educational background. The Ugandan Government is doing all it can to maximise available jobs and business opportunities for Ugandans, but still those jobs and opportunities are way less than what the public, especially in the oil-producing areas, believes. Some of the provisions[12] the Government has put in place include banning the IOCs from employing expatriates where

---

12   National content regulations under the Petroleum Acts.

there are Ugandans with similar qualifications, skills and competences. National content regulations also provide benchmarks on the employment of Ugandans. For instance, 20 per cent of management staff in IOCs and other international companies should be Ugandans at the start of operations, which should increase to 60 per cent after five years and 80 per cent within ten years. For technical staff, 30 per cent of all technical staff in international companies should be Ugandans at the start of operations, which should increase to 60 per cent in five years and 80 per cent in ten years, while 95 per cent of support staff and middle-level staff must be Ugandans. The regulations also ring-fence 15 categories of goods and services that will be provided exclusively by Ugandans.[13]

However, the Government has not been efficient in communicating these efforts, leaving the public at the mercy of the media, NGOs and politicians. These have spun the facts whichever way they pleased, depending on their motives at the time.

12.4   The Role of Politicians, Media and NGOs in Shaping Expectations

Expectations can be explicit or implicit, clear or fuzzy. They can be realistic or unrealistic; evidence based or opinionated (Bategeka et al., 2011, p.2).

Expectations, whether positive or negative, are largely shaped by the kind of information a person is consistently exposed to. Ever since oil was discovered in Uganda, there have been four main sources of information: politicians, the media, NGOs and Government (in partnership with the IOCs). Uganda has a vibrant and fast-growing media industry composed of print newspapers in both English and local languages, state- and privately-owned television and radio stations as well as a rising social media movement. Newspapers are popular in urban centres and provide the most extensive political and business coverage in Uganda. However, only 2 per cent of Ugandan households report print media as their primary source of information, according to a 2016 report from the Uganda Bureau of Statistics.

---

13   The goods and services 'ring-fenced' include transport, security, foods and beverages, hotel accommodation and catering services, human resource management, office supply, fuel supply, land surveying, clearing and forwarding, crane hire, locally available construction materials, civil works, environmental studies and environmental impact assessments (EIAs), communications and information technology (ICT) services, and waste management.

The most popular medium remains radio. According to the Uganda Communications Commission (UCC)'s third-quarter report of 2015, there were 292 operational FM radio stations. With advancements in technology, most mobile phones now come with a radio function. This means that the more than 19 million Ugandans who own mobile phones can practically access a radio station of choice that broadcasts in a language they are familiar with on their phones.[14] One can safely assume, then, that at least half the households in rural Uganda have access to one radio station at the minimum.

The majority of the rural population relies on radio for its daily dose of news and current affairs, including information on the oil and gas sector. Although UCC estimates that radio ownership by politicians stands at about 15 per cent, other media analysts claim that NRM politicians or businesspeople linked to the ruling party own about 70 per cent of all private FM radio stations, with the bulk of those based in the rural areas (Africa Centre for Media Excellence, 2015). Over the past decade, Ugandan politicians have discovered the importance of owning a radio station as both a source of revenue and, more importantly, a political mouthpiece to promote their political agendas. The hundreds of different radio stations in the country therefore broadcast material that serves those two interests. Inevitably, those radio stations that are owned by ruling party politicians will normally air programmes that are in support of the regime and its development programmes.

There is a strong relationship between the political inclination of the ownership of the radio and the kind of material that the station broadcasts. Kibazo and Kanaabi (2007) found, for instance, that proprietors interfere with operations, sometimes issuing instructions to prioritise or downplay specific stories. They also found that there is still a considerable amount of political interference in the broadcast sector, despite its liberalisation as exemplified in the following quotation:

> In Central, Eastern and Western Uganda, there are radio stations on which alternative political or religious views cannot be aired. … In other instances, editors and presenters are under instruction to propagate certain agendas and suppress news that is not in the interest of the station owners or their associates (Kibazo and Kanaabi, 2007, p.11).

---

14 Uganda Telecommunications Commission (July-September 2015, p.11), Post, Broadcasting and Telecommunications Market and Industry Report, retrieved from: https://www.ucc.co.ug/files/downloads/Q3-Market%20Report%20%20for%20Third%20Quarter%20-%20July-September%20 2015.pdf.

This influence is more common in upcountry radio stations, mainly because the radio managers have less influence and the communities are less exposed. Wasswa (2011) attributes this to financial pressure, largely unskilled man-power, excessive owner influence, as well as poor management, editorial and marketing skills. As a result, different communities in the oil-producing areas will have access to different types of information that will ultimately shape their expectations from the oil and gas sector. For example, interactions with different sections of people in Hoima District, which is a National Resistance Movement (NRM) stronghold where party candidate Yoweri Museveni garnered 74.7 per cent of the votes in the 2016 election, will reveal more positive expectations from oil than those with people in Nwoya District where the opposition is more dominant (only 41.64 per cent of the electorate voted for President Museveni).

Politicians have captured the radio waves upcountry and they can feed listeners with all sorts of information and misinformation to favour their own political agendas. For example, a baseline study on the impact of oil exploration on women and women's leadership in the Albertine sub-region reported some community concerns about oil as a result of different radio programmes in the oil-producing areas (Centre for Women in Governance [CEWIGO], 2012). Some quotations from that report are given below:

'I only heard from politicians when they were campaigning that if we voted for them they would fight for us to benefit from our oil'.
'We hear that our oil is already being taken away especially in Hoima and Buliisa districts.'
'I have heard from my MP that the oil is not there; that it has already been taken.'
'I heard that there is oil in Bunyoro and that whites had already camped around Lake Albert to exploit the oil.'
'I heard that there is oil production but the tender was awarded without consent of the area MPs... and that an oil refinery shall be constructed in Bunyoro.'

The second category of people who have captured the upcountry airwaves are NGOs, which dictate radio programming through sponsorship of talk shows and advertising. Through sponsored programmes, NGOs were able to educate communities about oil and gas issues, update them about recent developments and advise them on how to engage with Government and the international oil companies. In many ways they were the main providers of information to communities because Government was largely absent. This set them on a collision course with the authorities who perceived them as enemies of progress because of their ability to mobilise large groups of people to talk about issues which the Government held as sensitive.

It is NGOs that educated people about the 'Dutch disease', the 'Oil Curse' and aired videos of the Niger Delta conflict in Nigeria at their meetings and workshops. They told people to be cautious about their land and, where compensation was involved, encouraged them to ask for more. The NGOs questioned why the Government was keeping its contracts with the IOCs secret and called on people to put their leaders on the spot regarding oil transparency. International NGOs as well were critical sources of information and contributed a great deal to the local oil discourse.

In 2014, international campaigner Global Witness released a report exposing the details of some of the 'secret' contracts the Ugandan Government had with the international oil companies operating in the country (see Global Witness, 2014). That was the first time that Ugandans started getting a real sense of what the country had negotiated for its oil and gas resources. What was puzzling was that the report confirmed what several industry experts, including some employees of the oil companies, had claimed for some time: Uganda got a good deal, at least compared to many other oil-producing countries in Africa. According to the report, the country stands to retain anywhere from 80 to more than 90 per cent of the revenues that will be collected from oil, a considerably high take going by global industry standards. In addition, the contracts include a favourable revision of the royalty payments the oil companies will make to Government to factor in cumulative oil production so that they are not only based on daily production, potentially increasing the Government's earnings. The Ugandan Government also renegotiated the contentious stabilisation clause to leave room for it to introduce a new tax as production progresses, as well as clearer terms regarding payment of capital gains tax, a potential source of massive income when companies are either selling or acquiring shares in existing oil blocks.

All this information was brought into the public domain by the work of an NGO and it got Ugandans asking, 'Why the secrecy if Uganda got a good deal? What is the Government hiding? What are they not telling us?'. The political opposition fuelled this debate further and brought it to the floor of Parliament. It attempted to paint a picture that the Government could not be trusted and many key politicians had already pocketed bribes from IOCs to facilitate the latter's acquisition of oil concessions (Platform London, 2010).

According to Dr. Peter Mwesige the Executive Director at the Africa Centre for Media Excellence (ACME), media reporting on oil has—alongside NGOs' efforts— contributed to wider public knowledge about oil and gas.

> There is no doubt that the media here have really popularised that whole question of oil and tried to help people understand what is going on. I remember two years ago, 2011, that debate in parliament, it was broadcast live on television and for very many people it was the first time to get a sense of 'Wow! What is going on with oil in this country?' why this is a big deal, why this is important. And I have my cynicism about NGOs and all that but I quite frankly think that without the NGOs it could have been worse. Because a lot of Ugandans, including MPs, have only got to know about this oil story from workshops that have been organised by NGOs. They just didn't know what this whole thing was about, why it was important (Oil in Uganda, 2013b, p.11).

12.5   The Long Wait and its Impact on Ugandans' Perceptions

The delay in commencing oil production has had a sobering effect on Ugandans as the time lag has given them an opportunity to understand the sector better. The fluctuation in global oil prices has caused many to come to terms with the volatility of the sector and realise that oil may not fix all of Uganda's economic problems. In 2017, the Central Bank warned that the delay in starting pumping oil may cause debt distress by 2019 (Baryabarema, 2017). Uganda's external debt stands at over US$ 10 billion, largely because infrastructure projects like roads, a railway, an airport and hydropower dams, many of which are targeting the oil and gas sector, are yet to be operational.

It is not only the national debt that is getting out of hand. Even individual and corporate debt for many players in the oil and gas industry has become unmanageable. Many of the companies seeking a bail-out from Government to help them with their debt obligations borrowed heavily from commercial banks to invest in oil and gas-related businesses, but the slow development of the industry has meant that they are not able to meet their debt obligations (Muhumuza and Adengo, 2016). These include steel giant, Steel Rolling Mills, which invested in a new plant to ramp up production but has been unable to get a market for its steel. Although the Government is reportedly seeking ways of helping those businesses out, the experience has demonstrated how risky the oil and gas industry can be. Perhaps the biggest casualty eventually will be the legitimacy of the NRM regime, which based many of its political

promises on increased income from oil and gas. Before the oil prices plum-
meted, for example, the Government was assured of a refinery investor and
a host of other downstream investors, all of whom now seem doubtful. If the
Government cannot deliver on its promises of jobs, business opportunities
and enhanced service delivery, the population will probably continue to
withdraw its already diminishing support.

The 2016 presidential election revealed just how central the oil question is
to the President and the ruling party. At one of the campaign rallies, President
Museveni intimated that losing the election would by implication place control
of the country's oil and gas resources in the hands of the opposition, and he
was not ready to accept that. He said a victory by the opposition would force
him to resort to rebellion to regain political power. Moreover, Uganda's *Daily
Monitor* newspaper quoted the President as saying, '... Then you hear people
say "Museveni should go". But go and leave oil money? They want me to go
so they can come and spoil the oil money. These people want me to go back
to the bush' (Kafeero, 2015). The other candidates also routinely vowed to
manage the country's oil and gas resources better, ensure transparency and
accountability as well as equitable benefits for all Ugandans.

The presidential debate was the climax of the 2016 presidential campaigns.
It was the first televised debate that the country had conducted, and it was
an opportunity for Ugandans, especially the educated and elite, to assess the
potential of the candidates to run the country. As expected, oil was a central
issue. Some of the candidates had absolutely no idea about the sector, but
others challenged the President on his overbearing stance on the sector, lack of
transparency, secrecy of oil transactions and corruption. Yet again, the country
learned of President Museveni's tight grip on the sector. All the candidates
confessed that they had no clue about the country's oil and gas sector.

'I found it rather disheartening, absurd and archaic that none of the seven
contenders for the presidency of this country has had access to the Production
Sharing Agreements that Uganda entered into with the international oil
companies operating in Uganda', wrote James Muhindo after the presidential
debate (see Muhindo, 2016). Meanwhile at the community level, the delay
in commencing oil production has enabled some of the host communities
to mobilise themselves along tribal and ethnic lines to prevent those they
perceive as 'outsiders' from enjoying benefits of the extraction of oil and gas.
Tribal rhetoric from politicians was especially evident in the 2016 parliamentary elections, with many contestants calling out people from outside oil-rich
Bunyoro Region and urging their tribesmen to deny them access to land.

One shocking incident was in Kaseeta Parish, Kabwooya Sub-county in
Hoima in December 2014, when more than 70 houses were burnt and several

people injured after violence broke out between Bunyoro Kingdom loyalists and residents over the control of a seven-square-mile piece of land bordering the proposed crude oil refinery area. The land, which is also strategically located close to the Waraga, Nzizi and Mputa oil wells, was being claimed by Bunyoro Kingdom from squatters who kingdom officials claim are of Congolese origin. Eager to cash in on oil activities, kingdom officials had successfully persuaded the King to distribute the land amongst his subjects for them to set up income-generating projects to service the oil industry. Such incidents are likely to rise as the production phase kicks in, given the high rates of youth unemployment in the oil-producing areas.

12.6   Managing the Expectations

The latest projection from Government is that 'first oil' will be around 2022, after which the country expects to keep pumping crude for at least another 25 years, considering the current reserve estimates (The Daily Monitor, 2019). However, the expectations of the different stakeholders have to be managed properly for Uganda's oil and gas sector to flourish and make a positive contribution to the country's development. There is a need to strike a balance between the expectations of the Government, the oil companies, the host communities and the Ugandan population. The expectations of the Government and the oil companies are clear and detailed in the production-sharing agreements (PSAs) and other documents. As such, the expectations of the Ugandan public have to be understood and taken into consideration. As we have seen in some African countries, failure to manage the expectations of communities efficiently leads to undesired resentment of the oil companies operating in those areas. In extreme cases, the locals end up targeting those projects.

The first step in managing public expectations is to provide as much information as possible. Lack of reliable and accurate information from Government is the main cause of unrealistic expectations, as it leaves the public vulnerable to whatever messages come out in the media. The public, especially the host communities, need to be educated about the oil and gas industry, how it operates, what is possible and what is not. Government and the oil companies should dispel the illusion that the industry is like a very huge construction site where every able-bodied individual is assured of a job as long as he or she expresses interest. The Government should strive to provide timely information to all stakeholders including local communities, civil society organisations, the broader public, local government, Parliament and private sector on any developments in the oil and gas sector. The Government's communication strategy[15] needs to be applied.

Secondly, Ugandans should be supported to earn from the oil and gas industry. The Government must come out strongly on local content. Oil companies have expressed concern about the capacity of Ugandans to supply goods or services to the sector, claiming that they lack the requisite expertise and quality. The Government should therefore come up with training programmes that can build that capacity in Ugandans and then engage the oil companies so that they give due consideration to Ugandan suppliers. Once that capacity is built, then Government should consider providing finance to local service providers to enable them to compete with the well-capitalised international oil service providers operating in the country.

The Government should be strong on transparency. There is a fear amongst Ugandans that oil money will not be used to improve their living conditions, and most of it will be 'stolen'. A recent case in which the President awarded a select group of 42 government officials a special bonus amounting to 6 billion shillings (US$ 1.8 million) after the Government had won a court case against Heritage Oil and Gas following a tax dispute has reawakened these sentiments amongst Ugandans. The Government must be seen to be committed to proper utilisation and allocation of the oil revenues and must take a firm stand against corruption. Civil society should be given room to operate and monitor the oil and gas sector freely. The occasional censorship of the activities of NGOs operating in the Albertine Region should be stopped, so that they can freely interact with communities there. The Government has now embarked on steps to join the Extractive Industries Transparency Initiative (EITI) (Draku, 2019). This is commendable because it will enable Ugandans easily to track financial transactions in the sector. Proper use of oil money in itself is a good start to managing public expectations because it will stimulate government projects within the communities and improve, or rehabilitate, basic infrastructure. When people start seeing real change in their way of life, they will begin to appreciate the oil and gas industry.

The international oil companies should set up meaningful corporate social responsibility (CSR) projects. While production and refining are several years away, and so are the direct benefits, CSR is an ongoing business strategy which can be used to support the host communities. In some Albertine Region communities there is criticism of the projects that the oil companies

---

15   Two of the objectives of the communications strategy are to meet the information needs of the public through regular information dissemination, exchange and sharing; and to promote accurate and balanced coverage of Uganda's oil and gas sector through proactive communication.

have set up, while in others there is unanimous gratitude. These projects can be used to show the communities that the oil companies, and Government, are committed to improving their welfare. Prior to setting up a CSR project, the companies should consult with different stakeholders in the communities, including vulnerable groups like women. They should not only rely on district leaders and government officials. Communities should be given an opportunity to voice their needs. The companies should use such consultations also to establish what kind of projects would benefit the community most and where they should be located. This will ensure the sustainability of the projects even beyond the company's presence in the area.

An outcome of the NGO sensitisation initiatives in the host communities has been the selective empowerment of beneficiaries. This has altered the power dynamics in the communities as those that have attained the knowledge end up being more empowered than those that have not. Ultimately, they transform into opinion leaders on all matters oil, influence their peers and mobilise them to confront whatever issues they may face at the time. They are increasingly creating power centres which the oil companies and Government have to recognise and manage sensitively if their projects are to proceed smoothly.

12.7   Conclusion

Ugandans are undoubtedly expecting that oil and gas will be a useful addition to the list of the country's natural resources. A big part of the population may not know exactly how these resources will impact on the country positively or otherwise, but they know for sure how they would like to benefit if given the opportunity. The list of expectations is long, but the three key ones are employment, business opportunities and better public services. The Government of Uganda is in a good place right now. Despite the delays in starting production, they have had an opportunity to learn first-hand what good, or bad, oil can bring with it. Given that Uganda may not produce oil for another three to four years, it has plenty of time to correct whatever wrong impressions may have developed amongst citizens, as well as engage Ugandans on their expectations so that they know what to expect. But above all, the Government's biggest task should be to build trust and confidence with the population that oil money will be used for the greater public good and will not be stolen through corruption. The starting point in building this confidence is to give as much information as possible to the public so that they can follow developments in the sector, monitor performance and appreciate any challenges that may arise.

References

Aching, D. (2016, 21 January), 'Is Uganda Oil Production Still Viable? What Are the Alternatives?'. *The New Vision*. Retrieved from: http://www.newvision.co.ug/new_vision/news/1415347/uganda-oil-production-viable-venture-alternatives.

Acomai. I. (2017), 'Australian Firm Makes Bold Move into Uganda'. Retrieved from the *PLEXII* website: https://plexii.org/news/9-news/32-australia-s-armour-energy-makes-bold-move-into-uganda/.

Africa Centre for Media Excellence (2016), *Annual Report 2015*. Retrieved from: https://www.scribd.com/document/316760296/African-Centre-for-Media-Excellence-Annual-Report-2015.

Baryabarema, E. (2017, 27 January), 'IMF's Lagarde Says Uganda Needs to Rely Less on Credit for Infrastructure', *Reuters*. Retrieved from: https://www.reuters.com/article/us-uganda-imf/imfs-lagarde-says-uganda-needs-to-rely-less-on-credit-for-infrastructure-idUSKBN15B1V3.

Bategeka, L., J. Kiiza and S. Ssewanyana (2011), 'Oil Discovery in Uganda: Managing Expectations'. Economic Policy Research Centre and Makerere University. Retrieved from: https://www.mak.ac.ug/documents/EPRCUDICPaper.pdf.

Centre for Women in Governance–CEWIGO (2012), *Baseline Study on the Impact of Oil Exploration on Women and Women's Leadership in the Albertine Sub-region of Uganda*. Kampala, Uganda: Centre for Women in Governance.

Draku, F. (2019, 1 February), 'Uganda Cleared to Join Extractive Initiative', *The Daily Monitor*. Retrieved from; https://www.monitor.co.ug/News/National/Uganda-cleared-to-join-extractive-initiative/688334-4960686-t0khtq/index.html.

Global Witness (2010), *Donor Engagement in Uganda's Oil and Gas Sector: An Agenda for Action*. London: Global Witness.

—— (2014), *A Good Deal Better? Uganda's Secret Oil Contracts Explained*. London: Global Witness Limited. Retrieved from: https://www.globalwitness.org/en/reports/good-deal-better/.

Hamman, E. (2014), *Planning for the Future: A Demand and Supply Study on the Oil and Gas Sector in Uganda*. Retrieved from: https://unctad.org/meetings/en/Presentation/12-OILGASMINE%20Special%20Event%2015-16%20Oct%202014-HAMMANN-2-en.pdf.

Kafeero, S.D. (2015, 23 December), 'Opposition Fire Back at Museveni Over Oil Control', *The Daily Monitor*. Retrieved from: https://www.monitor.co.ug/Elections/Opposition-fire-back-at-Museveni-over-oil-control/2787154-3006804-view-printVersion-78du17z/index.html.

Kibazo, P., and H. Knaabi (2007), *FM Stations in Uganda: Quantity Without Quality*. Nairobi: Eastern Africa Media Institute (EAMI).

Matsiko, H. (2016, 15 July), 'Fight Over Museveni's Bail Out Money', *The Independent*. Retrieved from: https://www.independent.co.ug/independent-fight-musevenis-business-bailout-money/.

Ministry of Energy and Mineral Development (2016), *The Oil and Gas Sector in Uganda: Frequently Asked Questions*. Retrieved from: https://petroleum.go.ug/uploads/resources/FrequentlyAskedQuestin.pdf.

Muhindo, J. (2016, 26 January), 'Why Oil and Gas Was a Tie Breaker at the Presidential Debate', *The New Vision*. Retrieved from: https://www.newvision.co.ug/new_vision/news/1415639/oil-gas-tie-breaker-presidential-debate.

Muhumuza, M.K., and J. Adengo (2016, 22 July), 'FULL LIST: 65 Loan-stressed Firms Line Up for Shs1 Trillion Taxpayer Bailout', *The Daily Monitor*. Retrieved from: http://www.monitor.co.ug/Business/65-loan-stressed-firms-line-up-for-Shs1-trillion-tax/688322-3305166-d6h193/index.html.

Musisi, F. (2017, 4 January), 'How Govt Cleared Shs 6b Pay Out to Officials in Oil Tax Deal', *The Daily Monitor*. Retrieved from: http://www.monitor.co.ug/News/National/How-govt-cleared-Shs6b-payout-to-officials-in-oil-tax-deal/688334-3506674-8mbbpcz/index.html.

Nalubega, F., and B. Ongode (2013, 11 October), 'How Much Does the Ordinary Ugandan Know or Care About Oil?'. *Oil in Uganda*. Retrieved from: http://www.oilinuganda.org/features/local-content/just-how-much-does-the-ordinary-ugandan-know-or-care-about-oil.html.

—— and —— (2014, 27 August), 'We Want Our Share', *Oil in Uganda*. Retrieved from: http://www.oilinuganda.org/features/interviews/we-want-our-share.html.

Oil in Uganda (2013a, 19 February), 'Disappointed Rhino Camp Locals Still Hope for Oil', *Oil in Uganda*. Retrieved from: http://www.oilinuganda.org/features/environment/disappointed-rhino-camp-locals-still-hope-for-oil.html.

—— (2013b), 'Ugandans Deserve to know'. August 2013, Issue 6. Retrieved from; http://www.oilinuganda.org/wp-content/plugins/downloads-manager/upload/Oil_in_Uganda_Newsletter_August_2013.pdf.

—— (2015), *Invest Oil Money in Infrastructure, Health*. Retrieved from: http://www.oilinuganda.org/wp-content/plugins/downloads-manager/upload/oil_in_uganda_newsletter_march.pdf.

Ongode, B. (2013, 23 July), 'Petroleum Training an Attractive Option for Working Ugandans', *Oil in Uganda*. Retrieved from: http://www.oilinuganda.org/features/companies/petroleum-training-an-attractive-option-for-working-ugandans.html.

Platform London (2010, 15 December), 'Wikileaks Cable Shines Light on ENI Corruption in Uganda'. Retrieved from; https://platformlondon.org/2010/12/15/wikileaks-cable-shines-light-on-eni-corruption-in-uganda-heritage-offered-to-pay-bribes-in-congo/.

Ssekanjako, H. (2012, 1 June), 'Bunyoro King Storms Parliament Over Oil Revenue', *The New Vision*. Retrieved from: http://www.newvision.co.ug/new_vision/news/1302151/bunyoro-king-storms-parliament-oil-revenue.

The East African (2019, 14 February), 'Uganda Revises First Oil Production to 2022', *The Daily Monitor*. Retrieved from: https://www.monitor.co.ug/News/National/Uganda-revises-first-oil-production-to-2022/688334-4981204-guetcp/index.html.

Tullow Oil Plc (2011), *Annual Report and Accounts*. Retrieved from: http://www.tullowoil.com/Media/docs/default-source/3_investors/2011-tullow-annual-report.pdf?sfvrsn=4.

Wasswa, J.B. (2011), 'Media in an Era of Advertiser Recession: Rethinking the Business Models', *Uganda Media Review*, Issue 11, 27–32.

Young, N. (2012, 20 June), 'Colonial Agreement on Resources Still Stands Says Bunyoro King', *Oil in Uganda*. Retrieved from: http://www.oilinuganda.org/features/land/colonial-agreement-on-resources-still-stands-says-bunyoro-king.html.

Young, N. (2013, 7 August), 'Media Deserve Only Five Out of Ten for Promoting Oil Transparency', *Oil in Uganda*. Retrieved from: http://www.oilinuganda.org/features/interviews/media-deserve-only-five-out-of-ten-for-promoting-oil-transparency.html.

13

The Management of Social Tensions and Community Grievances in the Albertine Region of Uganda

Tom Ogwang

13.1   Introduction

The discovery of commercially viable oil deposits in the Albertine Graben in 2006 has negatively impacted local communities and consequently has led to numerous grievances (Holterman, 2014; NAPE, 2016; Ogwang, Vanclay and Van den Assem, 2018). The discovery of oil has also led to widespread tensions and social conflicts. Moreover, land and resource conflicts have morphed in Uganda, as the Government's and private sector's drive to exploit the country's natural resource wealth often conflicts with its human rights obligations, with long-lasting consequences for surrounding communities and the environment (de Kock and Sturman, 2012; Van der Ploeg and Vanclay, 2017). Many communities in the mid-western region of Uganda have been negatively affected by Uganda's emerging oil industry (Ogwang *et al.*, 2018; Ogwang and Vanclay, 2019; Ogwang, Vanclay and Van den Assem, 2019; Olanya, 2015) and consequently many of them have lodged complaints with the central Government (Holterman, 2014; NAPE, 2016).

The current chapter focuses on the emergent social tensions and conflicts linked to the oil exploration and development in Uganda. The chapter seeks to analyse how communities and different groups in society are being affected by the multi-facetted intrusions occasioned by the quest for oil. It also explores the different mechanisms and interventions that have been undertaken to address these tensions. The empirical analysis is based on extensive field research in Hoima and Buliisa, the two districts at the heart of the country's oil exploration and development. During this field research, about 40 in-depth interviews were conducted with district officials, oil companies' liaison officers, Bunyoro Kitara kingdom officials, Members of Parliament and civil society organisations (CSOs). These in-depth interviews were complemented by focus group discussions (FGDs) with different groups, including community elders, local council (LC) chairpersons and their executives in the communities affected as well as local community members. The study also benefited from secondary sources which included journal articles, reports from the line ministries and departments especially the Ministry of Energy and Mineral Development (MEMD), reports from civil society organisations, newspapers and newscasts.

The chapter is structured as follows. In Section 13.2, I will discuss and analyse the main sources of tensions and grievances associated with the oil exploration and exploitation. In Section 13.3, I will then analyse how these different grievances and tensions are being managed, and how far these interventions have been effective in this respect. Section 13.4 concludes.

13.2   Sources of Tensions and Grievances

According to Vanclay (2017, p.3), 'irrespective of their purpose, large-scale development and infrastructure projects... require land, and sometimes very large tracts of land'. Such projects also lead to economic and physical displacement. Natural resource exploitation and extraction is a fast-growing industry in resource-rich Africa, with adverse results for communities living in or around project affected areas (Avocats Sans Frontières, 2014; Bainomugisha, Kivengyere and Tusasirwe, 2006; International Alert, 2013; Mosbacher, 2013; Uganda Land Alliance, 2011). Activities carried out by various actors involved in natural resource exploitation and extraction—including government entities and private companies—have led to complex violations and abuses affecting an array of socio-cultural, environmental, political and social and economic development, with long-term and sometimes irreversible effects on people living in and around project-affected areas.

13.2.1 Environmental Concerns

Many studies have documented how oil exploitation is associated with negative social and environmental impacts (Aristide and Moundigbaye, 2017; Eggert, 2001; Ogwang et al., 2018; Söderholm and Svahn, 2015). The Uganda 2013 Strategic Environmental Assessment (SEA) of Oil and Gas Activities in the Albertine Graben observed that the discovery of oil and gas resources presented great socio-economic prospects for the Albertine Graben and the country at large, but it also noted that the area is of high ecological and biodiversity significance. This presents various challenges for environmental protection (Ministry of Energy and Mineral Development [MEMD], 2013; Tumusiime, Mawejje and Byakagaba, 2016). At the same time people in developing countries like Uganda depend on the surrounding environment for their daily livelihoods (Schwarte, 2008). The oil companies in Uganda (CNOOC, Total and Tullow) finished the exploration phase and are now heading into development, which will consequently lead to the production of Ugandan oil resources by 2020 (MEMD, 2017), which has been postponed again to 2022 (The Independent, 2018). Once produced, the crude oil will be partly refined in Uganda to supply the local market and partly exported to the international market.

The export to the international market will be through an export crude oil pipeline: the East Africa Crude Oil export pipeline (EACOP). This pipeline will be constructed and operated through a pipeline company whose share-holders are the Uganda National Oil Company, the Tanzania Petroleum Development Corporation and the three oil companies. The East African crude oil pipeline (EACOP) is 1,445 km long (with 296 kms in Uganda), and will transport crude oil from Kabaale in the Hoima district in Uganda to the Chongoleani peninsula near Tanga port in Tanzania. The pipeline route was selected by the Government of Uganda as the least cost (at an estimated tariff of US$ 12.2 per barrel) and most robust route. Due to the viscous and waxy nature of the oil, the pipeline will need to be heated along the entire route, making the EACOP the longest electrically heated pipeline in the world (MEMD, 2017). The pipeline will be buried (1.2 metres deep), and in some cases it will require to be bored under waterways and roads by using horizontal drilling. Some facilities will be above ground such as coating plants and pipeline storage yards, additional workspace for fuel, waste, etc. and access roads and borrow pits. The pipeline also involves pumping stations and pressure reduction stations (EACOP–TILENGA Uganda Scoping Report, 2017).

According to WWF and CSCO (2017), there are opportunities for increased employment and business growth because the EACOP is expected to provide a total of 5,000 jobs, of which an estimated 300 will be permanent and 4,700 temporary. However, the report also highlighted the fear of increased inequality resulting from the socio-economic changes associated with the new employment opportunities, which consequently will lead to income differentials as different local groups and individuals benefit or are negatively impacted upon unevenly from the induced socio-economic opportunities and challenges from the EACOP project. WWF and CSCO (2017) further observed that there are also concerns that more stress, crime and disruption will disrupt community cohesion as a result of rapid population growth from immigrations associated with the development of the EACOP project, and that these can increase stress, change individuals' patterns of interaction within communities, reduce community cohesion, and change a community's character.

The role of land and natural resources in conflict is attracting increased international attention (UN HABITAT, 2012, p.13). The concern in the Albertine region is that changes in land-use patterns such as agriculture, fishing, logging or hunting could increase as a direct consequence of land take or exclusion during the EACOP project, which could potentially lead to conflict (Kobusingye, Van Leeuwen and Van Dijk, 2017). According to UN HABITAT (2012, p.8), while 'environmental factors are rarely, if ever, the sole cause of violent conflict … the exploitation of natural resources and related environmental stresses can be implicated in all phases of the conflict cycle, from contributing to the outbreak and perpetuation of violence to undermining prospects for peace'. According to WWF and CSCO (2017, p.3), 'contamination of water, land and other basic livelihood necessities like oil spills and leakages could lead to chemical contamination of soil and water resources, exposure to fires and disruption of livelihoods'. It further suggests that 'oil pipelines are reported to cause disproportionate impacts on low-income and minority communities especially with regard to human rights violations in several areas around the world'. These impacts have been reported in African countries like Nigeria, Angola and South Sudan (Alozieuwa, 2012; Fidelis, 2010; UN HABITAT, 2012). There are also fears that the 'reduced State capacity and risk of armed conflict' due to 'oil dependence could skew the institutional development of the state because oil rents weaken agencies of restraint unlike in resource-poor countries' (WWF and CSCO, 2017, p.3).

According to a private consultant on oil and gas management and environment, most of the social tensions and grievances in the region stem from land, which he attributed to the influx of job seekers. He observed that:

Because of oil discovery, most people have stamped this area to fetch for opportunities and as a result they want land which is now scarce and on high demand. As a result, they end up grabbing other people's land and moving to forest reserves and swamps because almost 90% of the people in this area don't have land tittles and this has increased social tensions within in the community. If you went to court today you will find most of the cases are related to land. At the district level, the leaders who have got key information regarding on where certain infrastructures and oil related developments will take place, they quickly run to these places and grab off the land and title it and yet the land has got squatters (Private oil consultant Mr. R. Byaruhanga, Personal communication, November 2016).

During the construction of some roads in the region, there were also tensions and community grievances. One of the respondents claimed that during the construction of the 95 km Kaiso-Tonya road there was a lot of stone blasting, especially in one village called Kyenjojo which affected many houses and led to the deaths of animals like cows and the destruction of people's crops. Some women miscarried and most of these people have never been compensated for those injuries. These losses, according to him, were sources of grievances and were brewing tensions. He claimed that such people were 'potential candidates' who will cut the oil pipeline passing through their gardens because of the conflict that exists there.

Another respondent explained how the discovery of oil has affected the communities both positively and negatively, thereby creating tensions and grievances among the communities. He observed that the discovery of oil and gas in this region had increased a lot of expectations where people started to anticipate that there was going to be a lot of money. This has been documented by many researchers (Kiiza, Bategeka and Ssewanyana, 2011; Tumusiime *et al*, 2016). As a result, this led to the scramble for and partitioning of land, which worsened the land problems in the region, especially in Buhuka Kyangwali and Kyakaboga, Bugambe sub-counties in Hoima District. A local community mobiliser working in the area observed that a local organisation—Bunyoro Albertine Network of Civil Society Organisations on Environmental Conservation (BAPENECO)—conducted research to ascertain people's perceptions on oil and their involvement, and in one of its findings found that three cases of murder had happened between the Alur community and the pastoralists over land use and control. This, according to him, was one example of the tensions which have pitted these two communities against each other in the region.

13.2.2 Socio-economic and Political Concerns

According to local newspaper reports, in 2011 the Bunyoro kingdom, a traditional kingdom where most of Uganda's oil was discovered, made it clear that it wants the central government to pay it 10 per cent of revenues from the crude reserves once commercial production starts. An official from Bunyoro kingdom noted that the kingdom, which has had long-standing grievances against the central government, arrived at the final figure it is demanding after what he called 'intense discussions' by its Cabinet. He asserted that the *Omukama* King's cabinet deliberated over this issue for a long time and they had arrived at the figure of 10 per cent based on similar industry practices in other countries like Ghana. However, according to the Public Finance

Management Act (2015), central government will retain 94 per cent, while the local governments in the region will get 6 per cent. There is no specific mention of Bunyoro Kitara Kingdom in the Act. However, section 75(8) of the same Act (2015, p.69) states that 'the Government shall grant one percentage point of the royalty due to the Central Government to a gazetted cultural or traditional institutions'.

The kingdom has pointed to Article 36 of the 1955 Bunyoro Agreement which states that 'in the event of any mineral development taking place, a substantial part of the mineral royalties and the revenues from mining leases shall be paid to the Native Government of Bunyoro-Kitara'. Article 37 adds that '[a]ll natives shall have the right of fishing in all public waters…'. The surrounding communities along Lake Albert claim that fishing on the lake has some restrictions (International Alert, 2013; Ogwang et al., 2018; Vanclay, 2017) which have impacted on their livelihoods. These may result in major tensions and grievances. The kingdom is also demanding a publicly-funded university to be located in its area and a financial allocation to cover any environmental damage from petroleum production. There are fears that if the central government fails to meet the kingdom's demands, these grievances could produce hostility against oil companies and possible sabotage of oil installations, especially by the region's swelling ranks of unemployed youth.

A recurrent source of social tensions and grievances in the region is related to land grabbing and compensation (Ogwang and Vanclay, 2019; Olanya, 2015; Tusiime et al., 2016), some of which have been married with domestic violence. According to one respondent there was no element of gender sensitivity as far as giving compensation money was concerned. He observed that the moment men got the money they went ahead and did what pleased them rather than their families. For example, they marred more women, bought motorcycles (boda bodas) and alcohol, which led to domestic conflicts and some families broke apart. He further noted that while some people opted for relocation, many of them faced difficulties in moving on with their lives because of the Government's delays in relocating them.

In July 2013, the Africa Institute for Energy Governance (AFIEGO) in partnership with Oil Watch Network Uganda, and Publish What You Pay Bunyoro Chapter, mobilised the representatives of the project-affected persons for a 'dialogue' on the 'Violation of the Rights of People Affected by Uganda's Refinery Development'. This was in line with the principles of stakeholder engagement (International Finance Cooperation [IFC], 2007) and addressing issues related to project-induced in-migration (IFC, 2009), respectively. The dialogue brought together 25 participants comprising representatives from all the 13 affected villages of Kabaale which had over 7,000 people.

Other participants came from the districts of Kibaale, Buliisa, Masindi and Kiryandongo. During the meeting, a number of concerns were raised, in particular.

The failure to put regulations for the assessment and payment of compensation in place. It was noted that for the last 20 years the Minister for Lands, Housing and Urban Development had failed to make regulations for the assessment and payment of compensation as required by section 20 of the Compulsory Land Acquisition Act. This had left the people affected at the discretion of districts that are required to compile rates and the chief government valuer who endorses all payments. As a result, it remains difficult for one to challenge the rates in cases of disagreement.

The participants also noted that there was a conflict of interest and bias because it was inappropriate for the MEMD to allow the Strategic Friends International (SFI) company to conduct the Resettlement Action Plan (RAP) and at the same time to implement the plan through the ongoing compensation disclosures. This was irregular and falls below the required transparency necessary to guarantee respect for the rights and the future livelihoods of the local communities affected. The participants further observed that the MEMD and the SFI company had failed to make public the findings of the RAP for the last two years (2011 and 2012). By then, even Parliament and especially the Members of Parliament (MPs) representing the affected communities had no access to the RAP report. The participants were concerned that the SFI company was unable to avoid bias and conflict of interest in this case.

Furthermore, members were concerned about the secrecy around the contractual relationship between the MEMD and SFI. It was noted that there was no evidence that the services of SFI were procured through competitive processes and there was no guarantee that Ugandans would get value for money. Members were also aggrieved about the lack of competence on the part of SFI. They observed that while the SFI has been conducting several training sessions and research studies with a number of local districts and health centres across Uganda, there was no evidence to indicate any competence to deal with a project such as the proposed oil refinery in Kabaale that was scheduled to displace over 7,000 people. They pointed to the fact that the SFI and the MEMD had for two years failed to make public the RAP report, which brought its incompetence to the surface. In addition, they had also failed to advise Hoima district to put in place the 2013 compensation rates and were using an unapproved rate from 2011/2012. This, according to them, might lead to the possibility of the people affected opting to take the law into their hands in future.

In addition, the members were also concerned about the lack of respect for the right to information, public participation and access to justice necessary to guarantee common benefits, collectively termed as 'violation of access rights'. They asserted that Hoima district's local government, for instance, had ignored the need to involve the people in setting up and making decisions on compensation rates as required under the Land Act. Instead, the communities affected were being indirectly coerced to sign compensation forms without being given time to study them and make a decision whether or not to sign. This formed a basis for grievance among the project affected communities.

There were grievances related to several petitions to Parliament and government ministries which were not given much attention. Members felt that the grievances contained in these petitions were ignored. They noted that in May 2013 a delegation of 36 people representing all the 13 affected villages in Hoima and others from Buliisa petitioned the Parliament of Uganda, the Minister for Energy and Mineral Development, the Minister for Lands, Housing and Urban Development, the Minister for Bunyoro Affairs and the Hoima District Council, calling upon the Government to address the injustice and violation of their rights in the RAP process by MEMD and SFI. Therefore, this was interpreted by some locals as 'undermining' their grievances and integrity, and remained a permanent thorn in their relationship with the Government.

According to the Constitution, under Article 26, a person is entitled to adequate and prompt compensation for loss of any property rights. However, some of the people observed that the project-affected communities had been denied the right to negotiate their compensation or decide where to be resettled. They asserted that SFI had told the affected communities to sign documents for compensation, which were written in English, yet most of the affected communities cannot write or read English. To make it worse, they were not told the specific dates on which to expect their payments to enable them to plan properly for their future. As a result, the communities were subjected to a lot of speculation and anxiety.

Concerns over under-valuation of fruit trees such as mangoes were also raised by the members. They argued that UGX 80,000/= as the value of a mature mango tree under the 2012 rates was too small and did not take into account the fact that a mango tree could produce mangoes worth over UGX 100,000/= in a season. They also observed that it takes over six years for a new tree to grow before any harvesting can take place. Therefore, these six years should be compensated for at the rate of UGX 100,000 per season to cater for the years of deprivation as they waited for the new harvest.

In addition to the above, the proposed EACOP pipeline has already created concerns among the locals where the pipe will be constructed. This project will need land to build above-ground facilities (AGFs) like pumping stations, camps, and access roads among others. These will lead to displacements. According to the EACOP ESIA report (2018), the number of project affected persons (PAPs), with regards to temporary and permanent resettlement-related impacts, is estimated at 300–400 households. An estimated 1,700–3,000 households will be economically displaced. But, given the past experiences (Global Rights Alert, 2015; Imaka and Musisi, 2013), tensions are already building high among some communities which will be affected by this development which puts their livelihoods into uncertainty. According to IFC (2012, p.1), livelihood refers to the 'full range of means that individuals, families, and communities utilize to make a living, such as wage-based income, agriculture, fishing, foraging, other natural resource-based livelihoods, petty trade, and bartering'. IFC Performance Standard 5 (2012, p.1) recognises that 'project-related land acquisition and restrictions on land use can have adverse impacts on communities and persons that use this land'. According to IFC (2012, p.1), 'involuntary resettlement refers both to physical displacement (relocation or loss of shelter) and to economic displacement (loss of assets or access to assets that leads to loss of income sources or other means of livelihood) as a result of project-related land acquisition and/or restrictions on land use'. It further suggests that 'resettlement is considered involuntary when affected persons or communities do not have the right to refuse land acquisition or restrictions on land use that result in physical or economic displacement'.

This occurs in cases of; (i) lawful expropriation or temporary or permanent restrictions on land use; and (ii) negotiated settlements in which the buyer can resort to expropriation or impose legal restrictions on land use if negotiations with the seller fail (IFC, 2012, p.1). While some of the respondents were compensated, many complained of low rates for their land and crops. These, according to them, affected their livelihoods in many respects. This is why the Government and the oil companies should constructively engage with the affected communities to address any speculation regarding land acquisition and utilisation in the region. Reddy, Smyth and Steyn (2015, p.59) argue that anxiety, fear and speculation should be avoided because 'perception is reality if you do not engage then, people will create their own reality'.

Another source of social tensions and community grievances is related to suspicion, hatred and mistrust (Tumusiime *et al.*, 2016), which is mainly caused by a lack of information-sharing. One respondent claimed that important information is often concealed from the general population by being labelled 'classified' by the Government and oil companies. Many people have especially questions concerning the distribution and allocation of oil revenues. Illustratively, one respondent interviewed as part of this study, raised the following questions about the allocation of oil revenues: 'How much will the 6% given to local districts be? We also don't know where some of the crude oil which was drilled during oil testing went? Well we heard that some of this oil was sold to Nakansongola, others to Hima cement factory. Where did the money that came from it go? Where did the government put that money?' (Mr. K. Mugume, personal communication, November 2016). All these questions remain unanswered, so all these form sources of tension.

The area Member of Parliament for Buliisa county noted that there was still a feeling that oil and gas is a highly 'technical issue'. He was concerned that most people do not have access to information, and procedures for accessing oil-related documents are not known; oil contracts are not easily accessible. He wondered how an ordinary citizen can access information on the oil sector if the Members of Parliament cannot have ready access to some of the information. While he argued that participation was a right of all the citizens, many do not know that they have the right to participate and some believe that such issues belong to Government. He castigated the Government for thwarting their efforts in trying to prepare the public to participate effectively. In his view, public participation was constrained by lack of access to information, under-developed capacity, and lack of sensitisation. He argued that many stakeholders lacked the capacity to understand the content of the documents concerning oil and gas. He concluded that 'issues like the laws, content of the contract are severely lacking so even where information is availed many don't have capacity to comprehend the content' (Ssewante, F., personal communication, November 2016).

The above grievances are not new. For example, a number of studies have documented many concerns about the secrecy surrounding the operations of oil and gas companies and their dealings with the Government, which proved to be problematic at both the national and regional levels (Avocats Sans Frontières, 2014; Global Witness, 2013a; 2013b; Kiiza et al., 2011; Ogwang et al., 2018). For instance, in 2010 there was a parliamentary revolt over the undisclosed terms of agreements between the oil companies and the Government that were not made public. Parliamentarians accused some cabinet ministers of taking bribes from the companies in exchange for oil deals. After several verbal clashes and debates, in 2012 the Government disclosed to parliamentarians aspects of the oil deals it had with international oil companies, but details of the agreement remained confidential due to 'commercial interests', sparking further speculation about corruption and how these deals benefit the average Ugandan citizen.

This secrecy and lack of information is also replicated at local levels (Avocats Sans Frontières, 2014; Mawejje and Bategeka, 2013). There have been only minimal efforts, and in some cases no efforts, to enable community members to understand the legal requirements, procedures, processes, and the entire management framework of the oil and gas industry in the region. For instance, the Resettlement Action Plan (RAP) which is the most important document detailing terms and conditions for resettlement and compensation was not revealed initially to the project-affected people in Kabaale, Buseruka sub county in Hoima. Even the district leadership did not have access to it, leaving a huge communications void. Ideally the, RAP should not only be made available to the affected populations and their leadership, but should also be translated into languages that people understand so that they can make informed decisions.

According to a top local government official in Kibaale District, most of the sources of social tensions and community grievances arose from the displacement of people from their areas to pave way for oil infrastructures like the oil refinery, pipelines and the airport. He observed that whereas some people were compensated the money given to them was not enough and they have been complaining to this day. He further noted that since the discovery of oil, local communities and their leaders were not allowed access to areas with oil infrastructure. One of the respondents working with a community-based organisation observed that there were concerns over the 29 square kilometres which the Government acquired legally for the construction of the oil refinery in Kabaale in Hoima district. According to him there were some people who opted for relocation while others opted for compensation. He noted that the whole compensation process was punctuated with irregularities, ranging from under-valuation of property, and limited capacity training for the people on how to use their compensation money. For example, a person who got one million in a lump sum and had never got it before thought that all their problems were solved, which led to mismanagement of money.

According to him the problem was compounded by the fact that those who were outside the 29 square kilometres knew that those who were displaced were paid and decided to raise the price of land way beyond what the displaced people could afford with the money they received. In the end most of them ended up in wetlands and public forest reserves, leading to deforestation and environmental degradation. In addition, the community in the refinery areas claims that rates used for the valuation of their property were not communicated to them, and some claim that even after the completion of the property valuation there was no feedback on the value of their property, so they had no idea how much money they would get. This has led to dissatisfaction among the local communities, who questioned why the valuation team did not allow them to raise complaints before displaying details of the valuation.

Some locals also complained that the problem of low compensation was further compounded by the fact that the compensation agreements were in English. They argued that the majority of people cannot read or write English. There were allegations that some women thought they had signed land-use agreements, yet they were actually signing for compensation for destroyed crops, while others signed without knowing what they were signing for. There was also another concern by the respondents who claimed that the farmers were encouraged to produce a lot, hoping to get a bigger market from the oil industry. But this did not happen, as most of the supplies came from Kampala. The local communities do not ideally consume the surplus produced, thus discouraging the farmers from growing crops on a large scale. But one of the workers with the District Farmers Association observed that 'everybody wants to supply directly to the camps which is not possible. You find that many people want to enter the system and yet not all people can be taken on in this kind of arrangement' (Angeno, J., personal communication, November 2016).

13.3   Management Mechanisms and their Effectiveness

The management of social tensions and grievances mechanisms and their effectiveness are classified into formal and informal processes. In an interview with one of the staff members of ACODE, a pilot exercise to facilitate the locals acquiring customary land certificates had been introduced to help the community, especially those who could not afford to process freehold tittles easily. He said that people are now being helped to demarcate their land and acquire ownership of land. There is also sensitisation of the masses on how to resolve land-related conflicts. An important mechanism, which has worked at least for now, is the executive pronouncement of the President to stop the issuing of land tittles in Bunyoro region has to some extent helped to reduce the gravity of the problem. But this also meant that people who are well placed can continue processing these land titles at the expense of the local people.

According to one of the respondents, one of the mechanisms which a locally based NGO called Mid-Western Region Anti-Corruption Coalition (MIRAC) adopted in handling the grievances was to organise community round-table dialogues where the duty bearers and the communities are invited to share information concerning oil and gas-related topics and give feedback on the different issues happening in the area, but also amicably find solutions to different conflicts that are related to oil activities. The respondent stated that they bring different stakeholders like government officials who inform the people about the different government programmes in relation to oil and gas, but also listen to their grievances at the same time. According to him, when such government officials cannot offer sufficient answers to the questions asked, then they forward the matter to higher offices. He revealed that, for example, his organisation had petitioned different officers including those from the Ministries of Energy, and Mineral Development, and Lands, Housing and Urban Development (MLHUD). In particular, they petitioned the Ministry of MLHUD on the issue of land grabbing, and as a result of their interventions a total of 14 land tittles which were illegally acquired in Buhuka area, Kyangwali sub-county, were all cancelled. As an organisation, it felt proud of having contributed to this cancellation. The organisation is also involved in increased environmental civic consciousness. Amidst petroleum development, it tells people that environmental degradation and climate change are real. So, they encourage them to plant trees so as to prepare for it normally through tree planting; at times they also help the community to add value to its land and in case it is required for oil-related development then the people get more money through compensation.

According to a top official of Kibaale district local government, there are many different development partners, for example CSOs which are advocating for better management of the oil resource (Amara, P., personal communication, November 2016). Apart from the CSOs, there are also area Members of Parliament who were rallying the citizens on what can be done to manage the oil resource better. Their main concern was oil discovery and was awakening the masses about what they can do on the issues concerning oil. He also noted that, as local governments in the Albertine Graben, they held a workshop in Kampala with different stakeholders on what their contribution could be concerning the oil resources. As local governments from the region, they were also trying to lobby on how much oil revenues can be given because the current arrangement of 7 per cent (6 for the local governments and 1 for traditional leaders) was not 'fair'. As noted earlier, the sharing of the oil dividends is one of the key concerns which needs to be addressed by the Government.

The involvement of the cultural institution, for example the Bunyoro Kitara kingdom and cultural and religious leaders, is seen as important in trying to address the social tensions and grievances. These are also being augmented by Parliament and the local government councils. But even with some of these mechanisms in place, and despite the scrutiny and constant media coverage

TOM OGWANG

of the growing natural resource industry, including oil policies, laws and production agreements, little attention has been given to the legal recourse available for people and communities affected.

According to a study by Avocats Sans Frontières (2014), when asked whether they considered formal mechanisms as means of seeking redress or channelling their grievances 35 per cent of respondents in Buseruka sub-county stated that they had considered formal mechanisms as a means of obtaining redress, while 45 per cent stated that they did not consider the courts as possible redress mechanisms because they did not have any knowledge of the courts or how they functioned. The study further stated that half of the respondents noted that they did not use the courts because they could not afford the legal fees and other charges necessary to have a case filed. The study also revealed the distrust that formal justice mechanisms will meet their needs, citing corruption as the main reason. Some of the respondents assumed that corruption was the cause of delays in court proceedings, especially when the lawyer requested adjournments. The study noted that this points to other problems relating to lack of understanding of court procedures and processes.

Another factor presented as a barrier to accessing courts was the distance that most communities were required to travel. A person whose matter is before the magistrates' court was required to travel approximately 80km from Kabaale Parish to access the nearest magistrates' court in Hoima town council. Another person whose case was before the High Court had to travel over 150km from Kabaale Parish to Masindi town council where the High Court is situated (Avocats Sans Frontières, 2014). The formal mechanisms established by Ugandan law include courts of law (including the magistrates' courts, High Court, Court of Appeal and the Supreme Court), the Uganda Human Rights Commission and quasi-judicial mechanisms including local council courts.

Another mechanism introduced for the management of social tensions and grievances was the Resettlement Action Plan (RAP) Mechanisms. According to Avocats Sans Frontières (2014, p.47), the affected communities' lack of use of the formal justice mechanisms could also be partly explained by the dispute resolution mechanisms created by the Resettlement Action Plan (RAP). The research noted that discussions with district government officials in Hoima District revealed that affected communities had been sensitised about the RAP mechanisms, and had been advised that if they had any grievances related to RAP implementation, they could seek redress from these mechanisms. Within this framework, the community was expected to complain to the village RAP committee, who forwarded their complaints to Strategic Friends International.

Avocats Sans Frontières (2014) observed that similarly, according to the affected communities in Kabaale Parish in Buseruka sub-county, sensitisation was carried out by Strategic Friends International (SFI), the Resident District Commissioner (RDC) and the Ministry of Energy and Mineral Development (MEMD). The communities confirmed that during the sensitisation meetings they were told to use the RAP structures, which implied to them that the courts did not have the mandate to handle matters related to RAP implementation. However, some CSOs, like the Africa Institute for Energy Governance (AFIEGO, 2013), have since resorted to the courts on behalf of the people affected. People take their land-related grievances to different groups of people, for example some organisations that are fighting for the rights of the people. Some of the concerns are taken to Parliament so that they can be heard from there. Also, those who can are encouraged to process land titles because the 'land grabbers' cannot take lands away from people who have got land tittles because the locals will have ownership of the land already.

The other mechanisms which were proposed by the RAP are mediation fora constituted by representatives from the village councils, parish land committees, Ministry of Justice, a representative from the former Petroleum Exploration and Production Department (PEPD), now the Petroleum Directorate, Area District Councillor, a civil society representative, an area woman councillor, among others. In the event that an amicable decision is not reached, a complaint may seek legal redress in courts of law (Avocats Sans Frontières, 2014). At the village level, the RAP committee was elected by the community and composed of two community representatives and the local council 1 (LC 1). According to the community, they were informed that this RAP committee would be their first point of contact if they were dissatisfied with the valuation process. However, the village RAP committee only registers complaints from people who signed forms accepting the valuation outcomes and amount claimed as compensation. This therefore means that those who had grievances regarding compensation are left out of this arrangement.

According to Avocats Sans Frontières (2014), residents on land earmarked for the construction of the oil refinery indicated that they were to be paid compensation that ranged from 3.5 to 7 million Ugandan shillings (US$ 1,400–2,800) per acre of land, depending on the location. They indicated that this amount was too little to enable them to afford land of the same size elsewhere in the neighbouring communities. They also questioned why compensation rates were not uniform across the area marked for the refinery. While the people on the actual site of the refinery were to be compensated at the rate of at least 7 million Ugandan shillings (US$ 2,800) per acre, however, according to the residents some land was valued at 7 million while other land was valued at 3.5 to 6 million Ugandan shillings. These differing compensation rates, while all residents were displaced, became a source of stress and discontent among residents. The lack of transparency in the valuation process, the sole determinant of what a person is paid in compensation, led over 300 community members to refuse to sign the compensation claim form. Therefore, a person cannot be dissatisfied with the valuation process and at the same time sign the compensation claim form, which means that the limited scope of action of the village RAP committee was rendered ineffective for people to use to seek redress. According to Avocats Sans Frontières (2014, p.49), in the words of one of the people who rejected the valuation outcome and refused to sign the compensation claim form, 'the RAP committee did not help us at all; they just signed forms and received allowances. I thought they would have helped us voice our issues and give us feedback but they did nothing'.

Avocats Sans Frontières (2014, p.50) documented that Strategic Friends International (the RAP implementing agency) and MEMD were to be the next level of reference should the village RAP committee fail to resolve a grievance. The village RAP committee was required to forward the community complaints to Strategic Friends International (SFI). SFI did not handle issues of land revaluation for compensation. Instead, it convened community meetings together with the MEMD representatives to meet complainants. The community asserted that during these meetings their grievances were not dealt with, nor did they get answers from SFI or the MEMD representatives, who instead promised them that their issues would be resolved. On other occasions they were told to accept what was offered and stop impeding development (Kinyera, 2019). The Tilenga oil project in Buliisa district faced some resistance from the communities affected when it came to compensation rates for land acquisition for oil and gas projects (NTV Uganda, 2018; Ogwang and Vanclay, 2019).

In many places where there are cases of land disputes in Uganda, the communities normally approach the Resident District Commissioner (RDC) for assistance with their problems. According to Article 205 of the Ugandan Constitution, the RDC has two main tasks: coordinating the administration of government services in the district, and advising the District Chairperson on matters of a national nature that may affect the district or its plans and programmes, particularly in relations between the district and the Government. This mandate does not include judicial or arbitration functions. Nevertheless, despite this clear assignment of roles, the RDC is approached by individuals and communities because s/he is commonly viewed as the President's representative in a district. But in some instances they have been accused of supporting government programmes or siding with the rich against the local people.

According to Avocats Sans Frontières (2014), the perception of the RDC as the President's representative gives the community the misguided belief that, like the President, s/he has the power to grant favours, including the expeditious resolution of problems at the local level. Numerous groups and individuals have made appeals to the President for redress, compensation and the return of property. The communities pointed out that the RDC had not been helpful and had often dismissed their concerns. On one specific occasion, when people with complaints about the measurement and valuation of their land mobilised in large numbers to meet SFI and MEMD representatives, the RDC came with police and security personnel armed with tear gas and water cannons. They noted that although 'the tear gas and water cannons were not used, the presence of these items and the police and security personnel frightened them into not demanding answers from SFI' (Avocats Sans Frontières, 2014, p.51).

Avocats Sans Frontières (2014) further observed that the RAP mechanisms have created a perception that access to justice for RAP implementation-related issues can only be achieved through the executive arm of government, in which MEMD and RDC are located. This contravenes the doctrine of separation of powers and checks and balances enshrined in the Constitution of the Republic of Uganda which provides in Article 126 that judicial power shall be exercised by courts established under the Constitution. Subsequently, these findings showed the strong inclination of the people to utilise justice mechanisms they understand, are comfortable with and can afford, despite the fact that their choices are not based on their appropriateness to address the legal concerns and human rights issues they face. This is a legal vacuum that needs to be addressed to ensure access to justice and redress (Avocats Sans Frontières, 2014, p.51).

13.4   Conclusion and Recommendations

This chapter has analysed the major tensions and grievances that exist in the communities in and around the oil-rich Albertine region. It further examined the mechanisms and policies which have been implemented by the Government and other stakeholders, including international oil companies (IOC), to manage and mitigate the prevailing social tensions and grievances, and assessed how effective these mechanisms have been in resolving the tensions and grievances which have emerged as a result of the oil exploration- and production-related activities. While several studies (Kutesa, 2014; UNDP, 2016) have recognised that the extractive industry sector, especially oil production, could double or triple Uganda's current export earnings, some studies have also highlighted the dark side of this industry (Karl, 1997; Vokes, 2012; Mosbacher, 2013; Ogwang et al., 2019). It is therefore important that the different stakeholders need to take into account people's grievances in order to avoid the negative experiences of other oil producing countries.

Government should empower the local councils to handle the land issues at the local level, and where they are ineffective the cases should then be handled at the sub-county level. As there is still need for more land to accommodate the increasing demand for oil and gas infrastructure, it would be prudent to develop and provide a clear description of the potential extent/magnitude of displacement of persons/settlements including clear compensation and livelihoods restoration plans (LRPs). A well communicated compensation scheme (Honeyman, 2003) should be provided in the RAP to the potential and actual project affected persons (PAPs). The stakeholders should try to reduce suspicion among the locals by reducing the restriction on accessing oilfields to enable the locals to access firewood and medicinal herbs.

To avoid unnecessary and unrealistic expectations from these communities, it is recommended that the Government and the oil companies should develop clear management of expectations and anxiety plans. The process of this development should include the relevant stakeholders so that their voices are heard. Some of these could include providing upfront, clear, concrete and well communicated procedures for the provision of goods and services, hiring labour (both local and national), including their working conditions and duration. There is need for open, honest and realistic estimates (for example 5,000 for EACOP) to be provided with regard to labour requirements for the project, as well as training and transfer of knowledge. In addition, clear communication procedures should be introduced to allow for effective collection of complaints and responses to grievances of the people affected by the project's activities.

Furthermore, the stakeholders involved in the EACOP project and feeder pipelines should provide clear descriptions of how the pipeline's construction will be undertaken without causing significant environmental disturbance, for instance for forests, wetlands and other areas with vulnerable water conditions. It is also recommended that mitigation measures should be provided for all impacts that cannot be avoided. In summary, all the potential environmental and social consequences of these risks with regard to the pipeline should be addressed.

References

Alozieuwa, S.H.O. (2012), 'Contending Theories on Nigeria's Security Challenge in the Era of Boko Haram Insurgency', *Peace and Conflict Review*, 7(1), 1–8.

Aristide, M., and M. Moundigbaye (2017), 'Oil and Regional Development in Chad: Assessment of the Impact of the Doba Oil Project on Poverty in the Host Region', *African Development Review*, 29(1), 42–55

Avocats Sans Frontières (2014), *Human Rights Implications of Extractive Industry Activities in Uganda: A Study of the Mineral Sector in Karamoja and the Oil Refinery in Bunyoro*. Kampala: ASF.

Bainomugisha, A., H. Kivengyere and B. Tusasirwe (2006), 'Escaping the Oil Curse and Making Poverty History: A Review of the Oil and Gas Policy and Legal Framework for Uganda'. *ACODE Policy Research Series*, No. 20.

De Kock, P., and K. Sturman (2012), *The Power of Oil: Charting Uganda's Transition to a Petro-State*. Johannesburg: South African Institute of International Affairs.

Eggert, R. (2001), *Mining and Economic Sustainability: National Economies and Local Communities*, MMSD Report No. 19. London: International Institute for Environment and Development. Retrieved from: http://pubs.iied.org/pdfs/G00952.pdf.

Fidelis, A. (2010), *Implementation of Oil-Related Environmental Policy in Nigeria: Government Inertia and Conflict in the Niger Delta*. Doctor of Philosophy   Dissertation. Pietermaritzburg: University of KwaZulu-Natal.

Global Rights Alert (2015), *Acquisition of Land for the Oil Refinery: Tracking Progress in Resettling Project Affected Persons Who Opted for Land for Land Compensation*. Kampala: Global Rights Alert.

Global Witness (2013a), *The Benefits for Uganda of Joining the Emerging Global Transparency Standard for Extractive Industry Revenues*. London: Global Witness.

——— (2013b), *The Importance of a Transparent, Open and Fair Allocation Process for Uganda's Remaining Oil Rights*. London: Global Witness.

Holterman, D. (2014), 'The Biopolitical War for Life: Extractives and the Ugandan Oil State', *Extractive Industries & Society* 1(1), 28–37.

Honeyman, C. (2003), 'Grievance Procedures. Beyond Intractability'. Retrieved from the University of Colorado website: https://www.beyondintractability.org/essay/grievance-procedures.

Imaka, I., and F. Musisi (2013, 6 October), 'Oil Refinery: Residents Reject Government Pay'. *Daily Monitor*. Retrieved from: https://www.monitor.co.ug/News/National/Oil-refinery--Residents-reject-government-pay/688334-2019962-2fux9mz/index.html.

International Alert (2013), *Governance and Livelihoods in Uganda's Oil-rich Albertine Graben*. London: International Alert.

International Finance Corporation (2007), *Stakeholder Engagement: A Good Practice Handbook for Companies Doing Business in Emerging Markets*. Washington, DC: International Finance Corporation.

——— (2009), *Projects and People: A Handbook for Addressing Project-Induced In-migration*. Washington. DC: International Finance Corporation.

——— (2012), *Guidance Note 5: Land Acquisition and Involuntary Resettlement*. Washington, DC: International Finance Corporation.

Karl, T.L. (1997), *The Paradox of Plenty: Oil Booms and Petro-States*. Berkeley, California: University of California Press.

Kiiza, J., L. Bategeka and S. Ssewanyana (2011), 'Righting Resource-Curse Wrongs in Uganda: The Case of Oil Discovery and the Management of Popular Expectations', *The Journal of Humanities and Social Sciences*, 10(3), 183–203.

Kinyera, P.B. (2019), 'Land, Oil and Expressions of Citizenship in Uganda's Albertine   Graben', *Extractive Industry & Society*, 6, 110–119.

Kobusingye, D.N., M. Van Leeuwen and H. Van Dijk (2017), 'The Multifaceted Relationship between Land and Violent Conflict: The Case of Apaa Evictions in Amuru District, Northern Uganda', *Journal of Modern African Studies*, 53(3), 455–477.

Kuteesa, A. (2014), *Local Communities and Oil Discoveries: A Study in Uganda's Albertine Graben Region*. Washington, DC: Brookings Institute.

Mawejje, J., and L. Bategeka (2013), 'Accelerating Growth and Maintaining Intergenerational Equity Using Oil Resources in Uganda'. *EPCR Research Series No. 111*. Retrieved from; https://www.africaportal.org/publications/accelerating-growth-and-maintaining-intergenerational-equity-using-oil-resources-in-uganda/.

Ministry of Energy and Mineral Development (2013), *Strategic Environmental Assessment (SEA) of Oil and Gas Activities in the Albertine Graben*. Kampala: Government of Uganda.

—— (2017), 'Statement by the Minister of Energy and Mineral Development at the Signing of the Intergovernmental Agreement Between the Republic of Uganda and the United Republic of Tanzania for the East African Crude Oil Pipeline (EACOP) Project 26 May 2017'. Retrieved from: https://www.jamiiforums.com/attachments/349505503-uganda-minister-statement-on-iga-signing-may-2017-memd-final2-pdf.514981/.

Mosbacher, J. (2013), 'Fighting the Resource Curse: Uganda's Pivotal Moment', *The Washington Quarterly*, 36(4), 43–54.

National Association of Professional Environmentalists (NAPE) (2016), *Women-Led Action Oriented Research on the Negative Impacts of Oil on Women's Rights, Land and Food Sovereignty in Uganda's Oil Region 2015/2016*. Kampala: National Association of Professional Environmentalists.

NTV Uganda (2018), 'Lands Minister Betty Amongi, Buliisa Residents Clash over Oil Compensation Rates'. Retrieved from; https://www.youtube.com/watch?v=xOQNrz2i6b4.

Ogwang, T., and F. Vanclay (2019), 'Social Impacts of Land Acquisition for Oil and Gas Development in Uganda', *Land*, 8(7), 109–116.

——, —— and A. Van den Assem (2018), 'Impacts of the Oil Boom on the Lives of People Living in the Albertine Graben Region of Uganda', *Extractive Industry & Society*, 5(1), 98–103. Retrieved from: https://doi.org/10.1016/j.exis.2017.12.015.

——, —— and —— (2019), 'Rent-Seeking Practices, Local Resource Curse, and Social Conflict in Uganda's Emerging Oil Economy', *Land*, 8(4), 1–14. Retrieved from: https://doi.org/10.3390/land8040053.

Olanya, D.R. (2015), 'Will Uganda Succumb to the Resource Curse? Critical Reflections', *Extractive Industries & Society*, 2(1), 46–55. Retrieved from: https://doi.org/10.1016/j.exis.2014.09.002.

Reddy, G., E. Smyth and M. Steyn (2015), *Land Access and Resettlement: A Guide to Best Practice*. Sheffield: Greenleaf.

Scarborough, G.I. (1998), 'An Expert System for Assessing Vulnerability to Instability', in J. Davies and T.R. Gur (eds.), *Preventive Measures: Building Risk and Crisis Early Warning Systems*. Lanham, Maryland: Rowan and Littlefield.

Schwarte, C. (2008), *Public Participation and Oil Exploitation in Uganda*. London: International Institute for Environment and Development.

Söderholm, P., and N. Svahn (2015), 'Mining, Regional Development and Benefit-sharing in Developed Countries', *Resources Policy*, 45(1), 78–91.

The Africa Institute for Energy Governance (2013), 'Statement on the Violation of the Rights of People Affected by Uganda's Refinery Development'. Retrieved from: http://ugandajournalistsresourcecentre.com/statement-on-the-violation-of-the-rights-of-people-affected-by-ugandas-refinery-development/.

The Independent (2018, 20 December), '"First Oil" Date Moves to 2022 – Minister Muloni', *The Independent*. Retrieved from: https://www.independent.co.ug/uganda-now-to-get-first-oil-by-2022-minister-muloni/.

Tumusiime, D.M., J. Mawejje and P. Byakagaba (2016), 'Discovery of Oil: Community Perceptions and Expectations in Uganda's Albertine Region', 9 *Journal of Sustainable Development*, No. 6.

Uganda Land Alliance (2011), 'Land Grabbing and Its Effects on the Communities in the Oil Rich Albertine Region of Uganda: The Case of Hoima, Buliisa and Amuru'. Retrieved from: https://landportal.org/library/resources/uganda-landgr-201109/land-grabbing-and-its-effects-communities-oil-rich-albertine.

UN HABITAT (2012), 'Toolkit and Guidance for Preventing and Managing Land and Natural Resources Conflict: Land and Conflict'. Retrieved from: https://www.un.org/en/land-natural-resources-conflict/pdfs/GN_Land%20and%20Conflict.pdf.

United Nations Development Programme (2016), Human Development Report 2016: Human Development for Everyone, The United Nations Development Programme. New York: UNDP.

Van der Ploeg, L., and F. Vanclay (2017), 'A Human Rights-based Approach to Project-induced Displacement and Resettlement', *Impact Assessment and Project Appraisal*, 35(1), 34–52.

Vanclay, F. (2017), 'Project-induced Displacement and Resettlement: From Impoverishment Risks to an Opportunity for development?', *Impact Assessment and Project Appraisal*, 35(1), 3–21.

Vokes, R. (2012), 'The Politics of Oil In Uganda', *African Affairs*, 111(443), 303–314.

WWF and CSCO (2017), 'Safeguarding People & Nature in the East African Crude Oil (EACOP) Pipeline Project, A Preliminary Environmental and Socio-economic Threat Analysis. *WWF and CSCO Research Paper No. 3*. Retrieved from; https://www.wwf.no/assets/attachments/99-safeguarding_nature_and_people___oil_and_gas_pipeline_factsheet.pdf.

PART IV

INTERNATIONAL COMPARISON

14
Nigeria's Oil Governance Regime: Challenges and Policies

Ukoha Ukiwo

14.1   Introduction

This chapter attempts to discuss the different regimes that have evolved as Nigeria's post-colonial State seeks to govern oil. It argues that there are clearly four generations of regimes for the governance of oil in Nigeria. The chapter draws attention to the underlying pressures that underpin the emergence of each generation and ongoing efforts to address challenges in the successive regulatory and engagement frameworks. It is divided into five sections. This next section provides a background analysis of the Nigerian oil sector and seeks to explain its historical and contemporary challenges. This is followed in Section 3 with an examination of the first-generation governance regime for oil, which focused on ownership and control as well as production relationships. Section 4 focusses on the second-generation regime of oil that concentrates mostly on distributional and benefits issues. In Section 5, the paper addresses the concerns of third-generation regimes on environmental protection and sustainability. The sixth and concluding section explores contemporary efforts to address various challenges of oil governance through the instrumentality of an omnibus Petroleum Industry Bill.

14.2   Historical and Sectoral Overview of the Nigerian Oil Industry

For over two decades, Nigeria has been sub-Saharan African's largest producer of oil and the world's eighth largest producer of oil.[1] Nigeria's foray into oil production started in 1907 when exploration activities by Nigerian Bitumen

---

1   Nigeria's status as Africa's biggest oil producer/exporter has intermittently been undermined by production losses caused by militancy in the Niger Delta. For instance, between November 2015

Corporation (NBC) began. Exploration activities ceased with the onset of the First World War as the NBC departed the shores of Nigeria. Following the end of the war, D'Arcy Exploration Company and White Hall Petroleum also secured licences for exploration but returned the licences in 1923 after a frustrating exploration experience. In 1937, Shell D'Arcy, a merger between Shell and British Petroleum, commenced exploration activities.

However, it was not until the eve of the country's independence that oil was found in commercial quantities. The company's investment of over six million pounds over almost two decades yielded a significant find in Oloibiri in 1956 where oil was found in commercial quantity. By 1958, half a century after the commencement of exploration activities, Nigeria joined the league of oil producing nations by producing and exporting an average of 5,100 barrels per day. It is important to underscore this coincidence between independence and the commercial exploitation of oil because it explains the pervasive role of oil in shaping the character of the Nigerian post-colonial State. The discovery of exportable oil served to reinforce the foundational workings of the colonial enterprise in the framing of the Nigerian State as an extractive phenomenon. To the extent that the colonial State specialised in the extraction of rents from commodity production and the export and imports of finished products, the post-colonial period has witnessed continuities in the State's preoccupation with extraction and the appropriation of rents from oil.

A major discontinuity witnessed in the post-colonial period as a result of the ascendancy of oil has been the centralisation of ownership, control and appropriation of oil revenues. To be sure, while the central government representing the British Crown owned and controlled oil in the colonial period, this ownership and control was mostly titular and symbolic since it was fiscally inconsequential. This rentier orientation was inherited by the post-colonial State which, as shall become evident, extended its control in the oil sphere without making commensurate investments for the exploration and development of the sector.

The reaffirmation of central ownership, control and appropriation in the post-colonial period when oil graduated to become the mainstay of the Nigerian economy and cash cow of the Nigerian State came under stiff challenges from regional elites and peoples who were socialised into and had been accustomed to regionalisation of commodity export rent appropriation in the colonial period. The accumulated grievance of these elites partly found expression in the Twelve Day Revolution orchestrated for the stillborn Niger

and July 2016, Angola marginally overtook Nigeria as Africa's largest producer. See http://punchng. com/angola-overtakes-nigeria-as-africas-top-oil-producer/.

Delta Republic (1966) and Three-Year Nigeria Civil War that culminated in the abortion of the Biafran Republic (1967–1970). The resurgence of these sentiments and the attendant grievance since the late 1980s in the sites of oil extraction remain one of the greatest challenges that threaten Nigeria's aspirations towards petro-hegemony. By petro-hegemony I mean the conscious unmistakable efforts of the Nigerian political, social and economic power elites to instrumentalise oil for state building and nation building as well as regional and global prominence.

As at 2010, the proven oil reserve was put at 36 billion barrels. This reserve, which is one of the biggest in the world, is estimated to last for 46 years. Nigeria's low sulphur oil (Bonny light) is very much in high demand in North America and European markets (KPMG, 2014). Over the past decade production and export levels have averaged between 1.2 and 2.7 billion barrels per day after picking up in 2009 from an all-time low of 200–700 million barrels per day following the commencement of the amnesty programme for militants in the oil-producing areas of the Niger Delta. However, exploration and exploitation are still undermined by instability and crisis in the region, as well as declining levels of investments. The declining investments in the sector are the consequence of uncertainties engendered by the protracted debates in the Petroleum Industry Governance Bill. The challenges in the sector threaten the realisation of the national energy policy, the target of which is to build up reserves to 40 billion barrels and increase export to 4 million barrels per day (see Madueke, 2013).

The prospects for gas appear to be brighter, with Nigeria believed to have 5.39 trillion cubic metres in reserves, which is about 2.7 per cent of the world's gas reserves. The rich gas endowment of the country has led analysts to describe Nigeria as a massive gas basin with some oil reserves (see Madueke, 2013). The quality of the gas is also very high, with low sulphur content and rich liquids. However, 75 per cent of gas is currently flared in the process of oil production, given the country's poor technological base and lack of incentives for oil-producing companies to invest in gas reinjection and production. Only 12 per cent of gas is reinjected.

The significance of oil and gas is not only to be seen in their contributions to bolstering the country's stature in the global political economy but also with respect to its centrality to the Nigerian political economy. Since 1970, oil has accounted for not less than 80 per cent of public revenues and a minimum of 90 per cent of the country's foreign exchange. As Nigeria has moved from an agricultural commodity exporter to a rentier State since the 1970s, oil has come to define the strength and weakness of the Nigerian State. Both in national and international politics, the exercise and projection of state power have risen and waned as a result of vicissitudes and cyclical fluctuations in global energy markets. Instructively, the two cases of de-legitimation and loss of power by democratically elected governments—President Shehu Shagari through a military coup in 1983 and President Goodluck Jonathan through elections in 2015—occurred when Nigeria's political economy was severally affected by an oil glut and declining petro-dollars.

Recognition of the strategic risks of mono-cultural oil dependency has over the years spewed successive rhetoric and efforts at diversification. However, tackling oil dependency has been challenging with reform programmes ending as truncated visions and stillbirths. While successive Nigerian governments have expressed intentions to promote diversification, they have maintained a policy of monopolising access to and control of the oil industry. This quest for control is ironically evidenced by the decision of two Nigerian presidents who promised reform of the oil industry to insist on direct control of oil to retain the post of Minister of Petroleum Resources.

This is one of the contradictions of the Nigeria oil industry. Two other contradictions that the nature and character of oil exploration, exploitation and production have historically thrown up are worth highlighting at this juncture. First is the competing regional and national claim to ownership of oil arising from the fact that oil and gas resources are mostly produced from three basins located in Southern Nigeria. These are: 1) the Onshore Anambra basin; 2) the offshore Benin-Dahomey deepwater and ultra-deepwater basins; and 3) the Niger Delta shallow and deep offshore basins. Although seismic activities suggest the presence of oil and gas in other locations, notably Benue Trough and Chad Basin, exploitation and production have been in the three aforementioned locations in Southern Nigeria, with the Benin and Niger Delta basins accounting for most of the oil finds and products. The restricted endowment of oil and gas deposits continues to serve as a basis for contestation of national ownership of oil by communal and ethnic communities in oil-producing regions. This contestation has intensified since the late 1980s alongside rising ethno-regional tensions in the Nigerian federation. Second is the dominance of foreign technology and capital in the exploration, exploitation and production of oil and gas. The historical dominance of multinational oil-producing companies in production and the outward orientation of the industry in terms of both inputs and outputs has undermined the quest for national ownership and control.

Given these contradictions, I argue that it is hardly surprising that the regulatory institutions that have evolved over the years have primarily sought to address and/or mitigate the conundrum of regionalism versus nationalism as well as nationalism versus transnationalism/globalism in the oil and gas industry.

14.3   First Generation Oil Governance Regimes

The first category of regulatory institutions includes those that seek firstly to define ownership and control of oil resources, and secondly to define relationships needed for oil exploration, exploitation and production. In this vein, the first legislation on oil in Nigeria was the Nigerian Minerals Ordinance of 1914, enacted shortly after the Northern and Southern protectorates of Nigeria, which vested control and ownership of oil as all mineral resources in the Nigerian land and waters in the British Crown. It provided that prospective explorers for oil should secure licences from the Crown or its sworn representative. The legislation opened the doors to British companies to explore for oil in Nigeria, culminating in the monopoly concession granted to Shell D'Arcy to explore for oil throughout Nigerian land and waters in 1938. However, following the end of the Second World War and the push of the United States against colonial monopoly, other Western European and North American international oil companies (IOCs) mobilised to secure oil exploration licences in Nigerian oilfields. These pressures caused the Nigerian colonial state to relax laws that granted a monopoly to Shell D'Arcy. This relaxation led to successful licensing of major international oil companies to undertake oil exploration in Nigeria in quick succession as follows: Mobil in 1955, Tenneco in 1960, Gulf Oil and Chevron in 1961, Agip in 1962, and Elf in 1962.

Meanwhile, the Ordinance stipulated a production contract regime of a 50–50 profit-sharing arrangement between the oil company and the government. The main provisions of the statute were retained by the Mineral Act of 1958 and Petroleum Act of 1958, enacted as the country was being prepared for independence. It was only in the late 1960s that the Federal Military Government took decisive steps to gain greater control of the oil industry. This was accomplished through the promulgation of the Petroleum Decree 1969 (later called the Petroleum Act of 1969). The Act, which supersedes the Mineral Act of 1958, Petroleum Act of 1958 and Petroleum Control Law of 1967, gives extensive power to the Minister of Petroleum, acting on behalf of the Nigerian State, to exercise ownership and control over oil. The ownership clauses are evident in section 2 of the Act, which empowers the Minister to grant:

a)   a licence, to be known as an oil exploration licence, to explore for petroleum;

b)   a licence, to be known as an oil prospecting licence, to prospect for petroleum; and

c)   a lease, to be known as an oil mining lease, to search for, win, work, carry away and dispose of petroleum.

The Act also grants expansive powers to the Minister to exercise control over refining, distribution and pricing of petroleum products as well as the imposition of sanctions on actors who contravene the laws. As stipulated in section 8(1) of the Act, the Minister:

a) shall exercise general supervision over all operations carried on under licences and leases granted under this Act;

b) shall report annually to the Federal Government on the progress of the oil industry in Nigeria;

c) shall have access at all times to the areas covered by oil exploration licences, oil prospecting licences and oil mining leases, and to all refineries and installations which are subject to this Act, for the purpose of inspecting the operations conducted therein and enforcing the provisions of this Act and any regulations made thereunder and the conditions of any licences or leases granted under this Act or under any corresponding law for the time being in force in Nigeria;

d) may arrest without warrant any person whom he finds committing, or whom he reasonably suspects of having committed, any offence under this Act or any regulations made thereunder, and shall hand over any person so arrested to a police officer with as little delay as possible;

e) may by notice in writing require the holder of a licence or lease granted under this Act or any contractor working for the holder (or any servant or agent of the holder or the contractor) to appear before him at a reasonable time and place to give such information as he may require about the operations being conducted under the licence or lease, and every person so required to appear shall be legally bound to comply with the notice and give the information;

f) may direct in writing that operations under a licence or lease granted under this Act shall be suspended in any area until arrangements have been made which in his opinion are necessary to prevent danger to life or property;

g) may direct in writing the suspension of any operations which in his opinion are not being conducted in accordance with good oil field practice; and

h) may direct in writing the suspension of any operations where in his opinion a contravention of this Act or any regulations made thereunder has been or may have been or is likely to be committed.

The reasons for the dramatic extension of state control were the alleged duplicitous roles of IOCs in the Civil War, the challenges encountered by successive post-colonial governments in exercising control of the IOCs, and the country's application to join the Organisation of Petroleum Exporting Countries (OPEC). The membership of OPEC was particularly significant as OPEC's flagship policy was control of the oil industry by member States in furtherance of the objective to control supply and prices of oil. It is against this background that the post-Civil War era witnessed progressive steps by the Nigerian State to nationalise the oil industry. The Nigerian military government in 1973 initiated the First Participation Agreement and secured 35 per cent of the shares in IOCs which, by the Petroleum Act of 1969, were now incorporated in Nigeria. Barely a year after this, the Government upped its stake to 55 per cent. By 1979, the Government's equity had increased to 60 per cent. Following the nationalisation of British Petroleum the same year to influence the British position on the independence of Zimbabwe, the Nigerian Government extended its holdings to 80 per cent. However, with declining investments in the oil and gas sector, the Government decided to revert to 60 per cent equity in 1989 in the Fifth Participation Agreement and 55 per cent in the Sixth Participation Agreement in 1993.

Alongside strategic management of equity holdings, the State created institutions to exercise control over the industry. The Department of Petroleum Resources (DPR) and Nigerian National Oil Company (NNOC) were created in 1970 and 1971 respectively. In 1974, the DPR was upgraded to the status of Ministry of Petroleum Resources. However, in 1977 both the NNOC and MPR were abolished by the Act establishing the Nigerian National Petroleum Corporation (NNPC). The Act made the NNPC the Government's sole agent in exercising control and ownership of oil in the upstream, downstream and service sectors. The Act vested the following powers and roles on the NNPC:

a) exploring and prospecting for, working, winning or otherwise acquiring, possessing and disposing of
b) petroleum;
c) refining, treating, processing and generally engaging in the handling of petroleum for the manufacture
d) and production of petroleum products and its derivatives;
e) purchasing and marketing petroleum, its products and by-products;
f) providing and operating pipelines, tanker-ships or other facilities for the carriage or conveyance of
g) crude oil, natural gas and their products and derivatives, water and any other liquids or other
h) commodities related to the Corporation's operations;
i) constructing, equipping and maintaining tank farms and other facilities for the handling and treatment

j)   of petroleum and its products and derivatives;
k)   carrying out research in connection with petroleum or anything derived from it and promoting activities
l)   for the purpose of turning to account the results of such research;
m)   doing anything required for the purpose of giving effect to agreements entered into by the Federal Government with a view to securing participation by the Government or the Corporation in activities
n)   connected with petroleum;
o)   generally engaging in activities that would enhance the petroleum industry in the overall interest of Nigeria; and
p)   undertaking such other activities as are necessary or expedient for giving full effect to the provisions of this Act.

Principally under this governance framework, the NNPC enters into partnerships with IOCs for the purpose of oil exploration and production in the upstream sector. The partnerships take four major forms, namely: joint venture agreements, production-sharing contracts, service contracts and marginal field concessions. Production-sharing contracts have in recent years become more common as IOCs exercise caution in signing joint venture agreements, given the inability of the NNPC to meet its own funding commitments to exploration and production.

Efforts at nationalisation were not only restricted to initiatives to secure state ownership and control. There were also efforts to widen access to oil resources among the Nigerian public. This was implemented through institutionalisation of price control and uniform pricing in the downstream sector. Linked to the post-war national integration ideology, the policy sought to ensure that Nigerians from all regions enjoyed equal access to cheap petroleum products (see Ukiwo, 2008a; 2008b).

However, the perennial defaults in payment of joint venture funding commitments and continued foreign control of the industry, as well as oil theft and cross-border smuggling of subsidised petroleum products, have severely limited efforts at exercising national control and ownership. These lingering challenges have given rise to advocacy for reform of the sector. Since the return to civil rule in 1999, pressures for reform have revolved around the Petroleum Industry Governance Bill, which we shall return to shortly.

14.4   Second Generation Oil Governance Regimes

The second generation of oil governance regimes seeks to govern the distribution formula and relative share of all stakeholders of oil resources and revenues. From the outset, different Nigerian stakeholders have mobilised for access to benefits from the oil sector. For instance, one of the preoccupations of Nigeria's nationalists in the colonial period was to aggregate concerns of communities in sites of oil exploration activities whose interests were hardly captured by the Nigerian Mineral Ordinance (see Steyn, 2009). These early mobilisations were mellowed as independence approached because the nationalists clearly began to contemplate the potential role of oil in the stability of the post-colonial State.

It is hardly surprising therefore that the Independence Constitution of 1960 merely pandered to the interest of regional-based elite when it retained a 50–50 ratio of benefits between the regional and national governments based on the principle of derivation. The first step to reduce the percentage of revenues accruing to areas of derivation was the promulgation of the Petroleum Act in 1969 which reduced the share of states to 45 per cent while increasing the federal share to 55 per cent. Interestingly, the development did not generate much resentment in the oil-producing areas at the time because the oil-bearing areas had benefitted from the state creation exercise of 1967, which granted autonomy to minority areas in the former Eastern Region. Moreover, the adjustment was not considered a major incursion into the share of the sub-national units as the ratio accruing to the Federal Government was marginally higher than what was accruing to the state governments. This increment was also tolerated as a result of the increasing responsibility of the Federal Government in the Civil War and early post-Civil War years. The absence of any major social movement to resist the revised revenue distribution formula at the time no doubt contributed to the context in which the ascendant Federal Military Government was emboldened to further slash allocations to states on the basis of derivation from 35 to 20 per cent in 1975.

The gradual reduction of state quotas of oil revenues persisted when the revised revenue allocation formula of 1982 provided that 1.5 per cent of revenues accruing to the Federation Account would be shared on the basis of derivation. This reduction was undertaken by the short-lived civilian government in the Second Republic as the economic crisis, partly driven by oil glut and falling prices, set in. The resumption of military rule and expansion of the Federal Government by January 1984 witnessed further reduction in revenues accruing to oil-producing states on the basis of derivation, ebbing at 1 per cent by 1990. This development led to growing resentments in the oil-producing areas and gave rise to mobilisations for autonomy. Faced by self-determination movements in the oil-producing areas, the Federal Military Government established the Oil Minerals Producing Areas Commission (OMPADEC) in 1993, which was endowed with 3 per cent of oil revenues to address the ecological, social and economic challenges of the region.

However, the advent of OMPADEC did not address the quest and advocacy for autonomy and the reduction of federal control of oil rents. This is because OMPADEC was a federal intervention to address developmental challenges in the region. Much of its resources remained under federal rather than state control. The members and key officers of the Commission were appointed by and responsible to the President, the chief executive officer of the Federal Military Government. Consequently, OMPADEC did not satisfy the quest of the people for autonomy and greater benefits from oil production (see Ozo-Eson and Ukiwo, 2001). Little wonder that protests persisted in the region throughout the 1990s (see Human Rights Watch, 1999).

Part of the protests stemmed from perceptions of marginalisation by the peoples of the region. Not only was the successive diminution of the percentage of revenues that accrued to the oil-bearing areas linked to the minority status of the areas but also access to the oil industry in the forms of employment and business opportunities were perceived as favouring the people from major ethnic groups in Nigeria. Thus, the marginalisation of oil-producing minority groups became a salient manifestation of horizontal inequalities in Nigeria (see Langer and Ukiwo, 2009). A key moment for advocacy for the oil-producing minorities was the 1995 constitutional conference. Representatives of the minority groups campaigned for the percentage of revenue allocated on the principle of derivation to be increased to 50 per cent. Before the conference adjourned *sine die*, some consensus had been reached that a minimum of 13 per cent of revenues generated would be paid to originating states on the basis of derivation. This consensus informed the insertion of a provision for payment of a minimum of 13 per cent derivation revenues in the 1999 Constitution (Federal Republic of Nigeria, 1999; Uche and Uche, 2004).

Following the return to civilian rule in 1999, OMPADEC was abolished as it had become redolent of the corruption that pervaded the years of military rule. The newly elected civilian administration replaced OMPADEC with the Niger Delta Development Commission (NDDC). The take-off of the NDDC was initially marred by controversies, as the Federal Government initially declined to backdate payments of derivation revenues to benefitting states to 29 May 1999 when the Fourth Republic was inaugurated (see Edevbie, 2000). Regional elites and social movements in the Niger Delta were also peeved by the re-introduction of the offshore-onshore dichotomy in payment of derivation revenues. Under the policy first introduced in 1978, revenues from offshore oil which by international law belongs to the Federation were excluded in the application of the derivation principle. The enactment of the law, which occurred at a time when exploration for oil in deep waters showed promising results, had attracted protests in oil-producing states. The persistent protests by Niger Delta elites had influenced the military administration to abolish the policy. Thus, its reintroduction by the civilian administration undermined relations between the Federal and oil-producing States.

Furthermore, protests in the region were mobilised around poor funding of NDDC and dissatisfaction with the 13 per cent derivation revenues. These sentiments overshadowed the deliberations at the 2005 Constitutional Conference and led to its indefinite closure. The failure of the Niger Delta delegates to secure an increment in derivation from 13 per cent to between 25 and 50 per cent was one of the remote causes of the upsurge in militancy that saw militant groups taking action to stop oil production. In order to pacify the region, the Federal Government created a Ministry of Niger Delta Affairs in 2007 and granted amnesty to militants in the region.

However, these measures have not reduced grievances in the region. One of the sources of grievance is that derivation revenues have accrued to states rather than oil-bearing communities. Accrual of oil benefits to states is believed to have led to diversion and misappropriation of funds by state elites and their patrons. Thus, many state governors of the oil-bearing states are believed to have been constrained to transfer resources to political patrons outside their states to maintain relevance in the country's prebendal democracy (see Ukiwo, 2007). This grievance has led to advocacy for a community trust fund to which an additional percentage of oil revenues should be paid for the direct benefit of oil-bearing communities. This movement has canvassed inclusion of the community trust fund in the Petroleum Industry Governance Bill (PIB).

Apart from ethno-regional mobilisations for access, there have also been class-based mobilisations. These mobilisations can be traced to the colonial period as Nigerian technocratic and business interests complained about foreign domination of the oil sector. The indigenisation policies of the 1970s were partly aimed at addressing the concerns of the fledgling professional and business elites. However, indigenisation policies had their limitations in making Nigerians take control of the so-called commanding heights of the economy (see Ake, 1985) as IOCs retained control of the industry nearly 30 years after the initial attempts at indigenisation. It is against this background that the Government gradually introduced the policy on marginal field concessions which incentivised IOCs to cede holdings of unexploited fields in their leases to emergent indigenous oil companies.

In addition, persistent pressures for Nigerian participation has also led to the enactment of the Nigerian Oil and Gas Content Development Act (NOGIC Act) 2010. The main objective of the NOGIC Act is to increase the level of Nigerian content in the country's oil and gas industry. The Act defines Nigerian content as 'the quantum of composite value added to or created in the Nigerian economy by a systematic development of capacity and capabilities through the deliberate utilization of Nigerian human, material resources and services in the Nigerian oil and gas industry'. The 'NOGIC Act provides that first consideration shall be given to Nigerian independent operators, goods and services and also to Nigerians in employment and training. All fabrication and welding activities carried out in the industry must be performed in-country' (KPMG, 2014). It sets aside a levy of 1 per cent of contracts awarded in the upstream sector for payment to the Nigerian Content Development Fund, which is managed by the Nigerian Content Development Board.

The development has recorded some promising results, with indigenous companies increasingly entering into the upstream sector and service sector and also taking over onshore holdings currently being relinquished by the IOCs (see Madueke, 2013). Assessments of the policy suggest that some marginal gains have been recorded in engendering linkages and job creation (see Adedeji, Sidique, Rahman and Law, 2016). Since the introduction of the policy about 18 per cent of both oil and gas production is controlled by enterprises owned by Nigerian nationals (Mossman, 2017). It is envisaged that the Petroleum Industry Governance Bill (PIB) would further enhance indigenous participation in the sector.

14.5   Third Generation Oil Governance Regimes

Social pressures on oil exploration and production activities have also stemmed from concerns about the deleterious effects of hydrocarbons on the environment and attendant implications for livelihoods. A major complaint of locals was that the colonial Minerals Ordinance did not take due cognizance of the potential impact of exploration and exploitation activities on the environment (see Steyn, 2009). The Ordinance merely provided for compensatory payments for damage to economic crops in the course of exploration and production activities. Dissatisfaction with provisions for protection of the environment and remediation for damage continued through the colonial period, featuring prominently in the submissions of the peoples of the Niger Delta to the Henry Willinks Commission established by the Colonial Administration in 1958 to investigate the concerns of minority groups in Nigeria. The agitations intensified in the late colonial period as minorities sought regional autonomy, affirmative action and protection policies to forestall consolidation of their marginalisation in the post-colonial period. It is not surprising that one of the recommendations of the Commission was the establishment of a Niger Delta Development Board (NDDB), which *inter alia* was supposed to address ecological challenges and environmental protection.

As in the colonial period, the post-colonial State became increasingly faced with agitations by communities protesting about damage to their environment. These concerns led to clauses on environmental issues being inserted in different laws regulating the exploration for and production of oil (see Yalaju, 1999). The Petroleum Inspectorate Division was partly created to address the environmental challenges through monitoring of the operations of the IOCs. From its inception, oversight and monitoring of operations of the IOCs was hampered by the fact that it lacked real powers of prosecution, as well as by the absolute dependence of the Nigerian State on oil revenues. Given that oil exploration and production were increasingly a joint venture between the State and the IOCs, the state regulatory agencies became wary of imposing fines and sanctions on oil companies as the Government would have to pick up some of the bills—the quantum of potential fines and levies grew in proportion as the Nigerian State increased its equity in the joint ventures. The result is that throughout the 1970s and 1980s institutional weaknesses and petro-dependency undermined any effort to protect the Niger Delta environment. Symptomatic of this weakness is the longstanding inability of the Nigerian State to affirm and enforce the terminal date for gas flaring that has been extended on several occasions.

Aggrieved communities increasingly resorted to litigation to gain compensation for damage done to the environment and livelihoods (see Human Rights Watch, 1999). Obviously, protracted litigation due to the penchant of IOCs to appeal judgments of lower courts to higher courts and paltry awards based on contentious compensation rates tested the patience of communities (Frynas, 1999). Exasperated by the situation, some elements within the communities increasingly resorted to self-help by sabotaging vital oil infrastructures and imposing losses on IOCs and the Nigerian rentier state (see Ukiwo, 2011). To be sure, some of the sabotage of equipment stemmed from the intent not to punish IOCs for the damaged environment but to extract rents from them. This development was a culmination of the perverse incentives created by existing regulatory regimes which inadvertently established an order in which compensatory claims over pollution and destruction of the environment increasingly became the main means of accessing the benefits of oil production. The culture of compensation payments pitched communities against IOCs and the Nigerian State because the burden of proof rested on communities which had to prove that oil spills were not caused by sabotage.

The emergence of global environmental rights movements and their interconnection with local communities helped to amplify the voices of the communities in the Niger Delta in the 1980s. One result of this phenomenon was the rise of environmental rights groups in Nigeria, starting with the establishment of the Environmental Rights Action (ERA). ERA, which started as a project of the civil liberties organisations (CLO) and became an affiliate of the Friends of the Earth International. ERA subsequently encouraged the proliferation of similar movements including community-based groups that monitored, documented and published cases of oil spills and environmental pollution. Through international networking and advocacy, the environmental rights groups helped to question the environmental standards of IOCs. The groups also invoked international law and normative frameworks on environmental protection and best practices. This strategy increasingly pressured the Nigerian State to update its repertoire of laws on environmental protection as the existence of international law significantly constrained the capacity of IOCs and the Nigerian State to ignore environmental standards.

It is against this background that the Government created the Federal Environmental Protection Agency in 1988 and followed up with the enactment of the Environmental Impact Assessment Act 1992. The Act, among other things, provided for an environmental audit to be conducted before the commencement of exploration and production activities. Although the EIA regime was not exclusive to the oil industry, it had strong implications for the relations between the State, IOCs and oil-producing communities. However, the EIA regime suffered from poor implementation with reported cases of collusion between rent-seeking community elites and prospecting communities to organise phony consultation meetings required for the acquisition of an EIA certificate.

The growing incidence of oil spillage and the weakness of existing institutions further led to the establishment of the National Oil Spills Detection Agency (NOSDRA). NOSDRA was principally charged with managing the prevention and control of oils spills by interfacing between oil companies and communities. One of the instruments for the interface is the joint investigation visits (JIV) which, the NOSDRA Act stipulates, should involve oil companies, state ministries of environment and community representatives. The visits are intended to ascertain the causes of spills, the extent of the impact of spills and modality for response and remediation. Like the Petroleum Inspectorate Unit before it, the NOSDRA Act is weak and the agency is poorly resourced to check and manage oil spills. For instance, NOSDRA does not have helicopters and boats and routinely depends on the good offices of the IOCs to access sites of spills in the hard-to-reach creeks of the Niger Delta. The poor standing of NOSDRA and its ineffectiveness have eroded its authority and legitimacy, creating a situation whereby communities actually avoid rather than approach the agency for report and action on oil spills. Amidst the weakness of NOSDRA, which has not been addressed despite sustained advocacy for review of the NOSDRA Act, the Federal Government has established another agency called the Hydrocarbon Pollution Remediation Project (HYPREP) to lead the implementation of the United Nations Environment Programme (UNEP) Report on the Ogoni environment. Moreover, the Government's assumption that most of the spills stem from sabotage of equipment has led to securitisation. This is evidenced by the deployment of military and police forces to checkmate oil pollution and oil theft. The failed attempts to secure oil through troop deployment have also led the engagement of local strong militia groups to complement the securitisation agenda.

Contemporaneous to the mobilisations around the environmental challenge posed by oil are mobilisations intended to improve the governance of oil and its sustainability. This tendency has arisen largely from the international conventional wisdom that correlates oil with dictatorship, violent conflicts and state failure (see Omeje, 2006; Perouse de Montclos, 2014). Nigeria has been presented as a case *par excellence* of a country that failed to use oil to transform the lives of its people for good. A plethora of state-based and civil society initiatives have been mobilised to ensure that oil delivers benefits for a greater proportion of both living and unborn populations. These mobilisations crystalised with the enactment of the Nigeria Extractive Industries Transparency Initiative Act (NEITI) in 2004. The initiative, which drew inspiration from the advocacy of groups such as Transparency International, Extractive Transparency Initiative (EITI) and Revenue Watch Institute (RWI), has sought to enhance the monitoring, disclosure and publication of revenue flows in the industry and to governmental institutions.

While laudable, NEITI got a slow start as it took time to get government agencies and IOCs to respond and to conduct the necessary audits. However, even with the conclusion of the audits the NEITI Act was considered insufficiently strong as it depended largely on moral suasion and apportioned ridiculously low fines that are insufficient to restrain oil companies or state agencies. The weakness of NEITI stemmed not just from its voluntary provenance but from the inadequate stakeholder consultation, given the interest of President Olusegun Obasanjo (assisted by a reformist Finance Minister) to push through the legislation in order to gain international legitimacy. Although Nigeria gained legitimacy as one of the first countries to introduce an EITI law, the initiative did not enjoy widespread support in the political circles where it was considered a pet policy of the President.

What is more, the NEITI was unpopular among Niger Delta governors who superintended derivation revenues accruing to oil-producing states and saw the initiative as a subterfuge by the Federal Government to undermine their authority and weaken agitations for resource control in the region. The response of state governments and dominant elites in the Niger Delta to NEITI is understandable, given the tension between competing perceptions of the Niger Delta crises. While the Federal Government and the international community blame governance deficits, dominant Niger Delta elites implicate marginalisation and disempowerment for the development challenges (see Ukiwo, 2008a; 2008b). Consequently, while the Federal Government and the international community generally believe that existing resources should be better managed to promote development, the regional elites clamour for more resources, claiming that current resources are insufficient.

Similar tensions appear to have undermined mobilisations to create a regime to sustain gains of oil for future populations. Publication of reports of how trillions of dollars accumulated from oil have been frittered away and spent on conspicuous consumption by the elite as well as stark comparisons made between Nigeria and the oil-rich Gulf States have increasingly raised interests among reformist elements in government for the conservation of oil revenues. The growing interest in saving for a rainy day became the conventional wisdom as periodic fluctuations in oil prices undermined macroeconomic stability. This led to the creation of an excess crude account (ECA) where Government saved oil receipts in excess of projected incomes as a result of positive price fluctuations.

The ECA was established in 2004 to ensure that resources are saved to bolster revenues in periods of falling production and low prices. The Federal Government unilaterally transferred funds from the Federation account to the excess crude account and reverted to it when fiscal pressures mounted on the State. The ECA dispensation was fraught with controversy as many actors, especially state governors, challenged its illegality. The fact that the ECA was controlled by the Federal Government also raised suspicions of mismanagement of the account. Savings and administrations were criticised for making withdrawals from the ECA. For example, the Yar Adua and Jonathan administrations faced criticisms for allegedly depleting the ECA following a fall in global oil prices.

It is against this background that the Jonathan administration proposed the introduction of a sovereign wealth fund (SWF). The proposal was adopted by the National Economic Council and the National Assembly, which passed the Sovereign Wealth Investment Authority Establishment Act in 2011. The fund is made up of three major investments, namely: the Future Genera-tion Funds, the Infrastructure Fund and the Stabilisation Fund. They are respectively intended to serve sustainability and justice for the young and unborn, bankroll major infrastructural developments and provide short-term funds to stabilise the economy.

By its structure, the ownership of the SWF is as follows: Federal Govern-ment (45.83 per cent), states (36.25 per cent) and the 774 local governments (17.76 per cent) while the Federal Capital Territory (FCT) has 0.16 per cent. However, although there was considerable consensus around the passage of the SWF Act, its implementation has been dogged by controversies. The critical commentaries about the fund have mainly emanated from state governors who challenged the usage of the fund and frequently pressurised the Federal Government for bail-outs from the fund. Consequently, some state governments have challenged the constitutional basis of the SWF. For instance, Mr. Raji Fashola, Governor of Lagos State (2007–2015), who was one of the arrowheads of the mobilisations of the Nigerian Governors' Forum against the SWF said:

> I must be clear. I do not support it (SWF) not because I am against sav-ings; I disagree because for me there are fundamental and constitutional issues... The countries given as examples to support the initiative are either monarchies or emirates whereas Nigeria is a democracy ... How do we save money by an Act of the National Assembly when the Constitu-tion that created the National Assembly itself says that every monies that come into the accounts of the country must go to the Federation Account and that any monies standing in credit in that Account must be distributed between the states, local government and the Federal Government? ...Why do we save money when our entire infrastructure is over 40 years old? This country is running on an infrastructure that was built after the civil war. But the population we had then has multiplied in many folds.[2]

2   See Olusegun Adeniyi's column entitled 'Buhari and the Sovereign Wealth Dilemma', published in ThisDay on 22 October 2015, available at: http://newsexpressngr.com/news/detail. php?news=16581&title=Buhari-and-the-Sovereign-Wealth-Dilemma,-By-Olusegun-Adeniyi.

The frequent criticism of the SWF has the potential to contribute to its delegitimation. It is envisaged that the enactment of the Petroleum Industry Governance Bill would help to create a hospitable policy and political environment for the successful implementation of the sovereign wealth fund and the popularisation of its stabilisation and sustainability agenda.

14.6   Conclusion: Is PIB the Panacea?

After 60 years of oil production, the country adopted a national energy policy in 2004. Key elements of the policy include diversification, improved revenues for national development, cost effective, adequate and environmentally friendly supply, substantive indigenous participation and technological transfer and adaptation, robust private participation and better use of energy resources to project power and influence in the continent and globally for the attainment of national interest and foreign policy objectives. The current structure of the oil industry and extant regulatory frameworks is considered inadequate for the realisation of these laudable objectives. This explains why substantial attention has been trained on the PIB. The objectives of the PIB include the following:
1. To enhance exploration and exploitation of petroleum resources
2. To significantly increase domestic gas supplies especially for power and industry
3. To create a competitive business environment for the exploitation of oil and gas
4. To establish a fiscal framework that is flexible, stable and competitively attractive
5. To create a commercially viable national oil company
6. To create strong and effective regulatory institutions
7. To promote Nigerian content and
8. To promote and protect health, safety and the environment

Three main regulatory and institutional changes are proposed as follows:
1. The unbundling of NNPC as presently constituted through the creation of a national oil company that promotes indigenous operational capacity development
2. The creation of an asset management limited liability company to manage the JV assets on behalf of the federation
3. The excision of the Nigerian Gas Company (NGC) from NNPC as a separate partially privatised entity to cater for domestic gas marketing and gas infrastructure development.

In addition, the following policy objectives are expected from fiscal reforms proposed in the PIB:

1. To simplify the collection of government revenues,
2. To cream off windfall profits in the case of high oil prices
3. To collect more revenues from large profitable fields in the deep offshore waters, and
4. To create Nigerian employment and business opportunities by encouraging investment in small oil and gas fields.

Lofty as some of these objectives may appear at face value, it has been a herculean task to enact the PIB since 2000 when mobilisations commenced and 2011 when it was formally presented to the National Assembly. There are concerns that covert disagreements by powerful forces, including IOCs, may have stalled progress of the PIB in the legislature. Criticisms of the PIB also suggest that not much change would materialise as the proposed reform is light on transparency and accountability mechanisms, sustainable funding mechanisms and industry autonomy provisions and contains controversial provision for host community benefits (see Sayne *et al.*, 2012). There have also been concerns that some clauses of the PIB may lead to violation of existing contracts, retroactive applications and generally engender a situation where the responsibility crisis of the State worsens by relieving the State of its statutory responsibilities in securing social licence to operate and securing the sites of extraction (Okigbo, 2012).

As noted earlier, the delayed passage of the PIB has affected investment in both upstream and downstream sectors. This aggravated the damage to the sector which has been adversely affected by falling prices due to decreasing demand, increasing energy security in the US, which has historically been a major importer of Nigerian oil, and the challenges of human security in the Niger Delta. It is against this background that the NEITI Policy Brief made a clarion call that:

> The PIB ship should be rescued from a start-stop, unhurried and unco-ordinated mode and brought swiftly ashore. There is need for President Muhammadu Buhari to take the lead by investing his presidential capital on this all-important legislation, putting in place a mechanism for rallying the stakeholders to a consensus, and using this law as one of the pillars of the bridge to a much-needed economic recovery (NEITI, 2016, p.1).

However, such calls ignore the diverse stakeholders in the oil sector that have divergent interests in reforms. It even overlooks the possibility that relinquishing control of state oil—which full-scale reform would require—is not in the interest of key political and industry actors, including the powerful labour aristocracy. There seems to be no end in sight as President Muhammadu Buhari eventually withheld assent to the Bill, signalling that the PIG Bill will return to the next National Assembly to be constituted after the 2019 General Elections.[3] Thus, while the Nigeria oil sector is in dire need of reform to avoid collapse in view of maturing oil fields, declining investments and falling demand from longstanding customers (see Gupte, 2019), the prospects for reform in the oil sector remain precarious due to political economy factors. At the top political level, power flows from the barrel of oil. Control of oil and steady flow of revenues are vital to regime survival. Reform would require the easing of political control over oil. This is why reform is not attractive to incumbents. It is not only the top political actors that benefit from the status quo. Powerful IOCs reject elements of reform that would further erode profit margins without guaranteeing secure and hospitable operating environments. Labour unions in the sector reject reforms that would lead to privatisation and further liberalisation of the sector. The citizenry, accustomed to cheap fuel that they perceive to be their share of the national cake, reject reforms that would entail the removal of subsidies.

References

Adedeji A.N., S.F. Sidique, A.A. Rahman and S.H. Law (2016), 'The Role of Local Content Creation in Nigeria's Oil Industry: A Structural Equation Modelling Approach', *Resources Policy*, 49, 61–71.

Ake, C. (1985), *Political Economy of Nigeria*. London: Longman.

Edevbie, D. (2000), 'The Politics of the 13 per cent Derivation Principle'. Retrieved from: www.waado.org.

Federal Republic of Nigeria (1969), Petroleum Act of 1969. Retrieved from: http://lawsofnigeria.placng.org/laws/P10.pdf.

——— (1992), Environmental Impact Assessment Act. Abuja: Ministry of Environment.

——— (1999), Constitution of the Federal Republic of Nigeria. Lagos: Federal Government Printer.

——— (2012), Petroleum Industry Bill. Draft Bill. Lagos: Republic of Nigeria.

Frynas, J.G. (1999), *Oil in Nigeria: Conflict and Litigation between Oil Companies and Village Communities*. Münster: Lit Verlag.

Gupte, E. (2019), 'Nigeria's Oil Reforms in Limbo', *The Oxford Energy Forum*, 117, 10–12.

Human Rights Watch (1999), *The Price of Oil: Corporate Responsibility and Human Rights Violations in Nigeria's Oil Producing Communities*. New York: Human Rights Watch.

---

3   https://www.concisenews.global/2018/08/29/presidency-reveals-why-buhari-withheld-assent-to-pig-bill/.

KPMG Professional Services (2014), *Nigeria's Oil and Gas Industry Brief*. Lagos: KPMG.

Langer, A. and U. Ukiwo (2009), 'Subjective Realities: Perceptions of Identity and Conflict in Ghana and Nigeria', *Journal of International Development*, 24(4), 483–494.

Madueke, A. (2013), *The Future of Petroleum in Nigeria: Keynote Address*. Honourable Minister Ministry of Petroleum Resources at The Nigeria Economist's Group Summit. Retrieved from: http://www.nnpcgroup.com/PublicRelations/NNPCinthenews/tabid/92/articleType/ArticleView/articleId/457/The-Future-of-Nigerias-Petroleum-Industry.aspx.

Mossman, M. (2017, 29 November), 'How Nigeria's Oil Went Local'. *Foreign Affairs*. Retrieved from: https://www.foreignaffairs.com/articles/nigeria/2017-11-29/how-nigerias-oil-industry-went-local.

Nigeria Extractive Industry Transparency Initiative (NEITI) (2016), 'The Urgency of a New Petroleum Sector Law', *NEITI Policy Brief., Issue 2*. Retrieved from: https://www.minesandsteel.gov.ng/wp-content/uploads/2016/09/Policy-Brief-on-Petroleum-Sector-Law-Final.pdf.

Okigbo, A. (2012), Nigeria-Petroleum Industry Bill: History, Objectives, Institutions and Controversies', *Nextier Advisory Policy Brief*. Retrieved from: http://www.nextieradvisory.com/nigeria-petroleum-industry-bill-history-objectives-institutions-and-controversies-by-awele-okigbo/.

Omeje, K. (2006), *High Stakes and Stakeholders: Oil Conflict and Security in Nigeria*. Aldershot and Burlington, Vermont: Ashgate.

Ozo-Eson, P.I. and U. Ukiwo (2001), *The Niger Delta Development Commission: Towards a Development Blueprint: Proceedings of the Fourth Memorial Programme in Honour of Prof. Claude Ake*. Port Harcourt: CASS Publication.

Perouse De Montclos, M.A. (2014), 'The Politics and Crisis of the Petroleum Industry Bill in Nigeria', *Journal of Modern African Studies*, 52(3), 403–424.

Sayne, A., P. Mahdavi, P. Heller and J. Schreuder (2012), 'The Petroleum Industry Bill and the Future of NNPC'. Retrieved from the Revenue Watch Institute website: https://resourcegovernance.org/sites/default/files/rwi_bp_nnpc_synth_rev2.pdf.

Steyn, P. (2009), 'Oil Exploration in Colonial Nigeria', *The Journal of Imperial and Contemporary History*, 37(2), 249–274.

Uche, C.U., and O.C. Uche (2004), 'Oil and Politics of Revenue Allocation in Nigeria'. *Africa Studies Centre Working Paper, No. 54*. Leiden: Africa Studies Centre.

Ukiwo, U. (2007), 'Le delta du Niger face à la democratie virtuelle du Nigeria', *Politique Africaine*, 106, 128–148.

——— (2008a), 'Empire of Commodities', in M. Watts (ed.), *Curse of the Black Gold: 50 Years of Oil in the Niger Delta*. New York: Power House Books.

——— (2008b), 'Nationalization versus Indigenization of the Rentier Space: Oil and Conflict in Nigeria', in K. Omeje (ed.), *Extractive Economies and Conflicts in the Global South: Multiregional Perspectives on Rentier Politics*. Aldershot: Ashgate.

——— (2011), 'The Nigerian State, Oil and the Resolution of the Niger Delta Crisis', in C. Obi and S.A. Rustad (eds.), *Oil Insurgency in the Niger Delta: Managing the Complex Politics of Petro-violence* (pp.17–27). London: Zed Press.

Yalaju, J. (1999), 'Laws Regulating Oil Pollution in Nigeria: A Re-appraisal', *Current Jos Law Journal*, 5(5), 21–32.

15
Ghana's Oil Governance Regime: Challenges and Policies

Peter Quartey and Emmanuel Abbey

15.1   Introduction

Managing the economic gains from oil production has been a major challenge for many African economies. This is because of the perceived weakness in the governance structure not only of the oil industry but also for some of these economies as a whole. Indeed, several examples exist of African economies that have not been able to develop as expected following their discovery of oil, notwithstanding the significant change in revenues afterwards—Nigeria, Cameron and Gabon. While several lessons and policy recommendations have been extensively suggested, especially for the more recent economies that are now discovering oil, there is still some level of scepticism as to whether their governance structures are robust enough to withstand the challenges associated with the oil industry. This is because of the very visible deterioration in the social and economic infrastructure of their other natural resource sectors (mostly mining), with worsening situations in some of the most prominent communities of these countries where these resources are extracted.

These concerns are not very different in the case of Ghana. Since the UK-Irish firm Tullow announced that it had discovered oil around the Cape Three Points off Ghana's Western Region in June 2007, many have thought the economic woes of the country had come to an end because of the vast projected revenues. The significant high-end estimate of the expected revenue flow over the lifespan of the extraction process was seen as significant for the economic development of the country. Unfortunately, Ghana's history with the extractive industries has been very contentious. Aside from concerns about the country's inability to use revenues from the extractive sector to finance its development agenda properly, there is very visible deterioration in the social and economic infrastructure in some of the most prominent mining communities such as Obuasi and Prestea (Aryeetey, Osei and Quartey, 2016).

Fortunately, the Government of Ghana had a set of rules governing the oil industry (i.e. the Petroleum Exploration and Production Law, 1984), following existing regulations for some earlier oil discoveries in the 1970s, although production actually took place in very limited quantities from the Saltpond Fields in the 1980s. In particular, production was estimated to be a mere 700 barrels per day. This system of rules was recently comprehensively restructured to be in line with international best practices and also to support the Government's objective of providing an adequate and reliable supply of petroleum products and reduce the country's dependence on crude oil imports, through the development of the country's own petroleum resources. More recently new discoveries have been made, suggesting that the country even has commercial quantities of oil. Accordingly, the restructuring of the governance regime was supposed to deal with financial and environmental challenges that existed earlier on as well as to ensure local content and local participation in the oil industry.

This chapter presents an overview of the oil governance regime in Ghana. The objective is to review the existing regime and identify any policy challenges thereof. An attempt will also be made to tease out any relevant policy suggestions. More importantly, an attempt is made to identify the specific measures required to engender efficiency, transparency and accountability in the management of oil revenues as this underpins the governance regime of the most successful oil-rich countries. An understanding of Ghana's oil governance regime is critical to ensuring that the new oil resource becomes a blessing to the country and not a curse, as experienced by some other African countries extracting oil. It will also serve as a useful guide to other countries that are on the path of making new petroleum discoveries.

The rest of the chapter is structured as follows. Section 2 presents some stylised facts about Ghana's oil industry. Section 3 presents an overview of the governance regime. Section 4 elaborates on the challenges realised so far and what policy solutions have been offered. The last section offers some policy suggestions and the likely challenges with its restructured governance regime.

15.2   Background on Ghana's Oil Industry

The oil industry in Ghana is not completely new, as production has been taking place since the 1980s, albeit on a limited scale (PIAC, 2011). Unfortunately, no official records are readily available to show revenue being paid into the country's petroleum holding fund until the fiscal year 2010 (PIAC, 2011). Therefore, statistics about production volumes and receipts before 2010 are difficult to find.

Table 15.1: Total Production of Oil in Ghana (Barrels)

Year	Annual Production (mmbls)	Total Availability (mmbls)	Total Liftings (mmbls)	Liftings Ghana Group (bbls)	Stock Carried Forward (mmbls)	Proceeds from Liftings by Ghana Group (US$)
2010	1,181,088	1,181,088	0	-	1,181,088	
2011	24,195,895	25,376,983	24,450,155	3,930,189	926,828	444,124,723
2012	26,351,278	51,728,261	26,430,934	4,931,034	847,172	541,071,323
2013	35,587,558	36,434,730	36,048,290	6,793,449	386,440	628,580,078
2014	37,201,691	37,588,131	36,988,315	7,681,120	599,816	691,991,133
2015	37,411,661	38,011,477	37,167,225	5,730,090	844,252	374,292,488
2016	32,298,638	33,142,890	30,765,005	5,856,921	2,377,885	207,787,586
2017	58,658,063.54	34,641,855	32,311,961	Jub=5,742,876 TEN=4,038,375	2,329,894	Jub=302,634,338.36 TEN=198,765,753.93

Source: Republic of Ghana, Public Interest and Accountability Committee (PIAC), PIAC Annual Reports (Various Issues). Available at: http://www.piacghana.org/portal/5/25/piac-reports.

Currently, the major producing fields are the Jubilee field (which started production in November 2010), the Tweneboa-Enyenra-Ntomme (TEN, which started production in August 2016) and the Sankofa-Gye-Nyame (SGN, which started production in 2017). Conversely, there is the Saltpond Field, which has also been producing since the 1980s but on a very small scale. There are other major fields that are currently being developed, the major ones being the Deep Water Tano/Cape Three Points (DWT/CTP) Project, the Offshore Cape Three Points (OCTP) Project and the onshore (Voltaian) Basin project, which is the first oil exploration project in Ghana managed by the Ghana National Petroleum Corporation.

The major stakeholders in the oil fields of Ghana are Tullow, Kosmos, Anadarko, the Ghana National Petroleum Corporation (GNPC), Petro SA and ENI. For the Jubilee unit area, Tullow (the operator) owns 35.48 per cent, Kosmos owns 24.08 per cent, Anadarko owns 24.08 per cent, GNPC owns 13.64 per cent and Petro SA owns 2.73 per cent. For the TEN Development area, Tullow (the operator) owns 47.18 per cent, Kosmos owns 17.0 per cent, Anadarko owns 17.0 per cent, GNPC owns 15.0 per cent and Petro SA owns 3.82 per cent. ENI currently operates the Sankofa-Gye-Nyame project and owns 44.44 per cent. For the Saltpond field the current operator is the

Table 15.2:   Total Petroleum Receipts for Ghana

Year	Total Lifting (bbls)	Average Achieved Price (US$)	Proceeds from Lifting (US$)	Other Revenues (US$)	Total Annual Receipts (US$)
2011	3,930,189	113.08	444,124,723	-	444,124,724
2012	4,931,034	110.18	541,071,323	552,418	541,623,741
2013	6,793,449	106.95	628,580,078	218,187,106	846.767,184
2014	7,681,120	103.50	691,991,133	286,026,559	978,017,693
2015	5,730,090	52.36	374,292,488	21,880,422	396,172,909
2016	5,856,921	Jub: 46.07 TEN: 51.09	207,787,586	39,387,808	247,175,394
2017	Jub=5,742,876 TEN=4,038,375	53.16	Jub=302,634,338.36 TEN=198,765,753.93	39,011,343.61	540,411,435.90

Source: Republic of Ghana, Public Interest and Accountability Committee (PIAC), PIAC Annual Reports (Various Issues). Available at: http://www.piacghana.org/portal/5/25/piac-reports.

Saltpond Offshore Producing Company with GNPC owning a 45 per cent stake and Lushann-Eternit Energy Ltd owning 55 per cent.

Ghana's total proven oil reserve base, as at the end of 2015, was assessed at 1,247.5 million barrels of oil (MMBOE), comprising 898 million barrels of oil and 2,024 billion cubic feet of proven gas reserves (GNPC, 2016). Available production volumes are presented in Table 15.1. At least until 2017, production volumes have been increasing over time. It needs to be emphasised that production at the Saltpond field has remained completely shut down since 2015 and awaiting decommissioning because of an 'unresolved industrial issue with the offshore crew' (PIAC, 2018). Table 15.2 presents the corresponding total annual petroleum receipts obtained between 2010 and 2017. The total annual petroleum receipts increased over time until 2014 when they subsequently declined. The highest petroleum receipts received so far were in 2014, after which there was a decrease in 2015 mainly because of the decline in the average achieved price of crude per barrel. Similarly, oil rents (i.e. the difference between the value of crude oil production at world prices and total costs of production) as a percentage of GDP have also been increasing (see Figure 15.1).

Most of the petroleum receipts have accrued from the carried and participating interest on crude (see Table 15.3). Over time, there have been significant differences in the projected and the actual outturn of these revenue components because of the drastic changes in petroleum prices. The hardest hit in recent times is corporate income tax, thereby explaining its instability over time.

Figure 15.1:   Oil Rents (Percentage of GDP)

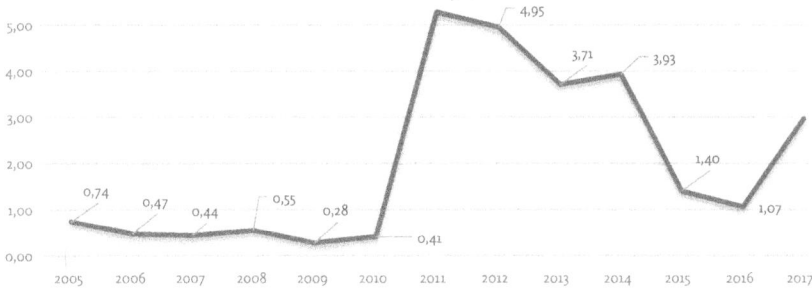

Source: Data drawn from World Development Indicators, The World Bank, 2018. Available at:
https://datacatalog.worldbank.org/dataset/world-development-indicators

Table 15.3:   Breakdown of Total Petroleum Receipts

	Carried & Participating Interest	Royalties	Surface Rentals	Corporate Income Tax	PHF income	Price Differen- tials	Gas
2011	72.49%	27.51%	-	-	-	-	-
2012	72.08%	27.88%	-	-	-	-	-
2013	53.57%	20.69%	-	25.63%	-	-	-
2014	51.01%	19.70%	0.18%	29.07%	0.01%	0.03%	-
2015	68.17%	26.30%	0.12%	5.15%	0.01%	0.11%	0.14%
2016	60.66%	23.40%	0.19%	11.95%	0.03%	-	3.76%
2017	67.62%	25.14%	0.29%	6.84%	0.11%	0.00%	0.00%

Source: Republic of Ghana, Public Interest and Accountability Committee (PIAC), PIAC Annual
Reports (Various Issues). Available at: http://www.piacghana.org/portal/5/25/piac-reports.

Table 15.4 below presents the allocation of the total petroleum receipts
acquired by the Government of Ghana (GoG) between 2010 and 2017. This
involves two major disbursements: a transfer to GNPC[1] and a net receipt
to the Government, with the latter further sub-distributed between the
petroleum fund (i.e. the Ghana Heritage Fund and the Ghana Stabilisation

---

1   The disbursement to GNPC is in respect of equity financing and a net carried and participating
interest.

Table 15.4:   Allocation of Total Petroleum Receipts by the Government of
Ghana (Mill. US$)

Year	GNPC	ABFA	GSF	GHF
2011	207.96	166.96	54.81	14.4
2012	230.95	286.55	16.88	7.34
2013	222.32	273,20	245.73	105.31
2014	180.71	409.07	271.76	116.47
2015	126,86	292.98	15.17	6.5
2016	88.6	98.38	29.51	12.65
2017	182.04	169.46	142.68	61.15

Note: Ghana National Petroleum Corporation (GNPC), Annual Budget Funding Amount (ABFA),
Ghana Sovereignty Fund (GSF), Ghana Heritage Fund (GHF).
Source: Republic of Ghana, Public Interest and Accountability Committee (PIAC), PIAC Annual
Reports (Various Issues). Available at: http://www.piacghana.org/portal/5/25/piac-reports.

Fund) and the Consolidated Fund to support the annual budget (Annual
Budget Funding Amount – ABFA). The guidelines for the disbursements
are contained in the Petroleum Revenue Management Act, 2011 (Act 815),
which was later amended in 2015 as the Petroleum Revenue Management
(Amendment) Act, 2015 (Act 893). In particular Act 893 stipulates that not
more than 70 per cent of the annual benchmark revenue[2] shall be paid to
the Annual Budget Funding Amount (ABFA) and not less than 30 per cent
of the benchmark revenue shall be paid into the Ghana Petroleum Funds
(GPFs). As at the end of 2017, the total accumulated petroleum receipts by the
Government of Ghana were US$ 3.994 billion, out of which 44 per cent was
transferred to the ABFA, 30 per cent to GNPC and 26 per cent to the GPFs.

Exploration activities suffered a major setback in 2014 following an interim
ruling of the International Tribunal for the Law of the Sea (ITLOS) regarding
a national border dispute between Ghana and Ivory Coast (PIAC, 2015). The
two countries have not been able to agree upon the location of their maritime
boundary, with Ivory Coast requesting Ghana to suspend all oil exploration
and exploitation activities in the disputed zone, which includes the TEN
project. The case got to the ITLOS after ten failed negotiation attempts.

2   Benchmark revenue = expected current receipts from crude oil + expected current receipts
from gas + expected dividends from a national oil company + corporate income tax + surface
rentals + any other revenue identified in the Petroleum Revenue Management Act (section C).

The interim ruling placed a moratorium on new exploration and drilling activities in the disputed areas. This affected the drilling of new wells in the TEN project as well as other blocks that fall within the disputed area, but not ongoing works. This was expected to affect the volumes of production from the TEN project.

The ruling in respect of the Ghana–Cote d'Ivoire maritime boundary dispute by the ITLOS was delivered on 23 September 2017 and was in Ghana's favour (PIAC, 2017). ITLOS ruled that there has not been any violation by Ghana of La Cote d'Ivoire's maritime boundary (PIAC, 2017). This has de-risked the uncertainty of the area and has led to the intensification of exploration by upstream petroleum companies in the previously contested area (PIAC, 2017).

15.3   Oil Governance Regimes

Oil governance regimes have a history. This history hinges on who the dominant players are and the power they exercise in terms of the set of rules guiding the industry. Mommer (2000) provides a useful review of the history of how these dominant players have changed over time. He asserts that before the First World War, private oil companies (which constituted the International Petroleum Cartel) established the first notable oil governance regime. These companies rented oil fields and paid a reservation cost to the landlords; accordingly, rules were formulated to guide the process, given this structure. However, as oil became an important asset immediately after the Second World War and when the power of the imperial countries over the Third World began to weaken, oil-exporting countries (which were mainly the imperial countries) started gaining control over their own oil fields (Mommer, 2000). This led to the introduction of a second oil governance regime, as these oil-exporting countries formed their own cartel, OPEC. Unfortunately, for many oil-consuming nations OPEC was a threat to the pricing of oil products (Mommer, 2000). Therefore, to ensure the security of supply and reasonable pricing, a third governance regime emerged from oil-consuming nations through the creation of the International Energy Agency (IEA) (Mommer, 2000). This basically has been the way oil governance regimes were established and the dominant role was played by the different actors.

More recently, and especially for many developing countries extracting oil, and given the opacity and perceived widespread corruption along the value chain of other natural resource extractions, the governance framework underpinning the Extractive Industries Transparency Initiative (EITI) is mostly relied upon. The initiative is a global effort to end the culture of opacity in the generation and use of extractive revenues and to ensure that resource extraction contributes to national development and poverty reduction. This framework encourages public disclosure of company payments and government receipts of extractive revenues as well as the demand for accountability in terms of how the revenues are used. The framework also requires countries publicly to disclose information on revenue management and expenditures, information on contracts and licences as well as the establishment of a legally mandated open contracting regime. This framework is supported by the Natural Resources Charter, which is organised around 12 core precepts offering guidance on key decisions governments face, beginning with whether or not to extract resources and ending with how generated revenues can produce maximum good for citizens.

For many African countries, there is the African Mining Vision (AMV),[3] which imposes an obligation on all African Union member States to align their governance arrangements and approaches to the management of their natural resources to a set of prescribed principles in line with international best practices as well as to the lessons drawn from the continent's century-old experience in mining. This focus affords the natural-resource-dependent African States the opportunity to integrate their natural resources into the rest of the national economy, and through that make a critical and sustainable paradigm shift from the enclave nature of resource extraction.

For the specific case of Ghana, the oil governance regime is a hybrid version; the people and government of Ghana own the oil, while international oil companies are doing the extraction, based on an agreement ratified in the Constitution of Ghana. Critical requirements from the EITI as well as the AMV have been complied with. Accordingly, the governance regime that guides the entire process focuses on two sub-sectors: the upstream and the downstream. The upstream sub-sector ensures the effective management of oil resources of the country and accelerates the exploitation and development of new hydrocarbon resources for the overall benefit and welfare of Ghanaians, present and future. The downstream sub-sector is to rehabilitate and expand petroleum refining, storage, distribution and marketing infrastructure as well as ensure fair distribution of petroleum products to all parts of the country and reduce the heavy burden of oil imports on the country's economy by accelerating the exploitation of indigenous hydrocarbon resources.

---

3   The Africa Mining Vision was adopted by Heads of State at the February 2009 AU summit following the October 2008 meeting of African Ministers responsible for Mineral Resources Development.

In Ghana, the key institution responsible for the upstream sub-sector is the Ghana National Petroleum Corporation (GNPC); meanwhile, the National Petroleum Authority (NPA) regulates the downstream sub-sector. The following laws regulate the upstream oil sub-sector:

– Ghana National Petroleum Corporation Law, 1983 (PNDCL 64)
– Petroleum (Exploration and Production) Act, 2016
  [previously, the Petroleum Exploration and Production Law, 1984 (PNDC Law 84)]
– Income Tax Act, 2015 (Act 896)
  [previously, the Internal Revenue Act, 2000 (Act 592)]
– The Petroleum Revenue Management Act, 2011 (Act 815).
– The Petroleum Commission Acts, 2011 (Act 821)
– Petroleum (Local Content and Local Participation) Regulations, 2013 (LI2204)
– The Petroleum Agreements.

The Ghana National Petroleum Corporation Law, 1983 (PNDCL 64) established GNPC as the national oil company of the upstream oil and gas industry. It gives GNPC the right to the development of the oil sector, oil exploration and production. The law sets out the functions, administration and corporate governance of the GNPC. The Petroleum (Exploration and Production) Act, 2016, replaced the Petroleum Exploration and Production Law, 1984 (PNDC Law 84). It contains provisions related to petroleum activities within the jurisdiction of the Republic of Ghana, including activities in, under and upon its territorial land, inland waters, territorial sea, exclusive economic zone and its continental shelf. The Act aims to provide for and ensure safe, secure, sustainable and efficient petroleum activities in order to achieve optimal long-term petroleum resource exploitation and utilisation for the benefit and welfare of the people of Ghana. The law makes all petroleum resources existing within the country's jurisdiction the property of the Republic of Ghana, which must be managed in accordance with the principles of good governance, including transparency and accountability. Broadly, the law caters for issues regarding area management, the provision of a reconnaissance licence, defines a petroleum agreement and has provisions regarding the exploration, development and production, transportation and storage, cessation, decommissioning and removal of facilities after the extraction. It also has provisions on health and safety, security and the environment as well as general requirements for petroleum activities in Ghana.

The Income Tax Act, 2015 (Act 896), previously the Internal Revenue Act, 2000 (Act 592), provides details of income and withholding taxes levied at the upstream stage of oil and gas operations. This law replaces any other law, including the Petroleum Income Tax Law, (1987), to the extent that provisions in those laws are inconsistent with provisions in this new Act. The Act also establishes activities in the petroleum industry as a special industry with the various tax elements defined in the Petroleum Agreement.

The Petroleum Revenue Management Act, 2011 (Act 815) provides the framework for the collection, allocation and management of petroleum revenue derived from upstream and midstream petroleum operations.[4] The Act establishes the Petroleum Holding Fund as the designated public fund at the Bank of Ghana to receive and disburse petroleum revenue due to the Republic, and these funds are to be transferred into the Ghana Petroleum Fund (a collection of the Ghana Stabilisation Fund and the Ghana Heritage Fund). The object of the stabilisation fund is to cushion the impact on or sustain public expenditure capacity during periods of unanticipated petroleum revenue shortfalls. The object of the Ghana Heritage Fund is to provide an endowment to support the development for future generations when the petroleum reserves have been depleted. Receipts into the Petroleum Holding Fund come from the following:

a) royalties from oil and gas, additional oil entitlements, surface rentals, other receipts from any petroleum operations and the sale or export of petroleum;

b) any amount from direct or indirect participation of government in petroleum operations;

c) corporate income taxes in cash from upstream and midstream petroleum companies;

d) any amount payable by the national oil company as corporate income tax, royalty, dividends, or any other amount due in accordance with the laws of Ghana; and

e) any amount received by the Government directly or indirectly from petroleum resources not covered by paragraphs (a) to (d), including where applicable capital gains tax derived from the sale of ownership of exploration, development and production rights.

---

4   Mid-stream operations are activities between the wellhead and refinery, transportation and storage. For instance, the activities of Ghana Gas constitute a mid-stream activity; they process natural gas liquids.

The Petroleum Revenue Management Act also establishes two key institutions: the Investment Advisory Committee (IAC) and the Public Interest and Accountability Committee (PIAC). While IAC advises on the management of the Ghana Petroleum Fund, PIAC ensures compliance with the Revenue Management Act while providing a platform for the public to debate whether spending prospects and management of revenues conform to development priorities as provided for in the Revenue Management Act.

Recently, the Petroleum Revenue Management Act, 2011 (Act 815) was amended as the Petroleum Revenue Management (Amendment) Act, 2015 (Act 893). The Act provides for the allocation of some petroleum receipts to the Ghana Infrastructure Investment Fund for the purposes of infrastructure development. The Act also makes provision for the composition of the Investment Advisory Committee and related matters as well as other amendments to revenue allocation.

The Petroleum Commissions Act, 2011 (Act 821), establishes the Petroleum Commission as the body to regulate and manage the utilisation of petroleum products and coordinate policies in relation to them. The Commission is also tasked to ensure compliance with health, safety and environmental standards in petroleum activities in accordance with applicable laws, regulations and agreements set forth by the Republic of Ghana. In addition, the Commission is to promote local content and local participation in petroleum activities as prescribed in the Local Content and Local Participation Regulations. The Commission, therefore, receives and stores petroleum data as well as managing the national petroleum repository upon request from the relevant Minister.

The Petroleum (Local Content and Local Participation) Regulations, 2013 (LI2204), were established to, amongst other things, promote the maximisation of value-addition and job creation for Ghanaians, develop local capacity, achieve a minimum local employment level and increase the capability and international competitiveness of domestic firms. It also seeks to create petroleum and related supportive industries and ensure Ghanaians have a degree of control over development initiatives. The law requires international companies to submit a local content plan, an employment and training subplan and succession plan, a programme for research and development as well as a technology transfer programme and report. In addition, the law requires international companies to provide their local insurance services content, legal services content, financial services content as well as data on the above issues to ensure monitoring, compliance and enforcement.

The Petroleum Agreement defines the duration of an exploration and extraction contract, the delineated area where the petroleum operations are to be carried out as well as possible sanctions and levies on production to

be paid to the Government. The applicable taxes as specified in the model petroleum agreements are as follows:
a) Royalty – 10 per cent
b) GNPC Initial Interest (Carried) – 10 per cent
c) GNPC Additional Interest (Paying) – 15 per cent
d) Petroleum Income tax – 35 per cent
e) Surface Rental – US$ 30/sq.km/year (Initial Exploration phase)

In addition, the Government of Ghana is signatory to the following international conventions that respectively define the rights and responsibilities of nations with respect to their use of the world's oceans, establish measures for dealing with pollution and for cooperation in the protection, management and development of the marine and coastal environment in the Atlantic Ocean:
–   United Nations Convention on the Law of the Sea
–   International Convention on Oil Pollution Preparedness, Response and Co-operation (OPRC)
–   Abidjan Convention (The Convention for the Co-operation in the Protection and Development of the Marine and Coastal Environment of the West and Central African Region)

Though the GNPC is the key institution responsible for the upstream oil industry, the following institutions also play an important role: the Ministry of Energy and Petroleum, the Ministry of Finance, the Bank of Ghana, the Parliament of Ghana, the Petroleum Commission, the Environmental Protection Agency, the State Enterprise Commission, the Public Interest Accountability Committee, the Auditor General and Ghana Gas. For instance, the Minister of Petroleum, in consultation with the Petroleum Commission, prepares a reference map showing areas of possible accumulation of petroleum within the jurisdiction of Ghana. The Minister of Finance monitors oil revenues that accrue to the State and estimates the benchmark revenue as provided for by law. The Bank of Ghana manages the petroleum account while the Ghana Revenue Authority accounts for the petroleum revenues. Lastly, Parliament ratifies all petroleum agreements.

The main law that regulates the downstream oil sub-sector is the National Petroleum Act, 2005 (Act 691).[5] This Act establishes the National Petroleum Authority as a body corporate with perpetual succession and a common seal, and may sue or be sued in its corporate name. The object of the Authority is to regulate, oversee and monitor activities in the petroleum downstream

5   This law is under review – National Petroleum Authority (Amendment) Bill, 2015.

industry and, where applicable, do so in pursuance of the prescribed petroleum pricing formula. The Authority, therefore, monitors the ceiling on the price of petroleum products, grants licences, maintains a register of licences granted and overall monitors standards or performance. The Authority also specifies the powers and functions of petroleum service providers, ensures that the downstream oil sector is liberalised, acts against the formulation of monopolies, receives complaints in the downstream sub-sector and settles disputes that may arise. The establishments operating in this downstream oil sub-sector are the Tema Oil Refinery (TOR), the Bulk Oil Storage and Transportation Company Limited (BOST), bulk storage depots and other service providers.

Particularly for the upstream oil sub-sector, the structure of Ghana's oil governance is similar to the Norwegian model—an administrative design that separates commercial functions from policy and regulatory functions. Ghana has a national oil company that engages in commercial operation (GNPC), a government ministry that directs policy (Ministry of Petroleum) and a regulatory body to provide oversight (PIAC). Regarding revenue management, the Norwegian model has a savings and a stabilisation fund; similarly, Ghana has a petroleum fund, which comprises a stabilisation and a heritage account. More importantly, regulations have been introduced to deal with inefficiencies that may be peculiar to the country, which may be absent from the more effective administrative regimes in Norway. One such action is the role played by PIAC.

Although the Norwegian model is by far the most recommended for many developing countries because of its reliance on separated functions, the development literature cautions in a general sense that governance strategies that work well in countries with mature institutions may be ill-suited to countries lacking certain institutions' endowments (see, for instance, Rodrik, 2008 and Moore and Putzel, 1999). Those who issue these cautions are quick to mention the examples of countries like Malaysia, Saudi Arabia and Angola that have performed creditably well in the absence of separated functions. Yet, Ghana's choice of the Norwegian model seems to depend heavily on its institutional and democratic development. Ghana's democracy is one that involves the separation of powers into different branches of government guided by a codified constitution.

One important milestone that has characterised Ghana's oil governance so far is the galvanised collective action of the civil society. Working together with the media and Parliament, civil society has played an influential role in the development of key legal and institutional frameworks for managing Ghana's oil (Gyimah-Boadi and Prempeh, 2012). For instance, immediately

Ghana began oil production in 2010, the country had no revenue-management law and no independent regulator. Several civil society groups called for a moratorium on the issue of new exploration licences until a new legal and regulatory regime was developed. Although the call was not entirely successful, it later led to the introduction of transparency in the management of oil revenues, with support from some Members of Parliament and some international organisations. These actions by the civil societies made the government realise that people were determined to participate in and to monitor the development of an appropriate policy and legal framework for the sector.

15.4   Challenges with Ghana's Oil Governance Regime

The oil governance regime in Ghana has had some challenges since production began in 2010. A few of the main challenges are summarised in the following paragraphs. When Ghana began its major oil operations in 2010, the country did not immediately have a comprehensive set of instructions for the oil industry. Most parts of the robust regulatory regime were established later. For instance, in 2010 the country did not have comprehensive provisions regarding the use of local content or the employment of locals by the international companies. A few guidelines existed in the previous Petroleum Exploration and Production Law, 1984 (PNDC Law 84). Yet, local community content was conspicuously absent.[6] This received criticism from communities very close to the oil field such as the Western Regional House of Chief. These communities were the first to experience the negative social and economic impact of extraction. In addition are other outstanding legal instruments such as regulations to the Petroleum Revenue Management Act, regulations to the new Exploration and Production Law, metering regulations as well as the Strategic Environmental Impact Assessment of the Volta Basin.

Aside from the incomplete governance framework is the poor sequencing of the entire governance framework, the anomaly of passing the Petroleum Revenue Management Act ahead of the Petroleum (Exploration and Production) Law. This is accompanied by a weak institutional collaboration which manifests itself in weak geological data-gathering, poor revenue collection as well as a lack of proper integration of the oil and gas sector into the rest of the economy.

---

6   Even though there are plans for such communities to benefit from corporate social responsibilities such as the retooling of bad roads and the improvement of social infrastructure.

Regarding revenue management, the 2015 Annual Report of PIAC cited some worrying instances of mismanagement. For instance, there were concerns about some extraction companies failing to pay their surface rentals. There were also concerns about the Government abusing petroleum revenues through many social intervention projects and, worst of all, not being transparent with the process of choosing them. In addition, the Government was cautioned to desist from spending more than the required budgetary allocation from oil revenues and ensure that the required parliamentary approval of revenue receipts to fund governmental projects were strictly adhered to. Furthermore, the committee expressed worry about the non-use of the funds for capacity building and recommended that a sizeable proportion of the petroleum revenues be channelled into the agricultural sector to boost productivity, giving its strategic importance to the people of the Republic of Ghana. Several recommendations have been made by PIAC to address these shortcomings, though there are still some instances of non-compliance.

Another challenge with Ghana's governance regime is the non-compliance with some key provisions in the country's legislative instruments for the oil sector. For instance, the Petroleum Revenue Management Act prescribes that all revenue reporting agencies must apply the same reporting standards. Yet, a report by the Ghana Extractive Industries Transparency Initiative (GHEITI) suggested that there was no standard format for reporting crude oil lifting for the year 2014 (GHEITI, 2015). Conversely, the Petroleum Revenue Management Act, 2011 (Act 815) entreats the Investment Advisory Committee to provide a benchmark on the returns from oil revenues; at least, for the year 2015 no such benchmark existed. There were also huge discrepancies in amounts stated for royalty, carried interest and participating interests. Lastly, there are concerns about the lack of transparency in the issue of licences to organisations interested in the exploration process as well as some oil companies not complying with the country's local content laws. The new Petroleum (Exploration and Production) Act, 2016 addresses some of these concerns.

In addition, there were some obstacles to ensuring full transparency regarding information reporting about the oil industry. For instance, the Petroleum Commission is required to have an online repository where information such as ownership of blocks, coordinates of oil blocks, allocation of blocks as well as annual payments is supposed to be reported. Currently, this online repository does not exist. However, some steps have been taken to address these concerns, and this includes the Petroleum Commission's commencement of activities to establish the online repository. In other perspectives, information about the issue of licences as well as the entire process of bidding for a licence is currently being made public.

There are also concerns about the effects of the oil industry on the type of political governance existing in Ghana. Some policy analysts fear that the oil industry will only worsen the already dysfunctional nature of contemporary Ghanaian politics and political culture, which is already described as factional, venomous and acrimonious (Gyimah-Boadi and Prempeh, 2012).[7] Within the limits established by the Constitution of Ghana, the party in power controls the Presidency and Parliament as well as making appointments to key ministries, departments and even agencies that are supposed to be independent by law. A typical example is the President appointing the executive directors and board of the Economic and Organised Crime Office—an institution that has the authority to investigate crimes involving financial loss to the State. A comparable institution, the Commission of Human Rights and Administrative Justice (CHRAG), which has the constitutional and statutory mandate to investigate corruption, abuse of office and human rights violation, has been rendered ineffective because of inadequate resources. Accordingly, issues of conflict of interest and self-dealing are routine amongst public officeholders.

Finally, there are concerns about non-compliance with key recommendations coming from bodies that are mandated to regulate the oil industry. The Ghana Extractive Industries Transparency Initiative (GHEITI) list several such recommendations that are still outstanding, with a few where no detailed information exists on their progress (GHEITI, 2015). It is important to mention that most of these recommendations are directed towards improvement in revenue management, as well as the introduction of transparency into the activities of the oil industry.

The major attempts made to address some of the above challenges can be found in the new Petroleum (Exploration and Production) Act, 2016 as well as in some of the existing laws. For instance, in the new Petroleum Act there is a local content law that addresses challenges regarding the use of local content and as well as the employment and training of locals for the oil sector; in addition, the law requires certain minimum equity for companies applying for a licence and compliance with the Insurance Act, 2006 (Act 724). There is also a commitment to open contracting; a committee was established to develop regulation in the Petroleum Revenue and Management Act; there was the establishment of an infrastructure development fund to support investments in infrastructure; there was the development of a national oil spill contingency; the Companies Act of 1963 was amended to provide for beneficial ownership; and the development of separate guidelines for the conduct of environmental and social impact assessment. The Revenue Management Law

---

7   This is because of the gaps in the legislative and institutional framework of the country.

also makes clear provision as to how petroleum receipts are to be disbursed and /or utilised. The new Petroleum Law further consolidates concerns about finance and the protection of the environment.

15.5   Conclusion and Policy Suggestions

Even though some steps have been taken to deal with the challenges identified in the previous section, there are still a few steps that need to be taken to ensure that oil does not become a curse to the country, but rather a blessing. Many policy analysts still worry about the local content law and the ability of local content to meet its requirements. There are also concerns about revenue mismanagement, giving the gaps in the legislative and institutional framework of the country. In addition, there are concerns about the lack of transparency in the industry. In that regard, the following policy suggestions are offered to deal with these likely challenges.

First, there is the need to use oil revenues consciously to develop an auxiliary industry since oil is a non-renewable resource, and sooner or later it will be effectively depleted. Ghana already has this policy direction and attempts are being made to modernise the agriculture sector including the recent Planting for Food and Jobs Programmes. Accordingly, steps have been taken to ensure that budgetary allocations from the petroleum fund are indeed channelled to the relevant sub-sector. For instance, PIAC has urged the Ministry of Finance to ensure that the allocated budget is disbursed and used to support interventions in agricultural mechanisation and post-harvest losses technologies. Unfortunately, there is no comprehensive guideline specifying any timelines as to when and how the country wants the agriculture sector to be modernised with proceeds from the oil revenues. More importantly, the agriculture sector has several important links with other key sectors of the economy, such as the manufacturing sector, and attempts should be made to strengthen these links.

Second, there should be further consolidation of the democratic governance system in Ghana since the ways in which political traditions are organised have a very strong influence on the extent to which the oil industry can also be effectively managed. This can be begun by the relegation of some powers given to the President to make appointments to the executive boards of institutions that are supposed to serve as checks on democratic governance. In addition, some opinion leaders have expressed concern about the President appointing chief executives for all the different districts in Ghana. They hold the view that such appointments should be made through a democratic system where people vote for such positions. We see this as key to ensuring that Ghanaians own their development process. Another area where democratic governance could be consolidated is the Government's commitment to passing the Right to Information Bill to increase transparency.

Third, to make Ghanaians feel a sense of ownership in the oil industry, an attempt should be made to adopt more cautious, transparent and flexible budgeting and transfer part of the incomes from the oil revenues directly to all Ghanaians during boom periods to reduce pressure for explosive spending followed by lock-in and fiscal crises during downturns. The transfer can take the form of utility subsidies. This is a policy suggestion offered by Sala-i-Martin and Subramanian (2012) for Nigeria; they argued that the solution prevails over the status quo of corruption and waste. Popularly known as the Alaska-style system, Palley (2014) also made a similar suggestion for Iraq, arguing that this will facilitate the political and economic reform of the country by building citizen ownership and engagement. We make a similar suggestion for Ghana and argue that such a process will increase individual and community participation in governance, and this will reduce the incentives for conflicts. Conflicts related to oil occur because of the politicisation in ways that make the control of oil resources the exclusive preserve of a few to the exclusion of the others. More importantly, such a system empowers civil societies effectively to serve as a check on the government as they will be having a large constituency interested in their activities. In the end, the quality of public institutions will be improved. Even though such a mechanism of transfer would be difficult to implement, given the context of Ghana where most people have no personal bank account. An alternative possibility, as suggested by Eifert *et al.* (2003), would be to use a transparent system of transferring the funds to communities, schools or local leaders.

Lastly, the country must implement prototypes of the OECD Anti-Bribery Convention and the UK's Extractive Industries Transparency Initiative. For instance, the Anti-Bribery Convention is a central international mechanism that many advanced countries have developed to prosecute payments from multinational investors to public officials in developing countries (see, for instance, Moran, 2006). On the other hand, the UK's Extractive Industries Transparency Initiative contains provisions that enhance transparency in the management of resource revenues (see Haaufler, 2010). While Ghana has institutions such as the EITI, tasked with some of these issues, they are poorly resourced and there are weaknesses in their legal frameworks. For instance, Ghana has an Extractive Industries Transparency Initiative and its legal support comes from the Mining Law. The country, therefore, needs to review the law and make it relevant to the oil industry as well as identify obstacles to the institution and possibly codify and institutionalise its actions.

References

Aryeetey, E., R.D. Osei and P. Quartey (2014), 'Managing Ghana's Oil Boom: Summary of Key Finding and Policy Lessons', in E. Aryeetey, R.D. Osel and P. Quartey, *Managing Ghana's Oil Boom for Structural Transformation* (pp.1–7). Accra: Institute of Statistical, Social & Economic Research.

Eifert, B., A. Gelb and N.B. Tallroth (2003), 'Managing Oil Wealth', *Finance and Development*, 40(1), 40–45.

Gary, I., S. Manteaw and C. Armstrong (2009), *Ghana's Big Test: Oil's Challenge to Democratic Development*. Washington, DC: Oxfam America. Retrieved from: https://www.oxfamamerica.org/static/media/files/ghanas-big-test.pdf.

Ghana Extractive Industries Transparency Initiative (GHEITI) (2015), '2014 Annual Activity Report', Accra, Ghana: GHEITI Secretariat, Ministry of Finance. Retrieved from: http://www.gheiti.gov.gh/site/index.php?option=com_phocadownload&view=category&id=28:2014&Itemid=54

Ghana National Petroleum Corporation (GNPC) (2016), 'Report to the PIAC on the Utilization of 2014 Share of Jubilee Crude Oil Revenue'. Accra, Ghana: Ghana National Petroleum Corporation (GNPC).

Government of Ghana (2010), 'Local Content and Local Participation in Petroleum Activities – Policy Framework'. Accra: Ministry of Energy, Government of Ghana.

Gyimah-Boadi, E., and H.K. Prempeh (2012), 'Oil, Politics, and Ghana's Democracy', *Journal of Democracy*, 23(3), 94–108.

Haufler, V. (2010), 'Disclosure as Governance: The Extractive Industries Transparency Initiative and Resource Management in the Developing World', *Global Environmental Politics*, 10(3), 53–73.

Mommer, B. (2000), *The Governance of International Oil: The Changing Rules of the Game. Oxford Institute for Energy Studies Working Papers WPM 26*. Retrieved from the Oxford Institute for Energy Studies website: https://www.oxfordenergy.org/publications/the-governance-of-international-oil-the-changing-rules-of-the-game/?v=d3dcf429c679.

Moore, M. and J. Putzel (1999), 'Thinking Strategically about Politics and Poverty. *IDS Working Paper 101*. Brighton, UK: Institute of Development Studies (IDS). Retrieved from: https://www.ids.ac.uk/files/Wp101.pdf.

Moran, T. (2006), 'How Multinational Investors Evade Developed Country Laws. *Center for Global Development Working Paper No. 79*. Washington, DC: Center for Global Development, Georgetown University. Retrieved from: http://dx.doi.org/10.2139/ssrn.984044.

Palley, T. (2014), 'Oil and the Case of Iraq', *Challenge*, 47(3), 94–112.

Public Interest and Accountability Committee (PIAC) (2011), *Report on Revenue Management*. Retrieved from; http://www.piacghana.org/portal/5/25/piac-reports.

——— (2012), *Report on Revenue Management*. Retrieved from: http://www.piacghana.org/portal/5/25/piac-reports.

——— (2013), *Report on Revenue Management*. Retrieved from: http://www.piacghana.org/portal/5/25/piac-reports.

——— (2014), *Report on Revenue Management*. Retrieved from: http://www.piacghana.org/portal/5/25/piac-reports.

——— (2015), *Report on Revenue Management*. Retrieved from: http://www.piacghana.org/portal/5/25/piac-reports.

——— (2016), *Report on Revenue Management*. Retrieved from: http://www.piacghana.org/portal/5/25/piac-reports.

———— (2017), *Report on Revenue Management*. Retrieved from: http://www.piacghana.org/portal/5/25/piac-reports.

———— (2018), *Report on Revenue Management*. Retrieved from: http://www.piacghana.org/portal/5/25/piac-reports.

Rodrik, D. (2008), 'Second-best Institutions', *American Economic Review*, 98(2), 100–104.

Sala-i-Martin, X., and A. Subramanian (2012), 'Addressing the Natural Resource Curse: An Illustration from Nigeria', *Journal of African Economies*, 22(4), 570–615. Retrieved from: https://doi.org/10.1093/jae/ejs033.

16
Kenya's Oil Governance Regime: Challenges and Policies

Germano Mwabu

16.1   Introduction

Opinions about the possible impact of oil exploration and production in Sub-Saharan Africa differ sharply. Some policy makers and academics see oil as a blessing for Africa, because oil revenues could be used to finance social and physical infrastructures that many African countries have been unable to undertake for a long time. Public infrastructure facilities, such as health and education systems, transport and communication networks, and research centres, are hard to build because of the lumpy nature of the investment that must be undertaken to construct them. Thus, the prospect of substantial oil revenues leads to higher welfare expectations in policy circles and local communities. Other policy makers and academics are more sceptical of the benefits that oil exploitation is likely to bring. Indeed, some of them see natural resources as a curse or a potential disease, because of their strong association with conflicts precipitated by groups that want to possess oil reserves exclusively for their selfish goals. In between a blessing and a curse exists a spectrum of viewpoints, one of which is that the oil resource itself is welfare-neutral. That is, it has no inherent potential to enhance or harm social welfare or the performance of an economy. Thus, any welfare or efficiency consequence of an oil resource depends on how it is extracted, managed, shared, and how its proceeds are deployed.

The view that oil is a curse is a description of society's complete failure in the management of oil, while the blessing perspective is a description of the polar case of success. The chapter argues that the kinds of welfare outcomes and economy-wide effects that are associated with oil critically depend on governance regimes that society designs and implements to get oil out of the ground, to use it to satisfy immediate population needs, to sustain its benefits for the future generations, and to improve the livelihoods of local communities. A governance regime to address these issues is proposed, based primarily on a review of a limited number of papers on oil and gas governance. The framework is used to point out what can be done to avoid the oil curse and to enhance the social and economic benefits associated with oil discoveries. The chapter examines all these issues with reference to Kenya, a country where oil exploration is in full swing.

The remainder of the chapter is organised as follows. Section 2 reviews the literature on the oil governance framework, with a focus on the Kenyan regime. Section 3 discusses challenges that might arise in applying the framework once the country starts producing oil on a commercial scale. Attention here is given to the adequacy of the legal and regulatory mechanisms (derived from the Constitution) in restraining rent-seeking and in averting ethnic conflicts that can be precipitated by disagreements in the sharing of oil benefits. Section 4 deals with optimal oil management policies and Section 5 concludes the chapter.

16.2   Natural Resources Exploration and Exploitation in Kenya

The extractives sector in Kenya (including the oil and gas industry) contributes only about 1 per cent to the country's gross domestic product (Institute of Economic Affairs, 2015). However, the economic and social roles of the sector have been changed by the recent discovery of oil. Although oil exploration started in Kenya in the 1950s, it was not until March 2012 that oil was discovered in Turkana by a UK firm, Tullow Oil plc. Even though the proven oil reserve is small, amounting roughly to 600 million barrels, there are good prospects for more discoveries. Since Turkana is within the proximity of the Ugandan region that is known to have considerably much larger reserves, there is reason to hope that large commercial reserves will be found in Kenya in the near future. Oil and gas explorations are also proceeding apace in the coastal region. Figure 16.1 shows the Kenyan region with oil and other areas with potential for more oil discoveries.

Figure 16.1 shows that the small quantities of oil and gas that have been discovered are in the northern part of the country, an arid and semi-arid region, occupied mainly by populations that depend on livestock and semi-sedentary activities for their livelihoods. However, as is also shown in that figure, the country has great potential for oil and gas discoveries. As is shown by the onshore and offshore exploration blocks, expectations of finding additional oil and gas reserves in Kenya are very high. Thus, despite the relatively small oil quantities ascertained, the policy makers

Figure 16.1:   Proven and potential oil and gas fields in Kenya

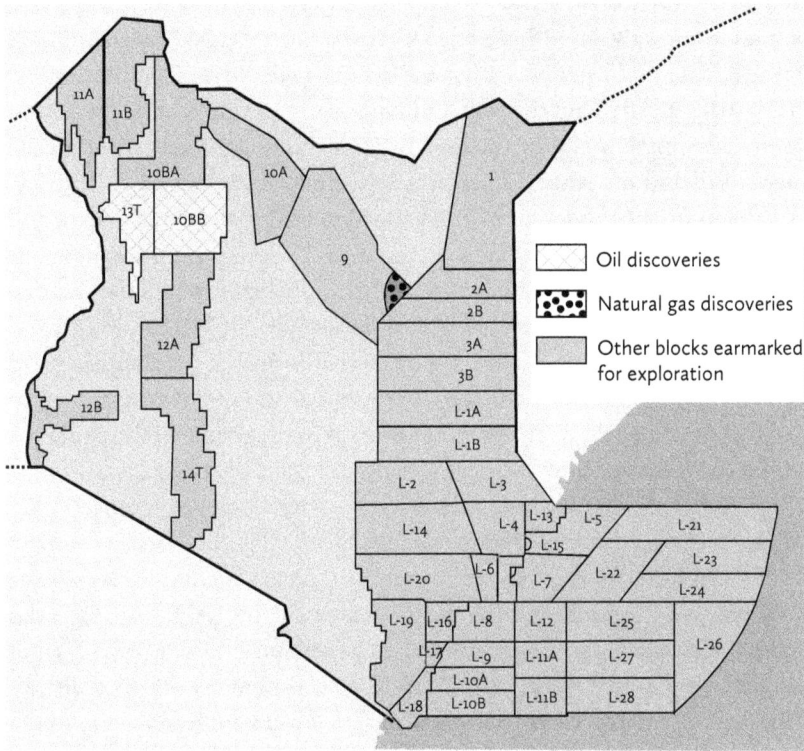

Source: Institute of Economic Affairs (2014, p. 2).

in Kenya have already begun developing a framework for governing its extraction and use.

Kenya's oil governance regime is contained in the new (August 2010) Constitution. The Constitution sets out, *inter alia*, the general principles to guide Kenyan citizens and other economic agents in pursuit of their private and social objectives. The principles related to natural resources and public affairs ensure:

–   fair land tenure and efficient land use;
–   environmental preservation and protection;
–   citizen participation in the management of natural assets;
–   fair benefit-sharing from natural resources and associated fiscal revenues;
–   transparency in the management of public services and assets;
–   access to information of a public nature.

The above principles were exercised by the Kenyan Parliament in 2013 (under the new Constitution) to enact a law establishing the mechanism for implementing *Vision 2030,* which inter alia states that 'oil development is for the benefit of the people with priority to be given to local communities'. The Parliament spelt out the principles specific to the governance of oil and gas in a number of policies and laws, e.g., the National Energy Policy, the Energy Bill and the Natural Resources (County Royalties) Bill. The new Parliament further updated the legislation governing the management and regulation of the biophysical environment and socioeconomic conditions in relation to the exploitation of oil and gas. The legislation amended the Environmental Management and Coordination Act, the Wildlife Policy and the Wildlife Protection Act, the Draft Wetlands Policy, the Land Act and the Land Registration Act, and the Community Land Bill. It is important to note that Kenya's oil governance framework is a component of the country's national governance framework as specified in the Constitution.

Figure 16.2 shows the interaction between Kenya's *oil* governance set-up and the *national* governance framework as specified in the Constitution. As can be seen from this Figure, the overarching structure for oil governance in Kenya, as in Uganda and in many other countries (Alba, 2009), is the national Constitution. The core of the oil governance framework is a set of oil-related policies and legislations. In Kenya, as in many other countries, oil governance is part of a broader national development framework. In the case of Kenya, the national development plan is Vision 2030—the country's long-term blueprint for economic, social and political prosperity. The first panel in Figure 16.2 shows the social institutions in which the natural resource governance framework is anchored, namely, the legal system derived from the Constitution. The second panel depicts the legislations specific to the governance of oil and gas. The next panels indicate laws that protect the environment and livelihoods in the process of exploiting natural resources more generally. Taken together, the policies and legislation shown in Figure 16.2 constitute the formal rules designed to govern the exploitation and use of oil in Kenya. Moreover, in addition to the formal rules and their enforcement, the oil sector is governed by numerous informal institutions, such as the local land use practices; the people's beliefs about the enforceability, duration and durability of exploration contracts; the established relationships between oil companies and local communities; and the norms for side payments made to obtain business licences.

Figure 16.2: Kenya's national and oil governance frameworks

Overarching		Constitution (2010)
		Vision 2030 (2010)
		Country Government Act (2012)
		National Policy for the SD [of...] Arid Lands
		Access to Information Bill (2013)
		Statute Law (Miscellaneous Amendments) Bill 2013
		Public Benefit Organisation (PBO) Act, 2013
Oil Governance		National Energy Policy (2014)
		Petroleum Exploration and Production Act (1986)
		Energy Act (2006)
		Energy Bill (2014)
		Petroleum (Exploration and Production) Act (1986)
		Mining Bill (2014)
		Natural Resources (Counties Royalties) Bill 2013
		Petroleum Master Plan (PMP) (in dev.)
Biophysical	**General Environment**	Environmental Mgt and Coordination Act (1999) and (2013)
		EIA and Audit Regulations (EIAAR) (2003)
		Draft EMCA (Deposit Bonds) Regulations (2014)
	Biodiversity	Wildlife Policy (2013)
		Wildlife Conservation and Management Act (2013)
		Land Act of 2012
		National Museums and Heritage Act (2006)
	Water	Water Policy (1999)
		Wetland Policy (2013)
		Water Act (2002)
		Wetland Regulations
		Water Quality Regulations
	Waste and Soils	EMCA (Waste management) Regulations (2006)
	Air and Noise	EMCA (Noise [...]) Control Regulations of 2009
		EMCA (Air Quality Standards) Regulations of 2007
Socioeconomic (N.B. Many safeguards incorporated in overarching legislation)	**Livelihoods**	Land Act (2012)
		National Land Commission Act 2012
		Land Registration Act of 2012
		Community Land Bill (2013)
		[...] Assistance to Internally Displaced Persons [...] Act (2012)
	Human Rights	Bill of Rights
		Private Security Bill (2014)
	Cultural Heritage	National Museums and Heritage Act (2006)

Source: Golombok and Jones (2015, p. 35).

It should be noted that Figure 16.2 is limited mainly to legal aspects of the oil and natural gas governance. In particular, other important governance issues, such as the procedures for awarding oil exploration and exploitation contracts; the mechanisms for monitoring exploration and production activities; methods of collecting and sharing oil taxes and royalties; the principles for investing the oil revenues for sustainable development are not included in this framework. However, these issues are also critical for the effective management of a country's oil resources and for averting the 'curses' and conflicts associated with the exploitation of natural resources. Alba (2009) extends the oil governance framework in Figure 16.2 in a way that addresses some of the above concerns. Alba's framework recognises the volatility, uncertainty and exhaustibility of oil revenue, and the technical complexities associated with oil extraction, processing and marketing.

The main contribution of Alba's paper to the analysis of the oil sector is the incorporation of local capacity building in an oil governance framework to ensure that professionals and entrepreneurs of host countries are equipped with the skills necessary to manage oil industries effectively, and to invest the oil revenue in ways that take into account the welfare of future generations and also recognise the fact that oil is an exhaustible resource. Further, Alba argues for transparency in the awarding of oil contracts to foreign and domestic firms alike, and in the allocation of oil revenue among communities and between central and local governments to avoid corruption—the root cause of social inequalities and ethnic conflicts (KIPPRA, 2011). Alba (2009, p.6) describes best practices in the award of contracts and licences as follows:

–   The sector law and regulations should define the legal and institutional framework for the exploration and exploitation of a country's hydrocarbon and mineral resources.
–   The role of state companies should be defined in the sector law, ideally separating commercial activities from the State's regulatory functions.
–   Licensing procedures and contract terms should take into account the geological, financial and country risks. Country, sector and market knowledge is needed to define appropriate licensing and contractual terms.
–   Transparent and non-discretionary procedures should be defined to attract investors.
–   The fiscal terms that determine the sharing of benefits between the Government and the investors should be progressive and preferably linked to project profitability to cope with changes in prices and different site conditions throughout the project's life.

–   The development of 'local content'—including local consultations and the
    use of local labour, goods and services—is a key aspect of hydrocarbon
    and mining projects.

In addition, Alba stresses the need to gather relevant geological information
for proper management of the oil sector, and notes that such data are important
for managing access to oil and gas resources, reducing land use conflicts,
providing a better understanding of the country's oil potential, and helping
to define sector policies and facilitating bidding processes. Another best
practice recommended in Alba's paper is the establishment of a 'one stop'
clearance shop, preferably in the Ministry of Mining or Natural Resources,
to handle all matters related to the extractive industries.

Kenya's oil governance framework largely addresses corporate, state,
environmental and fiscal issues in the extraction and use of oil. It says little
about the management of political, social and security risks that the country's
nascent oil sector faces and is likely to continue confronting in the future
(Patey, 2014). As already noted, oil in Kenya is located in Turkana County,
the homeland of the Turkana people. Since ethnicity and politics in Kenya
are intertwined, this location has social, ethnic and political implications for
oil governance. In particular, national institutions are needed for responding
to ethnic concerns about benefits from the Turkana oil and from localities
occupied by other ethnic groups. Although the Constitution states that oil is a
national resource and belongs to the national Government, this is not the view
of the local communities, who believe that the oil benefits (e.g., employment
opportunities) should be reserved to them (Patey, 2014). Demonstrations
have already been held by local communities over this issue, disrupting the
oil exploitation activities of Tullow Oil Company.

Recently, Tullow Oil Company threatened to suspend its activities following local disagreements. A Kenyan newspaper (*The Standard*) filed the
following report on the incident:

> Tullow Oil has threatened to suspend its operations in Turkana County
> just a day before a self-imposed deadline for the start of transportation of
> crude oil to Mombasa for export. The latest development has set off a chain
> reaction that will today see the Government announce suspension of the
> plan. The Standard has reliably established that for close to a month now,
> Tullow's employees have been unable to gain access to two of its sites where
> 40,000 barrels of oil that form the first batch of crude that is supposed to
> be transported to Mombasa is stored (*The Standard*, 2 June 2017).

Moreover, the surrounding communities view oil as a new scarce resource over which they should contest along the same lines as the traditional contestations for cattle, water and pasture (Patey, 2014), an issue that is a potential cause of ethnic conflicts. There are no established mechanisms as yet for dealing with risks that firms face due to ethnic rivalries over oil. Similarly, disputes have emerged between local communities and political leaders who have used their political positions to acquire or control land in the vicinity of oil wells. Again, mechanisms for resolving such risks are missing.

The greatest challenge facing oil governance in Kenya is the security risk, as terrorist groups can easily damage high-value oil investment or harm oil personnel. The areas where oil has been found (Turkana County) or where large reserves of oil and gas are likely to be discovered (the coastal region) have scanty security infrastructure, and are the ones most vulnerable to terrorist attacks. Moreover, absent from the current governance framework is a mechanism for the *safe* transport of oil and related products from production sites to harbours and ports for export. The *Standard* has described the insecurity that oil transport is facing as follows:

> Further, one of the seven companies contracted to upgrade the Kitale-Turkana road, which leads to the oil fields, has suspended works after three of its employees were attacked. ... In a letter sent to the Kenya Highways Management Authority (KeNHA), which The Standard has seen, Rowla Construction on May 20 said it had discontinued the construction of the road upgrade to the oil fields until the security of its staff was guaranteed (*The Standard*, 29 June 2017).

Apart from the insecurity problem, the investment that oil transportation infrastructure requires is too large to be undertaken by one oil company or by one country. Patey (2014) therefore proposes that Kenya, Uganda and, possibly, South Sudan combine efforts to build such infrastructure. However, as the *Standard* has reported, cooperation from Kenya's neighbours that are also beginning to develop their extractive industries may not be forthcoming (see *The Standard,* 29 June 2017). Safe transportation infrastructure for oil and gas is an integral component of the sector's governance structure. Thus, every effort should be made to construct it. The consequence for bad governance of a high-value natural resource, such as oil or gas, is underdevelopment, manifested by poverty and social conflicts (Institute of Economic Affairs, 2014).

16.3   Kenya's Oil Governance Regime

16.3.1 Guidelines from the Petroleum (Exploration and Production) Act

The Petroleum Act guides the contracting and negotiations between the Government and potential oil exploitation and production firms. It empowers the minister responsible for the energy ministry to start negotiations and the contracting processes once the decision to commence oil exploration or production has been made. Table 16.1 highlights some of the issues addressed by the law to ensure proper sharing of oil production activities and oil revenue among stakeholders and to guide negotiations and contractual processes under different circumstances.

As noted by the Institute of Economic Affairs (2014), the production-sharing mechanism detailed in Table 16.1 has a number of limitations, the main one being lack of provisions for corporate social responsibility that the corporate agents must fulfil. Other shortcomings include the absence of a compensation regime for locally recruited staff, and the lack of a company licensing timetable, as licence issue is on a first-come-first-served basis. There is also no formal provision for community participation in oil exploration or production activities. Since mechanisms for transfer of the business interests specified in production-sharing contracts are also lacking, investments in local oil ventures can happen only sporadically at best, limiting the steady growth of the local oil industry. The criteria for evaluating oil exploration or production are *ad hoc*, and this affects the quality of contractual agreements that can be concluded. Further, since the terms relating to environmental protection, conservation and management are not fully specified in production-sharing agreements, rigorous enforcement of the laws that safeguard the environment is not possible.

A new Bill (the Petroleum Exploration and Production Bill 2014) updates the original Act in important respects, but reportedly has not received presidential assent. The Bill sets out fees and levies to be paid by oil firms and specifies the formula for sharing the oil revenue. According to the Bill, when the oil sale begins, the National Government will get 75 per cent of the revenue, the county governments will take 20 per cent, and the local communities will receive 5 per cent. These sharing ratios will probably be heavily contested, given that the local communities host the oil and *are* the principals of county governments (see the Kenya Senate Bill on this issue below). Moreover, given the nature of Kenyan politics, the contestation is likely to have tribal dimensions that could precipitate ethnic tensions (*The Standard*, 2 June 2017).

Table 16.1:   **Kenya's Model for Oil Exploration and Production**

Subject of contractual negotiation	Comment on contractual terms
Oil exploration or production area	Map of a specified block size is provided with its coordinates.
Exploration period	Exploration is conducted in phases, with the initial period lasting 2–3 years, with the possibility of 2 extensions of 2 years each. Thus, the exploration period lasts 6–7 years.
Taxation	Taxes are paid in lieu for and on behalf of the contractor out of the government share of profit, i.e., the government share of the profit includes the tax amount that the oil company must pay the government.
Depreciation	This is a five-year straight-line depreciation for capital costs, which begins when production starts.
Ring fencing	Costs from one block are not allowed to be recovered from the proceeds of another.
Government participation	The minimum participation of the Government is 10 per cent of the expected proceeds. The government share is carried through exploration phase and paid in full during the development and production stages.
The cost recovery limit for the oil company	The absolute amount is determined by the negotiated gross revenue but cannot exceed 60% of annual revenues.
Profit oil split between the government and the investor	This is based on a Daily Rate of Production of profit oil on a sliding scale of 50/50 at the start of production, rising to a maximum of 78% in favour of the Kenya Government for profit oil of volumes of 100 k bbl/day onshore and 120 k bbl/day offshore.
Natural gas	In the case where the contractor considers that it is economical to produce natural gas, the contractor agrees to sell all or part of its share on natural gas to the Kenya Government, provided that the parties agree on price, volume, and terms of sale.
Supply of oil for domestic consumption	The contactor shall have the obligation to supply on a priority basis, the crude oil for domestic consumption.
Audit rights of government	The Kenya Government shall have the right to audit the joint venture accounts within 24-month period following the end of the accounting period.

Source: Author's compilation based on IEA (2014, p. 23–24).

16.3.2 The Income Tax Act as It Relates to Oil Companies

This Act is administered by the Kenya Revenue Authority on behalf of the Government of Kenya (Institute of Economic Affairs, 2014). The ninth schedule to the Income Tax Act regulates the taxation of oil companies. The following are examples of oil taxation to which the schedule applies.

Withholding Tax on Transfer or Assignment of PSC (production-sharing contracts) Rights
The ninth schedule to the Income Tax Act requires that assignment of rights under each production-sharing contract (PSC) be taxed as income. The law imposes a 10 per cent tax on the total value of the rights transferred (or assigned) for residents and a 20 per cent tax for foreigners. The taxed amount is the 'transfer gain', defined as the pre-depreciation difference between the proceeds and capital expenditure. The schedule is silent on the actions the Kenya Revenue Authority should take in the event of a transfer loss.

Tax on income derived from employment in oil-related activities
The income derived from employment in oil and gas firms is taxed on a 'Pay As You Earn' (PAYE) basis at the rate of 30 per cent. The employers must also collect social security contributions for remittance to the National Social Security Fund. It was not possible to establish the extent to which oil firms comply with the latter requirement.

Offsetting of Losses
Petroleum companies can offset losses incurred in a given year of production with proceeds from activities of the succeeding four years, including the years of the loss, a measure that essentially allows the oil company to reduce its tax burden. This tax measure is an incentive for risk-taking (see Mauritzen, 2017).

Determination of the Value of Sales for Tax Purposes
The schedule forbids transfer pricing practices across oil firms, as this affects the value of taxable sales revenue. This requirement, however, is hard to enforce without strict auditing of oil firms by the Kenya Revenue Authority.

Depreciation of Capital Expenditure for Tax Purposes
The schedule provides for a straight-line annual depreciation of 20 per cent, starting with the year the assets were deployed for commercial use or the year of production, whichever is more recent. It also allows full deduction of operational costs, such as the expenses of all kinds of drilling.

Capitalisation Rules for Petroleum Companies for Tax Purposes
The schedule stipulates rules for capitalisation of both foreign and local firms. In particular, it disallows the deduction of interest expenses from sales revenue for tax purposes if the loan amount or loan interest amount exceeds what is expected for short-term transactions. It sets no requirements for the debt-to-equity ratio that needs to be fulfilled for loan expenses to be tax deductible.

16.3.3 The Environmental Management and Coordination Act (EMCA)

The Act was passed by the Kenyan Parliament to 'provide for the establishment of an appropriate legal and institutional framework for the management of the environment' and 'improve the legal and administrative coordination of the diverse sectoral initiatives...necessary in order to improve the national capacity for the management of the environment' (as cited in Institute of Economic Affairs, 2014, pp.27–28). The Act establishes the National Environmental Management Authority (NEMA), the parastatal organisation responsible for general supervision and coordination of environmental matters in Kenya. However, EMCA is silent on measures to be taken by extractive firms to restore the integrity of the environment after their commercial activities have ceased. As a consequence, mining and extraction sites are abandoned without proper sealing, to the detriment of the environment.

16.3.4 The Sovereign Wealth Fund

Kenya's Sovereign Wealth Fund is mandated by the 2010 Constitution but is not designed to safeguard the oil revenues alone. The officers of the Fund comprise the President and a few members of the Cabinet. The objectives of the fund include building a sound savings base for the country; protecting and stabilising the budget and the economy from excess volatility in exports revenues; providing a mechanism for the diversification of the economy away from non-renewable commodity exports; assisting in dissipating unwanted liquidity; funding socio-economic development; and promoting strategic national objectives. The Sovereign Wealth Fund is a portfolio of three other funds, namely, the stabilisation fund, the infrastructure and development fund, and the future generations fund, which is financed by revenues from minerals, petroleum reserves, and exploitation of other exhaustible natural resources.

16.3.5 The Natural Resources (Benefit Sharing) Bill

The purpose of this Bill (by the Senate, rather than by the National Assembly) is to establish a method for sharing revenues from natural resource exploitation—particularly oil—between firms, the National Government, the county governments and the local communities. According to the sharing formula proposed, 20 per cent of the revenue from a natural resource, such as oil or gas, will be deposited into the Sovereign Wealth Fund, and the remainder (80 per cent) will go in a 60–40 per cent split to national and county governments, respectively. Moreover, the Bill mandates that 40 per cent of the amount received by the local governments be allocated to local communities.

A weakness of this Bill is that it does not specify the means by which the transfer of 40 per cent of the oil money received by county governments to local communities will be accomplished. Moreover, even if the transfer is actually made, it is not clear who would receive it in communities. Such monies can easily suffer the misuse and misallocations seen at the constitutional development funds that are typically under the control of a Member of National Assembly or of the ward development funds under the member of the county assembly. The establishment of legal and organisational institutions for receiving funds assigned to communities and investing them efficiently is needed. Such institutions would be managed by local people, with elected officials playing advisory and non-voting roles.

16.3.6 Institutional Architecture for Regulating the Oil and Gas Industry

The Kenyan oil and gas industry is regulated by constitutional institutions that govern the extractive sector, and these include:
- The Inter-Ministerial Committee on the Policy and Legal Framework for Geology, Mining
- and Minerals which implements policy and legal frameworks related to the extractive industry;
- The National Fossil Fuels Advisory Committee that licenses the petroleum industry;
- -The National Lands Commission that has the power to acquire private and public lands for natural resource exploitation;
- The Auditor General, an independent officer who audits and reports on accounts of national interest, such as of the national oil corporation, the courts, Parliament and political parties;

- The Controller of the Budget, an independent officer who has the constitutional power to authorise withdrawals from public accounts;
- The Legislature (National Assembly and the Senate), which inter alia ratifies agreements on the exploitation of natural resources and protects the interests of counties in such matters.
- The judiciary, a constitutional arm of government that handles specific disputes emanating from the extractive industry;
- The county governments directly control the regions with oil and gas discoveries;
- The National Oil Corporation of Kenya, a state corporation that collaborates with other oil firms in the upstream oil and gas ventures, and to some extent regulates the extractive industry.

16.4   Local Content and Gender Issues in the Governance of the Oil and Gas Industry

The policy, legal and institutional frameworks for governing the extractive sector contain little information about economic empowerment of local communities, and practically nothing about the participation of women in the extractive sector. The gender issue is tangentially covered in laws related to small-scale mining activities. Moreover, the laws on local content development are at the earliest stages, and have not begun seriously to address the issues of inclusivity and the safety of women in extractive industries. With regard to local content, oil firms and governments need to establish value-adding activities in upstream and downstream industries from which local communities can benefit. In particular, labour-intensive exploitation and production technologies should be given high priority.

Incentives should be designed for foreign oil firms to create opportunities for good jobs in local economies by training local entrepreneurs, transferring new technologies to them, and awarding contracts to local firms. There is evidence that the main foreign oil company in Kenya—Tullow Oil plc—is working closely with Kenya's National Oil Corporation to strengthen its procurement capacity and to create jobs in the area where oil reserves are being exploited, namely Turkana County. As reported by Kenya's National Treasury:

> Tullow Oil Kenya B.V. awarded National Oil the tender for the supply of bulk fuels, construction of a fuel station in Turkana and management of the fuel Distribution. One of the conditions of the contract with Tullow

entailed National Oil sourcing for a firm to supply the containerized stations as per specifications provided by Tullow. The proposed firm—Petrol Industry—provided specifications similar to those provided by Tullow in the post tender clarification on the tender awarded to National Oil. The total cost of the fuel storage facility and the dispensing pumps would be recovered within the Three (3) year contract if National Oil was awarded the tender. Pursuant to Section 74 (2) (b) of PPDA 2005 there is no suitable alternative for supply of containerized offices as Petro Industrial Solution (PTY) had the specifications required by Tullow Kenya B.V. (Kenya National Treasury, 2015).

The contractual partnership between Tullow Oil and the Kenya National Oil Corporation is in the spirit of the Senate Local Content Bill of 2016 which is yet to be enacted by Parliament (Kenya Gazette Supplement No. 115). Furthermore, in addition to the industrial side of local content development, provision of social services, such as education and health care—inputs into human capital formation—should also receive equal attention. In creating the infrastructure for local content development, care should be taken not to overlook protection and preservation of the natural environment—a form of capital that has sustained local communities for centuries.

16.5 Challenges in the Workings of Kenya's Oil Governance Regime

As is clear from the transport and safety problems already highlighted, Kenya's oil governance regime will face a number of challenges in the future.

First, an important challenge is likely to be in fulfilling or in managing the high expectations that people already hold about oil benefits. The quantity produced might be too little to be shared in the manner specified in the governance framework. For example, the revenue earned may be sufficient only for the sovereign wealth fund or just enough to augment the fiscal budget of the National Government—the owner of the oil. If reporting on the magnitude of oil earnings is not transparent, or is not sufficient, unnecessary conflict can arise among the stakeholders, particularly between the National Government and local communities, the custodians of the oil.

Second, a related challenge concerns the price of oil. Moderately large quantities of oil can be produced but sold at low prices, yielding little revenue. However, the critical question here is the effect the oil price has on oil production. There is evidence that a fall in oil price may not affect oil production

(Mauritzen, 2017) because oil firms tend to produce oil in excess of current demand so that extra oil can be stored and sold at better prices in the future. The evidence from Norway supports this viewpoint and shows further that low oil prices can divert exploration investments to oil production in existing fields (Mauritzen, 2017).

Third, a lack of transparency in reporting sales income can be a source of social tensions or disappointments. It is not at all clear how transparency in reporting can be convincingly conveyed to diverse ethnic groupings that tend to distrust each other, except members of their own communities (KIPPRA, 2013).

Fourth, even without information asymmetries between the stakeholders, the revenue from oil production may be insufficient to cover exploration and production costs or the large expense needed to heal the environment from exploration damage, raising legitimate inefficiency concerns on the part of the National Government. Such a circumstance can raise the risk of political and macroeconomic instability and hurt the whole economy.

Fifth, a somewhat different challenge is in using the governance framework to ensure that appropriate technologies are used to protect the environment during oil exploration, extraction and transportation. Oil exploration and production can plunge local communities into poverty if the activities damage the ecosystem beyond repair—via, for example, uncontrolled drilling, oil spills, the clearance of forested areas, disruption of aquifers, pollution of lakes and rivers, and via improper disposal of unwanted extraction material. Moreover, extraction dusts, noise, gases and debris can cause unanticipated health problems to local people.

Sixth, the aforementioned risks can be greatly reduced by making local communities aware of them, by involving the communities in the application of the framework, and by assigning them substantive interests in the oil industry. However, the assignment of business stakes has the potential for good and bad consequences for the environment. While it can restrain the oil firms from harming the environment, it can also be an incentive for the communities to align with oil companies to damage the environment for short-term commercial gains. The application of the governance framework should consider both short- and long-term dynamics in business relationships between communities and the oil industry.

Seventh, the most serious challenge facing the application of Kenya's oil governance framework arguably relates to averting or minimising conflicts in the control and use of oil. In the case of Kenya, this might appear to be a minor issue because of the existence of a solid and broadly based framework to that end—discussed in section 2. The challenge in its application is in sufficiently satisfying the interests of diverse ethnic communities that feel themselves to be equally entitled to oil benefits as the communities in which the oil is located.

Ethnic identities in Kenya are strong and are enshrined in the Constitution (promulgated by the Government in 2010), after landslide approval in a national referendum (Republic of Kenya, 2010). The Kenyan people are proud of their ethnic diversity—a phenomenon that the Constitution considers a national heritage. The reason Kenya's supreme law protects ethnicity is that ethnicity per se does no harm. It is a beautiful cultural phenomenon, especially as expressed in tribal songs, dances, some aspects of traditional medicine, costumes and methods of subsistence. The resilience of some communities to onslaughts of nature, such as droughts and floods, can inform the national response to natural disasters. However, some ethnic practices (such as the cultural mutilation of girls, early marriages and livestock rustling) are a constraint on inclusive development and should be discouraged. In this regard, it is important to note that unwelcome ethnic practices are not inherent attributes of some communities. Every community worldwide has some cultural aspect that needs changing in light of new knowledge and technologies.

Political parties or groupings have been organised along ethnic lines since the pre-independence days (Hino et al., 2012). The Constitution does not disallow political alliances along tribal gradients. Furthermore, politicisation of national issues along ethnic lines (negative ethnic politics), while generally not approved, is not illegal. As already reported by the Standard, there is little doubt that when the oil revenue begins to flow in large quantities it will be politicised along ethnic lines, and some ethnic tensions can be expected. It should be possible to find workable mechanisms for averting or managing such tensions.

The risk of rebel groups attempting to control oil enclaves should be expected, especially if large quantities of oil become available. The groups would be a formidable threat to the stability of the country if organised along ethnic lines. However, in the case of Kenya, such groups would also threaten the ethnic diversity of the country, as groups of that kind have secession tendencies. The country would certainly find ways of forestalling its activities. The challenge would be how to do so with a minimum of social conflicts. One way to that end is to strength public and civil society institutions that promote social cohesion. Such institutions (e.g., the National Integration and Social Commission, religious organisations and traditional leadership systems) can be empowered to bring different communities together to respond to a national crisis of that kind.

16.6   Policies for Oil-led Prosperity

Despite the development challenges posed by oil discoveries, it is possible to design and implement policies whereby oil revenues can be effectively used to reduce horizontal inequalities, to overcome extreme poverty, to address historical marginalisation, to diversify a country's economy, and to place a country on a higher growth trajectory. However, in order for Kenya really to benefit from its oil wealth, it will have aptly and proactively to deal with three important issues.

A first issue which requires proactive management is the prevention of the so-called 'natural resource curse', i.e. a situation in which oil wealth results in political instability and conflict rather than increased prosperity (see, for example, Auty, 1993). In particular, in a country without a strong rule of law or respect for norms of public order, some people or groups in society may attempt to use organised violence to gain control of the country's oil resources or other natural resource for that matter. Kenyan political leadership can reduce the risk of this type of economic violence by strengthening its internal security institutions and intelligence system.

A second issue which requires proactive management is the prevention of the so-called 'Dutch disease' (The Economist, 1977). The Dutch disease is a term coined by The Economist in 1977 in a description of the Dutch economy following its poor performance after massive oil and gas finds in the 1960s. Moreover, it is a metaphor for the over-concentration of investments in the oil (or other natural resource) sector, which exposes an economy to risks of depressions and recessions in the event of a decline in the demand for oil exports or in the case of a large decrease in international oil prices. There is evidence that a sudden increase in oil or gas prices can cause serious crises in the banking sector, and in the extreme case lead to a collapse of the banks. A partial cause of this malaise is the resultant non-competitiveness of export firms that hold large bank loans that the firms fail to repay (Kinda et al., 2016; Mlachila and Ouedraogo, 2017). The non-indebted export firms are also starved of credit by banks because banks know these firms are unlikely to meet their loan obligations. It is easy to see that this liquidity problem can easily cascade to all firms.

Policies that use a country's oil revenues to diversify the economy would strengthen the economy's resilience to adverse shocks to oil exports. The over-investment in the export sector starves the rest of the economy of the resources needed to develop agricultural and service industries, which tend to be labour-intensive and thus are capable of employing a large proportion of the population, in contrast to the oil sector which tends to be capital-intensive (thus creating high-wage jobs for a relatively small number of people). As already noted, the emergence of an oil enclave can increase supplies of international currency in the domestic economy and reduce the profitability of non-oil exporters. Moreover, the regional imbalance in investment resulting from oil discoveries can cause large social inequalities and extreme poverty. Thus, in addition to being used for diversification of economic activities, the oil revenues should be used to fight horizontal inequalities and extreme poverty. Policy makers should also strive to reduce macroeconomic and regulatory uncertainties as these reduce returns on oil stocks (Wensheng *et al.*, 2017). In general, policy uncertainty is not good for profitability of oil companies and is a disincentive for investments that add value to domestic products or create employment for local communities.

A third issue deals with the association between resource extraction and environmental degradation. The degradation adversely affects the welfare of the future generations and reduces the ability of the present generations to maintain their current living standards. Oil is part and parcel of the natural environment. Its extraction necessarily tears apart the environmental structure. Thus, without the repair of the environment—after oil extraction—it would continue to deteriorate as the oil reserve is run to exhaustion. It follows that without a programme to preserve the environment as oil is extracted, the country would end up without oil and without a usable environment. For example, the grassland that supported livestock in a pre-oil period may not be able to serve this purpose if the oil extraction is done in an environmentally unsustainable way. Furthermore, some habitats for fauna and flora would be destroyed due to the highly intrusive nature of oil exploration technologies.

The long-term consequence of uncontrolled extraction is under-development and widespread poverty. Although Hotelling (1931) has noted that exhaustion of one natural resource, such as oil or gas, need not thrust the whole country into extreme poverty, this situation can easily befall a community whose natural resource has been depleted or damaged irreparably. This reasoning reveals the need to preserve the local environment and to invest oil revenues in assets that yield returns into a distant future, if oil exploitation is to bring lasting prosperity. The Kenyan political leaders and their development partners should use Kenya's sovereign wealth fund to sustain oil benefits, and further rely on provisions of the Environmental Management and Coordination Act (EMCA) to preserve and protect the environment.

16.7   Conclusion

Oil exploitation is associated with three negative social externalities, namely, the natural resource curse, the Dutch disease and environmental degradation. Moreover, as noted by Hotelling (1931), exhaustion or degradation of a natural resource is a public bad that needs collective action to address. Taken together, the three externalities constitute large hidden social costs of natural resource exploitation in any country. The purpose of oil governance regimes worldwide should be to minimise these costs or avert them where possible. In the case of Kenya, the costs have not yet been incurred on a large scale because the oil industry is still at the embryonic stage. The costs will however increase considerably as soon as commercial oil begins to flow on a regular basis.

The oil governance framework discussed in section 2 will be an important tool for addressing the negative social externalities of establishing an oil industry in Kenya. If the framework is applied correctly, the country will prosper in both the short and long run. Recognising that social costs of extraction are negative externalities of establishing an oil industry is the crucial step in averting resource curses and Dutch disease. It is important to note that the cost of natural resource exploitation is not limited to negative social externalities associated with private outlays made by firms but also includes general equilibrium effects of such outlays and similar activities.

In assessing whether a natural resource such as oil or gas should be exploited, both the industry level and economy-wide costs and benefits should be considered explicitly. In the case of Kenya, oil production activities should be commenced on a commercial scale if the expected benefit of establishing the oil industry exceeds the associated social cost, including the expense of addressing negative social externalities. Such a cost-benefit calculation can help to avoid equating (at a later date) bad managerial decisions of the past to exogenously imposed curses or diseases.

There is need to stress that the problem of violent conflicts over a natural resource such as oil or gas among social groups is not inevitable. The conflict (curse or 'disease') often occurs due to a lack of institutional restraints on agents' self-regarding behaviours or because of unacceptably high level of horizontal inequalities that groups associate with natural resource exploitation. In the case of Kenya, the oil governance regime could address this issue through equitable provision of public goods across regions (including employment opportunities), and through acceptable sharing of political power across ethnic groups, as the ethnic structure of such power will in the Kenyan context invariably determine the degree of fairness in the allocation and use of oil proceeds.

References

Achuka, V. (2017, 2 June), 'Oil Export Plan in Limbo as Tullow Threatens to Pull Out of Turkana Oil Fields'. *The Standard Newspaper*. Retrieved from: https://www.standardmedia.co.ke/business/article/2001245230/oil-export-plan-in-limbo-as-tullow-threatens-to-pull-out-of-turkana-oil-fields.

Auty, R.M. (1993), *Sustaining Development in Mineral Economies: The Resource Curse Thesis*. London: Routledge.

Battaile, B., R. Chisik and H. Onder (2014), 'Services, Inequality, and Dutch Disease'. *Working Paper No. 6966*. Washington, DC: The World Bank.

Golombok, R., and M.I. Jones (2015), *Oil Governance in Uganda and Kenya: A Review of Efforts to Establish Baseline Indicators on the Impact of Oil Sector in Uganda and Kenya*. Nairobi: UNEP.

Hiroyuki, H., J. Lonsdale, G, Ranis and F. Stewart (2012), *Ethnic Diversity and Economic Instability in Africa: Interdisciplinary Perspectives*. Cambridge: Cambridge University Press.

Hotelling, H. (1931), 'The Economics of Exhaustible Resources', *Journal of Political Economy*, 39(2), 137–175. Retrieved from: http://supplier.treasury.go.ke/site/tenders.go/index.php/public/direct_view/275.

Institute of Economic Affairs (2014), *A Primer to the Emerging Extractive Sector in Kenya: Resource Bliss, Dilemma or Curse*. Nairobi: IEA.

Kamau, M. (2017, 27 April), 'Tullow Strikes More Oil in Latest Turkana Find'. The *Standard* Newspaper. Retrieved from; https://www.standardmedia.co.ke/business/article/2001237778/tullow-strikes-more-oil-in-latest-turkana-find.

Kangethe, K. (2017, 26 April), 'Three Exploration Companies Strike More Oil in Turkana'. *Capital FM Radio*. Retrieved from: https://www.capitalfm.co.ke/business/2017/04/three-exploration-companies-strike-oil-turkana/.

Kenya Institute for Public Policy Research and Analysis (KIPPRA) (2011), *Managing Kenya's Ethnic Diversity: Policies for Social Cohesion and Economic Prosperity*. Nairobi: Kenya Institute for Public Policy Research and Analysis.

Kenya National Treasury (2015, 17 March), *Tender for Supply of 3 Containerized Stations for Tullow Oil on Unit Rates at USD 79,158.07 for 3 units at the National Oil Corporation of Kenya*. Nairobi.

Kinda, T., M. Mlachila and R. Ouedraogo (2016), 'Commodity Price Shocks and Financial Sector Fragility'. *IMF Working Paper No. 16/12*. Retrieved from: https://www.imf.org/external/pubs/ft/wp/2016/wp1612.pdf.

Mauritzen, J. (2017), 'The Effect of Oil Prices on Field Production: Evidence from the Norwegian Continental Shelf. *Oxford Bulletin of Economics and Statistics*, 79(1), 124–144.

Mayorga Alba, E. 2009. Extractive Industries Value Chain: A Comprehensive Integrated Approach to Developing Extractive Industries'. *Extractive Industries and Development Series; no. 3. Africa Working Paper Series no. 125*. Washington, DC: The World Bank,

Mlachila, M., and R. Ouedraogo (2017), 'Financial Development Resource Curse in Resource-Rich Countries'. *IMF Working Paper No. 17/163*. Retrieved from: https://www.imf.org/en/Publications/WP/Issues/2017/07/19/Financial-Resource-Curse-in-Resource-Rich-Countries-44938.

Patey, L. (2014), 'Kenya: An African Oil Upstart in Transition'. *Oxford Institute of Energy Studies Paper, WPM 53*, 1–26. Retrieved from: https://doi.org/10.26889/9781784670115.

Republic of Kenya (2010), Kenya Constitution. Nairobi: Government Printer.

The Economist (2004, 5 November). 'The Economist Explains: The Dutch Disease'. *The Economist*. Retrieved from: https://www.economist.com/the-economist-explains/2014/11/05/what-dutch-disease-is-and-why-its-bad.

Wensheng, K., F. Perez de Gracia and R.A. Ratti (2017), 'Oil Price Shocks, Policy Uncertainty, and Stock', *Journal of International Money and Finance*, 70, 344–359.

PART V

A WAY FORWARD

17

Oil Wealth and Development in Uganda and Beyond: Conclusions and Policy Recommendations

By Ukoha Ukiwo, Pamela Mbabazi, and Arnim Langer

17.1   Introduction

The 2006 announcement of major oil finds in Uganda's Lake AIbert Basin generated much jubilation and trepidation. On the one hand, the jubilation arose from the improved prospects of this East African country fast-tracking its ascendancy to the status of a middle-income country based on the singular instrumentality of oil wealth. On the other hand, the trepidation that was felt both locally and globally stemmed from concerns about the fate of other developing countries that have had the fortune (or arguably misfortune) of discovering large quantities of oil or other natural resources.

In many of these countries the discovery, exploration, and exploitation of oil resources have been associated with mono-cultural economies, economic disruptions and vulnerabilities, mismanagement and corruption, subversion of democracy, and even violent conflicts. The 'poisonous' cocktail of these interlinked phenomena, which is often referred to as the 'resource curse' or 'governance curse' (see the Introduction to this book), has tended to moderate celebrations in developing countries which have discovered large quantities of oil or other natural resources. This is the context of this book, which is concerned with how well prepared Uganda is to manage its recently discovered oil wealth effectively, efficiently, and transparently. It is worth repeating that the question at the heart of this book is as follows: to what extent is Uganda ready to effectively harness its oil revenues for national and human development, thereby avoiding the oil governance curse?

The preceding chapters in this book have provided an in-depth analysis and deep insights into the diverse set of efforts and institutions that the Ugandan State has introduced in recent years in order to harness the country's oil wealth for national development. In this respect extensive attention was paid to the shortcomings and ongoing challenges of Uganda's oil governance regime. The comparative case study chapters have provided similar analysis on and insights from Nigeria, Ghana, and Kenya. Drawing extensively on the analysis and insights offered in the preceding chapters, in the current chapter we will draw a number of conclusions concerning Uganda's oil governance regime and the challenges the country is facing in effectively, efficiently, and transparently managing its oil sector and revenues. We will also formulate and reflect upon some possible policy options for harnessing oil for the benefit of the people of oil-producing countries in Africa.

17.2   Oil Governance Institutions in Uganda: Work in Progress

Uganda has recorded important progress in putting in place the necessary legislation to guide the nature of the relationship between the State, representing the Ugandan people, and the international oil companies (IOCs); the management of oil revenues for the common good of Ugandans; and the management of externalities associated with distortions to macroeconomic management and the pernicious effects of oil on the environment. The National Oil and Gas Policy, which is subsidiary to the Constitution of the Republic of Uganda, is the overarching policy framework that seeks to enhance the prospects of optimal benefits from oil (see, in particular, Chapter 2 by Mbabazi and Muhangi; and Chapter 3 by J. Oloka-Onyango).

The policy framework is codified in laws that stipulate the regulations in upstream, midstream, and downstream operations. Foremost among these laws is the Petroleum Exploration Development and Production Act, 2013, which has established the Petroleum Authority of Uganda, which is charged with regulating all operations in the petroleum industry as well as monitoring and ensuring compliance by all industry stakeholders. The Act also authorises the Uganda National Oil Company (UNOC) to manage the country's commercial interests in this sector. This principally involves transactions and partnerships with international oil companies (IOCs). Another key law was the Petroleum Refining, Conversion, Storage and Transportation Act 2013, which is a crucial piece of legislation with regard to attracting investment and the development of oil and gas infrastructure. Also worthy of note is the Public Finance Management Act 2015, which is aimed at ensuring that the country's oil revenues are managed in an accountable and responsible manner. Finally, the National Content Policy and Implementation Strategy and Plan has established mechanisms for guaranteeing that the oil industry is not dominated by foreign interests and ensures the involvement of Ugandans by providing rules for the employment of Ugandan citizens and patronage of Ugandan businesses in procurement and service provision in the sector. Uganda's Local Content Policy (LCPs) further emphasises the building capacity of local companies to participate actively across the entire value chain of the oil and gas sector. This support by government shall be extended to local companies by means of providing cheap credit through the recently proposed Uganda Development Bank (UDB), as well as supporting the acquisition of the latest equipment and technology to use across the entire value chain.

In order to achieve maximum returns and dividends on its oil wealth, Uganda uses the model of production sharing agreements (PSAs). Using this approach, the Government of Uganda believes it has obtained the best deals for Uganda in its negotiations with the international oil companies that participate in the upstream to downstream operations. Added to this is the fact that negotiations with neighbouring states, notably Tanzania through which Ugandan oil will be exported, have produced concessions and tax holidays which ensure that Uganda's oil will probably have one of the lowest costs of production at US$ 12.[1] This achievement came at the cost of abandoning earlier plans to transport the oil through Kenya (Patey, 2019). It should be noted though that the acclaimed capacity of Ugandan state representatives in deal-making has not come without costs (see Patey, 2015). In particular, protracted negotiations are seen to be one of the factors that have significantly delayed the time at which Uganda will be likely to achieve full production (now estimated to happen sometime in the period 2021–2023).[2]

Notwithstanding, the capacity of the Ugandan State to maintain its stance on negotiations at this early stage, when there is so much political and social pressure for the commencement of production, is a promising indicator of the strength necessary to ensuring that the country does not become vulnerable to the stranglehold of IOCs and vicissitudes of global energy markets.[3] Having said this, there are nonetheless a number of serious challenges in the legal and

1 See 'Uganda's oil production cost per barrel at US$12.2 is one of the best globally', retrieved from: http://www.infrastructure.co.ug/ugandas-oil-production-cost-barrel-us122-one-best-globally.
2 See, https://observer.ug/news/headlines/59159-uganda-s-first-oil-production-now-pushed-to-2021; https://www.monitor.co.ug/Business/Prosper/Uganda-slow-pace-towards-oil-production/688616-4594748-format-xhtml-xqd9oyz/index.html; and https://energy.economictimes.indiatimes.com/news/oil-and-gas/total-to-start-uganda-crude-oil-production-in-2021-at-the-earliest/64647798.
3 For instance, at the insistence of the Ugandan Government that Tullow Oil should pay capital gains tax, which it tried to avoid during protracted negotiations about the sale of its shares to CNOC and Total. See https://allafrica.com/stories/201811190539.html.

regulatory framework that engender concerns and raise suspicions about the motives of state actors and industry operators. Some of these concerns include excessive executive control, limitations of the oversight functions of Parliament, lack of transparency with regard to the contracts agreed with the IOCs, and limitations concerning local content development. Although the Ugandan Parliament has formally been given the power to oversee the licensing and governance processes, there are some clauses that have been capitalised upon by the executive to devalue the efficacy of the checks and balances that are included in Uganda's oil governance regime. These include provisions that allow the minister to negotiate with foreign companies and countries without recourse to the Parliament, since parliamentary approval is not necessary for the activation of the contracts. Parliamentary oversight is also circumvented by the fact that Parliament is not privy to the details of contracts entered into by the Government of Uganda with international oil companies (see Global Rights Alert, 2016).

The local content law is also seen as problematic for being ambivalent in its operationalisation of local content. One of the contentious issues is the law's designation of a national business enterprise as a business that has in its employ up to 70 per cent of staff members who are Ugandans. This provision, which is blind to ownership structure, is suspected of creating a window for fully-owned foreign companies to become 'Ugandan' by simply nationalising its labour force (Argom and Magona, 2017). Despite the observed limitations in its legal framework and governance institutions, Uganda appears to be relatively better prepared compared to earlier African oil-producing countries. It may be idealistic to assume even in the best of conditions that the whole gamut of legislation would be perfect from Day One. Arguably, perfection in the regulatory framework can only evolve from practice and experimentation over time based on a culture of learning. Moreover, as most of the chapters in this book have clearly indicated, it is risky to overplay the salience of the rules of the game, as the national experience suggests that it is not the dearth of good laws that afflicts the land, but rather a lack of consistency in the implementation and enforcement of existing laws. This experience is not dissimilar to the experiences of Ghana, Kenya and Nigeria.

In Uganda and these other countries, policy implementation and the functioning of institutions is contingent on the political economy. So far, the predominance of the National Resistance Movement (NRM) in the polity and the towering influence of President Museveni have created the stability required for engagement with national and global interests in the exploration processes. The institutions will be tested when Uganda commences full oil production and export in the next few years. A critical test will be how the NRM government under President Museveni will be able to preside over sustainable management of the oil revenues amidst expectations from diverse national actors. Another important variable is the longevity of the NRM regime as well as the Museveni presidency. With the constitutional reforms concerning presidential age and term limits successfully pushed through a number of years ago, Museveni is set to remain in power for the long haul. There is little doubt that the expected oil boom will contribute to mobilisations towards regime consolidation and tenure elongation and perpetuation. The continuation of the NRM regime is likely to guarantee short- to medium-term stability in institutions. The Ugandan one-party dominant system will likely allow for gradual reform of the sector characterised by the introduction of the piecemeal reforms that would contribute to regime legitimation and consolidation. This is evidenced by the acceptance of the executive and Parliament to join the EITI in 2019 after years of hesitation. The signing of the EITI suggests that the Government of Uganda is disposed to make Ugandans and the international community believe it is conforming to global best practice on the exploitation and production of oil.

17.3 Policy Options for Uganda and African Oil Producers

Experiences of oil-producing countries around the world point towards a number of policy options for Uganda and other oil-producing States in Africa.

17.3.1 The Role of the State

A fundamental issue to be addressed in order to prevent the resource or governance curse and associated impacts from taking hold is the role of the State in a country's oil exploitation and production process. The prevalent governance mechanisms evident in the case studies in this book, and in other African States for that matter, is one where the State plays a central and overwhelming role. The State is at once owner, law maker, monitor and regulator, investor, rent collector, and developer. The omnibus function of the State is evident in the mandate assigned to the national oil company (NOC), which usually personifies and represents state interests. National oil companies (NOCs) usually have a number of roles that go beyond profit maximisation and include oil wealth redistribution to the society, wealth creation for the nation, industrialisation and economic development, energy security especially for domestic consumption and stable exports, strategic foreign policy and participation in national politics (see James Baker Institute, 2007). However, these priorities often have implications for the capacity of national oil companies to maximise the value of oil reserves, replace reserves, expand production and attain technical efficiency (Jaffe, 2007).

The model of national oil companies did not originate in the African continent and it appears not to have served African countries particularly well. This is because of the self-negating and contradictory implications of its multifarious mandates. Prominent here is the contradiction between its roles as owner/investor and regulator. This creates a situation of conflict of interests that affects unbiased legislation, regulation and enforcement. In Nigeria, the NNPC—the national oil company—has shown serious deficiencies in the discharge of its many roles and responsibilities. As an investor, it has chronically defaulted on payment of costs of production and costs of maintenance with serious implications for investment in the sector. For over a decade, many investors have avoided the joint venture agreements (JVA) model because of the infamous incapacity and unwillingness of the Nigerian state investor to meet its cash obligations. By December 2018, the Joint Venture Cash Call (JVCC) stood at US$ 5.1 billion.[4] The Nigerian Government has sought to mitigate the risks by coming out of the cash call arrangement, which has made investors shun investments.[5] One area where investments have been affected is the downstream sub-sector of refining. With the national oil company owning all existing malfunctioning refineries that are sustained by state subsidies, investors have shied away from Nigeria, despite the extremely large domestic market. Instead, investors have been particularly attracted to the massively subsidised import of petroleum products to mitigate the perennial shortfall of refined oil products in Nigeria.

Another self-negating result of the omnibus mandate of the state oil company is evident in the context of environmental sustainability. State capacity to develop and enforce laws aimed at effectively preventing and/or curtailing environmental pollution is seriously undermined by the fact that the State is also an investor. As the leading partner in most JVAs, the State itself is bound to pick up a large proportion of the fines imposed for environmental breaches in the exploration and exploitation of oil resources. This removes the incentive to apply rigour in their enforcement as the State is at once enforcer and culprit.[6]

---

4   https://www.thisdaylive.com/index.php/2018/12/13/nigeria-owes-intl-oil-companies-5-1bn-says-nnpc/
5   http://www.nnpcgroup.com/PublicRelations/NNPCinthenews/tabid/92/articleType/ArticleView/articleId/693/Exit-of-Cash-Calls-Agreement-to-Usher-in-Investment-in-Oil-Sector.aspx.
6   Nigeria has been unable to end gas flares. There are indications that barely five years before the date fixed for ending gas flares, Nigeria has dropped in the global ranking on gas flaring. See https://www.premiumtimesng.com/news/headlines/297472-special-report-nigerias-gas-flares-increase-ahead-2020-deadline.html.

Another challenge associated with national oil companies relates to the State's control over the appointment of top management positions and boards of directors. This creates a context for nepotism and the politicisation of appointments, as evidenced in Angola, where the long-time president appointed his daughter to head the national oil company.[7] This may also lead to frequent changes in the executive leadership of the NOCs with implications for the strategic vision.

Comparative studies suggest that national oil companies are varied in their nature and missions, even though they may be largely similar in ownership structure (James Baker Institute, 2007). They have also achieved varying degrees of efficiency and results. Key lessons from comparative studies suggest that success factors include: 1) competition in the home industry; 2) competition in international exploration and refining; 3) strict monitoring of accounting and financial reporting practices; 4) investments in international stock markets, and 5) autonomous boards of directors and professional management (Jaffe, 2007). These factors contribute to the optimal performance of NOCs, because they moderate the impact of their pursuit of non-commercial national strategic objectives, keep them more focused on core business activities and ensure more probity and accountability. In Norway, for instance, competition in the home country created incentives for the State gradually to remove preferential treatment for Statoil, thereby enabling it to function more efficiently over time (see Gordon and Stenvoll, 2007).

It is noteworthy that Uganda and Kenya have established national oil companies and have sought to follow the model of separating the national oil company from the regulatory authority. While this is an important start, it should be noted that Nigeria also has a similar structure where the Ministry of Petroleum Resources[8] and the Department of Petroleum Resources (DPR) are statutory regulators. However, the relationship between the regulators and the NOC has remained complex. Although the Nigerian NOC was excised from the DPR, it has over the years become more powerful than the DPR. In fact, in the late 1970s when reforms in the sector led to the emergence of the NNPC, the Ministry of Petroleum and DPR were subsumed under the NNPC (see Nwokeji, 2007). This complex history and the imperatives of power politics—where the political leadership is drawn closer to the NOC and

7   Of course, the newly elected president sacked the former president's daughter in his bid to take control of the country. See https://www.theguardian.com/world/2017/nov/15/angolan-president-sacks-predecessors-daughter-as-state-oil-chief.

8   This ministry has had a chequered history. Originally excised from the Ministry of Mines and Power, it has been scrapped under some administrations and even when other administrations tolerated its existence the chief executive has retained the position of Minister of Petroleum.

at the best of times barely takes notice of the regulator—has had implications for the capacity of regulatory institutions. Clearly, there is a need for a clear separation of roles and the creation of the right incentives to subordinate the national oil companies to regulatory institutions, as is evident in Saudi Arabia and Norway. New oil producers such as Uganda, Ghana and Kenya have the opportunity to get it right from the outset. Nigeria's efforts to reform the industry and the NOC in particular have been stalled for the umpteenth time partly due to vested interests.[9]

17.3.2 Unburdening Oil

Africa's oil producers should make conscious efforts to unburden their oil. A recurrent concomitant of the discovery of oil is the explosion of expectations of the good life among the population and leadership. The historical role of oil wealth in transforming some poor nations to prosperous ones clearly shows that oil wealth may be a catalyst for national development. However, care should be taken to manage popular perceptions and communication to ensure that other sources of national wealth are not ignored in the craze to exploit oil for national development. Key priority sectors that have been supporting the economy, for example, the agriculture sector that usually employs a large proportion of the working population in most African countries, should still be prioritised since they are infinite resources compared to a petroleum resource which is finite. This fixation on oil as a source of national prosperity is often one of the sources of the 'Dutch disease', as aspirations for economic diversification become rhetorical.

Nigeria's experience is instructive in this context. Although economic diversification has featured as a priority national objective in successive Nigerian national development plans and annual budgets since independence, this has remained aspirational as a result of the fixation of the state and society on oil wealth. The fixation on oil is evidenced by the fact that all governments in Nigeria have privileged oil revenues in their national budgets. Nigeria's federal budget is usually based on projections of national production levels for oil and global benchmark prices. This practice, which may be rationalised on the ground that oil revenues account for up to 70 per cent of government revenues, diverts attention and investments from other sectors of the economy. This is because, since oil sustains the State, state policies are overly focused on

---

9   The main opposition candidate in the 2019 presidential elections promised to privatise the NNPC.

protecting the sector. This has gradually resulted in an enormous dependence on oil revenues and an economy characterised by monoculturalism.

As the chapters in this book have clearly shown, the governments of Ghana, Kenya and Uganda have also identified economic diversification as national priorities in order to avoid the Dutch disease. Oil revenues should serve as a lever to stimulate more investments in traditional and upcoming revenue-generating sectors in a competitive and efficient manner. While ensuring that a sustainable ratio of revenue from oil is reserved for the future generation fund, priority should be given to the development of infrastructure (including in rural areas) to foster traditional sources of livelihood and national income; the facilitation of human capital development through efficient education and health care systems; and the enactment of a policy framework that achieves the right balance between protecting national markets and attracting foreign investments in both the oil and non-oil sectors.

The role of society in unburdening oil is also important. The mythical perception in many oil-producing countries of oil as a 'national cake' that has to be shared among the citizenry has important policy implications. It undermines the efficient management of resources as the citizenry crave for subsidies as part of their share of the national cake. In strategic communications and practical examples, such as the avoidance of extravagance and conspicuous consumption, leaders of Africa's oil-producing countries should do away with the popular imagination that connects oil with sudden free wealth. This may be one of the benefits of transparency and openness in information on investment decisions and contract negotiations which is canvassed in virtually all chapters in this book. The people need to know that though a free gift of nature, oil, like corn and cocoa, costs money to produce. Therefore, it should not be disbursed freely. This might perhaps tame popular expectations that are often at the root of demands for subsidies and favour consumption over investment and saving for the future.

17.3.3   The Role of Politics and Leadership

Apart from institutional factors, the prospect of oil serving as a catalyst for national transformation is also contingent on the nature of a country's politics and leadership. In fact, in the context of developing countries, politics and leadership play overwhelming roles, given the tendency for institutional weaknesses which serve to undermine accountability (see Karl, 1997). Critical variables include the balance of power or nature of the political settlement, the role of oil in politics and the quality of leadership. A study of Indonesia and Nigeria found that these contingent factors alongside institutions explain why these two countries have experienced different development outcomes following the advent of oil (see Lewis, 2007). The nature of the political settlement is critical because it explains the patterns of conflicts likely to evolve as contending social forces mobilise to access oil resources. For instance, where oil is extracted from areas populated by minority groups, the State may ignore demands for compensation mechanisms and set the basis for grievances and dissent. This is likely to be the case if oil is extracted from an area whose people have a controlling coalition to threaten the State or at least the ruling coalition.

The nature of the political settlement is linked to the role of oil in shaping political identities and political contestations. It is important for the State to moderate the degree to which oil becomes the focus for political contestation. This is usually not an easy task, especially as the electorate usually develops a keen interest regarding the manifestos of political parties and their candidates concerning the proposed management and distribution of a country's oil revenues. For instance, during the 2016 Ugandan elections, different candidates and parties presented their different perspectives concerning the management of the oil sector (see Global Rights Alert, 2016). Much of the political instability associated with oil derives from the heightened stakes of controlling petro-states that not only attract many to the political contest, but also turn political contestations into zero-sum games (see Ross, 2001; 2008). This is often inimical to democratic development as incumbents circumvent rules to hold on to power perpetually.

The quality of national leadership is crucial to mitigating some of these effects. Historically, there is reason to suggest that countries that have managed oil wealth more efficiently for national development are those with established political settlements and effective leadership. Leadership efficacy involves being able to lead the country to achieve specific results for the public good. It involves rising above competing political actors to enforce rules and implement policies aimed at the attainment of strategic national objectives. While this may not always occur in democratic settings, it can be useful in the long term. This is evident in the developments in Uganda, where President Yoweri Museveni has clearly determined the direction for managing oil, against political actors seeking to undermine the developmental orientation of the State. As Hickey and Izama (2016) have observed:

> The president has deployed at least three strategic moves to countervail these tendencies, apparently driven by a genuine commitment to ensuring that oil wealth is used in line with his nationalist vision of development. These have involved efforts to control moves by other powerful members

of the ruling coalition to extract rents from the oil sector and central-
ize such rent-seeking; enabling the development of high-level technical
bureaucratic capacity within at least one mainstream government agency;
and resisting the temptation to link incoming oil wealth to populist election
pledges. Instead, he has repeatedly ear-marked oil revenue for investment in
agriculture and infrastructural development. Taken together, these moves
suggest possible routes through which even 'weak dominant' coalitions can
promote institution-building and development, when a leader is sufficiently
committed and is able to draw on investments in bureaucratic capacity from
an earlier phase of dominance (Hickey and Izama, 2016, pp.184–185).

All told therefore, auspicious political economy and the right set of institutions
are necessary for transforming oil into a beneficial resource for national
development in both old and new African oil producers. Uganda should
take these important policy reflections to heart if it wants to ensure that its
oil wealth will be used for the benefit of national development. The detailed
policy recommendations offered throughout this book can further help to
strengthen and improve the country's oil governance regime and ensure
that its oil wealth will be managed effectively, efficiently and transparently.

References

Jaffe, A.M. (2007), 'The Changing Roles of National Oil Companies in International Energy
    Markets: Introduction and Summary Conclusions'. Retrieved from the Baker Institute website:
    https://www.bakerinstitute.org/files/2462/.
James Baker Institute (2007), 'The Changing Roles of National Oil Companies in International
    Energy Markets'. *James Baker Institute Policy Brief*, No. 35. Retrieved from: https://www.
    bakerinstitute.org/files/420/.
Karl, T.L. (1997), *The Paradox of Plenty: Oil Booms and Petro States*. Berkeley, California: University
    of California Press.
Lewis, P. (2007), *Growing Apart: Oil, Politics and Economic Change in Indonesia and Nigeria*. Ann
    Arbor, Michigan: The University of Michigan Press.
Nwokeji, U.G. (2007), *The Nigerian National Petroleum Corporation and the Development of the
    Nigerian Oil and Gas Industry: History, Strategy and Current Directions*. Retrieved from the
    James Baker Institute website; https://www.bakerinstitute.org/center-for-energy-studies/
    role-national-oil-companies-international-energy-markets/.
Patey, L (2015), 'Oil in Uganda: Hard Bargaining and Complex Politics in East Africa'.
    OIES Working Paper No 60. Oxford: University of Oxford. Retrieved from: https://doi.
    org/10.26889/9781784670405.
Ross, M. (2001), 'Does Oil Hinder Democracy?', *World Politics*, 53(3), 325–361.
—— (2008), 'Blood Barrels: Why Oil Wealth Fuels Conflict', *Foreign Affairs*, 87(3), 2–8.

Illustration Credits

Every effort has been made to contact all holders of copyrights. Any copyright-holders who believe that illustrations have been reproduced without their knowledge are asked to contact the publisher.

Figure 5.1 is reprinted with permission from B. Bukenya and W. Muhumuza (2017), 'The Politics of Core Public Sector Reform in Uganda: Behind the Façade'. ESID Working Paper No. 85. Manchester: The University of Manchester.

Figures 6.1, 6.2, 6.3, 6.4 & 6.5 are reprinted with permission of the Economic Policy Research Centre, Kampala, from T. Doshi, F. Joutz, P. Lakuma, M.M. Lwanga and B. Manzano (2015), 'The Challenges of Macroeconomic Management of Natural Resource Revenues in Developing Countries: The Case of Uganda', Research Series No. 124, Economic Policy Research Centre, Kampala, Uganda.

Tables 7.1 and 7.3 are reprinted with permission from W. Wane and G. Martin (2016), *Education Service Delivery in Uganda*. Washington, DC: The World Bank.

Table 15.2 is reprinted with the permission of Ghana's Public Interest and Accountability Committee (PIAC) from PIAC (2015), Report on Revenue Management. Annual Report, Ghana.

Figure 16.1 is reprinted with the permission of the Institute of Economic Affairs from IEA (2014), *A Primer to the Emerging Extractive Sector in Kenya: Resource Bliss, Dilemma or Curse*. Nairobi: IEA.

Figure 16.2 is reprinted with permission from R. Golombok and M.I. Jones (2015), *Oil Governance in Uganda and Kenya: A Review of Efforts to Establish Baseline Indicators on the Impact of Oil Sector in Uganda and Kenya*, Nairobi: UNEP.

About the authors

EMMANUEL ABBEY
Emmanuel Abbey is a research associate at the Department of Economics, University of Ghana, working on various projects. He has a doctoral degree in development economics and was formerly an assistant lecturer at the University of Ghana. His research interest is in industrial organisation, technological innovation and the economics of education. His current position as a research associate has enhanced his interest in oil governance issues in Ghana.

KATHLEEN BROPHY
Kathleen Brophy is a Senior Program Advisor at Oxfam America working on fiscal justice and extractive industries governance. She formerly worked at Transparency International Uganda where she led work on extractive industry transparency and accountability for three years. Her areas of expertise include extractive industry revenue governance, corruption and public financial management.

BADRU BUKENYA
Dr. Badru Bukenya is a lecturer in the Department of Social Work and Social Administration at Makerere University, Kampala, Uganda. He is also currently a post-doctoral fellow at the Global Development Institute (GDI) of the University of Manchester. His research interests include civil society, the politics of service delivery, state and citizenship building, and governance of natural resources in Uganda.

JACKSON N. M. BYARUHANGA
Jackson Byaruhanga is a seasoned economist and long-term employee of the Bank of Uganda where, by the time of retirement, he was a manager responsible for financial sector regulation and supervision. He is among the pioneer researchers on local content policies in the oil and gas industry in Uganda and participated in the ground-breaking study for 'Enhancing National Participation in the Oil and Gas Industry in Uganda'.

MOSES ISABIRYE

Isabirye Moses is a professor at the Faculty of Natural Resources and Environmental Sciences, Busitema University. He is also a member of the national technical committee for developing environmental indicators and a monitoring plan to guide oil developments in the Albertine Graben.

WILSON BAHATI KAZI

Wilson Bahati Kazi graduated from the National Graduate Institute for Policy Studies, Japan, with a master's degree in public finance in 2002 and worked with the Uganda Revenue Authority (URA) from 1997-2007. He was an adjunct lecturer at Makerere University for 14 years until he left in 2018 to concentrate fully on his tax practice with Afrox Consulting Limited. His interests are oil and gas taxation, international tax planning and tax policy research.

CORTI PAUL LAKUMA

Dr. Corti Paul Lakuma is a research analyst in the Macroeconomic Department at the Economic Policy Research Centre (EPRC). His research interests include energy economics, business cycle modelling and fiscal policy. Dr. Lakuma has extensive experience modelling the macroeconomic impact of oil and gas revenues, and cost estimation of the upstream and downstream activities and facilities engineering of Uganda's oil sector.

ARNIM LANGER

Professor Arnim Langer is Director of the Centre for Research on Peace and Development (CRPD), Chair holder of the UNESCO Chair in Building Sustainable Peace, and Professor of International Politics at KU Leuven. He is also associate researcher at the Department of International Development at Oxford University, honorary researcher at the University of Western Australia (Perth) and Alexander von Humboldt Fellow at the University of Heidelberg in Germany. He has widespread expertise on issues of conflict and peacebuilding, the dynamics and persistence of horizontal inequalities, and social cohesion building.

JOSEPH MAWEJJE

Joseph Mawejje is an economist in the macroeconomics, trade, and investment practice of the World Bank. He is currently on assignment in South Sudan. He has previously worked as research analyst at the Economic Policy Research Centre (EPRC), Uganda's leading policy think tank. He has research interests in macroeconomics, the management of natural resources, and private sector development.

PAMELA MBABAZI

Prof. Pamela Mbabazi is currently the Chair of the National Planning Authority of the Government of Uganda. She holds a PhD in development studies from Mbarara University of Science & Technology, Uganda, an MA in development studies from Leeds University (UK) and an MSc in development planning and management from Kwame Nkrumah University of Science Technology. She has 20 years of training and research experience in development studies and has until recently been working with Mbarara University of Science & Technology in Uganda. Her key research interests include the changing nature and character of the State in Africa, governance issues, the political economy of oil, and peace building issues.

MARTIN MUHANGI

Martin Muhangi is a Deputy Director of the Uganda Investment Authority in the Department of Investment Promotion. He holds an LLM in petroleum taxation and finance from the Centre for Energy, Petroleum and Mineral Law and Policy (CEPMLP) at the University of Dundee (Scotland), where he attained specialised training in the legal, financial and commercial aspects of the international oil and gas industry. He has 22 years of experience in tax administration and a grounded experience in the negotiation of government protocols, the structuring of fiscal terms for the oil and gas sector and the formation of legal and institutional frameworks for managing the oil and gas industry.

ROBERTS KABEBA MURIISA

Roberts Kabeba Muriisa is Professor of Governance at the Department of Planning and Governance at the Faculty of Interdisciplinary Studies of Mbarara University of Science and Technology (MUST). He is a visiting Scholar at the University of Stavanger in Norway and the University of Oldenburg in Germany. He has conducted wide-ranging research and published extensively on issues of land governance as well as higher education and governance in Uganda.

CHRIS BYARUHANGA MUSIIME

Chris Byaruhanga Musiime holds a BA in environmental management from Makerere University and a postgraduate diploma in financial management from the Uganda Management Institute. He has for the past five years been a central player in civil society efforts advocating for a sustainably managed extractives sector in Uganda, initially as a manager of the oil governance project at ActionAid Uganda, and more recently as the Head of Programmes at the Africa Centre for Energy and Mineral Policy (ACEMP).

GERMANO MWABU

Germano Mwabu is Professor of Economics at the University of Nairobi. He was co-director of the AERC project on poverty income distribution and labour markets in Sub-Saharan Africa. He has also held the position of Senior Research Fellow, Director, Public Goods Project of the World Institute for Development Economics Research at the United Nations University, Helsinki (1996–1998) and Associate Professor of Economics at Kenyatta University (1994–1996).

JACKSON A. MWAKALI

Prof. Mwakali has over 30 years' experience in engineering research and practice. He pursued postgraduate studies and obtained both MSc and PhD degrees in structural engineering, becoming arguably the first Ugandan to obtain a PhD in structural engineering. He has published widely on issues of engineering as well as local content in Uganda's oil and gas industries.

JACQUELINE NAKAIZA

Jacqueline Nakaiza holds a master's degree in international relations and diplomatic studies from the Department of Political Studies of Makerere University. She is currently a PhD student at the College of Humanities and Social Sciences at Makerere University. Between 2007 and 2008, she was a research fellow at the Decolonisation Office at the United Nations headquarters in New York. Her current research interests focus on the governance of oil, peace and political stability in the Great Lakes Region.

TOM OGWANG

Dr. Tom Ogwang is lecturer in the Department of Planning and Governance at the Institute of Interdisciplinary Training and Research, Mbarara University of Science and Technology, Uganda. His research interests are the political economy of natural resources, the social and environmental impacts of extractive industries, international and regional security, governance, conflict and peace studies, with a specific interest in the Great Lakes Region.

J. OLOKA-ONYANGO

J. Oloka-Onyango is a Professor of Law at the Human Rights & Peace Centre (HURIPEC), School of Law, Makerere University. He has been a member and former chair of several local, regional and international human rights organisations, and was the Special Rapporteur on Globalisation and Human Rights of the United Nations (UN) Sub-Commission on the Promotion and Protection of Human Rights from 1998 to 2002.

PETER QUARTEY

Peter Quartey is Professor of Economics at the Institute of Statistical, Social and Economic Research (ISSER) and Head of the Department of Economics at the University of Ghana. He has published extensively on private sector development including SMEs, development finance, migration and remittances and poverty analysis.

SPECIOZA TWINAMASIKO

Specioza Twinamasiko is currently a PhD researcher at the Faculty of Interdisciplinary Studies at Mbarara University of Science and Technology (MUST) in Uganda. Her PhD research focuses on 'oil discovery and land compensation: risks and vulnerabilities to women's livelihoods and agency responses in Albertine Graben, Uganda'. She further holds an MSc in peace and development work from Linnaeus University in Sweden and has experience working with international research organisations.

UKOHA UKIWO

Dr. Ukoha Ukiwo is a Senior Lecturer at the Department of Political and Administrative Studies, University of Port Harcourt, Nigeria. He served as programme manager of the Nigeria Stability and Reconciliation Programme, a programme funded by the UK Department for International Development (DFID) and implemented by the British Council in partnership with International Alert and Social Development Direct. Dr. Ukiwo was also a member of the expert advisory panel of the Nigeria Natural Resources Charter and a global fellow at the Peace Research Institute, Oslo (PRIO). He has conducted extensive research on good governance and public policy issues in Africa, including the management of natural resources in Nigeria.

PETER WANDERA

Peter Wandera has been working at Transparency International Uganda as the Executive Director since 2012. He previously worked for over ten years at the Development Network of Indigenous Voluntary Associations (DENIVA) as the Assistant Executive Director, Human Resources and Administration. His current position at Transparency International has greatly enhanced his interest in public accountability issues, especially in the area of fighting corruption.

CPSIA information can be obtained
at www.ICGtesting.com
Printed in the USA
LVHW020307300120
645198LV00006B/53

9 789462 702004